Gender Constructs and Social Issues

Gender Constructs and Social Issues

EDITED BY

Tony L. Whitehead
and Barbara V. Reid

UNIVERSITY OF ILLINOIS PRESS
Urbana and Chicago

© 1992 by the Board of Trustees of the University of Illinois
Manufactured in the United States of America
1 2 3 4 5 C P 5 4 3 2 1

This book is printed on acid-free paper.

Library of Congress Cataloging-in-Publication Data

Gender constructs and social issues / edited by Tony L. Whitehead and
    Barbara V. Reid.
        p.   cm.
    Includes bibliographical references and index.
    ISBN 0–252–01831–1. — ISBN 0–252–06199–3 (pb)
    1. Sex role.   2. Social problems.   I. Whitehead, Tony Larry.
II. Reid, Barbara V.
HQ1075.G463   1992
305.3—dc20   91–11465
                                                                  CIP

To our children and to improved
intergender communications in the future.

Contents

Acknowledgments   ix

Barbara V. Reid and Tony L. Whitehead
Introduction   1

Part 1: Identity Formation

Anne Bolin
Coming of Age among Transsexuals   13

Michael V. Angrosino and Lucinda J. Zagnoli
Gender Constructs and Social Identity:
Implications for Community-Based Care
of Retarded Adults   40

John H. Storer
Gender and Kin Role Transposition as
an Accommodation to Father-Daughter Incest   70

Tony L. Whitehead
Expressions of Masculinity in a Jamaican Sugartown:
Implications for Family Planning Programs   103

Margaret A. Eisenhart and Dorothy C. Holland
Gender Constructs and Career Commitment:
The Influence of Peer Culture on Women in College   142

Part 2: Medical Issues

Dona Lee Davis
Gender and Elective Surgery in a
Newfoundland Fishing Village   183

Maureen J. Giovannini
The Relevance of Gender in Postpartum
Emotional Disorders   209

Part 3: Violence against Women

Lee Ann Hoff
Gender-Specific Network Influences
on Battered Women   235

Barbara V. Reid
A Man's Home Is His Castle: Spousal Rape
in Western Society   251

Catharine A. MacKinnon
Francis Biddle's Sister: Pornography, Civil Rights,
and Speech   261

Notes on Contributors   322

Index   325

Acknowledgments

We would first like to thank the people at the University of Illinois Press for their support in the production of this volume. Our first contact was with Elizabeth G. Dulany, who was managing editor when we began this process, and then Theresa Sears, who moved into this position and provided her support. All of the contributors found the copyediting of Jane Mohraz to be most thorough and are in general agreement that our essays are much more readable as a consequence of her diligent work. We would also like to thank our contributors for their patience and support. When volumes take a number of years to produce, as this one did, it is always embarrassing to run into contributors at meetings and to have to face their questions about the progress of the project. But it is great to have contributors, Dona Davis and Michael Angrosino in particular, whose response was always something like: "Hey, no problem, the paper is yours, regardless of how long it might take."

Whitehead is particularly grateful to research assistants who have helped him with the project over the years: Robert Aronson, who managed the project, and Linda Kaljee and Cindy Lollar for their editorial assistance. Gordon Karim assisted with the graphics and LaDonna Dickerson assisted with the typing. We would also like to thank our families for their support: Tony's wife, Karen, and their children, Malcolm and Anna; and Barbara's husband, Ralph, and their children, Sasha and James.

Barbara V. Reid and Tony L. Whitehead

Introduction

In the introduction to *Sexual Meanings,* Sherry Ortner and Harriet Whitehead (1981) point out that because gender issues had to be considered in cross-cultural discussions of marriage and kinship, which had long been a focus of anthropological studies, gender issues were being discussed, at least implicitly, even before the appearance of the feminist-inspired work of the past two decades. Rayna Reiter (1975) likewise mentions protogender interest in connection with the study of the division of labor. Yet it is only since 1975 that anthropologists have accepted gender studies as a legitimate subdiscipline within the field as a whole. There is now a growing trend toward integrating the concepts and findings of the anthropology of gender into the mainstream of the discipline (Moore 1988).

An impressive array of work has focused on explaining sexual stratification (Rosaldo and Lamphere 1974; Reiter 1975; Schlegel 1977; Etienne and Leacock 1980; MacCormack and Strathern 1980; Sanday 1981; Ortner and Whitehead 1981; Caplan and Bujra 1982; Sacks 1982; Strathern 1987, 1988). Each of these books elaborates on a specific theoretical framework, and each contributes to our ever-growing understanding of why societies have, by and large, developed gender systems in which the male portion of the population dominates the female. But it is also necessary to consider how the cultural construction of gender affects social issues other than gender stratification per se.

One goal of this anthology is to sensitize readers to the gendered aspects of a broad spectrum of social issues. In other words, we are concerned with the process of cultural construction as it relates to gender and specific social problems. We define *social issues* as controversial matters being disputed by members of society. It is not surprising that social issues often include a gender component, because the very power differentials that exist between men and women create problematic issues.

In this volume we seek to extend the work on the cultural construction of gender by looking at the impact of gender constructs on a variety of contemporary social issues. By examining how social issues are affected by gender constructs, we hope to demonstrate the applied relevance of the anthropology of gender. The term *gender construct* is used here to refer to the fact that the sense people have of their gender, of being a man or a woman, is culturally constructed; that is, gender is a cognitive and symbolic construct that helps individuals develop a sense of self, a sense of identity that is constructed in the process of interacting with others within a given human community. Being culturally constructed, gender definitions vary from culture to culture. Although the notion of gender constructs, or what Peggy Sanday (1981) calls "sex-role plans," has been explored theoretically and comparatively, it may also be applied to contemporary social issues. Gender constructs are guides to behavior, are reflected in the interactions of daily life, and are encoded into myth and ritual. They are likewise embedded in the ideology of any cultural system.

The dual nature of gender suggests a further relationship between gender constructs and social issues. Martin Silverman (1979) pointed out that gender can be thought of as both partial (because it is often considered as one factor among many, such as race, class, ethnicity, or generation) and encompassing (because as far as social relations are concerned, statements about men and women exhaust the possibilities). It is this dual nature of gender that informs this book, and all the contributors, in one way or another, illustrate that the issue they have chosen to study cannot be adequately described, discussed, or researched without reference to socioculturally determined gender constructs and sex-role plans.

Another theme unifying these essays is that however a culture structures its gender system, some groups within the culture become disadvantaged as a result. This brings us back once again to the problem of stratification and hierarchy. Since all ethnographic examples in this volume are set in the context of capitalistic, state-level societies, this stratifying effect should not be surprising. It is, however, important to remember that research into the social issues of more egalitarian societies may produce different configurations, and this volume does not attempt to explore the role of gender constructs vis-à-vis social issues in such cultural groupings.

The purpose of these essays is to explore social issues having gender constructs at their core and to demonstrate that the cultural construction of gender significantly affects the ways in which these issues are treated by the general public, academics, practitioners, and policy makers and that it has serious consequences for those most directly involved. These essays represent the value of taking a gendered perspective on social issues. We would like to see this gendered approach extended to the field of anthropology as a whole, to become the starting point for any topic of research, so that the importance of gender in all aspects of life will not be ignored by social scientists in the future, as it once was in the past.

The essays have been grouped into three sections according to the major problem discussed in each. Part 1 investigates identity formation as it is affected by gender constructs, particularly identity formation problems for transsexuals; retarded adults; fathers, daughters, and mothers in incestuous families; males dealing with reproduction issues; and college women making career decisions. Part 2 focuses on several medical issues affected by the cultural construction of gender, specifically the incidence of tubal ligations, hysterectomies, and postpartum depression. Part 3 examines violence against women, including wife abuse, marital rape, and pornography. Not surprisingly, several issues touch on more than one topic. For example, John H. Storer's essay on father-daughter incest exemplifies the rubric of both identity formation and violence against women. Although the essays are topically divided, they are all thematically related.

Personal identity, the theme of Part 1, is an aspect of human development closely tied to gender constructs, because every individual grows to adulthood with the knowledge that he or she will be not just a *member* of a given society but an American, Jamaican, or !Kung man or woman. Personal development is shaped by the process of cultural construction, with society setting the standards as to the acceptable range of behavior for males and females. There have been enormous changes in American culture where gender constructs are concerned; however, the majority of the population still has some fairly fixed notions about where the limits of masculinity and femininity lie.

Gender identity at times becomes problematic and requires a restructuring, as in the case of the transsexual who shifts self-concept from one gender to another. This is particularly crucial for societies such as our own, where gender categories are conceived of as an either-or proposition; that is, one must be male *or* female, and intermediate categories are not acknowledged or are unacceptable. That a binary schema of gender identity is culturally constructed becomes evident when we consider that Polynesian cultures, for example, recognize a so-called third sex—biological men who are permitted to dress and act as women (Caplan 1987; Shore 1981).

In chapter one, Anne Bolin describes the acquisition of female gender by male-to-female transsexuals. Bolin examined the ideological system of transsexuals by using the method of participant observation. She found that these emerging women rely on a model of life-cycle stages both to explain and to achieve their self-transformation. Making the connection between their own bodily changes and the cultural construction of puberty is crucial to transsexuals if they are to feel that their sex change has been accomplished. Transsexuals believe they are repeating the stage of adolescence, and when they successfully complete this stage, they will attain womanhood and the correct gender identity accompanying it. Intertwined with identity, then, is the cultural construction of psychosexual development.

There are other subgroups within society for whom the acquisition of the socially approved expressions of gender-appropriate sexuality becomes problematic. Michael V. Angrosino and Lucinda J. Zagnoli write about such problems with adult mentally challenged Americans. They have found that deinstitutionalized special-needs adults have been hampered in progressing beyond an adolescent conception of gender because their teachers, caretakers, and parents have stereotyped their sexuality. This has the effect of impeding the development of social competence, these authors argue, since such competence rests on the development of an appropriate gender identity. Because people in their environment deal with sexuality and gender formation in a simplistic manner, mentally challenged adults attain a conservative or "old-fashioned" conception of male-female relationships, which suggests that sex education and a more compassionate view of the sexuality of the mentally retarded are much needed components of programs for this population.

One strong and lasting influence on the development of culturally accepted gender constructs is the family—the context in which a child first learns the roles of daughter, son, mother, and father, through routine interaction with these roles. The family's contribution to psychosexual development is critically impeded in the case of parent-child incest because, as John H. Storer tells us in his essay, a persistent pattern of interaction emerges for which "no culturally defined performance rules exist." Even more critical is the obfuscation of the culturally accepted dyadic relationships between spouses and between parents and children. Storer analyzes these role obfuscations in twenty-eight cases of father-daughter incest and concludes that from the father's point of view, the daughter's status is elevated in the family while the mother's status is lowered. The tragedy of the gradual progress is that the pseudomaturity traits, which the daughter incorporates as a consequence of the father's attention and the mother's acceptance of them, are eventually used by the father to justify his behavior, while the mother is left powerless to intervene. Compounding this tragedy is the justificational system developed by the parents and surrounding societal institutions; the father is permitted to rationalize his deeds by adopting the role identity of "adulterer" and thereby escapes being labeled with the more onerous term "child-molester."

Even when a culturally acceptable gender identity is attained, this identity can often be problematic in certain situations. This is certainly evident in issues surrounding reproduction, both in the United States and abroad. Family planning efforts in Jamaica, for example, have often been geared to women and have operated on the assumption that lower-income males are irresponsible with regard to fertility. Tony L. Whitehead finds that the meaning of masculinity and the sex-role plan of society in general have far-reaching implications for male cooperation in such human service programs. It has been assumed there is a direct correlation between socioeconomic status and behavioral patterns for men. Whitehead, however, found that the cultural model of sexuality and its attendant gender constructs actually cut across economic levels and that *all* Jamaican men, motivated by the desire for higher status, share a set of binary oppositions structured by the polar concepts of respectability and reputation. Regardless of their economic status, all men valued both the responsible behavior associated with "respectability" and the irresponsible behavior associated with "reputation," which are simultaneously manifested at both the individual and cultural levels. Of course, Whitehead's structural analysis has implications for the gender constructs of other societies as well, and it suggests that contextual and seemingly contradictory cultural constructs of gender may be an important and perhaps overlooked factor, one that has implications reaching beyond theoretical concerns.

Gender identity is also problematic for young women striving for careers. Margaret A. Eisenhart and Dorothy C. Holland, in a longitudinal study of women students at two southern universities in the United States, found that, despite increased opportunities for women, many college women continue to make decisions that ultimately lead them into traditional roles in the work force. In questioning the students and their peer groups, they found that many women are pressured by their peers to embrace stereotypical gender constructs, which then impede their progress toward successfully completing their original career goals. The stereotypical gender constructs that dominate their informal friendship networks have a far greater impact on their career choices than does the more formalized superstructure of cultural values and institutions that suggest women's identity can be transformed in the educational context.

The feminist critique of the sexism inherent in Western scientific medical systems addresses gender as a factor in medically related social issues (Ehrenreich and English 1973, 1979; Turner 1987; Lewin and Olesen 1985; Martin 1987; Whelehan 1988). The articles in Part 2 examine the effects of the cultural construction of gender on two such medical issues.

In a modern-day Newfoundland fishing village, Dona Lee Davis learned that women of two successive generations justify drastic medical surgery affecting reproduction by the same cultural values underlying the symbolic construct of the good woman. The older generation, approaching menopause, has relied on hysterectomy as a type of preventive medicine, while their daughters, at the other end of the reproductive cycle, have been using tubal ligation as a preferred means of birth control. Both practices not only relate to villagers' conception of the good woman but also have been actively espoused by local doctors. In this instance sociocultural factors converge with the ideology of professionals in regard to women's health care. Although cultural change has resulted in vastly different reproductive practices for these two generations of women, at the level of values the gender construct of the good woman has been perpetuated. This illustrates the flexibility of moral systems when values are translated into practice.

Medical ideology also figures in Maureen J. Giovannini's analysis of postpartum depression. This disorder has been on the increase in the United States and Great Britain, and the medical profession has sought to explain it in terms of either hormonal changes or personality variables that supposedly lead to intrapsychic conflicts surrounding femininity. Looking at social environmental stresses during the postpartum period, which can be viewed as a life-crisis event, Giovannini advances a third explanation. She contends that where social support for the new mother is greater, the likelihood of depression is lower.

Part 3 of the book, Violence against Woman, examines three of the ways in which the cultural construction of gender in the United States fosters the victimization of women. Lee Ann Hoff's research on wife battering demonstrates the links between individual battered women in crisis, social networks, and the larger society. She points out the importance of the mother-daughter relationship in the adult psychology of battered women in the United States. The implicit attitudes of parents toward sex and violence are also important to the adult woman in terms of her acceptance of mistreatment. Society has constructed this problem in a way that leads us repeatedly to ask the wrong questions where the battered wife is concerned (e.g., "Why doesn't she just leave him?")

One specific form of husband-perpetrated violence is marital rape. Barbara V. Reid's essay notes the expansion of the concept of rape in recent times to include all forms of sexual intercourse in which one partner has not consented. This extension of rape beyond stranger assault has heightened our awareness of previously unrecognized types of this crime, such as date rape, acquaintance rape, and marital rape. Until recently, most Western nations adhered to a marital rape exemption, which protected men from prosecution for raping their wives. Reid explores the roots of this exemption in Western society (the implied consent of a wife to meet her husband's sexual demands, the unity of husband and wife as one individual, and the notion of the separation of public and private spheres) and concludes that they underlie not only the spousal exemption but also the way in which rape in general has been conceptualized in Western cultures. The most salient metaphor encapsulating the relation between the sexes where rape is concerned is ownership: women are considered the property of individual men. Reid's essay proposes that the challenge to this presumption of ownership has been advanced in Western society through two forms of discourse: one addresses the attainment of individual control over the body, and another seeks to redefine the contextual boundaries between public and private.

In the final essay of the volume, Catharine A. MacKinnon looks at the contribution pornography makes to the cultural construction of gender. Taking a feminist perspective on laws regarding pornography, MacKinnon enhances our awareness that the U.S. legal system is predicated on male-centered assumptions. Pornography as a legal issue serves to illustrate MacKinnon's contention that the presumption of the possibility of neutrality under the law ignores the unequal distribution of power where men and women are concerned and ultimately violates the civil rights of women.

Laws regarding pornography have been partially constructed around the public versus private spheres of activity, which serve as a dominant ideological base where the cultural construction of gender is concerned. This particular distinction affects all forms of violence against women, including wife battering and marital rape, the subject of the other two essays in this concluding section. Although this theory has sometimes been viewed as somehow biologistic (i.e., women's family roles determine their position in society), we employ it here to illustrate its centrality to the cultural construction of gender in Western society. Violence against women is carried out both in public and in private. Public rape and brutality encourage women to retreat into their homes for their own safety. Theoretically, husbands should protect their wives from the abuse; in reality, however, women may not be safe anywhere. Men's power over women is exercised in the home as well, which serves as a constant reminder that society is not really protecting women's rights or their bodies.

The issues presented here are but a few of the almost inexhaustible topics that could be analyzed in terms of gender. To name a few, everything from abortion rights to health care to homelessness to gun control has a gendered quality that should be included if social science research on such issues is to be considered an accurate or useful accounting of the problem. We hope to inspire such analyses where other social issues are concerned and to encourage readers to look at everyday life in terms of how society's gender constructs affect both ordinary behavior and extraordinary political and social controversies.

REFERENCES

Caplan, Pat, ed. 1987. *The Cultural Construction of Sexuality.* London: Tavistock.

Caplan, Patricia, and Janet M. Bujra, eds. 1982. *Women United, Women Divided.* Bloomington: Indiana University Press.

Ehrenreich, Barbara, and Deirdre English. 1973. *Complaints and Disorders: The Sexual Politics of Sickness.* Old Westbury, N.Y.: Feminist Press.

———. 1979. *For Her Own Good: 150 Years of the Experts' Advice to Women.* New York: Anchor.

Etienne, Mona, and Eleanor Leacock, eds. 1980. *Women and Colonization.* New York: J. F. Bergin.

Lewin, Ellen, and Virginia Olesen, eds. 1985. *Women, Health and Healing: Toward a New Perspective.* London: Tavistock.

MacCormack, Carol P., and Marilyn Strathern, eds. 1980. *Nature, Culture and Gender.* Cambridge: Cambridge University Press.

Martin, Emily. 1987. *The Woman in the Body: A Cultural Analysis of Reproduction.* Boston: Beacon.

Moore, Henrietta L. 1988. *Feminism and Anthropology.* Minneapolis: University of Minnesota Press.

Ortner, Sherry, and Harriet Whitehead. 1981. *Sexual Meanings: The Cultural Construction of Gender and Sexuality.* Cambridge: Cambridge University Press.

Reiter, Rayna R. 1975. *Toward an Anthropology of Women.* New York: Monthly Review Press.

Rosaldo, Michelle Zimbalist, and Louise Lamphere. 1974. *Woman, Culture, and Society.* Stanford, Calif.: Stanford University Press.

Sacks, Karen. 1982. *Sisters and Wives.* Urbana: University of Illinois Press.

Sanday, Peggy. 1981. *Female Power and Male Dominance.* Cambridge: Cambridge University Press.

Schlegel, Alice, ed. 1977. *Sexual Stratification: A Cross-Cultural View.* New York: Columbia University Press.

Shore, Bradd. 1981. "Sexuality and Gender in Samoa: Conceptions and Missed Conceptions." In *Sexual Meanings,* ed. Sherry B. Ortner and Harriet Whitehead. Cambridge: Cambridge University Press.

Silverman, Martin G. 1979. "Gender and Separations in Precolonial Banaban and Gilbertese Societies." In *Ideology and Everyday Life,* ed. Steve Barnett and Martin Silverman. Ann Arbor: University of Michigan Press.

Strathern, Marilyn, ed. 1987. *Dealing with Inequality: Analyzing Gender Relations in Melanesia and Beyond.* Cambridge: Cambridge University Press.

———. 1988. *The Gender of the Gift.* Berkeley and Los Angeles: University of California Press.

Turner, Bryan S. 1987. *Medical Power and Social Knowledge.* London: Sage.

Whelehan, Patricia, ed. 1988. *Women and Health: Cross-Cultural Perspectives.* Granby, Mass.: Bergin and Garvey.

Identity Formation

Anne Bolin

Coming of Age among Transsexuals

This essay is about rebirth, transformation, and becoming. It focuses on the transgender journey of a group of genetic males in the process of becoming women. The metamorphosis of these reluctant "men," known as transsexuals, is viewed as a patterned development having the characteristics of a rite of passage (Van Gennep [1908] 1960). This passage is dramatized by important stages and events that punctuate their progress toward the all-important surgical conversion—sex-change surgery.

The analysis is rooted in the meanings and symbols tradition in anthropology, developed by such scholars as Clifford Geertz (1973, 1983) and Victor Turner (1962, 1967, 1968, 1969, 1974, 1977), and symbolic interaction, principally the work of Erving Goffman (1961, 1967, 1969, 1970). This perspective adds a social dimension to understanding the transsexual's gender identity transformation, a subject that is usually considered from a primarily psychological vantage point. Gender identity is regarded here as socially mediated and dynamic rather than fixated and static. It is suggested here that the shedding and acquisition of identities as a life course phenomenon can be explicated by turning to one of anthropology's better "nomothetic" models: the tripartite model of rites of passage, which is discussed more fully later.

The research is based on two years of participant observation (between December 1979 and December 1981), followed by a year of follow-up and cross-checking, but far less intensive involvement, with a group of sixteen male-to-female transsexuals who were actively pursuing sex-change surgery when I began the investigation.

The term *transsexual* refers to individuals with a cross-sex identity, regardless of their surgical status. Since the transsexuals regarded themselves as females trapped in male bodies, feminine pronouns are used in referring to them.

The research population was informally organized through a grass-roots association identified here as the Berdache Society, which provided a variety of services, ranging from weekly support sessions to an extensive friendship network. The population was situated in a large urban setting of several million. The Berdache Society played an important role in establishing a transsexual strategy for pursuing the surgical conversion and in creating a subculture for identity transformation.

The Berdache Society consisted of approximately twenty-five transvestites, in addition to the sixteen preoperative transsexuals who contributed to the bulk of the research. Twelve of the sixteen represented a core group. I also corresponded with transsexuals throughout the United States and others locally who were not members of the Berdache Society (see Bolin 1988:40–48).

I attended Berdache Society meetings, engaged in informal open interviews mixed with focused discussions, and administered questionnaires (including the BEM Sex Role Inventory) to acquire information on their psychosexual history, their friendship networks, and their medical expenditures.

In the course of my research, seven of the core group of twelve transsexuals went full-time; that is, they went from cross-dressing on an intermittent basis to living as women on a full-time basis. Five of the transsexuals were full-time when I began the research. Two of the twelve underwent the surgical conversion during the period of participant observation. Between 1982 and 1987, subsequent to the surgical research, four more of this group underwent the surgical conversion. I visited three in the hospital immediately after surgery and discussed their experiences with them.

A point of definition is in order. Transsexuals share some of the characteristics of two other populations, gay female impersonators and transvestites, but they should not be confused here. Gay female impersonators, known in the argot as "drag queens," are men who cross-dress, generally as performers at public rituals or in shows. They form a subculture with oscillating boundaries and affiliations within the larger gay community. "Drag queen" presentation of self is in the tradition of the glamorous movie star or occasionally in the comedic mode. There is, however, never any doubt that the "true" identity of the performer is male (Newton 1972:57). The identity of female impersonators is consolidated through their shared homo-eroticism, not through gender-identity conflict, as in the case of the male-to-female transsexual.

Transsexuals in the research population clearly defined themselves as a category of people altogether different from transvestites, who cross-dress but do not have a cross-sex identity. From the transsexual view, transvestites are not women on the "inside," although they may occasionally appear as women on the "outside." Transsexuals therefore regarded themselves as more "authentic." They dressed as women because their identity demanded it. Transvestites, however, dress as women for other reasons, including fetishism, male role strain, or male protest (when the male role gets too tough, cross-dressing provides relief).

Although the transsexuals stratified cross-dressing populations into discrete identities, such psychiatric experts as Harry Benjamin (1966:17–19) propose that transvestism and transsexualism represent a continuum of cross-dressing behavior and identity. Based on re-search on over two hundred clients, he regards transsexualism and transvestism as variants of a theme of gender-identity dysphoria or dissatisfaction. The research population would ardently disagree. They viewed themselves as "normals" who are temporarily inhabit-ing the wrong bodies. They are therefore not "deviant" men, which is how they regard transvestites. They are women with ersatz phy-siques. This is clearly illustrated by one transsexual who pointed out that when transvestites visited, they left the toilet seat up. Even though this transsexual was preoperative, she saw herself as more "real" than transvestites. Transsexuals' construction of identity fol-lows Western cultural tenets in the construction of gender, which po-larizes the sexes on the basis of genital assignment.

Transsexual Identity and Rites of Passage

Rites of passage facilitate and ease individuals into new sta-tuses. It is therefore not unexpected that a group of transsexuals as-sociated through a self-help organization would develop and in some ways formalize their own rite of passage into womanhood. Like other rites of passage, the transgender journey of this group of transsexuals consisted of three stages: separation, transition or liminality, and incorporation.[1] These stages dramatized and punctuated the trans-sexual's progress into the new gender. The transgender rite of pas-sage was rich with ritual and symbolic metaphors of becoming, of transformation, and of the death of a man and the birth of a woman.

My research suggests that such ethnostrategies as a transsexually derived model for gender transformation can be valuable therapeutically. The individual is prepared for the new gender and a new sociocultural world through rites of passage, a process that is gradual and validating. Here, I focus on one stage of their transformation, a phase referred to by transsexuals and medical and mental health professionals as "transition."[2] Transition was *the* most critical phase of transsexual identity development. It was the period when they placed themselves under the therapeutic care of mental health professionals, began taking female hormones, prepared for the female role, and actually adopted it on a full-time basis. Transition had far-reaching implications because it involved the transformation of personal identity, social identity, and physical appearance.

One of the major mechanisms enhancing the maturation of their female personas was a transsexual ideological system. Through this they were the active participants in the creation of their own birth as women, explicitly using biological and social metaphors to explain how men could become women in a society that regards gender as an eternal verity. Physical feminization (as a result of female hormones) and adoption of the female role (passing) were reinterpreted; they were not peculiar to transsexuals but were inherent in womanhood per se. They perceived themselves as taking part in the same rite of passage that young genetic females who are in the process of becoming women do. This ideology was built on information available in the larger society and their own observations. It was consolidated in a biocultural model of womanhood that facilitated their belief they were becoming women, not just "like" genetic females but "as" genetic females.

Transsexuals were not, however, left completely to their own devices in the formulation of their journey. They had to fulfill guidelines established by medical policy, which outlined the formal steps that must be taken before qualifying for sex-change surgery. Medical policy provided transsexuals with a retinue of medical and mental health caretakers and a prescribed schedule of events, but transsexuals added a great deal symbolically by elaborating and refining the medical agenda. Through interaction with one another, transsexuals gave content and meaning to their journey. The medical model of how men become women was enhanced by transsexuals' own conceptions of the good, right, and proper way to approach womanhood. Through the Berdache Society, transsexuals developed norms, rules, myths, sanctions, explanations, and meaning, which became part of a transsexual ideological system. They imputed meaning to their experience, dramatizing their transformation with symbolic equations of male death and female rebirth. For example, they talked about their "birthdays" based on such markers as full-time status. What emerged as a conventional strategy for becoming women may be regarded as a rite of passage in which the ascribed status of male was transformed into an achieved female status.

The Tools of Analysis

To interpret, analyze, and explain the transsexual's gender change, a vigorous theoretical milieu in which the "native's" point of view is translated into the scientific is necessary.[3] This was provided by the rites of passage model originated by Arnold Van Gennep in 1908 and later refined by Elliott Chapple and C. S. Coon (1942) and several of the symbolic anthropologists, most notably Victor Turner (1967). The rites of passage model supplied the trifold conceptualization of stages—separation, transition, and incorporation—which accompany status changes (Van Gennep [1908] 1960; Chapple and Coon 1942). It seemed more than appropriate for transsexuals who indeed did separate themselves from their prior world, where they were men; underwent a transition where they gradually adopted, through a series of stages, the female role until they assumed the role completely; and finally were incorporated into society as women through the sex-change operation, which provided access to areas of interaction previously denied them (e.g., sexual intimacy as women). The rites of passage model furnished a framework for understanding the dynamics and processes of the transsexual's transition from male to female. This model was particularly valuable in revealing the cultural components of the transsexual's rite of passage into womanhood.

In addition, I found symbolic interaction a valuable interpretative and analytic tool, when combined with the rites of passage model. Symbolic interaction, originally devised by George H. Mead (1934) and currently articulated by Erving Goffman (1963), was especially useful in examining transsexuals' rites of passage for several reasons. First, it shared the underlying assumptions of the rites of passage model. Second, it meshed rather well with some of the theoretical cogs of that model. Third, it helped explain the personal and social identity transformations that accompany status change and incorporated stigma as an important facet of the transsexual's transition.

Synthesizing the rites of passage model and the symbolic interactionist approach resulted in a focused ethnography with descriptive, interpretative, and explanatory components. Ethnographic analysis was enhanced and given wider conceptual power by incorporating a model for transformation. The following sections provide a brief review of the rites of passage model and symbolic interaction, highlighting the major points and precepts of each.

Rites of Passage Model. Arnold Van Gennep devised the rites of passage model to account for the ordering and patterning of the ritual and ceremonial life of nontechnological peoples who are confronted with the inevitability of unsettling biological and social change. Van Gennep (1960:3) summarized the underlying premise for his framework in the following:

> Transitions from group to group and from one social situation to the next are looked on as implicit in the very fact of existence, so that a man's [and a woman's] life comes to be made up of a succession of stages with similar ends and beginnings: birth, social puberty, marriage, fatherhood, advancement to higher class, occupational specialization, and death. For every one of these events there are ceremonies whose essential purpose is to enable the individual to pass from one defined position to another which is equally well defined.

Van Gennep's rites of passage scheme is a powerful framework for viewing and interpreting the similarities in ceremonies and rituals indigenous peoples devised to cope with the crisis associated with changing social positions in the group. These are conceived of as rites of passage, which mark an individual's transition from one social world to another. As mentioned earlier, the rites of passage in their complete form have three distinct phases: separation, transition, and incorporation (3). Since each of the three phases may in itself be a bona fide rite, a rite of transition could have its own three phases of separation, transition, and incorporation (12). Each of these phases marks the individual's change of status in the group, and each is imbued with supernatural and symbolic components dramatizing each phase of the neophyte's social movement.

The rites of separation symbolically remove one from a previous social existence. The transition rites are liminal or threshold rites in which an individual is prepared to rejoin his/her group or society. The rites of incorporation or "aggregation" integrate the individual back into his or her society or group (21). Incorporation may actually be the neophyte's physical return to group or village life, if he or she had been physically removed through a rite of separation or symbolically removed, but it is primarily a social return (46). Van

Gennep construed the rites as expressive metaphors of change of social position, saturated with symbols of "death, rebirth and resurrection" (67).

Elliott Chapple and C. S. Coon (1942) refined the model. They continued Van Gennep's interest in the ritual and symbolic components of rites of passage; however, they focused on the significance of social relations (Posinsky 1962:387). Of consequence for this research is their attention to rates of interaction.

The concept of interaction rates added a dynamic facet to the model and brought human relations explicitly into the cultural system. Separation was viewed not only in symbolic terms but also as a phase in which interaction between the neophyte and his/her previous social relations was reduced or completely eliminated (Chapple and Coon 1942:48). In transition, the individual interacts with the new system of which he or she will eventually become a part. Finally, in incorporation, the individual is returned to his or her previous social environment, but in a new status and in different symbolic relations with people (506).

Chapple and Coon regarded the changes in personnel and social relations in society as inherently disturbing. They thus considered how the elements of symbol in rites of passage eased and facilitated individuals' transitions from one position to the next and enhanced the capacity of the broader cultural group to adjust to these disquieting changes (308).

Symbolic Interaction. To enhance an essentially macro-perspective from anthropology, the micro-perspective of the sociological theory of symbolic interaction was integrated. Erving Goffman, although not the source of the school of symbolic interaction, is certainly one of the most well-known proponents and popularizers of the approach (see Goffman 1961, 1963, 1967, 1969, 1970, among others). Goffman has remained untroubled by the anthropological controversy over the existence of secularized rituals. With little ado, Goffman has assumed a priori the rituals of social relations. He has conceptualized rituals in much the same way that anthropologists do. Goffman's definition of ritual (rather elusive if one seeks an exact statement) emerges from the contexts of his discussions (e.g., Goffman 1967) and is congruent with Jaquetta H. Burnett's (1975:46) secularized anthropological definition as "formalized interpersonal behavior." For Goffman, rituals are firmly ensconced in the social relations of interaction. Like symbolic interactionists preceding him, he focuses on individuals whose statuses and identities are actively and creatively negotiated in ritualized and standardized presentations. People are the dynamic facilitators of their cultural environment as it is translated, manipulated, and given meaning in human interplay.

Goffman's perspective is in the tradition of George H. Mead, who is credited with establishing the school of thought in his work, *Mind, Self and Society* (1934). He contributed the concept of the self as important in understanding interaction and the notion that interaction itself is crucial in ascribing meaning to an experiential domain (Blumer 1969:5). The self is a self-conscious, interpretive facet of the individual, who is able to separate him/herself from others yet has the capacity to take the part of the other. The self is considered the significant variable in understanding the dynamics of meaning in the interactive process (Blumer 1969:80). Mead's three underlying premises characterize the school of symbolic interaction and the relations of self, interaction, and meaning: (1)"human beings act toward things on the basis the meanings have for them"; (2) "the meaning of such things is derived from or arises out of the social interaction that one has with one's fellows"; and (3) "these meanings are handled in, and modified through, an interpretive process used by the person in dealing with the things [she or] he encounters" (Blumer 1969:1).

Social relations are thus viewed as the continual process of interpreting others' actions and one's own actions, and meaning is an essential attribute of this process. People are envisaged as active participants in their cultural matrix, where meaning is not merely superorganically imposed but interpreted by individuals "creating their social reality and sense of self as they engage in community life and as they interpret and evaluate the meaning of their interactions with others" (Kaufman 1981:54). Because people are active, not just reactive, agents in the creation of meaning, the context (or the social environment) in which they interact assumes meaning as part of the interpretive process (Kaufman 1981:54). Symbolic interaction as a school of thought thus focuses on the dynamic aspects of the creation of meaning as an ongoing modus operandi of the self.

Transsexual Identity Transformation

The transsexual gender journey was a "becoming." It was a multifaceted transition that was a total process and implied much more than a simple switch of status. The process of becoming involved the transmutation of the *personal identity*, defined here as how a person conceives of her/himself, including one's gender identity; gender-role identity—"a set of expectations about what behaviors are appropriate for people of one's gender" (Kessler and McKenna 1978:11–12); self concept, and world view—"the way we see ourselves in relation to all else" (Redfield 1953:85–86).

The process also involved the transformation of social identity. *Social identity* is defined as a "pattern of observable or inferable attributes [that] 'identifies' . . . the self and others; his [her] identity is a socially labeled object which is of great concern and frequently revaluated both by the person and others in the groups in which he [she] is a member" (Miller 1963, quoted in Schwartz and Merton 1975:196). It also includes the construct of gender role (sex role) as those culturally approved behaviors associated with males and females. Facets of gender-role or sex-role identity are defined as "interests, activities, dress, [and] skills" socially approved for the two genders (Kessler and McKenna 1978:2, 11–12). Social identity is how an audience perceives and endorses the individual as a role occupant or member of a category fulfilling role prescriptions, meanings, and scripts (Goffman 1963:2; Vernon 1965:125).

Personal identity is closely tied to social identity since self-perception is, in part, determined through interaction whereby others respond to the social identity performance. This has been called the "looking glass self" (Cooley 1928, quoted in Vernon 1965:145); we see ourselves (to some degree) as others see us. During the transsexual's rite of transition the personal and social identities were transformed into integrated components of the whole; change in one identity had ramifications for the other.

Personal identity is envisaged as a hierarchy of identities, where one identity is primary and others are subidentities around which one organizes the self. During the transsexual's identity transformation, the primary identity of transsexual and the subidentity of female gained ascendancy. The emergence of this identity was facilitated through interaction in the Berdache Society, where it became clear what it meant to be a member of the category "transsexual." This was enhanced by other transsexuals' furnishing social identity reinforcement for one's presentation (social identity) as transsexual.

The female subidentity was a *felt* but not a *lived* identity at the time most individuals joined the Berdache Society. As transsexuals entered the Berdache Society and as they entered the rite of transition, their social identity underwent change. They would increasingly dress as females, attempt to pass undetected in public more frequently, and in effect live two lives (referred to here as the dual role phase). At some point they would "go full-time" and live as females

100 percent of the time. Living the female social identity and gaining reinforcement for their performances from their "own" (other transsexuals) and unknowing audiences fed into their personal identity as females. The female identity became a primary identity once the label "transsexual" was accepted and mediated through group interaction (see Goffman 1963:19, 66).

The primary identity of female, for a time, carried the subidentity transsexual. This was associated with transsexuals' focus on passing, a central theme in the rite of transition. With passing they learned to hide their transsexual stigma. They engaged in techniques of information control to hide their male genotype, history, and past social identity. At some point during full-time status, they transformed their personal and social identity to the point that they viewed themselves as "natural" women who were comfortable occupants of the female role, and they rejected their transsexual identity as well as the term *passing*, for they were now merely being who they really were: females. This had been accomplished with the aid of hormones that feminized their bodies. Physical feminization was an important part of their becoming and their personal and social identity transformation, because it enhanced their self-perception as females and their role performances.

This view of identity is in the constructionist tradition in anthropology, which regards identities as socially created and brokered by gender cues, including cultural meanings associated with somatotypes, such as body contours, degree of muscularity, roundness or softness, body modifications and mortifications, speech (including paralanguage, language expression, and communication patterns), and sartorial expression. The position taken here is that the rites of passage transsexuals undergo foster the development of their sense of self as females as part of the gender attribution process, whereby transsexuals come to learn to present themselves successfully as women, embodying cultural meanings of physical, verbal, and nonverbal expressions. This is a learning process for the transsexual that is crucial to the ultimate establishment of a fully developed female identity. According to Holly Devor (1989:140), "gender status is learned by displaying the culturally defined insignia of the gender category with which one identifies."

Transsexuals support the "incorrigible proposition" that there are only two genders—male and female (not in-between); these are "natural" and are determined by the genitalia (Garfinkel 1967:116–85; Feinbloom 1976:150; Kessler and McKenna 1978:112–41). Yet the reality is one of which transsexuals are all too aware. In the everyday process of living one's gender, gender is attributed on the basis of gender cues—insignias that are visible, not hidden from view, such as the genitalia. Transsexual gender theory incorporates two seeming contradictions: first, gender is a socially constructed phenomenon that transsexuals learn (I maintain this is escalated through a rite of passage); second, although gender is learned, it is based on an ideology of the biology of genital differences. Subscribing to this logic, transsexuals must have the surgery, because women are people with clitorises and vaginas, just as men are people with penises and scrotums. Although they endorse this view, transsexuals acknowledge that in the course of their physical feminization produced by female hormone therapy and while learning the art of passing, they become, in fact, women with penises for a time. They therefore know that the genitalia are not a determinant of gender. In addition, they recognize that gender identity, the component transsexuals regard as the core criterion of gender, is independent of genitalia and gender roles.

Holly Devor (1989:145–54; 1987:12–14, 34–38) posits that although Western society proposes a gender schema (belief system underlying the construction of gender) based on genitalia as the determinant of one's status as a woman or a man, in actuality the attribution process is the reverse; that is, one's social presentation of self leads others to assume one's sex and the presence of the concordant genitalia. Transsexuals, therefore, acknowledge the dominant gender schema as one that affects them. Because of this gender schema, they pursue sex-change surgery instead of opting for a potentially stigmatizing alternative, such as an androgynous presentation. In intimate relationships and women's backstage areas, such as restrooms, locker rooms, or circumstances in which the attire is so skimpy that the male genitals cannot be hidden (e.g., bathing suits), the genitals can be problematic as vehicles for discrediting the female presentation. Yet, for the majority of public interaction, transsexuals know that if their display of gender cues is convincing as females, people will assume they are "natural" born women. Transsexuals are thus social scientists themselves, independently discovering the actual operation of the gender attribution process and the articulation of gender in everyday life (Devor 1989).

Rites of Passage as Therapy

The rite of transition was endowed with symbol and meaning expressed in rituals punctuating the transsexual's transformation into womanhood. Ritual referents were manifested as symbols of the birth of woman and the death of man. These accented the transsexual's progress in the rite of transition. The identity transformation mirrored the three phases of the rite of passage: separation, transition, and incorporation.

The rite of transition was specifically a rite of exit from a former male role and entrance into a female role. It was a journey through "liminality," where transsexuals were "betwixt and between" (Turner 1974:13–14, 231–33; Middleton 1973:388), for they were no longer males and not yet complete women. In transition, they became women with penises. The resolution was the rite of incorporation, in which a "neovagina" was constructed and they conformed to the cultural minimal requirement for claiming the female gender. Their transformation involved making "order out of disorder" (Middleton 1973:388) and normalcy out of stigma (Turner 1967:94).

Status (positions in society) transformations include role (behaviors associated with status) transformations as well as changes in concepts of self or identities. Victor Turner (1967, 1968, 1969) has provided a broadly applicable theory of religion, originally based on his research on Ndembu rituals. Because of its focus on ritual and rites of passage, Turner's theory of religion is relevant to the identity transformation that occurs during transsexuals' rites of passage. As individuals enter the transition phase, they have the unique opportunity to recognize their common humanity unencumbered by the structures of society. Turner (1969) refers to this as "communitas." Communitas, or the recognition of a sense of human bondedness, emerges from tension created by structures of society pushing and pulling individuals apart. Societal structures separate people by creating distinctions, roles, statuses, hierarchies, and rules that restrain. This separates people from their shared humanity, which is glimpsed through anti-structure, the antithesis of structure. Anti-structure, "the reverse of structure, is the segment of the world within which statuses, roles, and norms do not occur. Anti-structure exists outside structure, between structural categories, and at the bottom of structure" (Cohen and Eames 1982:242). During transsexuals' transitional period, given the Western logic of gender constructs, they are between structure, for they are women with penises—neither properly males nor females.

As shown cross-culturally, individuals in marginal periods, such as initiates, must be closely constrained and watched since those outside structure are theoretically unpredictable (Douglas 1966 in Frayser 1985:145). Similarly, transsexuals are under the careful scrutiny of their caregivers during the period of transition.

Transsexuals' creation of a biocultural explanation of their transformation as a neoadolescence (discussed later) incorporates elements from the Western gender system that regards biology as paramount. Their biocultural model of womanhood, based on this Western logic of gender and the cultural construction of adolescence, anchors the transsexuals in a dynamic interaction between structure and antistructure, providing a framework for what could be overwhelming nothingness—the nothingness that comes of being neither male nor female.

The transsexuals' rite of passage, particularly their rite of transition, is therapeutic. It facilitates the transformation of their identities from fantasies of womanhood to a lived womanhood, which in turn contributes to their psychic transformation. They undergo a resocialization process as others respond to the female persona and presentation.

Rituals ease individuals' transitions into and between statuses and unquestionably include what can be regarded as therapeutic components for disquieting changes. That status transformation is problematic and has ramifications on identity is axiomatic. As the individual undertakes separation, liminality, and incorporation, the identity, both social and personal, undergoes incredible transformation. The male personal and social identity is dispersed and literally melts away. It is gradually replaced by the development of, first, a transsexual personal identity and, later, a female gender identity, accompanied by physical changes that represent feminization. A social identity transformation occurs as well. The female role becomes a more "natural" presentation as the transsexual learns to present gender cues associated with females in this society.

The rite of passage transsexuals participate in is therapeutic in another sense. As the transsexual comes to acknowledge herself as a transsexual in quest of surgery, she is thrust into a personal status crisis. Since status changes incorporate identity changes, rites of passage facilitate identity transformation by separating the individual from the previous status so that new learning can occur and a new self can emerge. This is not unlike the mazeway resynthesis that Anthony Wallace describes for leaders of revitalization movements, whose transformation is facilitated by extreme stress (Bourguignon 1979:325–26).

Like initiates, transsexuals are subjected to extreme stress throughout the first two phases of the rites of passage. As suggested by Suzanne Frayser (1985:145–49), rites of passage are very similar to the Western therapy defined here as "an interpersonal process whereby patients or clients work toward achieving desired changes in thinking, feeling, or behavior with a therapist, a professional trained in the behavioral sciences" (Grant 1982:337). Like Western therapy, rites of passage "cushion" identity change and "restore equilibria" (Posinsky 1962:388).

The therapeutic components of ritual and the processes of healing are well described by anthropologists (e.g., Dow 1986). Rituals, like therapy, ultimately help an individual establish and re-create relationships that have been interrupted by the individual's crisis (Dow 1986:59), which in turn reduces anxiety and allows for a new self to emerge. Undoubtedly, the cathecting of feeling through ritual expression is a part of this (Posinsky 1962:376–81). According to Gardner Murphy, the individual acquires selfhood or personal identity (as discussed here) through the mechanisms of "identification and role playing, projection and introjection; that is, by activities that are 'interwoven with experiencing other individuals' " (Murphy 1947, quoted in Bock 1988:198). Individuals in a therapeutic process participate in the same process that transsexuals do. Both the individual in therapy and the transsexual involved in rite of passage have the opportunity to find and create a new self. This self is in part socially constituted, through interaction, as it is "tried out" and experimented with.

The transsexuals' transformation was similar to the therapeutic one in other arenas as well. Their transformation involved the psychic process of dissociation, whereby irrelevant past learning is filtered out and replaced with relevant information (cf. ritual learning, Wallace 1966 in Myerhoff 1982:121), just as occurs in the course of the therapeutic process. Other psychic processes that take place in therapy can be seen in transsexuals' transformation as well, including reinforcement from the environment for their new interactions as woman (Myerhoff 1982:121).

In summary, the rites of passage in general, and transsexual rites of passage specifically, are therapeutic for the individual. In addition, the Western therapy process and the individual's rites of passage function similarly in terms of psychic transformation.

The Rite of Transition

The term *transition* is a double entendre of etic (scientific) and emic (insider) meanings. In the rites of passage model it is the liminal phase between statuses, where the individual is no longer in a previous status and not yet of a new status. It is a state of ambiguity, reconciled by incorporation into the new position in society (Turner 1967:94, 1974:13–14; Middleton 1973:388). Medical and mental health caregivers use the term to describe the period in transsexuals' lives when they seek caregiver help with an agenda designed to weed out the women from the men. It is a period characterized by transsexuals' recognizing themselves as members of that category and one in which they set about the task of pursuing sex-change surgery. From the caregiver perspective, transsexuals are "in transition" when they go to a therapist, begin taking hormones, prepare for and actually assume full-time status, and work in the role of women. Transsexuals accept this medical/mental health terminology and refer to themselves as "in transition," using the same parameters.

Whether consciously or unconsciously, caregivers have chosen a term that is the symbolic equivalent of birth. Transition is a medical term associated with childbirth. It refers to the period of maximal cervical expansion prior to the actual birth of the child. Correspondingly, transition for transsexuals is the period prior to their final rebirth, when they become at last complete females, both socially and physically. They return once more to the setting of their first birth, the hospital, where medical professionals, who first declared that "it's a boy," now declare them female. If the obviousness of the analogy has escaped the caretakers, it must still be seen as more than just an ironic coincidence, reflecting the power of symbolic expression where changes in life situations are often expressed through biological analogues (see Van Gennep 1960:3).

In many instances, transsexuals were consciously aware of their symbolic rebirth and were active participants in creating their own birth, overtly using biological and social metaphors to explain their progress in becoming. In this manner, as they looked and acted the part more convincingly, they felt more womanly in identity. The agendas marking their progressive integration into society as women were transformed into something more than the mere accomplishment of such tasks as passing and going full-time. They became symbolic dramas of cultural myths about sex roles, gender, and identity such that transsexuals became women by reference to genetic women (cf. Read 1980:16). As will be discussed later, the transsexuals became women by going through the same process that genetic women do.

When transsexuals entered transition, they led double lives. At work, they continued to present themselves as males, but at home the actual social identity of emergent women was manifested by more frequently dressing as females. At the same time, their bodies were becoming feminized as a result of taking female hormones. When in the female role and in the process of learning to pass in public, transsexuals learned a myriad of techniques to cover their male physical attributes, verbal and nonverbal aspects of the male role they so long occupied, and any other information from their male past likely to disrupt their female role performance. The more they practiced passing, the more naturally they acted as women. During this dual role phase, they gradually became habituated to their performance as women, and it no longer required the self-conscious effort that it did at first. Full-time status provided the opportunity for their role presentation to become almost second nature. This was, however, a processual experience, beginning in the early phases of dual role occupancy and continuing through full-time status.

Needless to say, the male role could become problematic for transsexuals as their bodies feminized and they became more natural (i.e., less self-conscious) in their social identity performance as women. However, as passing behaviors increased, the male social identity was also in increasing jeopardy. The results of physical feminization could be hidden to some degree for some time, although changes became noticeable as fat was distributed in the female direction and breasts developed. Electrolysis also was either initiated or continued throughout transition. Other indications of changes occurred during the double phase in preparation for full-time status. Transsexuals grew their hair longer in anticipation of a more culturally female hairdo. Many took voice lessons and learned to alter the pitch and intonation patterns of speaking. Because transsexuals worked on learning to alter their voices, it became difficult for them to switch back and forth between male and female voice and speech patterns demanded by their double lives.[4] These factors, along with their habituation to the body language and proxemic behavior characteristically associated with females, could alter their presentation as "normal" men. They would then take pains to hide the effects of feminization so they would not discredit their status as males. Fellow workers, however, often discerned the changes in their appearance and performance. According to the transsexuals, their coworkers usually suspected they were homosexuals.

The transsexuals progressed from a potentially stigmatizing phase prior to transition, where cross-dressing was hidden, to dual role status, where there was even greater risk for stigmatization. The double life ceased when transsexuals felt they had feminized to the point that it could discredit their male status. The additional effort required to conceal their female attributes when in the male role triggered their going to full-time status. At this point, they made the decision to change jobs and set aside money for a period of unemployment or notified people at work that they would be changing genders.[5]

In addition to a social identity transformation that had been occurring through hormones and a marked improvement in passing, a personal identity transformation took place. The female identity was in the process of gaining ascendance over the primary transsexual identity. As they increasingly dressed as women, they felt they really were female. The male role now required additional effort. This produced an internal stress that propelled transsexuals into full-time status. One transsexual felt "positively schizophrenic." Dressed as a woman in public, she had to pass as a female; dressed as a male, she had to present herself as the man she no longer considered herself to be. The period in which they were hormonally becoming females and were learning the art of passing by spending more and more time in the female role was a time of personal identity growth, which would ultimately lead to the rejection of the label "transsexual." This happened with, and was exacerbated by, full-time status. But again this was a gradual process of rejection, coterminous with the emergence of a full-fledged female identity. Dressing the part of women, habituation to the female role, and audience reinforcement all contributed to the waxing of the personal identity as females.

One major mechanism fostering their becoming, in terms of personal and social identity, lay in transsexual ideology, where physical feminization and learning to pass were reinterpreted as inherent in womanhood per se, not as something peculiar to transsexuals. Transsexuals perceived themselves as undergoing the same rite of passage that young genetic females participated in as they became women. This ideology was built on a biocultural model of womanhood, as well as their own experience watching and observing young females as they were growing up.

Biological Maturation as the Idiom for Womanhood

Genetic females' maturation is a biological and cultural development, marked by physical and social changes in status, whereby biological growth is culturally designated and given broader social meaning (Turner 1967:93). In Western culture, puberty for genetic females is a period of transition, during which they will emerge as women from the previous state of being little "girls."

A point of explanation is in order. Adolescence is a culturally constituted phenomenon and its recognition varies cross-culturally and even historically. For example, it was not until 1904 that adolescence was given status as a distinctive phase in the life course in the United States (Myerhoff 1982:110). Adolescence came to be regarded as evidence of the power of biology in affecting human behavior. This biocentric view is still an established part of Western gender constructs, although in 1928 Margaret Mead challenged the prevailing "raging hormone" theory of adolescence with her work *Coming of Age in Samoa*. Barbara Myerhoff (1982:110) eloquently notes that "separations are socially imposed upon its [life's] natural continuity, divisions established, cut-off points provided, distinctions made." Puberty as a cultural phase therefore may or may not be marked by biological changes. As a Western social construct, however, puberty is regarded as biologically constituted, a phase characterized by *Sturm und Drang* (storm and stress) and clearly indicated by the development of secondary sexual characteristics. It is the alleged "raging hormones" of adolescence that also give it its reputation as a phase of sexual awakenings and experimentation with behaviors that are portents of adult status. Transsexuals undertook their own neopuberty, a construction of a construction resting on a bed of biocentrism.

Although transsexuals were physically transforming themselves into hermaphrodites through hormone usage, transsexual ideology reinterpreted this as a maturation period or a period of puberty in which they were approaching womanhood the way genetic females do. As a result of hormones, fat was redistributed so that transsexuals developed breasts and hips, and the waist consequently appeared smaller (and might actually have become smaller) in proportion to the other dimensions. According to Anthony Gottlieb, these changes take about as long as genetic females' puberty does (1980:6).

Transsexuals' biological maturation was an idiom for their womanhood. Feminization then became more than just a biological change. It was a symbolic referent expressing cultural perceptions of the meaning of biological changes and facilitating the development of a primary identity as female. The idiom, through the meaning transsexuals derived from genetic females, was transformed into something more; they were in reality becoming women, not just "like" but "as" genetic females. As a consequence, the primary transsexual identity assumed an increasingly subordinate position, and the female subidentity became crystallized into a primary identity.

Their physical puberty was recognized as a life stage that all women encountered. They were, in fact, becoming women as women do, not like gay female impersonators and transvestites, whom they regarded as creatures of artifice. Transvestites and gay female impersonators were metaphorical women, while transsexuals were becoming "real" women, for they were encountering the same physical changes that accompany girls' transition into womanhood. This aspect of their transition was one in which their phenotypic changes became a symbol of transsexual parturition as women. It was a symbol of an inner process given substance by the outer change.

Transsexuals have turned the outward inward. Their maturation was a key not just to passing (although it certainly gave credibility to the social identity dance) but also to naturalness since they no longer needed breast or hip padding. Their physical feminization eventually led transsexuals to reject the notion of passing and the label "transsexual," because they were presenting themselves as they were: women.

Transsexuals were very conscious of their maturation. They wore their newly developing breasts proudly, declaring "that's all me." They were keenly aware of their own breast development and that of other transsexuals. They again were "as" genetic women, developing at different rates. As soon as some breast development was perceivable, they discarded padding and brassiere inserts and wore thin bras or no bras at all. They kept track of growth by brassiere cup size. Changing from an *AA* cup to an *A*, or from an *A* to a *B* cup size, was a significant event, announced and shared. Their fascination with their breast development was akin to that of genetic females in puberty.[6]

Despite the drop in libido that is a well-known concomitant of hormone therapy, transsexuals' breast growth was accompanied by a sense of impending sexuality. Because their breasts became tender and sensitive as they enlarged, and because in our society breasts are erotic symbols, transsexuals were immensely aware of themselves as sensual beings. In plain words, they felt sexy about having breasts on their bodies, even though libidinal interest had declined. In this way, they viewed themselves as genetic females, whose puberty is culturally regarded as a period of sexual and sensual awakenings.

The transition period in which they were developing was verbally acknowledged as their own puberty: "I'm in puberty now" or "I'm just a teenager," reckoning age based not on actual chronology but on the biosocial analogy. Another transsexual's words on the changes during her readolescence are instructive: "How resilient this human anatomical form of mine seemed to be. How it seemed to meet the challenge of the direction of this new and different hormonal-directed development. My skin softened, my pores became smaller and more refined and I fought with the problems of teenage complexion (in my forties). My appearance seemed to youthen."

In the present discussion, then, puberty is viewed not just as a biological event but also as an event reconstructed in cultural denotation. Transsexuals utilized the concepts of their own culture to construe their own transgender experience. This fostered a metamorphosis from the cocoon of a little girl, where the female identity was a mere fantasy, to full womanhood, where the female identity emerged as cause and effect of the social meaning given "neopuberty."

Transsexuals' neoadolescence contained the same paradox that their ethnotheory of gender had. Their biological maturation was reinterpreted in terms of the current "raging hormone" theory of puberty. This was represented in a playful game that began with the statement, "You know you're on hormones when . . . ," often followed with some gender stereotype or such clever construction as "you have an uncontrollable urge to put down the toilet seat." In addition, these transsexuals often reported that they felt more emotional, clearly linking gender stereotypes and biology. On the other hand, they knew that adolescence was a period of learning about one's gender and that they were involved in a resocialization process, one in which they had a second chance to learn a gender.

As "pubescent" females, transsexuals experimented with the images of adult womanhood available in American society. They explained that genetic females in puberty wobble in high heels and wear outlandish high-fashion makeup and exaggerated clothing as they investigate women's culture. Transsexuals viewed their own early passing attempts as analogous to this experience. They looked back on their hyperfeminine and superchic clothing, their exaggerated makeup and hairdos, and their learning to walk in high heels as part of their puberty. These extremes were regarded as legitimate because genetic females themselves must experiment as teenagers before a mode of presentation is finally arrived at. They were, therefore, the same as genetic females, who experiment with and exaggerate the cultural accoutrements of womanhood during this period.

For transsexuals, genetic girls' rites of passage into womanhood were their own. It was part of transsexual rhetoric that physical and social maturation was the idiom of their own becoming. Their puberty was not just a metaphor but a "reality" of transformation that accompanied and organized the development of a female gender identity and the learned parameters of that identity.

No Longer a Transsexual

Full-time was the period in which the final transformation of the female identity occurred. During full-time, transsexuals had the opportunity to become completely habituated to their female role performance. They became much less self-conscious about passing. Passing unfolded as an incrementally spontaneous performance that became "natural" (Kessler and McKenna 1978:121–25). By extension, they also became natural women. This was a process of creating a lived history as women, women who had undergone puberty and who were establishing their adult status as females. Their transition was a reiteration of their progress out of ambiguity and into coherence (Turner 1967:94). They were on their way to becoming whole people.

Going full-time was an important event in the lives of transsexuals. After their double lives in which they became more like women as a consequence of the dynamics described, full-time status gave transsexuals access to really "being" women. It was here that "doing" (or enacting and living in Kessler and McKenna 1978:126) the female status everyday, including interacting with others only as women, gave transsexuals an inside edge on knowing how it felt to be female. Transsexuals agreed there was something magical about the full-time position because of the internal changes in identity and perspective that occurred. By analogy with genetic women, part of what made them women was their doing womanhood everyday, and this was what all transsexuals had to do if they were ever really to become women.

As transsexuals felt like, acted like, portrayed, and approximated genetic women, they began to reject the label "transsexual." This was manifested in "affiliation cycles" in the Berdache Society, where affiliation with their own declined (see Goffman 1963:20, 38). They had, by becoming full-time women, tasted "normalcy" and were accepted by naive audiences as natural women. And "presumably the more an individual is allied with normals, the more he [she] will see him[her]-self in non-stigmatic terms . . . " (Goffman 1963:107). Transsexuals were presented with the choice of remaining transsexual, and hence being stigmatized by continuing group association, or becoming women, "normal" members of society.

All transsexuals in the group wanted to disappear into society as women. They had spent a lifetime of not belonging and feeling out of place in their male gender roles. Unlike many other minorities, they wished to escape their stigmatized transsexual status, not destigmatize transsexualism. If they continued to affiliate with other transsexuals in the Berdache Society meetings, they would continue to be labeled "transsexual." Although they had learned a great deal from the Berdache Society, it had outlived its usefulness. In response to the question of why they did not continue to attend meetings, the transsexuals replied, "They are all younger than me"; "I've outgrown the group"; "It has nothing more to teach me"; or "I've been through all the stuff they're talking about, and it bores me."

During full-time, the transsexuals continued to associate with their own age-mates, construed in terms of physical feminization and passing ability. These were people who in transsexual argot were "as far along." The full-time (and even postoperative) transsexuals would return to the group meetings for ceremonial visits, where they acted as models of "normalization" (Goffman 1963:30–31), showing the younger transsexuals what they could look forward to as they progressed through transition. By returning to the group, they acted as models of becoming for the other younger transsexuals and revealed inside information about problems and successes in full-time.

The Berdache Society was regarded as a temporary association and a temporary phase of a transsexual identity. It provided support, reinforcement, information, and instruction on passing, role models, and an ideological system with norms for how men become women. Transsexuals all recognized the importance of the group in their lives, and they recognized there would be a time when they would leave the group. This was invariably correlated with anticipating and going full-time. For example, even Sasha, the transsexual director of the Berdache Society, had severed ties with the group to some degree, although she continued to attend the transsexual weekly meetings (an important part of the Berdache Society's services) in her official capacity. She had, however, discontinued meetings at her home, explicitly to create a more normal environment, where she could preserve her reputation with her neighbors as a natural woman. This occurred when she moved to a new apartment and had the opportunity to create a network of people who knew her only as Sasha the woman, not the transsexual.

From a single event in the Berdache Society meetings, it was possible to assess the transsexuals' progress in transition and to recognize those who were beginning to disaffiliate or had disaffiliated from the group. Invariably, Sasha (who because of her position as director was in some ways unique) began the meetings with "I'm Sasha and I'm a transsexual," followed by introductions all around the group. Those who were about to separate, were in the process of separating, or had separated from their own would introduce themselves by their female names only. An introduction such as, "Hi, I'm Ginny," left poignant silences as the others waited for the identifier that never came. This clearly pointed to two stages and respective identities for neophytes. The youngsters followed the name with the label transsexual or an occasional "don't know."

With this simple act, those approaching or in full-time status not only expressed their primary identities as women but rejected the label "transsexual" as stigmatizing. Being transsexual was an identity phase to be outgrown as one became a woman and sought normalcy. Whereas the label "transsexual" had once been a godsend, providing a category around which to focus their identity, it now became a dirty word, a discreditor of the claim to womanhood.

As they became established in the female role, progressed from ambiguity to order, and incrementally integrated into society, their penises became glaring symbols of the limits of their incorporation into the female role and indicative of the fragility of their incorporation into society. During full-time status, the desire for surgery intensified as the penis increasingly was perceived as an attribute discordant with the female identity. It perpetuated their subidentity as transsexual and was a constant reminder of their past. After surgery, the transsexuals tried to forget about their male history, although to some extent they would always have a transsexual subidentity because they would always have to edit part of their history. After the surgery, however, the transsexual subidentity became less important as a component of their total identity.

Their success in the full-time role and their ability to pass and to get jobs as women indicated to their mental health caregivers their readiness for surgery. If they had done all this and still wanted the surgery, the caregivers considered them a good surgical risk and recommended them for the surgical conversion. Their female identities and their social identity performances thus legitimized them in the eyes of those who controlled the surgery.

The tension created by the incongruity between penis and identity led transsexuals to request their primary caregivers for an evaluation for surgery. The more they lived full-time, the more they wanted the surgery; the longer they had lived full-time (a minimum of one year), the more inclined their caregivers were to provide them with favorable evaluations. They were, at this point, totally prepared for surgery. The agenda they had followed and the transsexual ideology underlying the agenda had served to "soften each blow" (Coon 1971:9) of the transition. They were finally ready, and there was no turning back.

The surgical conversion punctuated the culmination of their transition. It was their passage out of liminality and was a symbolic and ritual event dramatizing their exit. Surgery consummated a journey that was regularized, patterned, and clearly defined.

Becoming was the crux of the rite of transition. It was a multidimensional passage, including the components of personal identity, social identity, and physical transformation, shadowed by phases in their rites of transition whereby one status was transformed into another. Becoming was an inside-outside transformation, where the development of the personal identity (psyche, mind) was matched by a social identity transformation (role, sex-role identity, and so forth) and physical transformation (body), and these three domains of becoming dovetailed into a paradigm of passages dramatized by a rite of transition.

NOTES

1. Henceforth, the term *transsexuals* will be used to refer to this research population, but it should not be construed to mean all transsexuals.

2. Portions of this essay are based on my book *In Search of Eve: Transsexual Rites of Passage* (1988). I would like to thank Bergin and Garvey for permission to use those sections. This essay, however, represents a reconceptualization and expansion of my previous work.

3. The emic ("native" insider) and etic (scientific outsider) distinction is seriously challenged as a false dichotomy in postmodernist writing. Clifford Geertz (1973) has suggested experience far and experience near concepts as an alternative. George E. Marcus and Michael M. J. Fischer (1986) provide an excellent critical review of the field.

4. Voice lessons were undertaken at various times during transition. Many waited until after they had gone full-time, because it required too much effort to switch in and out of male and female voice patterns.

5. The strategy endorsed by transsexuals was to quit one's job and then go full-time, living on savings for awhile until a new job as a woman could be acquired. The worst strategy, sometimes unavoidable, was to go full-time on the job. One transsexual had pursued this strategy, violating other transsexuals' beliefs about the proper scheduling of events in transition. Under the influence of her therapist Hope, Lydia had chosen "androgyny" as the idiom of her transition. She had informed her employers of her transsexualism and was gradually feminizing herself. She was not like the transsexuals who had lived a double life, attempting to hide the effects of physical feminization but gradually allowing them to be apparent. Hope endorsed this strategy as one in which the individual would go through a phase of being recognized as neither male nor female but as "embracing both." Other transsexuals thought this was a poor strategy, a violation of the rules of conduct of "the

way" a transsexual should pursue womanhood. Transsexuals supported the notion that there are only two sexes. For the transsexual to pass as a woman was one foot in the door of normalcy in a dual gender system. Androgyny to transsexuals was an unnecessary and stigmatizing route to womanhood.

6. It must be pointed out that these transsexuals were, with the exception of one, over thirty years old. Their perceptions of little girls' puberty as a cultural phenomena were influenced by the era in which they grew up. The cultural information about how little girls experience puberty, which was also responsible for the transsexuals' biocultural model of womanhood, may reflect some cultural lag. Many Americans are rearing children in a nonsexist milieu. The nontraditional socialization of children will undoubtedly affect the manifestation of children's rites of passage into adulthood and influence the meaning of puberty as a biocultural phenomenon.

REFERENCES

Benjamin, Harry. 1966. *The Transsexual Phenomenon.* New York: Julian Press.
Blumer, Herbert. 1969. *Symbolic Interactionism: Perspective and Method.* Englewood Cliffs, N.J.: Prentice-Hall.
Bock, Philip. 1988. *Rethinking Psychological Anthropology.* New York: W. H. Freeman.
Bolin, Anne. 1988. *In Search of Eve: Transsexual Rites of Passage.* South Hadley, Mass.: Bergin and Garvey.
Bourguignon, Erika. 1979. *Psychological Anthropology.* New York: Holt, Rinehart and Winston.
Burnett, Jaquetta H. 1975. "Ceremony, Rites and Economy in a Student System of an American High School." In *The Nacirema*, ed. J. P. Spradley and M. A. Rynkiewich. Boston: Little, Brown.
Chapple, Elliott, and C. S. Coon. 1942. *Principles of Anthropology.* New York: Holt, Rinehart and Winston.
Cohen, Eugene, and Edwin Eames. 1982. *Cultural Anthropology.* Boston: Little, Brown.
Coon, C. S. 1971. *The Hunting Peoples.* Boston: Little, Brown.
Devor, Holly. 1987. "Gender Blending Females." *American Behavioral Scientist* 31:12–40.
———. 1989. *Gender Blending: Confronting the Limits of Duality.* Bloomington: Indiana University Press.
Dow, James. 1986. "Universal Aspects of Symbolic Healing: A Theoretical Synthesis." *American Anthropologist* 88:56–69.
Feinbloom, Deborah H. 1976. *Transvestites and Transsexuals: Mixed Views.* New York: Delcorte Press.
Frayser, Suzanne. 1985. *Varieties of Sexual Experience.* New Haven, Conn.: HRAF Press.
Garfinkel, Harold. 1967. *Studies in Ethnomethodology.* Englewood Cliffs, N.J.: Prentice-Hall.

Geertz, Clifford. 1973. *The Interpretation of Cultures.* New York: Basic Books.
———. 1983. "From the Natives' Point of View: On the Nature of Anthropological Understanding." In *The Pleasures of Anthropology,* ed. Norris Freilich. New York: New American Library.
Goffman, Erving. 1961. *Encounters.* New York: Bobbs-Merrill.
———. 1963. *Stigma: Notes on the Management of a Spoiled Identity.* Englewood Cliffs, N.J.: Prentice-Hall.
———. 1967. *Interaction Ritual.* Garden City, N.Y.: Doubleday.
———. 1969. *Strategic Interaction.* New York: Ballantine Books.
———. 1970. *Gender Advertisements.* New York: Harper and Row.
Gottlieb, Anthony. 1980. "Transsexualism and Sexual Identity." Paper presented at the Vail Psychiatric Conference, Feb. 2, Beth Israel Hospital, Denver, Colorado.
Grant, Igor. 1982. "Psychotherapy: Brave New World or Requiem for Misguided Idealism." In *Anthropology of Medicine,* ed. L. Romanucci-Ross et al. South Hadley, Mass.: Bergin and Garvey.
Kaufman, Sharon. 1981. "Cultural Components of Identity in Old Age: A Case Study." *Ethos* 9:51–87.
Kessler, S. J., and W. McKenna. 1978. *Gender: An Ethnomethodological Approach.* New York: John Wiley and Sons.
Marcus, George E., and Michael M. J. Fisher. 1986. *Anthropology as Cultural Critique.* Chicago: University of Chicago Press.
Mead, George H. 1934. *Mind, Self and Society.* Chicago: University of Chicago Press.
Mead, Margaret. [1928] 1961. *Coming of Age in Somoa.* New York: Morrow Quill Paperbacks.
Middleton, J. 1973. "Some Categories of Dual Classification among the Lugbara of Uganda." In *Right and Left: Essays on Dual Symbolic Classification,* ed. R. Needham. Chicago: University of Chicago Press.
Myerhoff, Barbara. 1982. "Rites of Passage: Process and Paradox." In *Celebration,* ed. Victor Turner. Washington, D.C.: Smithsonian Institution Press.
Newton, Esther. 1972. *Mother Camp: Female Impersonation in America.* Englewood Cliffs, N.J.: Prentice-Hall.
Posinsky, S. H. 1962. "Ritual: Neurotic and Social." *American Imago* 19:375–90.
Read, K. 1980. *Other Voices: The Style of a Male Homosexual Tavern.* Novato, Calif.: Chandler and Sharp.
Redfield, R. 1953. *The Primitive World and Its Transformations.* Ithaca, N.Y.: Cornell University Press.
Schwartz, G., and D. Merton. 1975. "Social Identity and Expressive Symbols." In *The Nacirema,* ed. J. P. Spradley and M. A. Rynkiewich. Boston: Little, Brown.
Turner, Victor. 1962. "Three Symbols of Passage in Ndembu Circumcision Ritual." In *Essays on the Ritual of Social Relations,* ed. M. Gluckman. Manchester, England: University of Manchester Press.

———. 1967. "Betwixt and Between: The Liminal Period in Rites de Passage." In *The Forest of Symbols*, ed. V. Turner. Ithaca, N.Y.: Cornell University Press.

———. 1968. *The Drums of Affliction*. Oxford: Clarendon Press.

———. 1969. *The Ritual Process: Structure and Anti-Structure*. Chicago: Aldine.

———. 1974. *Dramas, Fields and Metaphors: Symbolic Action in Human Society*. Ithaca, N.Y.: Cornell University Press.

———. 1977. "Process, System and Symbol: A New Anthropological Synthesis." *Daedalus* 106(3):61–80.

Van Gennep, A. [1908] 1960. *The Rites of Passage*, trans. M. B. Vizedom and G. L. Caffee. London: Routledge and Kegal Paul.

Vernon, G. M. 1965. *Human Interaction*. New York: Ronald Press.

Michael V. Angrosino and Lucinda J. Zagnoli

Gender Constructs and Social Identity: Implications for Community-Based Care of Retarded Adults

In this essay, we accept the position of M. Kay Martin and Barbara Voorhies, who contend that "the recognition of males and females is universal, but the typical behaviors ascribed to them vary greatly from one society to the next" (1975:2).[1] Gender is therefore a matter of identity, which has three principal facets: *attributed status* (that which is assigned by society), *subjective status* (that which one thinks one fulfills), and *optative status* (that which one wishes to fulfill) (Harrington and Whiting 1972:488). The key to developing a well-balanced personality—one in which the individual is in relative harmony with his or her social environment—is to develop a balance among those three facets of identity.

These assumptions, however, are based on ethnographic descriptions of normative behavior. What, then, of people who for one reason or another have been socialized outside the mainstream? How can they first develop an image of self and then balance that image with one that others hold of them?

These questions have relevance, of course, to many racial, ethnic, or religious groups in pluralistic societies, members of which must, at some point (in public education, in the job market), adjust their behaviors to meet the expectations of the majority. The social and psychological consequences of such a dichotomized socialization are well documented (see, e.g., DeVos 1975). It has particular poignance in the case of those who cannot readily make an autonomous, informed decision about entering the mainstream and do not necessarily appreciate the consequences of doing so. Such are the mentally retarded adults who have entered the community as a result of the policy of deinstitutionalization (Lerman 1981) that has prevailed for the past decade.

On the basis of our experience in working with retarded adults in both community programs and individual counseling, it is our contention that despite all constraints, retarded people develop gender constructs to go along with their burgeoning physical sexuality, although these constructs are skewed by the countervailing forces of denial and suppression.[2] This essay addresses the following questions: What is the nature of gender constructs among retarded adults? In what ways are such people socialized into the acceptance of such constructs? How do those constructs differ from those of the mainstream? In what ways are they similar? What are the implications for the evolution of a reasonable policy of deinstitutionalization and community care?

We place gender constructs in the larger context of social identity, since gender is but one factor, along with race, ethnicity, religious affiliation, social class, and age, defining identity (Babad, Birnbaum, and Benne 1983:17). Identity has both objective and subjective components, and one of the critical problems in defining the social identity of deinstitutionalized retarded adults is that the subjective and objective elements of the gender part of that identity have not been allowed to develop in a balanced fashion.

Moderately or mildly mentally retarded children born since 1970 have grown up in school systems and other care facilities that operate under an explicit philosophy of "normalization" (Wolfensberger 1972). It is certainly possible to criticize such programs on both philosophical and practical grounds, but at least they have the virtue of providing a consistent socialization environment (at least as consistent as that provided to "normal" children).

On the other hand, those who are now adults very likely either endured the ghetto of CRMD (Children of Retarded Mental Development) classes in public schools or grew up in one or another type of custodial institution at a time when concepts like "least restrictive environment" (Shelton v. Tucker 1960; Wyatt v. Stickney 1972; New York State v. Carey 1975; Halderman v. Pennhurst State School 1977), "dignity of risk" (Perske 1972), "mainstreaming" (MacMillan 1977), and "normalization" (Frank 1975; Nirje 1980) were but faint hopes in the hearts of clients' rights advocates. As a result, their deinstitutionalization places them, as individuals, at a significant disadvantage and jeopardizes the aims of the community care movement as a whole.

The poor preparation of retarded adults for life in the community is compounded by the lack of appropriate support systems in the community itself. Retarded adults do not have the capacity to locate and utilize support services without some assistance, which is often not forthcoming. The result can be a feeling of social isolation and, for some, eventual reinstitutionalization.

The problem is further complicated by the widespread notion that "habilitation" of institutionalized mentally retarded adults in preparation for community placement involves mostly "life-skills training" (telling time, making change, taking care of personal hygiene). Mental retardation specialists have long recognized that successful adaptation to the community involves more than the acquisition of these simple skills; it requires the development of a true social competence (see, e.g., Dingman 1973:90). Yet the linked questions of adult sexual functioning and an identity that includes one's gender awareness—both of which should play a part in any realistic construct of social competence—have tended to be ignored. For example, the American Association on Mental Deficiency has developed a widely used scale to measure "adaptive behavior" (Nihira 1975). This scale is typically used to test clients' readiness for community placement. Out of nearly one hundred items, only four deal with sexuality, and these questions are grouped under the far from optimistic rubric "sexually aberrant behavior." They ask whether a client engages in "inappropriate masturbation," exposes his/her body inappropriately, has homosexual tendencies, or exhibits sexual behavior that is "socially unacceptable" (e.g., is overly seductive in appearance or action, hugs or caresses too intensely in public, lifts or unbuttons clothing to touch intimately, engages in sexual relations in public, is overly aggressive, has raped others, is easily taken advantage of sexually).

Similarly, several states have adopted adaptive behavior scales to monitor their own clients. Tennessee's Community Skills Profile (Tennessee Department of Mental Health and Mental Retardation 1980) is an example of a reasonably sophisticated, sensitive instrument, and yet out of its 239 separate items, only seven even touch on sexuality, and they again fall in the category of "inappropriate behavior." There is no formal recognition in such scales that the adaptation of an adult to a social setting requires more than knowing when *not* to do certain things in public. The development of a positive sexuality is not a factor in such scales. If the recognition of clients' biological sexuality has been slow to develop, the incorporation of training for the development of appropriate gender identities has been truly retarded.

There are two prevailing stereotypes that may account for this state of affairs. On the one hand, there is a nostalgic view (fostered perhaps by such retarded characters as Benjy Compson in *The Sound and the Fury* or Mickey Rooney's television role as "Bill") that retarded people are sweet-souled innocents, perpetual children with a transcendent wisdom-of-the-heart. Since our culture tends to equate innocence with an absence of sexuality, this view leads to the stereotype of the retarded adult as a kind of angelic neuter, who might, perhaps, need to be protected from sexual victimization but is not expected to develop an adult's sexual orientation. On the other hand, there is the "dumb brute" view that equates mental retardation with a general tendency toward disinhibition and depicts retarded men as grotesque monsters swept by uncontrollable lusts and retarded women as undiscriminating nymphomaniacs (see Evans 1983:254–59 for further discussion of sexual stereotyping of mentally retarded people). The persistence of these two clichés is not unlike the paradoxical view of primitives once held by even fairly enlightened Westerners: they are at once "noble savages" to be idealized and "bloodthirsty barbarians" who need to be fended off and controlled. These views were relatively harmless as long as retarded adults were far-off abstractions rather than next-door realities. A result of deinstitutionalization to a community that continues to believe in these clichés, however, is that neither the retarded people nor their putative hosts are well prepared for the true nature of the other.

Given the general unwillingness of even liberal caregivers to agree that mentally retarded adults do, in fact, have "normal" sex drives (whatever that means), it is not surprising that habilitation programs are structured to deny or suppress the need for sex education in the development of social competence. When the attitudes of denial and suppression are supported by the caregivers themselves, there may be a perpetuation of stereotypes through the staff training and development system. As a result, the mentally retarded adult may experience not only confusion about who they are as social entities but also confusion about the nature of the outside community, as represented to them by the staff members. It is therefore reasonable to expect that these clients are placed in a most confusing position: a veritable identity crisis.

In the following section we explore a model of identity formation in an attempt to understand the particular deviation represented in the socialization of deinstitutionalized retarded adults. As Paul Koegel has pointed out, current retardation researchers have begun to reexamine "the basic tenet that mental retardation is a pathology solely indigenous to the individual" (1978:1). Koegel is part of a research team of anthropologists, sociologists, and psychologists exploring "the manner in which socialization shapes the life experiences of mentally retarded persons" (1). Our view, as elaborated below, is a variation on the interactional perspective advocated by Koegel and his associates.

Sexuality and the Mentally Retarded: A Review of the Literature

There is no dearth of literature dealing with the sexuality of mentally retarded people, although the bulk of it is written from a behavioral-psychological perspective aimed at the needs of special educators. Relatively little of it addresses the question of how sexuality fits into a more general pattern of adaptation to the community. Moreover, there is relatively little recognition of this essay's thesis that sexual *behavior* is only one facet of the larger issue of the developing social identity, which includes learning the *meaning* of "male" and "female" in a particular social context.

General Features of Sexuality

According to Rosalyn Kramer Monat, mildly retarded persons may be characterized by the capacity to engage in behavior similar to average or normative psychosocial sexual behavior in society; to explore, adapt, and control sexual impulses and urges similar to the way people of normal intelligence do; to respond to verbal modes of sex education/counseling/therapy; and to develop appropriate adaptive skills (1982:3). Moderately mentally retarded people, by contrast, may be characterized by their delayed development of secondary sex characteristics; difficulty in developing general adaptive and psychosocial sexual behavior; reliance on a primary reward and reinforcement system; and limited capacity to respond to verbal sex education/counseling/therapy. The condition of severely and profoundly retarded people will not concern us here, since they are unlikely to be living independently in the community.

Monat is one of a band of sex educators who have championed the need for thorough sex education and counseling as an ongoing and integral part of the process of preparing institutionalized retarded people for life in the community and who have developed various packaged courses suitable for this purpose (see also Amary 1982; American Association for Health, Physical Education, and Recreation

1971; Bass 1974; Blom 1971; Champagne and Walker-Hirsch 1982; Delp 1971; Edmonson 1980; Education Development Center 1978; Frith 1976; Goodman 1973; Gordon 1971; Graham-Bafus 1980; Greenbaum and Noll 1982; Hamre-Nietupski and Ford 1981; Jacobs 1978; Johnson 1973; Kempton 1983; Koscierzynski and Karpen 1977; Lebrun and Hutchinson 1977; Meyen and Carr 1967; Money 1971; Ogle 1983; Perske 1973; Riches 1978; Rinckey 1975; Russell and Hardin 1980; Secker 1973; Sengstock and Vergasos 1970; Shindell 1975; Souma 1974; Steward 1973; Thurman, Bassin, and Ackerman 1976; Vockell and Mattick 1972; Walter 1982; Zelman 1976; Zylla and Demetral 1981). The anthropologist John Price conducted a survey of associations for mentally retarded persons throughout North America. He received little or no response to questions dealing with sex education and related policies because, it seems, the issue is still in the formative stage (1985:267).

From this literature we may discern three general problems that inhibit the implementation of good sex education programs. First, there is an inadequate preparation of professional staff (Brantlinger 1983; Meyen and Retish 1971). Some evidence suggests that professional caretakers typically do not even expect retarded clients to act in gender-appropriate ways and hence do not bother to model such behavior (Copeland and Weissbrod 1976). Second, there tends to be an overreliance on stereotypical role behaviors and "expected" patterns of sexuality when such gender issues are confronted at all (Cegelka 1976; Rosen 1970). Perhaps most important, there is the problem of parental resistance. Parents' fears for (or sometimes of) their retarded children as sexual beings form a profoundly conservative force (Dupras and Tremblay 1976; Turner 1970). George Tarjan (1973) has characterized the limitation of the retarded person's capabilities, coupled with the hesitance of society at large to admit to retarded people's sexuality and the protective conservatism of parents, as a "tri-polar conflict" that inhibits the adaptation of mentally retarded adults in the community.

Legal Perspectives

The right to marry is fundamental to all citizens, including retarded ones, although some states limit the capacity of retarded persons to exercise that right because of their inability to grant "valid consent." Since not all mentally retarded people are incapable of understanding contractual obligations, there is increasing awareness on the part of constitutional experts that exclusion is not appropriate as a blanket rule. Exclusion is also no longer the rule with regard to their competence to act as parents. Cases now tend to be judged on individual merits.

Moreover, mentally retarded persons may seek and be given birth control information through normal channels of purchase and prescription. No state prohibits a physician from prescribing birth control to a mentally retarded patient not living in an institution.

For the mentally retarded, involuntary sterilization was historically the most important legal aspect of sexuality. Most states began promulgating sterilization laws in the early 1900s, a process ultimately endorsed by the U.S. Supreme Court (Buck v. Bell 1927). These rulings presumed that retardation was necessarily hereditary, which has proved not to be true in the vast majority of instances. The prevailing legal opinion at this time is that the decision to bear children is within the area of individual privacy protected by the Constitution. It is now up to the state to demonstrate that in particular cases sterilization will accomplish legitimate state goals and will do so with minimal infringement on personal rights. Similarly, involuntary abortions are now widely considered to be constitutionally indefensible. (See Lottman 1982 for a full discussion of the sterilization issue; Friedman 1976:112–24 for a comprehensive overview of the sexual rights of mentally retarded persons living in the community; and Haas 1979 for an analysis of the larger social context of fertility control among retarded persons.)

Sexuality and Adaptation

The small but growing body of literature on the life-ways of retarded people in the community owes much of its inspiration to the work of the anthropologist Robert Edgerton and his research associates. His pioneering study *The Cloak of Competence* (1967) established a tradition of viewing deinstitutionalized retarded adults as people capable of adjusting to the world outside the institution. Their adaptation relies on two strategies: the ability to deny their retardation (and hence to avoid situations in which that lack of competence might be discovered), and, if that fails, to find one or more "benefactors" who can mediate between them and the demanding outside world. Leaving aside the question of the possible long-term, nontherapeutic nature of these strategies and their tendency to reinforce dependence, it is clear from Edgerton's research that mentally retarded people are not helpless. They are able to exploit elements in their social environment to meet their perceived needs. They do so, however, in ways into which they have been socialized in the institution. In other words, they are "culture-bearing" people in the sense that anthropologists would understand that term. In that respect, they are not altogether dissimilar to people of normal intelligence. (See also Edgerton 1979; Edgerton and Bercovici 1976; Evans 1983; Kaufman 1984; Koegel 1978.)

If retarded people are capable of using resources to help them cope with the stress of community life, anthropological practice would lead us to an investigation of how they themselves view the process they undergo. The most important reason to include the anthropologist in studies of the community adjustment of deinstitutionalized retarded adults is to clarify the "insider's perspective" on a process commonly described only by caretakers or other advocates. This point is reinforced by Robert D. Whittemore and Paul Koegel's report on the results of their survey of community-based clients (1978:68).

Barbara Edmonson (1979) points out that retarded people develop their views about sexuality on the basis of their experiences, quality of instruction, and personal interests rather than on the basis of IQ— just like "normal" people do. In this regard, the findings of G. Abelson and Maria Paluszny (1978) take on special significance. Their analysis of an administration of the Michigan Gender Identity Test to a sample of both retarded and normal students indicates that the formation of a gender identity is a function of mental, not chronological, age. Yet if staff members fail to expect the retarded client *ever* to be of an age to formulate such constructs, they will not bother to structure experiences that will help the formation of a sense of identity.

Andrea G. Zetlin and Jim L. Turner identify those factors responsible for the development of identity (which they term "self-perception") among noninstitutional retarded adults (1984:115–19). They are, in order of importance, parental practices and expectations, the number of years of independent living, and the availability of support services offered by community care agencies. In sum, "these data demonstrate the plausible link between past environment and circumstances and characteristic attitudes and ways of thinking about oneself" (117).

The basic problem in this literature is that although we can be certain that retarded people can become adept at adjusting themselves to changing environments, and that they develop evaluative perceptions of themselves as people ("acceptors," "qualifiers," "vacillators," or "deniers," in Zetlin and Turner's terminology), we have little basis for appreciating the role of gender constructs in the adaptation process. Even as sophisticated a scheme as that of Zetlin and Turner discerns retarded people's perception of themselves *as retarded people*—they are asked to identify themselves in terms of how they react to their handicap and how they will work the rest of their lives around that crucial issue. For our purposes, however, one's identity is involved in a more comprehensive process of developing a character, a sense of one's strengths resulting from having undertaken the kinds of conflicts suggested by the adaptation process outlined by Zetlin and Turner.

We therefore turn to an analysis of our own informants to understand the components of gender identity as they perceive them. We then attempt to link these gender constructs back to our larger theory of the growth of the social identity so we can make some recommendations for modifying the public policy of community care for the deinstitutionalized.

Methodology

The Study Population

Our informants form an "opportunistic," rather than a random or stratified, sample because they were chosen from among the particular client populations with which the authors work. Since these clients have been diagnosed as having emotional disturbances or psychiatric disorders in addition to mental retardation, they cannot be taken as representative of retarded people as a group. It would be advisable to compare our findings with research designs that could incorporate control populations. Our current limited results, however, might be taken as suggestive of trends in the larger population.

Our group consists of fifty men and twenty-three women. The men range in age from eighteen to forty-two. Ten of the male respondents are black. The others are white or Hispanic. All spent one or more periods of incarceration in state institutions prior to joining Opportunity House, a pseudonym for a private, nonprofit program under contract to the state of Florida to provide residential, vocational, and academic services to its clients, all of whom are male. Clients of Opportunity House progress through a behavior modification–based series of groups, beginning with closely supervised group homes (in a rural town twenty miles from Tampa) and work crews, through minimally supervised apartment rentals (in the city) and individual job placements. The fifty men in our sample represent all levels of adaptation in the program.

The women range in age from nineteen to fifty-nine. Four of them are black; the others are white or Hispanic. Thirteen of the women are currently living in the community with support from family and friends. The remaining ten live in minimally supervised group homes, boarding homes, or halfway houses. All of them are receiving psychiatric care (individual or group counseling) at a nonprofit community mental health center in a rural Florida County. Since this center is a comprehensive facility, the women are also able to receive psychiatric evaluations, chemotherapy, and counseling. Community networking, which is part of both the center's case management services and the halfway house, is provided to appropriate clients. Social services (e.g., housing, food stamps, adult and child protective services) are also arranged. The majority of the women in this group have been psychiatrically evaluated and at some point in the past five years have been on psychiatric medication. More than half of the individuals have been psychiatrically hospitalized at least once.

The Survey Instrument

We chose to administer the inventory associated with the Essential Adult Sex Education (EASE) Curriculum (Zelman 1976) to generate some quantifiable data about our informants' perceptions of their sexuality. This instrument was developed as part of a curricular package and was designed to be administered in pretest/posttest fashion in conjunction with the course. None of our informants studied the curriculum, so that all responses may be taken as indications of their beliefs independent of special training. (Their "uninformed" status is by no means atypical of deinstitutionalized retarded adults, as noted above.)

We chose this particular instrument for two reasons: it does not isolate gender issues but deals with sexuality and interpersonal behavior in a comprehensive fashion; it has been validated nationally and had been distributed through the Secondary Education and Adult Basic Education departments of the county school system, which made it more palatable to agency authorities than any instrument we introduced "cold."

The EASE survey is divided into four sections, testing knowledge about basic biological processes; sexual behavior (both "normal" and "deviant"); sexual and reproductive health; and interpersonal relationships. It is cast in a true-false mode, except for a series of questions asking respondents to identify parts of male and female bodies on drawings. Although the questions are supposed to be asked in a standardized manner, it is permissible to substitute common terms for technical ones in those instances where it is not the technical term itself that is being tested. Each of the four sections can be scored separately, although a composite score can be computed as well. The instrument, which contains ninety-four items, is difficult to apply to retarded subjects with limited verbal abilities and attention spans, and it is conceivable their confusion or boredom with the test biased the results. However, since all the respondents share these disabilities, there is no internal bias involved.

Qualitative Data

The administration of the EASE survey was embedded in a larger process that might be considered participant observation. Angrosino is an officer of the Board of Trustees of Opportunity House and has worked with its clients as a classroom aide for four years. He had previously worked with community programs in Tennessee in conjunction with research on the relationship between the state and its community service vendors (Angrosino 1981). Zagnoli is a licensed mental health counselor at a community mental health center and is also in private practice; she has worked with numerous retarded clients over the past five years. In these capacities, both authors have had the opportunity to conduct extensive interviews with retarded members of the study population and others in similar circumstances. We have also been able to observe and interact with them in residential, classroom, work-related, and social settings. Agency staff, social workers, and other service providers were also interviewed for this project.

Survey Data Results

Male Respondents

The median composite score for male respondents was 62.60, indicating a generally low (but certainly not disastrously bad) level of understanding of sexual apparatus and process. Of the four subsections, the median score was highest for health (72.52) and lowest for behavior (57.77). These findings are certainly in keeping with what the literature would suggest; deinstitutionalized retarded adults are bombarded with lectures about "hygiene," but they are given little encouragement, let alone opportunity, to experiment with behavior (cf. Edmonson and Wish 1975; Hall and Morris 1976).

The fourth subsection, dealing with personal relationships, probably says the most about gender constructs, about being a "man" or a "women," and about how the two deal with each other. We therefore endeavored to correlate the respondent's general adaptive level with his knowledge about such relationships. Each client was scored from zero (living under close supervision) through four (in the more or less independent apartment program). Computation established significant correlations only at the extremes of the scale. That is, the men in the zero group consistently have the lowest scores in this section, while those in the four group consistently have the highest. The three intermediate groups demonstrate varying degrees of knowledge. (The relatively small size of the sample and the possibly confounding effects of the respondents' emotional and psychiatric problems must be taken into account before making firm generalizations.)

The suggested scoring key that accompanies the EASE indicates a generally "liberal" view of gender and interpersonal relationships. The following items in this section were most likely to have been answered incorrectly by our male respondents, regardless of the adaptation level: you have to kiss on the first date; a man should always pay for the date; you must have sexual intercourse if you are going steady; a married man should never do any cooking or cleaning; it is okay for girls to ask boys for a date. Our respondents, from the most dependent to the most streetwise, are thus operating on a somewhat stereotypically "macho" model of maleness. Denied other models, they apparently fall back on the most clear-cut images—the man as strong protector and sexual aggressor, the woman as servitor. Sex is seen as the sine qua non of the relationship. It is quite possible that these attitudes reflect the cultural backgrounds of the clients rather than their experiences in institutions for the retarded. These responses, however, were from men not only from low socioeconomic status and ethnic or racial minority groups but also from white, middle-class (or even affluent) backgrounds.

The following items, on the other hand, seemed to discriminate the poorly adapted from the streetwise informants: you can get a bad reputation if you have sexual intercourse with all your friends; friends can hurt your feelings; when you are with a group of friends, you have to do what they want to do; if someone asks you on a date, it is better to go even if you don't like the person who asked you; everyone is your friend. These data suggest that adaptation to the community is accompanied by a growing awareness of the integrity of the person—one does not necessarily have to go along with the crowd to be "cool." In fact, the desire to be seen as "my own man" is a factor that shows up in the interview results quite frequently.

A series of questions about the institution of premarital engagement and the relationship between marriage and childbearing/rearing was inconsistently answered by respondents at all adaptive levels, perhaps indicating considerable guessing. Even the most socially adept of the men, those who have begun to think of themselves as "my own man," have not consistently associated the roles of husband and father with the attributes of the "real man." Cutting across all class and ethnic lines among our respondents is the view that a "real man" is a domineering, sexually aggressive tower of strength detached from the responsibilities of family life.

Female Respondents

The median composite score for female respondents was 73.20, a finding in keeping with the general trend in the literature that suggests retarded women are better informed about sexual matters than are the men. Of the four subsections, the median score was highest for health (78.56), as it was for the men, and lowest for basic biology (but at 65.80 still higher than the biology score for the men). More important, the median score on the behavioral section was 77.60, almost as high as on the health section, a vast difference from the distribution of scores for the men. The women were clearly far more knowledgeable about interpersonal relations than were the men.

Partially because of the relatively small size of the female group, it was not possible to establish any statistically significant correlations between adaptive level and knowledge about interpersonal behavior. However, the trend is toward women in the lowest adaptational group (group one in this case) having the lowest scores, those in group four having the highest.

Although the majority of the women answered "correctly" the questions in the behavior section that the men tended to answer incorrectly, their comments to the interviewer indicated that they held more traditional views, or had had more traditional experiences, but knew what "normal" people expected. It is worth noting that the majority of the women come from rural communities, as opposed to the men, whose backgrounds are more diverse.

Unlike the men, who split on the issue of personal integrity versus going along with the crowd depending on their level of adaptation, the women evinced no clear pattern of response. Individualization is probably less of an issue for the women than it is for the men. It is acceptable for a woman to be part of the crowd, even if she is "high functioning," while the men place a real premium on their personal identity as a badge of adaptation.

Although none of the men in our response group had ever been married, at least five of the women had been or are currently married. One of the men fathered a child out of wedlock but had never acted his parental role; at least five of the women have had babies and have been actively involved in raising their children. It is therefore not surprising the women at all levels of adaptation consistently answered more questions correctly about the institutions of engagement, marriage, and childrearing than the men did. The one question the women did not, as a rule, answer correctly was whether "you have to get a ring to be engaged," once again indicating a very old-fashioned viewpoint. The findings are compatible with those of a survey about sexuality conducted in Toronto among mentally retarded adults (Price 1985:267).

Qualitative Data Results

Male Respondents

The tentative survey conclusions are reinforced by the qualitative data. Two general problems stand out from the unstructured interviews: the absence or inconsistency of role models; and the presumption that retarded people, if they are to be "gender conscious" at all, can actively develop their identities only with other retarded people. The respondents themselves expressed concern about both of these issues, while their caretakers were generally aware of the former but not the latter.

The men at Opportunity House have relatively few occasions to act like grown-ups. The agency hosts two major parties per year, but the men cannot invite dates. There are occasional mixers with other residential programs for retarded adults, but these parties do not always work out very happily. After one such event, at least six of the men reported gleefully that they had met a new girlfriend who had given them her picture. Unfortunately, it was the same woman in each case. It may be significant that all the men caught in this predicament were white. The black men, as a group, tended to affect a more streetwise demeanor (regardless of what they actually know) and were openly scornful of their white friends' gullibility. "Gotta check it out first," they agreed.

The apparent promiscuity of the woman in question should not, however, be taken too seriously. From all indications, she was simply trying to be friendly and gracious (the party was held at "her" agency's facility) but chose a socially inappropriate way. The real problem was the men's stereotypical view of male-female relations. A woman could not just be "friendly"; her slightest gesture of friendship could only be taken to mean she was ready to "do it." It is worth noting that at least four of the six men had only a hazy notion of what "doing it" meant.

Masturbation is a way of life to most of the men of Opportunity House. It is a practice tacitly encouraged by the staff as long as it is done "discreetly." None of our informants, however, indicated he had any particular set of fantasies to accompany the act, which has a purely physical function. None of them assumes masturbation is in any way a substitute for "doing it" with a woman; many of them were not even aware it was a "sexual" act at all.

Men in Opportunity House's apartment program are theoretically free to make dates and other social engagements at their discretion. Having a live-in girlfriend, however, would not be tolerated. The staff members like to point out that the one graduated client currently enjoying what they believe is a "healthy" sex life is a man who had had *no* sexual experience prior to coming to the program or while he was in the semi-independent apartment phase of the program.

The problems of lack of knowledge, social ineptitude, and nonmainstream gender constructs do not arise in a vacuum. Staff respondents were quick to point out that virtually all the clients come from what they characterize as "peculiar" family backgrounds. That is, regardless of ethnicity, race, or income level, most of the clients come from families that had mentally retarded parents unable to cope with the demands of raising a retarded child, had had some sort of structural disruption (divorce, remarriage, unwed parents without permanent ties to one another), or had given up the client at an early age to foster or institutional care. However, the black men seem to be "universally better social compensators" relative to their IQs, in the words of one staff member. The white retarded adults seem more comfortable adopting a helpless, dependent role, while the black men face the stresses of retardation plus disrupted family life with a show of independent bravado.

This link between the family (disturbed though it may be in the lives of many of these clients) and current gender constructs is of particular poignance when one realizes that the only other women in their world are staff members in positions of authority. The men tend, in fact, to equate the staff women with their mothers. This is by no means an unheard of phenomenon among young schoolboys of normal intelligence, but for the respondents there is no opportunity to move to a different model of relating to adult women. The fix on the mother (who is not, in most cases, a figure of particular warmth or stability) is thus both ambivalent and hard to shake. One psychologist suggested, with fine Freudian insight, that the men's desire to be dominant in relations with women reflected their basic desire to prove to their mothers that they really were "all grown up."

Most of the black men reported having had some sort of sexual experience prior to coming to Opportunity House, although the white men who did so proffered the more baroque elaborations about their experiences. The psychologist suggested that the white men, bereft of real experience, developed richer fantasy lives, although that explanation does not address the question of why the black men had opportunities—or took advantage of opportunities—unavailable to the white men.

Homosexual activity undoubtedly figured heavily in these earlier experiences, including those unspoken experiences found in the records of the white men. These experiences may have been in the form of abuse at home, in jail, or in the institution. Most of the men, however, seemed very reluctant to discuss the issue, having picked up on their caretakers' disapproval. The official policy of Opportunity House is that no sexual acts per se are considered socially inappropriate, as long as they are practiced with discretion. The fact is, however, that given the circumstances of life at Opportunity House, sexual encounters tend to be homosexual, if they occur at all,[3] and the staff tends not to regard such acts with calm acquiescence, regardless of how discreetly they are conducted. The Opportunity House psychologists note that few cases of true preferential homosexuality exist among the clients, although circumstantial (opportunistic) homosexuality is quite common. The men in our group are intent on upholding the image of real men as sexually dominant; a dominant homosexual partner is not considered "queer," although the passive partner may be so labeled. Most of the men had been the passive recipient (willing or otherwise) of homosexual advances, but because they cannot square that fact with their view of their maleness, they deny it. One respondent, in fact, broke down in tears during the administration of the EASE and confided that he had been raped in jail before coming to Opportunity House. "I know it's bad," he said, "but I didn't want to do it, so maybe God won't punish me." In short, despite the official policy of toleration, homosexual activities among clients at Opportunity House are actively discouraged.

Recently, there was a case of a male staff member who was caught sexually abusing some of the clients. The presumption was that they were incapable of giving informed consent to someone in a position of authority over them. He was fired.[4] The obverse of this abusive situation is not unknown. Clients may develop "crushes" on female staff members, usually along the "mother" lines suggested above. The response of the female staff members can be critical: if they respond in kind (as some have done), they may inadvertently lead the client into a relationship for which he is emotionally unprepared; but if they are too cold in their rebuff, they may set back the man's ability to express his sexuality. The female staff members are officially required to comport themselves as "professionals" at all times, but the fact that they are women, regardless of their demeanor, is not lost on the clients. In one recent case, a female staff member fell in love with one of the clients. On an outing to a drive-in movie, she frequently sent her other charges away to buy refreshments. They nonetheless discovered her kissing her beloved. When the story came out, the man initially denied it. Then the program director confiscated a tape cassette the woman had sent to him declaring her undying devotion. He was punished—presumably only for lying about it, not for having been willing to kiss her back. She was dismissed, and the client professed relief. He admitted he didn't know how to handle a "real woman" (as opposed to a retarded woman). The other men put up a macho, joking front about the whole episode. "All I got to say," said another of the clients, "is, What's *he* got that I ain't got?"

The question of socialization into gender constructs extends beyond the opportunities (or lack thereof) for actual physical encounters between the sexes. In a habilitation program such as that of Opportunity House, for example, the major training is always in traditional male roles—carpentry, mechanics, heavy janitorial work. The men are constantly taught that it is bad to continue to be dependent and that they must learn to support themselves (but not necessarily to support a family). The men are encouraged to help prepare meals at the group home, but that is never their major responsibility. Those in the apartment program cook and shop for themselves, but they say that in the best of all possible worlds they would not have to do so much "woman's work." It may, therefore, not be surprising that few of the men express any desire for a family-style home life; as nice as it would be to have a woman to do the housework, the other responsibilities that go along with marriage are considered beyond their capabilities just now. They seem, by and large, to have accepted this staff evaluation of their capabilities.

The staff members believe an ongoing sex education program would be desirable, not so much because the clients would retain many specific pieces of factual information but because discussions of sex would at least serve to demystify it. They think it is the "forbidden fruit" aspect that is disruptive. But, as this essay has indicated, training should focus on not simply the mechanics of sex but also the development of constructs of gender and interpersonal behavior.

However, it is still considered a somewhat dangerous, liberal notion to allow the clients the "dignity of risk" and to use the ensuing faux pas as "teachable moments" toward a more healthy social identity, as would be done with people of normal intelligence.

The attitudes of the men of Opportunity House are encapsulated in the story of one female staff member who was accused by one disgruntled client of allowing herself to be "felt up." This story quickly made the rounds but proved to be false. At a group meeting, the woman tearfully confessed that she was very hurt, not because of the accusation itself but because none of the men in the program had risen in her defense. The men were deeply chastened and professed that it is the duty of a man to protect the honor of "his" women. They noted ruefully that this woman's husband always picked her up after work, and they approved of the fact that although she was a working woman, she still had some man who was able to take care of her. They said they would like to be in a position to do likewise and were sorry they had failed this test of their adult manhood.

Female Respondents

Despite their limitations, the women in our survey population want to identify with mainstream expectations. Consequently, these women often claim to be romantically linked with someone, even in the absence of an appropriate courtship. One woman habitually announces to her family that she is "engaged" to a man she has met the day before. Nothing develops from these encounters, but the woman fulfills, at least in her fantasy, a desire to be just like everyone else. Often, a retarded woman exaggerates any attentive response from a man to fit her desire for a "relationship." Another woman in our study has a history of frequent "relationships," many of them one-sided. In some cases, the man in question was not even aware of the woman's feeling of commitment. Neither of these women appears to be delusional in the psychotic sense, but they are capable of living with delusions regarding their contacts with men. These delusions are their way of meeting the emotional need for what they think is socially acceptable behavior.

Retarded adult women know what they expect of their men, but they do not always have a clear expectation about themselves. They appear to expect the relationship to take care of itself as long as the man is in charge. Short-term, often intense liaisons frequently occur with men who are more intelligent or socially adept. In these situations, the women may be seen by the men only as sex objects, regardless of the romantic expectations of the women. In one such relationship, a woman ended up pregnant with twins, who were subsequently delivered in a state psychiatric hospital.

As this example indicates, retarded adult women are often sexually active but do not take appropriate precautions, even when they are aware of birth control measures and the consequences of sex. Stories of one woman's insistence on having sex "in the bushes" near her adult high school class led her doctor and her parents to advocate birth control measures for her. She tried a variety of devices, and her parents (who were reluctant to accept her sexual activity) agreed to undergo counseling, but to no avail. The result was her more or less voluntary acquiescence to sterilization.

Longer relationships appear to occur more frequently when a retarded woman develops a relationship with a comparably or even more markedly retarded man. One successful couple has a history of several psychiatric hospitalizations between them, and they are currently active participants in the welfare system. Nevertheless, the relationship itself continues to be stable and fulfilling for both. Problems found in couples of normal intelligence (insecurities, jealousy, difficulty in communicating) occur in these retarded relationships as well. Another married retarded couple frequently deals with the woman's desire to have a baby, a problem that often leads them to counseling or crisis intervention sessions. Since she has a history of explosive behavior and is on extensive psychotropic medication, getting pregnant would be an unhealthy choice for her. However, the desire exists and continues to be an issue to be dealt with by the two of them and their families, doctors, and counselors.

Several of the women in our survey population had had children. Among the women who are currently raising their children, there is a constant fear of losing custody through state intervention. One woman cried during the administration of the EASE when she realized there were questions she did not understand. She feared her ignorance might indicate that she was not a fit parent or, worse, that she was "crazy." When reassured that it was a confidential survey and the results would not be used against her, she finished without further incident.

Learning appropriate parenting skills is critical for the retarded women since many of them are involved with the protective services of the state. Their counseling sessions typically focus on parenting and one-to-one instruction. Since women are believed to be the primary childrearers, parenting education is a vital part of a woman's life skills. How to set limits and how to be consistent in following through with children, common concerns of mainstream parents, are typical issues for retarded parents as well. Extended family support often provides the modeling of parent skills as well as the supervision that enables retarded people to be successful parents themselves. A number of the women with children do, in fact, live with their parents.

Of the women surveyed, no one indicated that sexual behavior other than the traditional male-female relationship was either desirable or part of their experience. Such behavior has probably occurred, but the women have learned to be discreet about their experiences. Masturbation was recognized by many of the women and acknowledged as a common behavior. They generally did not consider it deviant or shameful, and, unlike the men, they recognized that the practice could fulfill certain needs they identified as explicitly sexual. Despite the rural and strictly Christian background of most of the women, only one indicated masturbation was wrong according to the Bible. More reflective of the general trend was the blunt answer of one woman, who responded to the question about masturbation by pointing to her middle finger and indicating it should be worn down by now, given all its use over the years.

For the most part, the women in this study perceived themselves in a traditional light. They believed that a "successful" woman has a relationship in which she is taken care of and is primarily responsible for the children, if any come. Nothing in our interviews indicated that any of these women felt a need to "find themselves" in the world of business, although many did have hobbies outside the home. Although most of the women receive financial support through state agencies, they felt they were the ones primarily responsible for the care of their households. More than half indicated that it was appropriate for men to help, but they did not expect them to do so. Similarly, many said the idea of Dutch-treat dates or of women asking men to go out was appealing, and they did not believe these were common experiences. Since the women are living in the community with minimal professional supervision, it is reasonable to suggest they are exposed to the social influences of the mainstream. In addition, the lack of specialized support services forces most of these women to seek out services from the community at large. As a result, much of what they believe is based on that which is taught to the general population through schools, churches, media, and the family. Unlike mainstream women, however, they do not have a real opportunity to experience a different set of options and thus accept the standard view as the only appropriate one. The retarded women's inability to comprehend the consequences of some behaviors (e.g., sexual activity) is not dissimilar to that of mainstream adolescents.

Conclusions

Conceptual Issues

Retarded people, like everyone else, have goals to which they aspire. When such aspirations are periodically blocked, the result is psychosocial stress. A perception of conflict, however, is intrinsic to the process of personality development. The resolution of the conflicts built into social and cultural institutions leaves the individual with a series of virtues (strengths), such that the emergent identity is a composite of both personality (behavior, attitude) and character (a moral awareness of self). Retarded people experience the conflicts built into the social and cultural institutions shaping the lives of people of normal intelligence. They are also frustrated because their disability prevents them from being the kind of people they would ideally like to be. More important, they are, by custom in our society, generally treated as a dependent class (regardless of their individual capacities). The great paradox of normalization and deinstitutionalization is that retarded people are told simultaneously that there are values, behaviors, and positions deemed worthy of striving for and that they will probably never be able to achieve those goals. This paradox becomes a self-fulfilling prophecy if mainstream caretakers deny retarded people some of the basic attributes of striving by not allowing them the opportunity to experience conflict and to learn and grow from those encounters. Retarded people may thus be seen as analogues to people in colonial and postcolonial societies, who are systematically excluded from metropolitan benefits they have been taught are the only ones worth having.

Retarded people therefore have the same option as colonial people: they can develop a value system that is a locally acceptable alternative to that of the mainstream. That system will be an amalgam of superficially discordant parts: attributed status as helpless dependents, which they must learn to reject; subjective status, which is responsive to the circumstances of their immediate situation; and optative status, which must strike a balance between the unobtainable goals of the mainstream and the reasonable goals of "habituated" retarded people living autonomously in the community.

Gender constructs are central to the development of an adult identity because they speak not only to who we are but also to how we relate to significant others in our social environment. It is therefore necessary to understand how retarded people themselves conceptualize gender as an important clue to understanding how they evaluate who they are and what they would like to know.

The Ethnography of Selfhood

Although our sample is admittedly a biased one, some tentative conclusions may be advanced on the basis of our interaction with these particular people.

1. Both men and women hold what may be considered very old-fashioned views of "male" and "female" and the relationship between the two. The women are more cognizant than are the men of what mainstream people believe, but they seem to share the men's attitude that liberal (less rigid) standards of role behavior are not really desirable. The women are much more knowledgeable about sexual process than the men are, but this knowledge has not been translated into a more highly developed gender awareness.

2. Both men and women are aware that sexual expression is a legitimate and desirable facet of an adult social identity. They would agree that being denied the right to sexual expression condemns them to permanent dependence. The women, however, tend to believe that there is at least an ideal link between a sexual relationship and a permanent bond of marriage and parenthood and that their femininity is tied to being a wife and mother. The men, on the other hand, seem content to define their masculinity in terms of the sexual liaison itself instead of linking it to being a husband and father.

3. There is a common belief in a rigid and unchangeable division of gender; homosexuality may be practiced, but it challenges clear-cut notions of gender uniqueness too much to be considered a valid lifestyle. In sum, men are breadwinners; they are independent and need to be in a position where nobody can tell them what to do. They are sexually aggressive and are the dominant (i.e., decision-making) partners in all relationships. They are not interested in being tied down to permanent responsibilities and are most concerned with personal gratification. Women are supportive helpmates who need the stability of a more or less permanent bond with a strong man. They would like to be nurturant and take great comfort from family and community.

4. The men are far more likely to be self-conscious about their handicap than the women are. It is apparently easier for a retarded woman to "pass" (particularly in a rural community where complex technical skills are not demanded of her) by establishing a relationship with a "normal" man. The retarded men are not particularly

hopeful about establishing relationships with "normal" women; indeed, their emphasis on being "my own man" may well reflect their belief that a permanent relationship is not possible for them (they do not consider a relationship with a retarded woman at all desirable).

Black retarded men seem less anxious on this score than their white counterparts. That is, the black men seem willing at least to entertain the possibility of their being attractive to "normal" women, although they are not any more interested in being tied down to family responsibilities than the white men are.

5. To a certain degree, the retarded people we work with are not dissimilar to mainstream people. Many of the aspects of gender summarized above are congruent with attitudes found in certain mainstream communities (rural white or urban black). People in the survey population, however, tend to uphold far more clear-cut standards than those of their mainstream compatriots. They are less comfortable in experimenting with options. This conclusion is compatible with the point often raised about the adolescent identity crisis: people caught in the conflict between the call to adult responsibility and the allure of childhood safely tend to establish very clear, "ideological" allegiances to certain values as an anchor in the storm.

Implications for Policy

Further research, with larger, more systematically selected samples in which the biases of psychiatric disorder are controlled, is certainly needed. (Note, for example, the slight, but perhaps significant differences between the viewpoints expressed by our informants and those reported in Robert D. Whittemore and Paul Koegel's study [1978].) Nonetheless, a sensitivity to gender constructs analyzed in the context of the model suggested here might well contribute to the evolution of the policy of deinstitutionalization currently dominating the lives of retarded adults.

Deinstitutionalization has been described as a philosophy or a moral crusade as much as a social policy (Willer, Scheerenberger, and Intagliata 1978). V. Bradley (1978:5–6) describes several milestones in this development, including the affirmation by the President's Panel on Mental Retardation (1963) that mental retardation is preventable and subject to amelioration; the passage of the Mental Retardation Facilities and Community Mental Health Centers Construction Act (1963); the enactment of the Medicare and Medicaid Programs (1965), which enabled disabled people to secure long-term care in their local communities; the creation of the President's Committee on Mental Retardation (1965), a permanent national advisory board; the successes of the civil rights movement, which led to an awareness of the rights of many disadvantaged citizens; the growth of public interest legal advocacy, resulting in judicial decisions expanding the rights of the developmentally disabled; the announcement (1971) of a national goal to return one-third of all institutionalized mentally retarded persons to "supportive community living," coupled with the presidential directives to enforce the rights of the mentally retarded and other handicapped persons, particularly in the field of housing; the inclusion of a mandate (in the amended Rehabilitation Act of 1973) to require states to address vocational rehabilitation problems of the severely disabled as a first priority; and the extension of federal programs (e.g., Supplemental Security Income and Title XX of the Social Security Act) to provide federal aid for services for the developmentally disabled.

During the course of this evolution, deinstitutionalization has come to stand for a set of related "core values," including equal justice, human dignity, equity in the allocation of social resources, individualization, normalization, right to reside in the least restrictive environment, right to treatment, protection from harm, efficiency of service programs, economy of the human service system, and effectiveness of the developmental program (Bradley 1978:17–8).

Unfortunately, the high moral tone and the lofty expectations of deinstitutionalization that dominated social policy in the 1970s (affecting the chronically mentally ill, the aged, and other dependent institutional populations, as well as the retarded) fell on hard times in the 1980s. The lack of community preparedness has been a perennial problem (Maluccio 1980:92), leading to the phenomenon of the homeless deinstitutionalized person wandering the streets of cities across the United States unable to locate appropriate services. This issue has become a staple of investigative reporting in both print and broadcast media, and there is every indication that legislative action may soon reverse the swing of the pendulum. The institution is being increasingly talked about as the most humane placement for many of these people and (more ominously in these days of tight budgets) as the most cost-efficient alternative. (See, for example, Florida's 1984 amendments to its comprehensive Mental Health Act, which moved dramatically away from an emphasis on client rights to a concern with the rights of the community.)

Deinstitutionalized retarded adults are placed in a most disagreeable position by this shift in public attitudes toward social policy. One aspect of their identity that is most widely misunderstood is their sexuality. Yet the extremely cautious socialization procedures advocated by their current caregivers condemn them to a perpetual sexual adolescence in which the ability to develop adult gender awareness is significantly hampered. These practices help reinforce the image of the retarded as sexually uncontrolled and unable to learn appropriate gender roles and, hence, as unfit adult members of our society.

Our data suggest retarded adults are capable, despite the barriers set in their way, of developing an awareness of themselves as adult men and women. If anything, their views of themselves in these roles are even more old-fashioned in their conservatism and moralism than are those of society at large. (It may be worth noting that Whittemore and Koegel's more liberal-minded respondents live in the Los Angeles area, while ours live in a more conservative part of the Sunbelt.) It therefore seems both feasible and desirable to insist that since retarded adults are going to become sexual beings anyway, habilitation programs should be structured to include comprehensive sexuality education as an integral part of their activities. Such education should stress not only the mechanics of process but also the values that guide all adults—retarded or not—in making decisions. This is a question of general public mental health. People with a primary diagnosis of mental retardation are frequently denied mental health services (counseling in coping skills is one example) because of the overly rigid dichotomization of human services. These programs should logically include the families or significant others in the life of the retarded adult. Learning to use social networks in a creative sense (not in the sense of finding "benefactors") would be an important part of developing a mature gender awareness.

The gender constructs of retarded adults *can* evolve beyond the stage of the adolescent identity crisis as long as the conflicts of adulthood are made available to them. The task is to prepare them to cope with those conflicts, for to continue to deny that those conflicts apply to them is to condemn them to emotional as well as intellectual retardation. In the current political atmosphere, such a condemnation implies a defeat for deinstitutionalization, for the inept adults we have created can only find their way back to the very institutions we emptied with so much fanfare.

NOTES

1. The authors acknowledge the assistance of Virginia Kiefert and Geraldine Tierney in the preparation of this essay.
2. Only about 20 percent of retarded people have intellectual deficits that are associated with major organic dysfunction (Edgerton 1979:4).

3. At least one incident of the use of a household pet for sexual stimulation was reported; the perpetrator was severely reprimanded.

4. This man had been accused of similar behavior at facilities in another state. He had apparently had his record cleared by authorities on the condition that he leave the state. Infuriated at not having been warned about this man's history, the Opportunity House administration and board of trustees mobilized other residential programs for children and dependent adults and lobbied successfully to get the state to provide more thorough background checks of prospective direct service employees.

REFERENCES

Abelson, G., and Maria Paluszny. 1978. "Gender Identity in a Group of Retarded Children." *Journal of Autism and Childhood Schizophrenia* 8:403–10.

Amary, I. B. 1982. "Social Awareness, Hygiene, and Sex-education for the Mentally Retarded/Developmentally Disabled." *Journal of School Health* 52:71.

American Association for Health, Physical Education, and Recreation. 1971. *A Resource Guide in Sex Education for the Mentally Retarded.* Washington, D.C.: Sex Information and Education Council of the United States.

Angrosino, Michael V. 1981. *Quality Assurance for Community Care of Retarded Adults in Tennessee.* Mental Health Policy Monograph Series, No. 11. Nashville: Vanderbilt Institute for Public Policy Studies.

Babad, Elisha Y., Max Birnbaum, and Kenneth D. Benne. 1983. *The Social Self: Group Influences on Personal Identity.* Beverly Hills, Calif.: Sage.

Bass, M. S. 1974. "Sex Education for the Handicapped." *Family Coordinator* 23:27–33.

Blom, Gaston E. 1971. "Some Consideration about the Neglect of Sex Education in Special Education." *Journal of Special Education* 5:359–61.

Bradley, V. 1978. *Deinstitutionalization of Developmentally Disabled Persons: A Conceptual Analysis and Guide.* Baltimore: University Park Press.

Brantlinger, E. 1983. "Measuring Variation and Change in Attitudes of Residential Care Staff toward Sexuality of Mentally Retarded Persons." *Mental Retardation* 21:17–22.

Buck v. Bell, 274 U.S. 200 (1927).

Cegelka, Patricia T. 1976. "Sex Role Stereotyping in Special Education." *Exceptional Children* 42:323–28.

Champagne, Marklyn P., and Leslie W. Walker-Hirsch. 1982. "Circles: A Self-organization System for Teaching Appropriate Social/Sexual Behavior to Mentally Retarded/Developmentally Disabled Persons." *Sexuality and Disability* 5:172–74.

Copeland, Anne P., and Carol Weissbrod. 1976. "Difference in Attitude toward Sex-typed Behavior of Non-retarded and Retarded children." *American Journal of Mental Deficiency* 81:280–88.

Delp, Harold. 1971. "Sex Education for the Handicapped." *Journal of Special Education* 5:363–64.

DeVos, George. 1975. "Ethnic Pluralism: Conflict and Accommodation." In *Ethnic Identity: Cultural Continuities and Change*, ed. G. DeVos and L. Romanucci-Ross. Palo Alto, Calif.: Mayfield.

Dingman, Harvey F. 1973. "Social Performance of the Mentally Retarded." In *Sociobehavioral Studies in Mental Retardation*, ed. R. K. Eyman, C. E. Meyers, and G. Tarjan. Los Angeles: American Association on Mental Deficiency.

Dupras, Andre, and Regina Tremblay. 1976. "Path Analysis of Parents: Conservatism toward Sex Education of Their Mentally Retarded Children." *American Journal of Mental Deficiency* 81:162–66.

Edgerton, Robert B. 1967. *The Cloak of Competence: Stigma in the Lives of the Mentally Retarded*. Berkeley: University of California Press.

———. 1979. *Mental Retardation*. Cambridge, Mass.: Harvard University Press.

Edgerton, Robert B., and S. Bercovici. 1976. "The Cloak of Competence—Years Later." *American Journal of Mental Deficiency* 80:485–97.

Edmonson, Barbara. 1979. "What Retarded Adults Believe about Sex." *American Journal of Mental Deficiency* 84:11–18.

———. 1980. "Sociosexual Education for the Handicapped." *Exceptional Education Quarterly* 1:67–76.

Edmonson, Barbara, and Joel Wish. 1975. "Sex Knowledge and Attitudes of Moderately Retarded Males." *American Journal of Mental Deficiency* 80:172–79.

Education Development Center, Inc. 1978. *Starting a Healthy Family*. Newton, Mass.: Education Development Center.

Evans, Daryl Paul. 1983. *The Lives of Mentally Retarded People*. Boulder, Colo.: Westview.

Frank. J. L. 1975. "Normalization." *Mental Retardation* 13:25.

Friedman, Paul R. 1976. *The Rights of Mentally Retarded Persons*. New York: Avon Books.

Frith, Greg. 1976. "Sex Education." *Pointer* 20:85–87.

Goodman, Russell. 1973. "Family Planning Programs for the Mentally Retarded in Institutions and Community." In *Human Sexuality and the Mentally Retarded*, ed. F. F. de la Cruz and G. D. La Veck. New York: Brunner/Mazel.

Gordon, Sol. 1971. "Missing in Special Education: Sex." *Journal of Special Education* 5:351–54.

Graham-Bafus, Suzanne M. 1980. "The Effects of a Course in Family Life Sex Education on Knowledge regarding Sexuality of Mentally Retarded Adults in a Community Residential Facility." *Dissertation Abstracts International* 41:57–58.

Greenbaum, Madeline, and Sandra J. Noll. 1982. *Education for Adulthood: A Curriculum for the Mentally Retarded*. Staten Island, N.Y.: Staten Island Mental Health Society.

Haas, Laurel M. 1979. *The Mentally Retarded and the Social Context of Fertility Control*. Working Paper No. 9, Socio-Behavioral Group. Los Angeles: Mental Retardation Research Center, School of Medicine, University of California.

Halderman v. Pennhurst State School, 446 F. Supp., 1295 (E.D. PA 1977).

Hall, Judy E., and Helen Morris. 1976. "Sexual Knowledge and Attitudes of Institutionalized and Noninstitutionalized Retarded Adolescents." *American Journal of Mental Deficiency* 80:382–87.

Hamre-Nietupski, Susan, and Allison Ford. 1981. "Sex Education and Related Skills." *Sexuality and Disability* 4:179–93.

Harrington, Charles, and John W. M. Whiting. 1972. "Socialization Process and Personality." In *Psychological Anthropology,* ed. F. L. K. Hsu. Cambridge, Mass.: Schenkman.

Jacobs, Judith. 1978. "The Mentally Retarded and Their Need for Sexuality Education." *Psychiatric Opinion* 15:32–34.

Johnson, Warren R. 1973. "Sex Education of the Mentally Retarded." In *Human Sexuality and the Mentally Retarded,* ed. F. F. de la Cruz and G. D. La Veck. New York: Brunner/Mazel.

Kaufman, Sandra. 1984. "Friendship, Coping Systems and Community Adjustment of Mildly Retarded Adults." In *Lives in Progress: Mildly Retarded Adults in a Large City,* ed. R. B. Edgerton. Washington, D.C.: American Association on Mental Deficiency.

Kempton, Winifred. 1983. "Teaching Retarded Children about Sex." *PTA Today* 8:28–30.

Koegel, Paul. 1978. *The Creation of Incompetence: Socialization and Mildly Retarded Persons.* Working Paper No. 6, Socio-Behavioral Group. Los Angeles: Mental Retardation Research Center, School of Medicine, University of California.

Koscierzynski, Sandy, and Mary Lou Karpen. 1977. *Life Education for Mentally Impaired Persons: A Curriculum Guide.* Monroe, Mich.: Monroe County Intermediate School District.

Lebrun, Simone, and Peggy Hutchinson. 1977. "Human Sexuality: Expanding Self-awareness in a Leisure Setting." *Journal of Leisurability* 4:6–8.

Lerman, Paul. 1981. *Deinstitutionalization: A Cross-Problem Analysis.* Rockville, Md.: U.S. Department of Health and Human Services, Public Health Service, Alcohol, Drug Abuse, and Mental Health Administration, National Institute on Alcohol Abuse and Alcoholism.

Lottman, Michael S. 1982. "Sterilization of the Mentally Retarded—Who Decides?" *Trial* 18:61–64.

MacMillan, D. L. 1977. *Mental Retardation in School and Society.* Boston: Little, Brown.

Maluccio, Anthony N. 1980. *Alternatives to Institutionalization: A Selective Review of the Literature.* Saratoga, Calif.: Century 21.

Martin, M. Kay, and Barbara Voorhies. 1975. *Female of the Species.* New York: Columbia University Press.

Meyen, Edward L., and Donald L. Carr. 1967. *A Social Attitude Approach to Sex Education for the Educable Mentally Retarded.* Iowa City: Special Education Curriculum Development Center, University of Iowa.

Meyen, Edward L., and Paul M. Retish. 1971. "Sex Education for the Mentally Retarded: Influencing Teachers' Attitudes." *Mental Retardation* 9:46–49.

Monat, Rosalyn Kramer. 1982. *Sexuality and the Mentally Retarded: A Clinical and Therapeutic Guidebook.* San Diego: College Hill Press.

Money, John. 1971. "Special Sex Education and Cultural Anthropology." *Journal of Special Education* 5:369–72.

New York State v. Carey, 393 F. Supp. 715 (E.D. NY 1975).

Nihira, K. 1975. *Adaptive Behavior Scale (1974 Revision).* Washington, D.C.: American Association on Mental Deficiency.

Nirje, B. 1980. "The Normalization Principle." In *Normalization, Social Integration and Community Services,* ed. R. Flynn and K. Nitsch. Baltimore: University Park Press.

Ogle, Peggy. 1983. *Being Human: A Resource Guide in Human Growth and Development.* Tallahassee, Fla.: Developmental Services Program Office, Department of Health and Rehabilitative Services.

Perske, R. 1972. "The Dignity of Risk and Mental Retardation." *Mental Retardation* 10:24–27.

———. 1973. "About Sexual Development: An Attempt to Be Human with the Mentally Retarded. *Mental Retardation* 11:6–8.

Price, John A. 1985. "The Metropolitan Toronto Association for the Mentally Retarded and Its Policy Formation, Successes and Failures." *Human Organization* 44:264–67.

Riches, Vivienne C. 1978. *Social Development Training Project.* North Ryde, Australia: Macquarrie University School of Education.

Rinckey, David J. 1975. "A Curriculum for Teaching Human Sexuality to Mentally Impaired Adolescents." Master's thesis, Central Michigan University.

Rosen, Marvin. 1970. "Conditioning Appropriate Heterosexual Behavior in Mentally and Socially Handicapped Populations." *Training School Bulletin* 66:172–77.

Russell, T., and P. Hardin. 1980. "Sex Education for the Mentally Retarded." *Education and Training of the Mentally Retarded* 15:312–41.

Secker, Leonora. 1973. "Sex Education and Mental Handicap." *Special Education* 62:27–28.

Sengstock, Wayne L., and Glenn A. Vergasos. 1970. "Issues in Sex Education for the Retarded." *Education and Training for the Mentally Retarded* 5:9–103.

Shelton v. Tucker, 364 U.S. 479, 1960.

Shindell, Paul E. 1975. "Sex Education Programs and the Mentally Retarded." *Journal of School Health* 45:88–89.

Souma, Alfred M. 1974. *Social Living: A Curriculum for the Educable Mentally Retarded Student at the Secondary Level.* Fitchburg, Mass.: Fitchburg State College.

Steward, Kathy L. 1973. "Curriculum Guide in Sex Education for the TMR." Unpublished manuscript.

Tarjan, George. 1973. "Sex: A Tri-polar Conflict in Mental Retardation." In *Sociobehavioral Studies in Mental Retardation*, ed. R. K. Eyman, C. E. Meyers, and G. Tarjan. Los Angeles: American Association on Mental Deficiency.

Tennessee Department of Mental Health and Mental Retardation. 1980. *Community Skills Profile*. Nashville: Tennessee Department of Mental Health and Mental Retardation.

Thurman, Richard L., Jeff Bassin, and Teel Ackermann. 1976. "Sexuality, Sex Education and the Mentally Retarded: One Educational Approach." *Mental Retardation* 14:19.

Turner, Edward T. 1970. "Attitudes of Parents of Deficient Children toward Their Children's Sexual Behavior." *Journal of School Health* 40:548–49.

Vockell, Edward L., and P. Mattick. 1972. "Sex Education for the Mentally Retarded: An Analysis of Problems, Programs, and Research." *Education and Training of the Mentally Retarded* 7:129–34.

Walter, Esther. 1982. "Continuity of Sexual Education Programs Serving People with Mental Handicaps." *Sexuality and Disability* 5:9–13.

Whittemore, Robert D., and Paul Koegel. 1978. *Living Alone Is Not Helpful: Sexuality and Social Context among the Mildly Retarded*. Working Paper No. 7, Socio-Behavioral Group. Los Angeles: Mental Retardation Research Center, School of Medicine, University of California.

Willer, B., R. Scheerenberger, and J. Intagliata. 1978. "Deinstitutionalization and Mentally Retarded Persons." *Community Mental Health Review* 3:1–12.

Wolfensberger, Wolf. 1972. *The Principle of Normalization in the Human Services*. Toronto: National Institute on Mental Retardation.

Wyatt v. Stickney, 344 F. Supp., (M.D. Ala. 1972).

Zelman, David B. 1976. "The Development and Evaluation of the Essential Adult Sex Education (EASE) Curriculum for the Mentally Retarded." *Dissertation Abstracts International* 37:3557.

Zetlin, Andrea G., and Jim L. Turner. 1984. "Self-Perspectives on Being Handicapped: Stigma and Adjustment." In *Lives in Progress: Mildly Retarded Adults in a Large City*, ed. R. B. Edgerton. Washington D.C.: American Association on Mental Deficiency.

Zylla, Therese, and G. David Demetral. 1981. "A Behavioral Approach to Sex Education." *Sexuality and Disability* 4:40–48.

John H. Storer

Gender and Kin Role Transposition as an Accommodation to Father-Daughter Incest

This essay discusses father-daughter incest and how families in North American culture are able to function and adapt to it, despite the alleged strength of the prohibition against sex between immediate kin. The incest taboo has occupied the anthropological imagination since the beginning of the discipline because of its seeming universality, but the act of incest has been largely ignored because of its seeming rarity. In the past decade, however, it has become evident that in at least one society (the United States) one variety of incest (father-daughter) is far from rare.

Perhaps the most convincing estimate of the prevalence of father-daughter incest is David Finkelhor's 1978 survey of undergraduate students (Finkelhor 1979). In this sample, 1.3 percent of the females reported having had sexual contact with their fathers, while 9 percent reported having had sexual contact with some male kin. This is the most convincing survey to date because it was not derived from contact with the legal system or referral to a helping agency and because participants were assured of complete anonymity through the use of unsigned and uncoded questionnaires. Finkelhor's study suggests not only that father-daughter incest frequently occurs in North American families but also that these families persevere and continue to function in spite of dealing with the "grisly horror" of incest.

After encountering families in which father-daughter incest has become established for a period of time, one is struck by the similar characteristics virtually all exhibit. Moreover, the literature repeatedly mentions the existence of an "incestuous family pattern" (e.g., Geiser 1979; Giarretto 1976; Kroth 1979; Renvoize 1982). The characteristics typifying these families are:

1. Social isolation: These families appear to maintain few social relationships outside the nuclear family and express a pronounced "we versus they" attitude toward the outside world. This attitude is often manifested in the way the family physically isolates itself, often living on the outskirts of town, on the end of a dead-end street, or behind tall walls or hedges.

2. Religiosity: Although no particular sect or religion seems to be correlated with father-daughter incest, vocal and rigorous religious participation by the entire family is common.

3. Incapacity of the mother: This is a general way of referring to such things as chronic illness, physical handicap, mental retardation, mental illness, closely spaced children, and the need to care for an aged parent. It is interesting to note that these incapacities may or may not affect the father's sexual access to her.

4. Pseudomaturity of the daughter: In addition to the anticipated sexual precocity, this includes such areas as household budgeting, childcare, housekeeping, and etiquette.

5. Transposition of roles within the family.

I have not elaborated on this last characteristic because this phenomenon is central to understanding the family's adaptation and contributes to shaping the other characteristics. The existence of such a predictable and repetitive family structure indicates that, in this culture, a family's response to incest is the product of interpreting and enacting culturally determined rules and shared understandings about behavior toward kinsmen rather than the product of the behavior of deviant family members. The purpose of this study is to identify and analyze these rules and shared understandings, not to offer insight into the origin of the incest taboo and not to identify which families and individuals risk father-daughter incest. To my knowledge no study in social anthropology has dealt with the act of incest within the nuclear family as it occurs throughout a society.

This research makes contributions on two distinct levels. First, it contributes to understanding the structure of the North American nuclear family and the options available within the set of primary kin roles. One aspect of this is to describe which aspects of role performance are necessary for the maintenance of the nuclear family and which are optional. Second, this research contributes to understanding the incest taboo in the United States as it operates in society, in contrast to how it operates as part of codified legal and value systems.

The data for this study are derived from my child abuse and neglect investigatory caseload, encompassing a four-year period from

1980 to 1984. The core of these data consists of twenty-eight cases. In twenty-three families a sexual relationship existed between the natural father and daughter. In two cases there was grandfather-granddaughter incest; in two, stepfather-stepdaughter incest; and in one, a sexual relationship with mother's paramour.

The data were gathered by interviews conducted during one to ten or more sessions with virtually all combinations of family members (entire family, daughter alone, father alone, mother and daughter, etc.). Also, interviews were often done with nonnuclear family members and other individuals involved with the family (e.g., school teachers, neighbors, and pastors). Additional contacts were made with family members and relevant others (as many as two hundred contacts for a single family) to manage the logistics and aftermath of the investigation.

The present study centers on explaining how the actors in three interrelated social categories (father, mother, daughter) use the social raw material available to their categorical relationships to adapt, in a persistent and patterned way, to a behavior (incest) for which no performance rules exist. This calls for an analysis that goes beyond traditional rule-centered role theory. Ward Goodenough (1965) and Roger M. Keesing (1970) have provided concepts that facilitate this analysis.

The analytical categories defined by Goodenough are the proper starting point for a discussion of role behavior. *Social identity* is used to refer to the social position, while *status* is reserved for the rights and duties attached to it. *Social persona* is the combination of social identities salient in a given social situation. For example, a man may be adult, male, father, plumber, and veteran but the identities of plumber and veteran are not likely to be important in the context of disciplining his child. An *identity relationship* is a dyadic relationship between two social identities; likewise a *status relationship* is the reciprocal rights and duties relevant to a given identity relationship. For example, the rights and duties relevant for the identity "doctor" would not be the same for a doctor interacting with a nurse as for one interacting with another doctor. *Role* is reserved for the sum of all behaviors appropriate to all the relationships in which an identity can legitimately participate (e.g., doctor-nurse, doctor-patient, doctor-doctor).

Since Goodenough isolates some of the structural components of a status-role system, I use his terminology to describe the phenomena he has identified. There are many aspects of roles Goodenough did not treat, however. Roger Keesing has identified some of these.

Keesing calls for a "building block" model of analysis, which relates specific behaviors to the constituent units of a social position rather than to the position itself. For example, the position "father" can be viewed as being made up of the building blocks "adult," "male," "immediate kinsman," and the like. The sum of the behaviors enacted with each building block are called composite roles by Keesing.

Keesing's work is particularly important for understanding father-daughter incest because it obviates relating specific behaviors to specific social categories. He sees these role entailments as ideal and probabilistic (Keesing 1970:446). Keesing's emphasis on contexts is also important for understanding father-daughter incest. The "complex networks" within which relationships are embedded is one element of context. Another is the "scene" that Keesing describes as a culturally defined and labeled event (Keesing 1970:432). As is the case with social identities, he assumes not monolexemic labeling but rather the native's identification of the presence of sufficient definitional criteria.

The Father-Daughter Dyad

A sexual relationship between father and daughter is not encapsulated in a specific event. It is generally assumed that most fathers at times respond sexually to physical contact with their children (see, e.g., Renshaw 1982:2–6). It is also assumed that most fathers do not act on this. In fact, as a rule, the lessening of physical contact expected in this culture at puberty can probably, in part, be attributed to the additional sexual potential of the relationship.

There were no cases in my sample in which the father instigated sexual activity without having previously derived some sexual gratification from physical contact initiated for some other purpose, including ordinary displays of affection (hugging, kissing, cuddling), bathing, and, in one case, discipline. Visual stimulation was also frequently cited as a source of sexual stimulation: "She would run around half naked even after she started developing."

At this point, the father does not see himself as altering his relationship with his daughter. According to the typical daughter's perception, however, the father's behavior toward her has changed noticeably. She sees him becoming increasingly attentive and, in particular, seeking out the kinds of situations that provide sexual stimulation. Of course, the child does not recognize the sexual motivation for this behavioral change.

This unilateral behavioral change on the part of the father begins the process of altering the role relationships between father and daughter. It also stimulates a set of behavioral responses on the part of the daughter in accordance with the new, complimentary role configuration she adopts. One of the building blocks of the identity "daughter" is "female," as "male" is for the identity "father." All father-daughter relationships have gender-based behavioral components, but prior to incestuous sexual contact, the father stresses her gender in ways inappropriate to the child's age. As one daughter put it, "When I was a real little kid he didn't pay too much attention to me, but in 4th or 5th grade, a year or so before he started doing anything, he started paying a lot of attention to me, and how I looked and how I acted. He would give mom hell if she sent me to school in just jeans and a top. He also started buying me clothes. He really liked skirts with knee socks. I would have fashion shows for him, trying things on. I loved it. I thought I was really special."

At this time, such factors as "looking good and smelling good for daddy" are also stressed. More direct is the father's attention to female physiology and anatomy. Several daughters reported that at age nine or ten they were periodically questioned about breast size and pubic hair. As the father stresses the feminine component of the daughter role, the daughter also accentuates it in interaction with the father. The father rewards feminine behaviors, and the daughter, who values the attention, adopts them.

The second major role shift in this preincestuous stage is that the child is usually placed in a special, unique category, apart from other siblings and the world at large, She is often designated by the father as his "best friend," and the child is overtly told she is the most important person in his life. More important, she is treated like a best friend. She is given extra time, money, and consideration; defended in altercations with other family members; and made privy to secrets, including gossip about other family members.

It must be remembered that at this point sexual contact has not yet taken place and the daughter is, on average, somewhat less than nine years old (see Table 1). The duration of this period is impossible to

Table 1: Ages of Family Members at Onset and Discovery of Incest

	Father	Mother	Daughter
Onset	37	33	9.4
Discovery	41	37	13.3

pinpoint because there are no demarcating events. It fades directly into the period of sexual contact.

There seem to be no regularities surrounding the stages of sexual contact, other than that they occur in the sequence described here. There is no set duration for a stage and no set age for a daughter to be moved from one stage to the next. A father and daughter may stay in stage one or two for years and never progress, or intercourse may be attempted almost immediately.

In no cases did sexual contact begin in a form that could be classified as violent rape. However, coercion was always used in some form, and in no case had the child reached the age of informed consent. The types of sexual contact practiced fall naturally into three stages (see Figure 1). The first stage consists of the father's fondling the breasts, buttocks, and genitals. The second consists of mutual masturbation and oral or anal intercourse. The third consists of genital intercourse.

Figure 1: Stages of Sexual Contact

Stages	Type of Contact
Presexual contact stage	"courtship" behavior "special" relationship
First Stage	fondling
Second Stage	mutual masturbation oral and anal intercourse
Third Stage	genital intercourse

The first stage of sexual contact does not mark a radical departure from the "special" relationship of the father and daughter. At this age the child usually does not have the sophistication or resources to mount much resistance, and the nonintrusive nature of the sexual contact is not, in itself, very traumatic. The aspect of the relationship that is threatening to the child appears to be not the change in the nature of the physical contact but the way the father negotiates the relationship.

The most important element of the father-daughter relationship introduced with sexual contact is not the sexual contact itself but the need for secrecy. Fondling is usually introduced gradually, in the context of bathing, showering, being put to bed, or playing, such as mock wrestling. Norms concerning modesty are learned and understood by age nine or ten, but these norms include different standards vis-à-vis family members. Younger daughters (under twelve) therefore, do not readily classify fondling as an assault on their modesty. The sexual content of fondling begins to be recognized at about age twelve, and breaking modesty norms consequently becomes an element of first-stage sexual contact. Below this age daughters reported fondling as a neutral, if not pleasurable, experience. If it were not accompanied by other behavioral changes on the part of the father, it likely would not be recalled as being distinct from the stage of heightened affection that preceded it.

The need for secrecy introduces a number of new role elements and behaviors. The first change that daughters can readily identify is a new "scene." Preincestuous physical contact could occur spontaneously in any context, but first-stage sexual contact must occur at places and times safe from observation and interruption. Although details may vary from occasion to occasion, it becomes a recognizable category of event due to the common elements of privacy and the father's role as the active agent in organizing it: "I always knew when we were going to 'play' like that because he would say I needed a bath when I wasn't dirty or he would have something to show me in the back bedroom or in the barn."

Of course the need for secrecy is ongoing. This is usually accomplished by two transactions. The first is a simple threat: "Don't tell anyone or I'll punish you." The second is adopting the roles of coconspirators: "Let's keep this just our secret. This kind of playing is something only you and I will do, we won't tell anybody else." Most fathers use both ploys. They are, in part, contradictory. The first emphasizes the rights attached to the identity "father" as disciplinarian, rule-maker, and authority figure. The second elevates the daughter to peer status as coconspirator, abrogating the power differential contained in father-daughter and adult-child relationships.

From the daughter's point of view, however, the net result is not as contradictory as it might seem. As noted above, the incestuous family tends to be a traditional, father-centered structure in which the father exercises the most authority. It is contradictory that he introduces punishment as a means of assuring silence about behavior he himself has instigated. Normally, since one of the components of the father identity is "head of the household," the father is the ultimate arbiter of the family's behavior. Behavior he has instigated is therefore good, right, proper, and open to the family's scrutiny. He can, however, enforce his threat of punishment by virtue of the power differential inherent in the adult-child relationship, without the authority implied by either the father-daughter or head of household-family member relationship. Since the power used to enforce the daughter's silence is not legitimized by the authority attached to either of the kin-based relationships, her silence becomes open for negotiation. At least one father consciously recognized this shift: "After it first started I was scared to death, guilty as hell and totally confused. I was afraid that if I didn't make a big deal out of it she would let it slip accidentally. I was just as afraid that if I was too hard on her she would get mad and tell, or, almost as bad, that she would be scared of me and stay away."

Although daughters may not be able to verbalize the transactions taking place in the first stage, the sexual contact "scene," they have two negotiable commodities: their silence and sexual access. The daughter has the ability to negotiate, but usually little negotiation takes place at this time. As stated before, first-stage sexual contact is not, in itself, very averse to the daughter. What is averse is her father's nervousness, shortness of temper, and touchiness that surround the new kind of playing. Although the daughters found these behavioral changes unsettling, they reported they derived sufficient benefits from the new nature of the father-daughter relationship that they were rarely motivated to terminate it at this point.

The enhanced levels of affection, attention, and companionship begun prior to sexual contact continue at an even higher level. In fact, a sense of the direction the father-daughter relationship takes at this time can be conveyed by metaphorically labeling it a "courtship." It is clear that in addition to sexual gratification the father is seeking attention, affection, and understanding from the relationship. As one father put it, "I didn't know I was hurting her. I wouldn't hurt her. I care more about her than the rest of the whole damn family put together. My wife is either laying in bed with a headache or out spending money, and the other kids leave the room when I walk in. Susan [the daughter] is the only one who appreciates how much I do. How could I hurt her?"

A courtship requires that an actor assume the social identity of "suitor." Although the father does not label the relationship a courtship or himself a suitor, he has some cultural knowledge of strategies required to press his suit successfully. These strategies can be implemented without causing other family members or the wider society to relabel either the father-daughter relationship or the father's social identity, primarily because there is considerable overlap in the duties attached to both the father and suitor social identities (see Figure 2). Additionally, behaviors unique to the suitor identity will be activated only in private.

Figure 2: Duties Shared by the Father and Suitor Social Identities

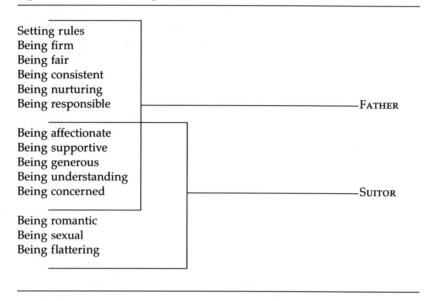

Setting rules
Being firm
Being fair
Being consistent
Being nurturing
Being responsible
                                                    ———Father

Being affectionate
Being supportive
Being generous
Being understanding
Being concerned
                                                    ———Suitor

Being romantic
Being sexual
Being flattering

For the daughter, courtship furthers the process of elevation vis-à-vis the father. As the object of courtship, the daughter is expected to become the father's confidante: a listener, sympathizer, and adviser for his life problems. These functions can be performed by any number of social identities with which the father may have a relationship (e.g., girlfriend, various kinsmen, counselor, priest). An adult male can "grammatically" choose individuals occupying these and other social identities for establishing a confidant-confidante relationship. Two components seem to be distributed across the range of permissible identities: (1) being nonantagonistic to the father's best interest, a component a daughter shares, and (2) being adult, a component a preteenage daughter cannot share. In becoming the father's confidante and romantic and sexual partner, the daughter is forced to assume many adult behaviors. She generally incorporates other adult behaviors and competencies into her repertoire, including childrearing, housekeeping, money management, and becoming impatient with and intolerant of her age-mates because they are so "immature." In the incest literature, this precocity is generally called pseudomaturity.

The shift from first-stage to second-stage sexual contact incorporates more changes than does any other shift in the progression of father-daughter incest. The only overt changes are in the kind of sexual contact itself. These changes, however, are enhanced because the daughter is likely to be older and more sophisticated and because the cumulative effect of previous sexual contact is made more manifest in the day-to-day functioning of the family.

As stated earlier, the start of second-stage sexual contact does not correlate with either the age of the daughter or the duration of previous sexual contact. Regardless of their age, daughters find the mutual masturbation and the oral and anal intercourse of stage two more repugnant than the fondling of stage one. The reasons cited for this are (1) digital penetration and anal intercourse are frequently painful; (2) direct manipulation of the genitals transgresses a modesty norm; (3) oral-genital contact is inherently "dirty," "unsanitary," and hence disgusting; (4) ejaculation is associated with defecation and urination and is therefore abhorrent; (5) fellatio is physically uncomfortable ("It chokes me when he puts it in my mouth"); and (6) their father's loss of control upon orgasm produces fear, bordering on terror ("It's like he's having a fit or heart attack or something").

Whatever the reason, the daughter becomes much more motivated to avoid sexual contact and starts implementing strategies to achieve that end. The simplest strategy is avoidance; she avoids being alone with the father. The second most popular strategy is refusal. The same reasons are given to the father that are given to the social worker: pain, disgust, and fear. The father's response to her refusal crystallizes the elaborate multiplex relationship that characterizes father-daughter incest.

Since the second stage of sexual contact continues for a period of months or years and fathers and daughters maintain a number of conflicting identity relationships throughout, most fathers and most daughters respond in all of the following ways at one time or another. If the daughter refuses him, the father can respond as the:

1. Gentle and concerned lover: This identity generates profuse apologies along with promises to be more gentle and understanding in the future. It can also move him to purchase lubricating jelly or even to drop back to stage-one sexual contact until the daughter is deemed ready.

2. Nurturing father: Instead of apologies, this identity produces explanations of how this kind of activity is something many girls do not like at first but need to learn to appreciate in order to become sexually fulfilled adults. Promises are made about going slow and explaining what is happening. It also prompts the purchase of lubricating jelly.

3. Dutiful provider: This identity stresses how badly the father needs the kind of release only the daughter can provide. An accounting is made of how much the daughter has received and how little she has given. She must comply to do her part for the family. This identity seems to be activated only if the other two fail. It is partly a response to the daughter's ingratitude in her refusal to accept the appropriateness of the lover and nurturer identities.

As the father implements these strategies, the daughter responds with corresponding counterstrategies. To the father-lover she can (1) continue to refuse, (2) refuse with qualifications, or (3) accede to his wishes. If she continues to refuse he can (1) accept the refusal, (2) make a counteroffer ("If you will X, I will Y"), or (3) invoke either the nurturer or provider identities.

Recall that by this point in the father-daughter relationship the daughter has likely become accustomed to receiving privileges and gifts from her father, in association with sexual contact. She previously might not have solicited them, but they open a new arena of bargaining now that she is motivated to refuse sexual contact. If the daughter's terms are reasonable, the father will likely meet them because he is seeking approval, attention, and affection, as well as sexual gratification. He is more likely to receive these payoffs by maintaining the less demanding suitor identity than by adopting another strategy. Daughters have cited such things as two dollars, being taken fishing, and being allowed to go to a basketball game as the "price" on specific occasions.

All the cases with which I dealt contained some elements of a lover-lover relationship. Most also contained a "father as sex educator–daughter as pupil" element. This adds additional complexity to the relationship. During first-stage sexual contact the "scene" of courtship is separated from other scenes of father-daughter interaction. When the father-educator identity is introduced into the sexual contact scene, the authority differential inherent in the father-daughter (kin identity) relationship is injected into a context that has been reserved for the confidant-confidante or lover-lover relationship.

Although it would seem that adding sexual content to the educator-pupil relationship would make the lover-lover relationship untenable, this is not the case. Sex education is apparently an "education" scene and not a "sex" scene. Outside of the sexual scene, the expected elements of the parent-child relationship are maintained to a surprising degree throughout the incestuous relationship. Sex education, as a strategic transaction on the part of the father, centers on arguments as to why the daughter needs to develop sexual proficiency. Instruction on specific techniques is left to sexual contact scenes in which the older, more experienced lover instructs the younger, less experienced lover. Thus dual socialization process, or theory-practice distinction, involves two types of scenes about which the child will already have learned. For example, explaining why good grades are necessary for getting into college is different from actually helping a child with his or her homework. If sex education motivates a daughter to reenter the lover-lover relationship, an equilibrium will be reestablished until her aversion to second-stage sexual contact overcomes the father's ability to motivate. If this occurs, the father-provider identity may become salient.

Most cases of father-daughter incest that end through discovery terminate at a time when the provider identity has become the predominate strategy for maintaining the incestuous relationship. The arguments the dutiful provider presents to his daughter include: "The world outside the family is so stressful I need sexual release to function"; "I have given you so much, you owe me sex"; "Your mother is sick [or frigid, pregnant, selfish, etc.], so there is no one else to take care of me"; "I support the whole family and I need sex, so to refuse is to let the whole family down"; "Daughters are supposed to do this for their fathers. It is your duty [often supported with child pornography]"; "If you don't do this, it proves you don't love me."

The reasons these arguments lead to instability and the potential dissolution of the family are:

1. They break down the discreteness of the courtship scene. By presenting sex as something the father needs without reference to the daughter, the "specialness" of sexual contact is lessened, removing it as a motive for maintaining the sexual relationship and for remaining silent.

2. Over time daughters are presented with clearly contradictory information, such as "mothers are supposed to do this but she is turning me down" and "daughters are supposed to do this."

3. Making sexual compliance an issue of parental control makes sex an issue in scenes that are cued or defined by control issues ("I know I didn't clean my room but I did have sex with you this week"). This transaction would be "ungrammatical" if sex were confined only to a peer relationship.

4. The father has created a set of conditions that legitimize the continuance of a sexual relationship, regardless of the wishes of his daughter. This removes the secondary rewards of affection, attention, and companionship for both father and daughter and makes sex the only reward the father can get. This changes the "courtship" scene to a "sexual encounter" scene. This makes sexual contact even more averse for the daughter because the nonaverse elements have been removed.

An additional confusion of scenes occurs because the father displays behavior equally appropriate to a "jilted lover" identity and the "father-provider" identity. He is suspicious, quick to anger, overprotective, jealous, and easily hurt. Fathers express two major concerns at this time: their deteriorating relationship will cause the daughter to expose him; she is rejecting him because she is sexually involved with someone else. His response is to forbid the daughter to interact with friends, to interrogate her about time not strictly accounted for, and to forbid her participation in school and community activities. The result is that father and daughter become antagonistic. The daughter's efforts at avoidance intensify, and sexual contact becomes more coercive. It still by no means constitutes forcible rape. It involves such strategies as sneaking into the daughter's bedroom late at night so she cannot resist without awakening the family and being forced to test the sincerity of the father's threats.

At this point it is appropriate to discuss the significance of the third stage of sexual contact, genital intercourse. The introduction of genital intercourse is not strongly tied to the previous course of the father-daughter relationship. Not all fathers attempt intercourse; nor is there an identifiable set of precipitating circumstances. However, an identifiable pattern appeared in the fifteen cases in which intercourse occurred.

This shift to the third stage is much more significant to the father than to the daughter. Genital intercourse may or may not be more averse for the daughter than previous forms of sexual contact were. The father maintains a certain amount of gentleness and concern for the daughter's physical well-being in introducing genital intercourse. Daughters as young as six or seven have been introduced to genital intercourse without physical damage or memorable discomfort.

Genital intercourse is more significant to the father for several reasons. One is the somewhat mystical significance of "going all the way," apparently a carryover from his socialization into the identity of suitor. Second, upon discovery it becomes more difficult to argue that the daughter was merely misinterpreting play or affection as a sexual act. Third, the rigidly religious father is likely to view genital intercourse as the point at which he technically has become an adulterer. Fourth, the act of genital intercourse transforms the daughter into a nonvirgin.

This last reason is particularly significant. The maintenance of the sexual purity of one's daughter is a value very much espoused by incestuous fathers. It is frequently cited as a reason for the isolation of the daughter and as a justification for the incest itself: "I thought that if I kept her satisfied at home she wouldn't go looking for it somewhere else." It is also central to one of the primary duties of the parent identity: one must not knowingly harm (devalue or corrupt) one's child. It is probably safe to say that causing one's child to lose her virginity constitutes harm in this culture.

The way the fathers, without exception, dealt with this conflict was to assume or suspect that the daughter has been sexually active with someone else prior to the father's attempt at genital intercourse. This is not entirely rationalization on the father's part because fully half (twelve out of twenty-three) of the daughters admitted to being sexually active with someone other than the father at the time of discovery.

Even though sexual contact is limited to a specific sexual scene throughout most of the course of father-daughter incest, an inevitable by-product is that the daughter becomes "sexualized." By this I mean she has learned that flirtatious and seductive behavior is likely to be rewarded. This behavior is not likely to attract a great deal of attention until the beginning of adolescence, when her peers are likely to start appreciating the sexual content of her behavior.

Fathers are aware of their daughter's sexualized behavior all along. Since it is a gradual process, they are unable to perceive their role in causing it and often sincerely believe it has been the daughter who has escalated sexual contact. This perception (1) allows the father to see himself as the victim of his daughter's sexuality; (2) justifies his desire to isolate his daughter, based on the need to keep her out of trouble because she is "wild" (a duty attached to the culturally legitimate parent identity) rather than based on his sexual jealousy (a right attached to the culturally illegitimate lover identity); (3) allows the father to maintain a sexual relationship with the daughter, based on the premise that it keeps her from seeking sexual gratification under more dangerous circumstances (parent identity) rather than based on his own desire for sexual gratification (lover identity); and (4) allows him to display and act out his hurt, anger, and frustration, based on his being the parent of an acting-out child rather than on his being a rejected lover.

Genital intercourse often begins just as the daughter's sexuality is becoming a more general issue. Of the fifteen fathers who engaged in genital intercourse, six cited menarche as their cue to begin, while four cited the development of secondary sexual characteristics. By the early teenage years, when these events occur, the daughter will likely have learned that most daughters do not have sex with their fathers and that it is called incest, which is illegal. They also have probably begun to incorporate their peer group's standards of sexual attractiveness, which for reasons of age does not include their father.

The daughter has also learned that although sexual activity has become an abiding interest for her age group, being sexually active and sexually experienced is not the norm for that age group. In addition to having been socially isolated from her peers, she now becomes isolated because of her different range of experience. The father seeks to maintain her isolation both because of his fears that forming close friendships will increase the likelihood of the daughter's exposing the incest and because of sexual jealousy. As the daughter gets older, the opportunities for extrafamilial social activity increase. Correspondingly, the frequency with which the father needs to control these activities increases. The result is that the father and daughter are almost constantly at odds over control issues and sexual access.

At this point actual sexual contact between father and daughter rarely takes place when the lover identities and the courtship scene are salient. Sexual contact is maintained through such threats as "No one will believe you, they will think you are crazy and send you away"; "I will kill or harm you"; "They will put me in jail and the family will starve"; and "They will know it's your fault because you have screwed so many other guys."

As indicated earlier, most cases of father-daughter incest are probably never reported to the authorities and are terminated only when the daughter leaves home. Nor do all cases reach this final stage. Five of the cases were reported inadvertently, in the sense that the daughter told friends about the incest but did not expect anything to be done about it. The friends or their parents brought about the intervention. In other cases, professionals (teachers, social workers, counselors,) noticed symptomatic behavior and elicited accounts from the child. In any case, this adversarial relationship represents the structural conclusion to the father-daughter incest process. It is the pattern most often seen at the time of incest reports and the pattern described in the retrospective, first-person accounts of adult incest victims (see, e.g., Armstrong 1978; Finkelhor 1979:185–215). This pattern can apparently constitute a disequilibrium that leads to discovery or an equilibrium that allows the incestuous family to persist, depending on the idiosyncrasies of the particular family.

The Mother-Daughter Dyad

To a large degree the changes that take place in the mother-daughter relationship reflect the ongoing changes taking place between the father and daughter. Although there may be predisposing elements in the mother-daughter relationship, these are as yet undiscovered due to the impossibility of identifying potentially incestuous families prior to incest.

The changes in the mother-daughter relationship are grounded in the daughter's usurpation of behaviors, rights, duties, and obligations normatively attached to the mother or wife identities. In the "traditional" nuclear family power structure common to incestuous families, the mother and daughter identities share a number of building blocks at the outset. Each building block was found to have behaviors appropriate to the particular context.

Since the nature of family interaction before the beginning of the preincestuous "romantic" stage must be reconstructed from family members' recollections, it is impossible to know what conditions existed before the father-daughter relationship began to change. There is, however, a consensus among mothers that "things used to be different, we used to do things together. He paid attention to me and seemed to respect me. I think we used to have a good marriage."

Because entrance into the presexual contact stage is not marked by a specific event, alterations in the mother-daughter relationship are in step with alterations in the father-daughter relationship. The alterations are gradual. The father's time, attention, energy, and money exist in finite quantities. As more is given to the daughter, some portion must be taken from the mother. Mother and daughter thus become rivals for these scarce resources. This rival-rival relationship causes the same type of elevation to peer status for the daughter vis-à-vis the mother that is taking place with the father.

Mothers and daughters are often rivals for the fathers' time and attention in other kinds of families, but the rivalry is much more direct in the incestuous family. The fact that some of the father's attention is being given in a "courtship" scene makes for a situation in which the mother must compete for what normally are exclusive rights attached to the adult, lover, and sexual partner components of her wife identity.

The course the mother-daughter relationship takes as the father-daughter relationship progresses is not a linear course of increasing jealousy and rivalry. Instead of asserting her rights to her husband's affection and attention, most mothers bow to the younger and more attractive rival. They are able to do this and maintain both their marriage and a relationship with their daughter because (1) the overtly sexual behavior on the part of father and daughter is confined to private sexual scenes; (2) most of the observable behaviors displayed by father and daughter are not radical departures from, but exaggerations of, acceptable interactions between father and daughter, adult and child, and family member and family member; and (3) in the traditional incestuous family there is already a power differential between husband and wife, and the power differential between mother and daughter has begun to even out because of the daughter's incipient elevation vis-à-vis the mother, which imposes even more limits on the mother's power and thus her ability to alter the situation.

The powerlessness of the mother in incestuous families has often been noted (Kroth 1979; Renshaw 1982; Renvoize 1982). The tendency for the mother to be incapacitated or absent has attracted particular attention. In these cases, out of twenty-five relevant (father or step-father incest) families, ten mothers can be termed absent or incapacitated. Two were dead, one had a chronic heart condition, three were retarded, one was addicted to prescription drugs, and three were neurotic or psychotic to the point of incapacity. In addition, I would categorize all but three of the rest of the mothers as naive and unsophisticated. For example, although one mother was of normal intelligence, was a high school graduate, and had a driver's license, she did not know the location of the county courthouse, even though she had lived within two miles of it her entire life.

Moreover, only two (8.7 percent) of the twenty-three living mothers were employed at the time of discovery. This contrasts with recent figures indicating that 64 percent of mothers with school-age children are employed (Knox 1985:277). While this to some degree reflects the high rate of incapacity among mothers, it also reflects a functional incapacity in terms of complete economic dependence on the father. This factor probably also contributes to their lack of sophistication.

It can probably be said that mothers are not aware of the changing nature of sexual contact as such. Since the first stage of sexual contact enhances, rather than alters, the "special" and romantic nature of the father-daughter relationship, there is no change in the mother's response of jealousy and rivalry.

In addition to the initial response of jealousy and rivalry, a secondary response reflecting the daughter's elevation to peer status begins. The first manifestation of the daughter's shift to stage two is change in her behavior. Because the father is in large part treating her as a peer, interactionally as well as sexually, she becomes knowledgeable about areas inappropriate for her age. She also is positively reinforced for "adult" styles of conversation and interaction. She does not limit the use of these precocious styles to interactions with her father but assumes them with her mother and siblings as well. If one assumes that one of the primary methods of socialization is rewarding the successful emulation of adults, the mother is able to encourage and promote her daughter's precocity while maintaining the mother identity.

However, since the father is not placing limits on the degree to which adult-like behavior can progress or keeping a play-work distinction intact, the daughter begins to develop true competencies beyond what are normally regarded as within a child's capabilities. The mother is not in a position to curtail this development directly. Pride in the accomplishments of one's child is an expectation of the parent identity, and the mother directly benefits from the development of the daughter's skills in performing household duties and childcare. As the daughter takes over some of the mother's rights in terms of attention, companionship, and sexual access, the mother's loss is tempered by the fact that the daughter is also taking over some of the mother's less pleasant duties.

A curious phenomenon is that as the daughter develops additional competencies, the mother seemingly "forgets" competencies she previously possessed (see Figure 3 for the process). I have interviewed mothers who, prior to marriage or children, worked at responsible jobs, lived alone, budgeted, and dealt with government agencies and other demanding tasks; however, when presented with the prospect of the dissolution of the family and faced with resuming these tasks, they pleaded total inadequacy. Daughters also frequently take responsibility for other tasks, such as planning meals and taking care of younger siblings. This even is carried to the extent that the daughter is the one who deals with younger siblings' school teachers when problems arise. It is usually unacceptable for daughters to assume parental duties because it would be exploitative or harmful, but it is less unacceptable if the parent assumes an "incapacitated" identity.

Figure 3: The Process of Mothers' Losing and Daughters' Gaining Competencies

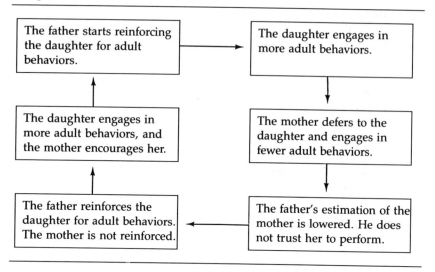

Although confirming data do not exist, it would seem that this loss of competence is motivated by the mother's search for a legitimate justification for allowing the daughter to assume behaviors normally attached to an adult identity. Of course, in cases where the mother is incapacitated prior to the onset of incest, the daughter would be forced to assume adult behavior due to the mother's incapacity, thereby facilitating the assumption of other adult behaviors, possibly including a sexual relationship with the father. This is not to say that a mother's incapacity causes incest, because many families with incapacitated mothers are not incestuous and many incestuous families do not have incapacitated mothers.

For the duration of incest, the mother-daughter relationship is fraught with ambivalence on the part of both mother and daughter, caused by the jealousy and resentment resulting from the daughter's usurpation of many of the mother's rights and duties vis-à-vis the father, and by the dependency the mother has on the daughter. There seems to be a certain ebb and flow to this ambivalence, depending on not only the personalities of the particular mother and daughter but also the quality of interaction between father and daughter at a given time.

As the father-daughter relationship reaches the point where sexual contact begins to become averse the mother-daughter relationship can undergo several different kinds of alteration. Like fathers and daughters at this stage in their relationship, most mothers and daughters use various identities, exercising all of their options at one time or another.

One response is for the daughter to accept the father's argument that this would not be happening if the mother were satisfying him sexually. As a result, the daughter is going to view the mother as lazy, irresponsible, and the cause of her having to cope with the father's advances. Since laziness, irresponsibility, and exploitation of one's child are incongruent with the parent identity, the daughter's elevation vis-à-vis the mother is furthered, as is the process of the daughter's gaining and the mother's losing competencies. If the mother has some identifiable incapacity when the daughter takes over the mother's sexual duties, the "invalid mother" and "dutiful daughter" identities become salient. These identities are culturally approved and have already been adopted by the mother and daughter in other scenes.

Another universal element of the daughter's response is anger and resentment at the mother's failure or inability to alter the situation. Although children's anger at parents is hardly unique to incestuous families, the daughter's anger at the mother does make it more likely for the daughter to remain more tolerant of the father and appreciative of the privileges, attention, and gifts that he can still bestow.

A second set of responses, usually coexisting with the first, entails creating building blocks (see Figure 4). As the daughter is elevated to a peer-peer relationship with the mother, identity relations requiring peer-peer "building blocks" are sometimes activated, including friend-friend, confidante-confidante, sympathizer-sympathizer, and adviser-adviser. The mother and daughter share the experience of mutually running the household and caring for other children in the family. They also share the task of dealing with the husband-father, who is usually the sole source of material goods for the household and ultimately has sole authority in affairs concerning the household. The mutual problem of dealing with the father sometimes has the effect of giving the daughter even more power in the family than the mother has, because the daughter often has more influence with the father than the mother has. This frequently results in the mother's being unable to enforce the authority granted to her by the mother identity, because the child can ask for various kinds of reprisals from the father. As a consequence, neither the mother nor the father can effectively discipline the child.

There are, however, scenes in which the parent-child and mother-daughter relationships are maintained throughout the period of sexual contact. In some scenes, involving special skills (such as sewing)

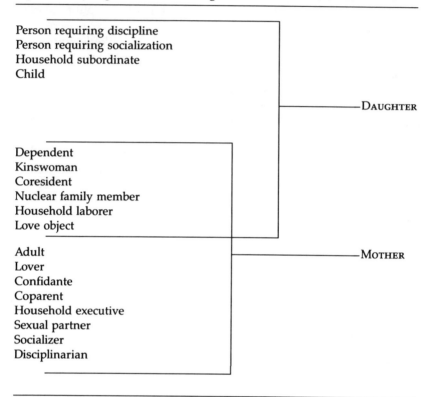

Figure 4: Building Blocks of the Daughter and Mother Identities

Person requiring discipline
Person requiring socialization
Household subordinate
Child

——————DAUGHTER

Dependent
Kinswoman
Coresident
Nuclear family member
Household laborer
Love object

Adult
Lover
Confidante
Coparent
Household executive
Sexual partner
Socializer
Disciplinarian

——————MOTHER

or adult identity rights (such as signing checks and making contracts), the mother remains more competent than the daughter. There are also scenes in which parental control and authority are so blatantly needed to maintain the family that mother and father are certain to support one another against the daughter.

At the point sexual contact becomes averse for the daughter, she frequently (in eleven cases) tells her mother about the sexual relationship with her father, despite the father's efforts to ensure against this eventuality. In only one case did telling the mother about the sexual relationship lead to its discovery by authorities. There has been considerable speculation as to how much mothers in incestuous families are aware of the father-daughter sexual relationship. In none of the cases presented here did the mother admit to firm suspicion. There is no compelling reason to doubt their lack of awareness. The behaviors that could be observed by the mother are not overtly sexual, and changes in the father-daughter relationship are very gradual. Also, there is evidence (Langworthy and Storer 1985) that incest as a category of activity is viewed as an abstraction that one does not encounter or have to deal with in everyday life. Most important, those changes that directly impinge on the mother, those that cause the mother to assume a rival identity, cannot be countered by assigning a sympathetic "exploited child" identity to the daughter.

When the daughter tells the mother about the sexual relationship with the father, the mother looses the freedom to interpret the relationship innocuously and is forced to take some kind of action. With the exception of the mother who did report incest to the authorities, the course of action entailed (1) confronting the father about the incest, (2) having him deny any impropriety, (3) accepting his denial, and (4) labeling the daughter either a liar, a troublemaker, or mentally ill.

At this point the mother has nothing to gain by believing the daughter. To believe her means she must take steps to end the incest. Because of the power differential between husband and wife, she cannot do this without outside intervention. Outside intervention likely means dissolution of the nuclear family, untenable for the economically dependent wife. Also, the act of believing the father is a powerful gambit in the rival-rival component of the mother-daughter relationship. It gets approval from the father and directs disapproval toward the daughter. More mundane, but equally important, in this culture adults are supposed to have a firmer grip on reality than children have, since children are given to all sorts of fanciful imaginings, and incest is not a contingency one expects to encounter.

When it becomes evident the mother cannot terminate the incest, the mother-daughter relationship stabilizes into an uncomfortable alternation between mutual hostility and mutual sympathy. Of course, hostility and sympathy were elements of the mother-daughter relationship since stage one, but the mother's hostility is now based on a direct threat to the family's existence as well as the competition for the husband's attention. The rival-rival, friend-friend, and parent-child relationships are still periodically salient, but in most day-to-day activities the building block of the mother-daughter relationship that most clearly shapes behavior is the conuclear family member–conuclear family member relationship. The mother can no longer perform the mother identity duties of control, discipline, nurturance, and education, and the daughter can no longer perform the daughter identity duties of obedience, learning, and respect. The only duty attached to this identity, that is to say common to all identities within the nuclear family, is the duty to cooperate and refrain from conflict enough to allow the family to function. One daughter articulately expressed her conscious efforts at maintaining the salience of this identity: "Once I knew for sure that my dad wasn't going to stop and my mom wasn't going to do anything I figured I would just shut up and put up with it. I didn't want to get sent to some home and I didn't really want my dad to go to jail, and as long as I didn't make any waves Mom mostly ignored me and it was easier to give in to Dad than to argue with him. I guess it would have been like that until I graduated if he would have let me see Bryan [her boyfriend]. Besides, someone had to take care of the kids, Mom is such a loser."

Mothers and daughters can reach this breakdown in the mother-daughter relationship even if the daughter has not told the mother about the incest. The daughters reported that they assumed the mother must have known about the incest and had chosen to do nothing about it. In some instances, the daughter actually believed her father's statement that she must have sex with him because her mother could not or would not, and she assumed the incest had her mother's blessing if not her complicity. Some daughters stated they believed the mother found sex with him just as odious as they did. The belief that the mother is exposing her daughter to an averse activity to save herself from it brings about the same result that the mother's failing to act after disclosure did.

As is the case for the last stage of the father-daughter relationship, a family may adapt to the situation or fail to adapt, which leads to discovery.

The Husband-Wife Dyad

It is in the marital relationship that the nuclear family's response to father-daughter incest makes visible the factors that allow for the persistence of the family. As is the case with the father-daughter and mother-daughter dyads, there may be preexisting conditions necessary for father-daughter incest to occur, but these are unknown.

In the case of long-established father-daughter incest, informants are best able to recall relationship changes that are most recent. It is easier to recall specific events, such as first intercourse or "the time I told my mother about the incest," than to recall the exact time a relationship in flux changed in quality. In the case of the incestuous family, the husband-wife relationship reacts to the changes in individual behavior caused by father-daughter sexual contact rather than to the secretive contact itself.

The presexual contact stage and the first stage of sexual contact is marked by the husband's turning, with ever-increasing frequency, to the daughter for the performance of a variety of behaviors attached to the wife identity. Even before sexual contact begins, the father has "fallen in love" with the daughter, thereby depriving the wife of her right to be the husband's primary romantic partner. Since the "courtship scene" is conducted in private, the wife cannot directly associate the change in her husband's behavior with changes in the father-daughter relationship, but she first notices that her husband is not turning to her for conversation, consultation about family matters, and recreation to the extent he might have previously.

There is wide variation in the amount of "togetherness" a given couple experienced prior to incest. Incapacitated wives were more distant from the husband than were other wives, but even wives who were incapacitated reported an increasing distance and coldness over time.

The typical response to this distancing is for the wife to assume her husband is having an affair with another woman. This, of course, is true, but the daughter is not the suspect. There are no doubt culturally prescribed behaviors for wives to perform when they suspect their husbands are having affairs. These, however, are not a factor in the course of father-daughter incest. Without exception, every wife who mentioned suspicions about her husband having an affair discounted the possibility because it was logistically impossible. Obviously, this is because husbands stay at home. They go to work on time and come home immediately afterward. According to the reports of all family members, fathers rarely seek outside relationships, sexual or otherwise.

Lacking "the other woman" as an explanation for the change in her husband's behavior, the wife is forced to assume her husband is responding to her own inadequacy. Although the sexual and romantic nature of the father-daughter relationship is not directly perceivable, it is apparent to the wife that her husband is turning to a child for things she, as an adult, should be better able to provide. This strengthens her assumption that it is her own inadequacies causing the husband to direct his attentions elsewhere.

While the wife can assert her right to her husband's time, attention, and affection, she cannot legitimately demand it be taken away from the daughter to be given to her. The husband can respond he is merely performing as coparent and performing well. To demand that the husband divert his attention from the daughter is to fail in her performance as coparent.

Her belief that she is inadequate is enhanced by the fact that her daughter, a child, is perceived by the husband as more interesting, intelligent, knowledgeable, and fun to be with. The father positively reinforces precocious behavior and negatively reinforces the mother's displays of competency. The mother is encouraged or forced by the father to leave the arena open for the daughter's virtuosity, that is, to refrain from doing some valued task the daughter can also do. Moreover, because the father is "in love" with the daughter, the daughter's least efforts will draw praise and the mother's best efforts will be ignored.

This entire process sets up a feedback loop that ensures the mother's loss of competency and the daughter's precocity. Of course, a high proportion of the mothers are, in fact, incompetent due to incapacity. These mothers quickly become dependent on the daughters for the performance of necessary tasks. To a certain extent nonincapacited mothers also become dependent on their daughters through their loss of competencies.

This condition of distance and dependency can exist indefinitely. One of the primary factors allowing for the persistence of the incestuous family is that the incest process itself makes the wife increasingly less able to stop it. In fact, not only is she unable to stop the incest when her daughter discloses it but she frequently attempts to reestablish the prediscovery equilibrium when authorities learn about it.

Recall that daughters become increasingly "sexualized" throughout the course of incest. Recall also that half of the daughters are sexually active with someone other than the father at the time of discovery. This is at an average age of 13.3 years. One national survey (Hass 1979) indicated that only 7 percent of girls were sexually active by age thirteen and only 31 percent by age sixteen.

In addition to acting out sexually, many girls acted out in other ways: three had been runaways, two were involved with drugs, two had been caught shoplifting, and one had been arrested for trying to pick a man's pocket. Even if the daughter had not been acting out in a way to attract attention to herself, the mother likely noticed with disapproval her precocious sexuality.

The daughter's acting out underscores the point that by the third stage of sexual contact the daughter has likely become a "problem" to both the mother and the father. Her credibility is not high. She has seemingly gone out of her way to cause trouble before, and her sexuality lends weight to the father's counteraccusations that she is fantasying the incest because of her obsession with sex or that she seduced him. The wife is quite motivated to believe her husband.

The fact that the wife does believe her husband has puzzled most outsiders (such as social workers and the police) who have worked with incestuous families. The wife is able to recount such incriminating factors as the deterioration of the marital relationship, the favoritism the father shows the daughter, the unusual efforts the father has made to get the daughter alone, the daughter's heightened sexuality, and her external view of the whole courtship, and yet she still acts as if either the daughter is lying or her daughter is the seductress and her husband the victim. I have been astonished repeatedly during interviews when a mother expresses anger at her husband, not for exploiting her daughter but for cheating on her. This is articulated in a context in which she is aware I am judging her fitness as a parent. This displays a considerable degree of nonparticipation in one of the basic norms of the wider society, but it does accurately reflect the social reality operating in the incestuous family.

The mother directly observes the romantic nature of the father-daughter relationship. She does not see the sexual contact. What she can observe is the daughter enjoying the attention and perquisites of her relationship with the father. Since the child begins to act out about the same time the sexual relationship becomes averse, the mother can assume that the worsening father-daughter relationship is the result of the daughter's becoming a "problem" rather than the changes in the nature of sexual contact.

Whether the child tells the mother only or the incest is somehow reported to the authorities, the only viable transaction for the mother is to ensure the continued economic support of her husband and the continued social support of the nuclear family. In fourteen cases in which the mother had some control over the family's disposition upon investigation, eleven chose to have the daughter removed from the home rather than have the father restrained from the home by court order. This is not a callous sacrifice of the daughter but is, from the mother's perspective, the most responsible way to serve the best interests of the nuclear family.

To believe the daughter would necessitate ascribing an "incestuous father" identity to the father. Assuming the father is married and the daughter is a child, the "incestuous father" identity contains the building blocks "child molester" and "adulterer." Ward Goodenough (1965) postulates the existence of cultural rules that specify which social identities can be combined to constitute a person's "social persona," or sum of salient identities, in a given social scene. Child molester, which contains the building blocks of felon, pervert, and harmer of one's child, cannot be "grammatically" combined with the husband and father identities, although adulterer can be grammatically combined with the husband and father identities without causing the disintegration of the nuclear family. While adultery is proscribed, there are culturally acceptable ways of dealing with a husband who is an adulterer without breaking up the family. The same is not true for a husband who is a child molester.

The practice of ascribing the adulterer identity to incestuous fathers is not limited to family members. I first considered the importance of the adulterer identity after talking to two incestuous fathers who had sought religious solace for their action, one before the president and elders of the Church of Jesus Christ of Latter-day Saints, the other before a Roman Catholic priest. In both cases religious authority chose to treat the cases as simple cases of adultery: "They felt it would be in everyone's best interest." A similar response was given by a fundamentalist pastor who took the initiative in intervening with a father.

These were decisions made by individuals, but they point to the fact that there is no institutional means of dealing with father-daughter incest while maintaining the family. It also indicates that practical decisions were made to choose the less severe of two interpretations of an action. It also implies other segments of the wider society believe that maintaining the nuclear family is more important than recognizing and punishing the "grisly horror" of incest.

The rival component of the mother-daughter relationship and the "courtship" between father and daughter facilitate the adoption of the adulterer identity. The father has already physically and emotionally withdrawn from his wife. He has also become secretive and defensive. These behaviors are consistent with both the adulterer and incestuous father identities.

The salience of the adulterer identity is further reinforced by the triadic interaction of mother, father, and daughter. If the daughter were allowed to assume the social persona of daughter-victim, the mother would have to reciprocate with protective behavior. She cannot do this without contradicting the husband-adulterer persona.

As discussed earlier, the symptomatology of sexual victimization in young girls includes sexual acting out, running away, and drug use, and a majority of the daughters in these cases engaged in one or more of these activities. The daughter's symptomatology ascribes to her another identity in American culture, that of "slut." The daughter-slut persona is compatible with the husband-adulterer persona. It also carries with it a set of duties and obligations for the parent persona. There are culturally prescribed ways of dealing with daughters who are sluts.

This persona is conducive to the maintenance of both the husband-adulterer persona and the father-lover persona. This is because a jealous lover and the father of an acting-out child share many of the same instrumental behaviors: hurt, anger, concern, disappointment, and an enhanced need to control. The daughter perceives these behaviors as indicative of the jealous lover, which has been the father's salient identity with her. The wife can perceive the same behaviors as indicative of a concerned father, supportive coparent, and remorseful adulterer. The persona formed by these three identities is one the mother can perceive as indicating that her husband is recommitted to performing his duties in a culturally legitimate way, when the reality is that it reinforces the relational skewing that originally began the cycle.

The Family through Time

I have described the process a family undergoes when a father begins a sexual relationship with a daughter. To a large extent the process was explained by reference to the interactions of the subunits or "building blocks" of social identities, closely following the work of Roger Keesing. It still remains to describe how the act of a father deriving some sexual pleasure from fondling his daughter can lead to a considerable regularity of reciprocal behaviors that ultimately changes the structure of the family.

To do this one must first look to Keesing's belief that neither identities, building blocks, nor scenes need be monolexemically labeled. Without labels actors must have some means of perceiving and responding to these unlabeled actors and situations. In the case of the incestuous family, the patterns or gestalts of interrelated behaviors provide cues to the actors that another actor is occupying an (unlabeled) identity. The behaviors making up these patterns are much more diffuse than the fairly discrete acts that are usually associated with "rights and duties." They can consist of such things as "being flirtatious" or "being withdrawn." These, of course, are behaviors that can be performed by practically any identity, but when they are part of a pattern they can allow one to distinguish salient identities and generate appropriate responses.

Time and the processual nature of relationships are the factors that allow the structured nature of the seemingly unmarked behaviors to appear. A clue to the role of time in uncovering structure is to be found in Aaron Cicourel's notion of "reconstructed logic" or "evaluating 'what happened' and connecting it to others or some wider group or community" (1974:29).

Although Cicourel does not overtly say this, one can continue to evaluate "what happened" in light of data gained from succeeding interactions and reflexively use old information to interpret the present interaction more effectively. I conceptualize this as a series of transparencies being placed one over the other as an actor goes through a series of interactions, from one point in time to another. Although a pattern may not emerge for some time, the interrelatedness of certain behaviors contained in an interaction will eventually become perceivable. The pattern does emerge.

It would seem that some interactions produce more "noise" than others, "noise" being behavior not related to an identifiable pattern. The less clear the pattern, the more likely an actor responds either to a misperceived pattern or to isolated behaviors. This seems to be what is happening early in the incest process. Initially, many of the "suitor" and "father" behaviors are the same, making a pattern difficult to perceive. When the daughter and mother respond to what they perceive as isolated behaviors, they also draw from culturally coded repertoires of patterned behavior, which means, in a sense, that they "over-act." If the father presents the daughter with a behavior that is part of a culturally coded peer pattern, the daughter is likely to respond with a behavior drawn from a peer pattern as she has learned it. The "suitor" pattern of behavior may not yet be perceivable, but the pattern of behavior associated with the "peer" building block of the "suitor" identity may already have come into focus. The daughter is thus reinforcing the father by giving him a pattern of behavior to which to respond. The pattern is "grammatical" and is a subset of the behaviors associated with the suitor identity, which the father is attempting to enact. It is possible to envision the processual aspect of father-daughter incest as a series of these behavioral transparencies overlaying previous interactions.

Conclusion

. . . there is always this curious dialectic between the fact and the idea, between action and thought, between constructs of the mind and the activities of men. But both sides of the dialectic can be regarded as emanating from the same traditional "structure" behind both the thought and the act. It is noteworthy to observe how the form of the "structure" varies in a given region like the dialects of language. Yet the variations appear as logical permutations of a limited set of principles. Again like language, the principles are clearly not embedded in the utilitarian particularities of specific social systems. They appear to be certain fundamental principles of organization which are behind the various manifestations of specific social patterns. In this sense what we call "social structure" corresponds to a grammar which relates the activities of individuals to one another and makes communication and order possible in social life (Yalman 1967:376).

It may seem curious to quote at length from a work on South Asian kinship in a study of father-daughter incest in the United States. The problem Nur Yalman set out to solve was how a set of structural principles and an ideology surrounding it could survive intact in patrilineal, matrilineal, and bilateral descent systems, while crossing lines of space, ethnicity, language, and religion. He brilliantly separates this common structure from the "noise" of local variation. He derived his inspiration from Edmund R. Leach's essay in which he made the point that "generalized structural patterns are not restricted to any one, manifest structural type" (1961:7) and likened the elements of this generalized structural pattern to the topological relationship of elements in mathematics.

The problem I set out to solve is how a family can maintain the generalized structural pattern of the nuclear family in U.S. culture while the structured interactions of the persons within the family are dramatically altered. Although Yalman's problem and mine are on a vastly different scale—his based in entire subcultures over many generations, mine in single families over a few years—we both seek to discover how this dialectic between fact and idea, action and thought, and constructs of the mind and activities of individuals forms a single, processual system.

For the incestuous family, this dialectic utilizes the same store of cultural knowledge available to all families. It also operates under the same constraints affecting other social groups. Internally, it must perform the same work required of all nuclear families. It must acquire and distribute adequate material goods and provide sufficient nurture, education, and protection to allow its individual members to function. Externally, it must maintain interfaces with other social institutions in such a way as to ensure the wider society's tolerance and meet its own needs. To maintain itself, the nuclear family must also provide its members with the *perception* that their needs are being met at a level consistent with their expectations.

The incestuous family can operate within these constraints and still maintain a sexual relationship between father and daughter. I attribute this ability to the latitude available in perceiving social identities in relation to perceiving behavior patterns.

Structural social anthropology has projected a particular kind of internal dialogue to account for regularities in social interaction. This dialogue consists of one actor's perceptions of another actor's social identity vis-à-vis her own: "He is an X to me." The next line of dialogue is, "Because he is an X, I expect him to do X behavior." The third line is, "Because he is an X to me, I am a Y to him, and therefore he is entitled to Y behavior." Of course, our actor would also simultaneously process a context or "scene" to determine if she is interacting with an X or with another social identity.

In reality, this dialogue appears to be a gross oversimplification. In addition to perceiving the other's identity and using that knowledge to generate behavior, the actor can perceive a pattern of behavior and respond with a reciprocal behavior pattern. These patterns may or may not be labeled. They may be attached to no particular social identity or to any number of identities. There also must be cultural codes that allow an actor to respond to a pattern of behavior with a pattern that is "grammatical" and furthers the actor's goals. The cultural codes linking isolated behaviors into patterns and constructing appropriate reciprocal patterns would constitute Keesing's "operating norms."

There are, then, four variables involved in the negotiation of an interaction that shape the flow and outcome of the interaction: the actor's identity, the other's identity, the actor's behavior pattern, and the other's behavior pattern. Rules for assigning patterns of behavior to identities and for recognizing patterns amidst the behavioral "noise" of an interaction must exist.

There are many more internal dialogues if these four variables are considered, including the following:

1. Since he is an X to me and yet is engaging in $X1$ behavior, he is viewing me as a Y and expecting $Y1$ behavior.
2. Since he is an X to me and yet is engaging in $X1$ behavior, I should reciprocate with only those behaviors common to both the Y identity and the $Y1$ pattern.
3. Although he is engaging in $X1$ behavior I want to keep the X-Y identity relationship salient and therefore will only respond with Y behavior.
4. Although he is an X to me and is engaging in $X1$ behavior, the pattern this behavior forms when viewed in conjunction with two

previous interactions indicates an *X3* pattern. I should therefore assume a *Y3* behavior pattern.

5. Although he is an *X* to me, he is engaging in *Z* behavior. *Z* behavior is not appropriate to any of our identity relationships, but the reciprocal response to *Z* behavior is *Z* behavior.

6. Although he is an *X* to me, he is engaging in *X3* behavior, which is only appropriate in "scene" *A*. In scene *A*, people who are *X3* to me become *X4* to me. I therefore should assume an *X4* identity and *X4* behavior pattern.

This by no means exhausts all possible internal dialogues, but it does counter the simplified assumption that actors merely need to know the rights and duties attached to their social identities and perform them.

This is not to say I am postulating a process as unstructured and contingent as some symbolic interactionist characterizations. The process I propose simply recognizes the fact that the more multiplex elements a dyadic relationship contain and the more interactions the dyad has, the more variables the actor must process to negotiate the relationship successfully. It also clarifies that identifying and understanding these variables cannot be accomplished only by formally eliciting the categories and behavior patterns that are labeled or by minutely describing single interactions, commonly done in small group research in social psychology.

Father-daughter incest cannot be understood without considering the temporal dimensions. Incest is not a practice that has a set of cultural rules telling one how to conduct it, yet in family after family the incest process follows the same course and produces the same family structure. The culture does not have rules for the conduct of incest, but it does have rules for interacting with daughters, fathers, lovers, rivals, adulterers, and the like. Rules specify what behavior patterns are appropriate in interaction with a given identity. Many of these patterns overlap. Some behaviors are appropriate in interaction with several different identities, usually because these identities may share several building blocks.

Yalman borrows Leach's description of topology as the geometry of rubber sheeting in describing how the structure of the marriage alliance system in Sri Lanka and South India is pulled and distorted, yet still preserved, as it adapts to local conditions. In much the same way, the incestuous family pulls and distorts identity relationships within the nuclear family to accommodate father-daughter incest. The ability of the incestuous family to function in the face of this distortion is often attributed to the psychological defense mechanism of denial. I cannot deny that denial may be a factor, but to deny something one must at least unconsciously perceive it. The incestuous family does not perceive the same interactions the outsider perceives. When they are accurately perceived, the contradiction between thought and action has been exposed. The rubber sheeting often tears.

REFERENCES

Armstrong, Louise. 1978. *Kiss Daddy Goodnight*. New York: Hawthorne Books.

Cicourel, Aaron. 1974. *Cognitive Sociology*. New York: Basic Books.

Finkelhor, David. 1979. *Sexually Victimized Children*. Riverside, N.J.: Free Press.

Geiser, Robert L. 1979. *Hidden Victims: The Sexual Abuse of Children*. Boston: Beacon.

Giarretto, Henry. 1976. "Treatment of Father-Daughter Incest: A Psychosocial Approach." *Children Today* 5:2–5.

Goodenough, Ward. 1965. "Rethinking Status and Role: Toward a General Model of the Cultural Organization of Social Relationships." In *The Relevance of Models for Social Anthropology*, ed. M. Banton. London: Tavistock.

Hass, A. 1979. *Teenage Sexuality*. New York: Macmillan.

Keesing, Roger M. 1970. "Toward a Model of Role Analysis." In *A Handbook of Method in Cultural Anthropology*, ed. R. Naroll and R. Cohen. Garden City, N.Y.: Natural History Press.

Knox, David. 1985. *Choices in Relationships: An Introduction to Marriage and the Family*. Hagerstown, N.Y.: Harper and Row.

Kroth, J. A. 1979. *Child Sexual Abuse: Analysis of a Family Therapy Approach*. Springfield, Ill.: Charles C. Thomas.

Langworthy, Nancy, and J. Storer. 1985 "Is Incest Really Taboo in America?" Paper presented at the 84th Annual Meeting of the American Anthropological Association, Washington, D.C.

Leach, Edmund R. 1961. *Rethinking Anthropology*. New York: Humanities Press.

Renshaw, Domeena C. 1982. *Incest: Understanding and Treatment*. Boston: Little, Brown.

Renvoize, Jean. 1982. *Incest: A Family Pattern*. London: Routledge and Kegan Paul.

Yalman, Nur. 1967. *Under the Bo Tree*. Berkeley: University of California Press.

Tony L. Whitehead

Expressions of Masculinity in a Jamaican Sugartown: Implications for Family Planning Programs

The purpose of this essay is to introduce a comprehensive model for understanding the meaning of masculinity in a Jamaican community and to suggest the applicability of the model for the development of family planning services for lower-income males and their families. The model is based on a reassessment, critique, and expansion of Peter J. Wilson's (1973) description and analysis of reputational and respectability traits exhibited by West Indian males. The model emerged from an analysis of data collected during the summer of 1971, the full calendar year of 1974, the summer of 1975, and the summer of 1983. Although a number of research methods were used, the primary method underlying the model is the exploration and analyses of "meaning" encoded in people's use of language as it relates to male mating and family practices.

The essay reports on the study's analysis of such words as *big, little, strong, weak, good*, and *wicked*, frequently used by men in the Jamaican community to describe men. It was found that big and little were contrasting pairs representing class or vertical connotations. That is, a big man is one of high social status, and a little man is one of low social status. This is similar to the way these terms have been found to be used in other regions of the world, most notably the Pacific (Sahlins 1963; Weiner 1983) and West Africa (Vincent 1968), but not necessarily with the same reference to political power.

All men in my Jamaican study community, Haversham (a pseudonym), want to be big. Yet while *big* and *little* are references to status, expressions of *strength* and *goodness* are means of achieving bigness, whereas *weakness* and *wickedness* are traits that keep a little man little or cause a big man to lose his bigness.

Traits of strength are further categorized into what Wilson (1973) has classified as "respectability" and "reputational" traits. These two categories of traits are used as contrasting pairs in Haversham (see Figure 1), as Wilson noted for Providencia. In Haversham, however, these categories are *not* sex specific (women are respectable, men are reputational), as Wilson argues, nor are they class specific (big men are respectable, little men are reputational), as the family planning staff with whom I talked would insist. All men are expected to express respectability and reputational traits because they are both attributes of strength, and all men are measured by the influential community of men to which they belong for their ability to exhibit strength. Where big men and little men differ is in the manner in which strength is expressed. These differences are made possible by inequities in social status, characterized primarily by differences in access to material resources. Moreover, the maintenance and expression of contrasting traits is not a function of a "national personality conflict," as suggested by Madeline Kerr (1963), or "normative dualism," as suggested by M. G. Smith (1966), but is mediated by the indigenous view of "balance."

The best way to describe what Havershamians mean by balance is to discuss the contrast: unbalanced. A man who is weak is unbalanced. An unbalanced man might lack the capacity, resources, or will to exhibit strength (respectability and reputation) and goodness, or he might overexpress such traits. That is, an overexpression of either strength/goodness or weakness reflects a lack of balance, which can lead to wickedness if it continues. The epitome of wickedness is homosexuality.[1]

Because of his circumstances (lack of access to resources), a little man is at base in a state of imbalance. He therefore must continually struggle to exhibit strength and, to a lesser extent, goodness. Because of his lack of resources, he is continually at risk of being metaphorically "fucked over" by big men. The metaphor here refers abstractly to the wickedness of homosexuality but concretely to the little man's continually being embarrassed by having to defer to, and having his women seduced by, big men. Also because of limited resources, the little man's exhibition of strength is slanted more toward reputational than respectability traits. In the exhibition of strength, the community of little men allows itself to stretch the boundary of reputational traits before considering one of its members imbalanced. This feature is similar to Hyman Rodman's (1963) concept of the "lower-class value stretch" in Trinidad.

Figure 1: The Cognitive Construct of Masculinity in Haversham

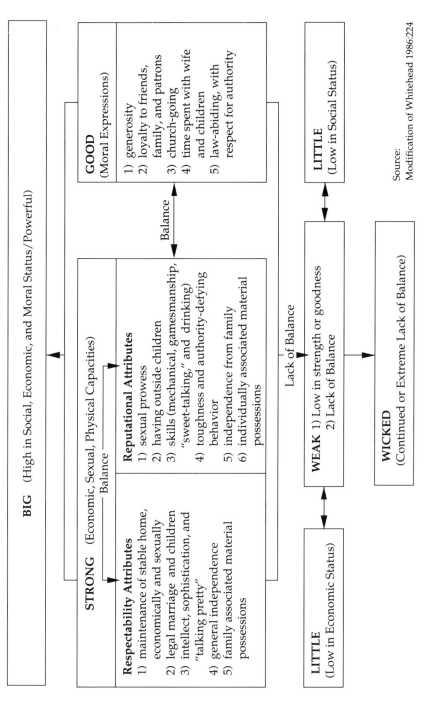

BIG   (High in Social, Economic, and Moral Status/Powerful)

STRONG   (Economic, Sexual, Physical Capacities)
—— Balance ——

Respectability Attributes
1) maintenance of stable home, economically and sexually
2) legal marriage and children
3) intellect, sophistication, and "talking pretty"
4) general independence
5) family associated material possessions

Reputational Attributes
1) sexual prowess
2) having outside children
3) skills (mechanical, gamesmanship, "sweet-talking," and drinking)
4) toughness and authority-defying behavior
5) independence from family
6) individually associated material possessions

Balance

GOOD
(Moral Expressions)
1) generosity
2) loyalty to friends, family, and patrons
3) church-going
4) time spent with wife and children
5) law-abiding, with respect for authority

Lack of Balance

WEAK 1) Low in strength or goodness
2) Lack of Balance

LITTLE
(Low in Economic Status)

WICKED
(Continued or Extreme Lack of Balance)

LITTLE
(Low in Social Status)

Source:
Modification of Whitehead 1986:224

This essay discusses this cognitive analysis in more detail and suggests that it is in the analysis and use of such constructs that human services programs, such as family planning, can become more effective.

Background and "Breakdown"

During the summer of 1971, as a consultant to the National Family Planning Board (NFPB) of Jamaica, I talked to family planning doctors and nurses in almost every parish on the island (Whitehead 1971). I found they shared the opinion that the greatest barrier to the success of family planning programs was the "irresponsible" mating behavior of lower-income males: "They are only interested in impregnating as many women as they can and spreading 'picni' [children] all over the island" (fieldnotes from Whitehead 1971). A similar opinion was expressed by non–family planning personnel. They maintained that money and children are important symbols of masculinity in Jamaica and that men compensate for lack of money by engaging in irresponsible mating behavior.

These views of male reproductive irresponsibility are supported by a sociological tradition regarding West Indian and Afro-American family structure, yet I could find few references to male-focused research.[2] In most of this literature, references to male attitudes and practices were gleaned from interviews of female respondents. I therefore decided to return to the island in 1974 and carry out a male-focused ethnographic study related to family planning in Haversham, a Jamaican community of about 8,000 people.

Using the information gathered during 1971 and the accounts in existing literature, I entered the field with a research design in which male familial attitudes and practices were hypothesized to be primarily correlated with socioeconomic status. Using a multimethod approach to data collection,[3] I soon came to find, however, that the phenomena I was studying could not be so simply defined. While I found some differences in family behavior and attitudes between men of lower income and those of high income,[4] there were many more unexpected similarities (Whitehead 1986). Moreover, I found most men receptive to contraception,[5] and when I did encounter opposition to family planning it was related to complex definitions of masculinity. My fieldwork was also disconcerting because I saw what I thought were contradictory attitudinal and behavioral patterns within the same men (Whitehead 1986). How could men of both lower- and higher-income status sit around and speak disparagingly about men who consumed so much rum and ganja (marijuana) that they could not support their families, while they themselves were consuming great quantities of rum and ganja? How could men who know from experience the difficulty of finding steady work, and who sometimes work two or three jobs simultaneously when they do find work, quit or get fired because they didn't feel like working or because they decided to go to Montego Bay and have fun on a workday?

Not until after completing my fieldwork did I learn from Michael Agar (borrowing from Gadamer 1975) that what I was suffering was "ethnographic breakdown"—a "disjunction between worlds . . . the fieldworker's world and the field community's world . . . the fieldworker's expectations are not met, something does not make sense, one's assumption of perfect coherence . . . is violated" (Agar 1982:783). The fieldworker's world is influenced by his/her research design, particularly when the research is hypothesis driven. According to Agar, however, breakdown is not a stage to dread but is, in fact, when the intellectual process in ethnography begins.

In the field, I not only had problems defining my independent variable (economic status) but also found my dependent variable (reproductive and familial irresponsibility) to be culturally invalid. How could I distinguish between who was acting responsibly and who was acting irresponsibly when the same individual exhibited both behaviors?

Perusing the plethora of West Indian family literature supporting the view of irresponsible male behavior, I soon found that none of it defines with any degree of precision what is meant by irresponsible behavior so that it can be distinguished from responsible behavior. The closest paradigm is Wilson's (1973) concept of respectable and reputational behavior. Although Wilson's model is not completely satisfactory, it did lead me away from Gadamer's stage of breakdown toward the more desirable stages of resolution and coherence (see Whitehead 1986). Before moving on, however, a description of the research setting and its history is in order.

Haversham: Past and Present

As I have stated elsewhere (Whitehead 1978), Haversham may be viewed as a microcosm of not only the larger Jamaican society but also other societies within the British West Indies. These societies have traditionally experienced "persistent poverty" (Beckford 1972) due to a long history of slavery, monocrop agriculture, colonialism, a continual outflow of capital (Jefferson 1972), and great inequities in the internal distribution of income (Jamaica Government, Department of Statistics 1973). Even though the larger Caribbean Islands' decision after World War II to industrialize did contribute to impressive growth spurts in their national economies (as measured by gross national product), high rates of unemployment and underemployment have continued to the present (Jefferson 1972).

The long history of slavery and colonialism left the majority of the populations of these societies unprepared to take advantage of the jobs offered by the new industries (Manley 1974). For example, while the move toward industrialization brought an 885 percent increase in the gross national product between 1950 and 1972, the unemployment rate during that period increased from 17.5 percent to 22.5 percent. In 1974, underemployment resulted in 62.5 percent of Jamaica's labor force earning less than J$10 per year (US$11 in 1974). The impact of such employment figures was aggravated by the fact that between 1966 and 1973 the cost of certain food staples increased by more than 400 percent (Whitehead 1978:819).

Haversham is the site of one of the earliest sugar estates in the British West Indies, dating back to the late seventeenth century. In the 1920s, a sugar factory was constructed in the community. Following World War II, the town experienced rapid industrial and population growth as additional factories were opened. Both skilled and unskilled laborers moved into the area to take advantage of the new economic opportunities (Whitehead 1978:819); however, as in other areas of the Caribbean, there were problems. Although the increase in job opportunities improved the economic status of the community as a whole, rates of unemployment and underemployment actually increased because most people had neither the technical nor the literacy skills to take advantage of the new jobs. At the time of my extensive fieldwork (1974–75), Haversham was a good example of a West Indian community experiencing "development without employment" (Demas 1965). Although the sugar factory and three of the food processing plants offered full-time employment to more than 1,200 workers, and the nearby bauxite factory offered full-time employment to almost 3,000 workers, the majority of the people in Haversham were either chronically unemployed (only able to pick up menial labor) or irregularly employed (employed for agricultural work seasonally or employed two to three days per week).[6] Personnel managers complained of severe labor shortages because the new technology required a literacy rate beyond that of the local population.[7]

Components of the Gender Construct of Havershamian Males

My major problems with Peter J. Wilson's (1973) paradigm have been discussed elsewhere (Whitehead 1986), but briefly they include (1) a lack of precision in defining the attributes of reputation and respectability and how they are different; (2) the exclusive association of respectability traits with Europeans and West Indian females and reputation traits with West Indian males; and (3) the implication of a racial dialectic between persons with European or female attributes (respectability) and persons with West Indian male attributes (reputational).

From various sections of his book, I was able to discern that for Wilson (1973) attributes of respectability included going to church, believing in God, having a legal marriage, maintaining a good home, providing excellent care of the family within the home (74–75), and having "all the children in her belly" (150). Reputational attributes included having self-confidence (74), fathering children, fighting, arguing, and shouting (151), possessing sexual prowess and skills of sweet-talking and sweet-singing, having money and buying gifts for girls (257), being generous to and supportive of friends and family (123–78), and having skills in drinking and gambling (156).

As one can see, Wilson's attributes of reputation are similar to what others view as irresponsible behavior. Problems accrue, however, when Wilson associates respectability traits with Europeans and reputational traits with the West Indians. This component of his argument renders the paradigm open to charges of racism, given that all societies, not just European societies, value some of the respectability traits (e.g., having socially accepted marriage, having children in unions defined as legal by that culture, and providing for and protecting that family). Moreover, men in most human societies practice such reputational traits as fighting, arguing, shouting, and sexually conquering women (sexual prowess).

Wilson's "revolutionary" call for replacing respectability traits with reputational traits can be considered not only anti–West Indies but also sexist—his call for male attributes (reputational traits) would replace female attributes (respectability traits). Although I found reputational traits in Haversham were practiced primarily by men, respectability traits are not exclusive to women. Rather, men exhibit both sets of traits and thus have available a broader range of ways to express their masculinity and to symbolize gender differences.[8] As youth, men are allowed the freedom to express reputational traits almost exclusively; however, as they age and gain access to resources, they increasingly display respectability traits and, in turn, expect to be given social roles and statuses associated with responsibility and respect.

I found a similar dialectic in the gender construct of males in Haversham, but it was highly influenced by the historically entrenched political economy outlined in the preceding section. Utilizing an ethnosemantic approach, I found that *respect, reputation, responsible,* and *irresponsible* were part of the lexicon of Havershamians, but they represented more complex constructs than those offered by Wilson or health and family planning professionals. Indeed, they were not used as frequently as the descriptors *big, little, strong, weak, good,* and *wicked.* These adjectives were used to describe both men and women.[9] Further analysis revealed that these concepts, along with respectability and reputations, were all part of a total gender construct, which is illustrated in Figure 1.

I quickly discovered that *big* and *little* referred to social status.[10] Money, level of education, and occupation are important measures of social status (as they are elsewhere), but a man's sphere of influence is also important. A big man[11] has a broad sphere of influence, including a number of people with whom he has never had personal contact. A little man, on the other hand, has a very small sphere of influence, usually including only intimates. The littlest man is one with no sphere of influence.

A *strong* (respectable) man is one who is legally married, has children, provides well for his home and family, shows intellect, sophistication, and the ability to "talk pretty" (speak standard English), and possesses "respectable" material goods, such as land, a home, and furnishings. It is believed the exhibition of such traits of strength helps a little man achieve bigness by bringing him to the attention of big people, who are believed to value these traits. At the same time, a strong man is also expected to exhibit such reputational skills as mechanical abilities, intellect, gamesmanship (in dominoes and cards), success in "sweet-talking" women, and the ability to drink rum and other alcoholic beverages.

Reputational traits can help the little man achieve bigness in several ways. First, these skills are carried out in the company of men of both lower and higher socioeconomic status, and they allow a man to demonstrate his superiority to his peers as well as to higher-status males who may become friends or patrons. As a friend, the little man expects to share in (borrow) some of the big man's status. As a patron, the big man can help elevate the status of the little man by enhancing his brokering capacity.

The brokering capabilities of the little man are viewed by the other little men as a means of helping them achieve access to economic (labor and capital), political, health, educational, legal, and informational resources. If the little man in the community needs work, his broker is periodically able to provide short-term work that comes from the broker's patron, who is rewarded by an abundance of cheap labor when he needs it. Sometimes the patron is a political candidate or a supporter of a certain candidate, and he may come to the broker to secure votes. These votes are secured because of past favors the patron has bestowed upon his client, the little man.[12]

A broker may be asked by little men to go with them and their family members to the hospital in Kingston because "they [the brokers] know how to talk to all of them doctors and nurses up there." A broker may be approached to talk to the big people to help a little man's child get into a technical school. A broker may be asked to approach a visitor from Canada, England, or the United States to request sponsorship in one of these countries, where "a man can make something of himself" (see Whitehead 1984 for more discussion of the little men's broker).

Brokers also provide information about the world outside Haversham by making themselves aware of what is happening in national and international news and by disseminating this knowledge in rumshop arguments. The broker is listened to by little men, and he is used to intervene with big people because of his argumentative skills.[13] Such skills are displays of intelligence or "smarts."

A broker's intelligence is exhibited not only by the information he shares or his debating skills with little men but also by his willingness to enter into a debate with a big man in the company of other little men. This behavior is admired because historically the role of little men in Jamaica has been to defer to big men in public interactions. In fact, in rural Jamaica, not only do little men defer but they avoid situations in which such interactions might occur. If a situation cannot be avoided, the little man tries to use a broker as a mediator with the big man. If the use of a broker is not possible, the little man in the company of a big man will speak only when spoken to, will avoid eye contact, and will present a low opinion of himself while flattering the big man (Whitehead 1984:562). Havershamians refer to such deference behavior as the "buccra-massa," in reference to the historical tradition of slavery when one didn't dare "buck the master." Over rum, there are also jokes about the little man's having to drop his pants all the time and be "fucked" by big men.

The little man who dares confront the big man is greatly admired for "bucking the master." Not only does his defiance of authority imply great intelligence but it also expresses strength and courage. It is not just the substance of the debate that is deemed important but also the deed itself.

Although the majority of little men dare not "buck the massa,"[14] the defiance of authority is an important attribute of reputational strength because it supports independence. For the majority of little men, however, the "exhibition" of defiance and independence is verbal—tales of past deeds they hope will be supported by peers. This exhibition is usually carried out in conjunction with the exhibition of independence from one's partner (simply by being out with other men) and with another reputational skill—drinking rum or smoking ganja (marijuana) without experiencing what are considered ill effects. During my fieldwork, however, ill effects, including violent crimes and imprisonment, did occur in association with acts of defiance of authority or simple "hell-raising." Jamaican males displayed an affection for guns and an admiration for the exploits of "gunmen" in 1974, although gun-related violence was a great social concern.[15]

Traits of *goodness* (respectability) include being loyal to family, friends, and patrons; being generous to family, friends, and clients; going to church; being family oriented; and being a law-abiding citizen with respect for authority. In rum-shop gatherings, a little man or a broker aspiring bigness can display an attribute of goodness— generosity (or "sharing" his bigness)—by buying drinks for his friends. A man with ambitions for achieving bigness is expected to exhibit traits of goodness if he wants to come to the attention of big people, who, of course, hold the keys to such status.

Within the social segment of males, respectability and reputational traits are thus part of the gender construct of strength, which along with goodness is a trait that big men use to stay big, little men use to gain bigness, and both classes of men use to avoid the status of weakness or wickedness.

Stated in another way, a big man can be weak if he does not show attributes of strength; a little man is in a weak position by virtue of his circumstances. Yet the little man *must* exaggerate his skills of strength to overcome an appearance of weakness. Men are expected to be strong and women weak, and littleness makes a man vulnerable to weakness and "womanness"—an unnatural state of man and the extreme of wickedness.

Sources of Masculine Strength as They Relate to Marriage, Sex, and Reproduction

In Haversham, there are three sources of masculine strength and goodness: material, physical, and metaphysical.[16] The dominant material sources of masculine strength and goodness are landowner-ship and money. Historically, land has been a very important commodity in the West Indies, and it continues to be so today.[17] Whereas land was only a symbol of freedom following slavery (Wilson 1973), it has now come to symbolize strength as well. In Haversham, a man does not have to own a plantation to be a strong man; he can simply own a few acres that provide enough food for the family and extra food for sale at a sizeable profit in the internal market system. Men speak of the loss of land as similar to the loss of one's "balls" (a symbolic castration). A number of the men live on family land owned by their partners or the partner's consanguine kin. These men are frequently not considered the heads of their households (Whitehead 1978). Given the importance of household leadership to masculine role identification, this is another form of symbolic castration.

The ownership of a house (and a small piece of land) in Haversham appears to be related to marrying late in the life cycle.[18] The ownership of property serves as an indication that a man is able to take care of a woman properly, and it acts as a protection against infidelity on the part of a woman. Men in Haversham feel that a man should not marry until he has a home for her or she will surely take up with a man who can provide her with one (Whitehead 1976). Marriage is a risky business for a young man who is struggling to find steady employment and has very scarce resources. This is exemplified by the following statement made by a small storekeeper in Haversham:

> You see, Tony, my father helps me. He helps me get this store because he is a big man now. But not always. Not always. Once me father had nothing, and me mother left him for some other man. My father was very vexed. And it was because of this that he worked so hard to get what he has now. He said it would never happen to him again. But it happened to me. My baby's mother run away with another man too, because then I was young and wasn't interested in doing nothing for "self." That's why, Tony, I don't think that a man should marry until he has something, especially a house . . . something to show the woman that he can take care of her.

Money is even more important than land as a material source of masculine strength. The man with money is the strongest of men and is able to exhibit the greatest reputational and respectable traits, including the attributes of goodness and bigness. The family provider role is the core respectability attribute and is the most important one for the adult male in Haversham. Both men and women believe that the male should be head of the household; yet, if a man is not the primary money earner or, as mentioned above, is not the owner of the land upon which the family resides, he may not be considered the head of the household.

Money, or the lack of it, has also been found by scholars of West Indian family structure to be a primary reason given for marriage late in the life cycle (e.g., Blake 1961; M. G. Smith 1966; R. T. Smith 1963; Wilson 1973). Money allows a man to buy a house (land) and enables him to pay for a wedding. An expensive wedding is another indication of a man's material strength. Money also allows a man to buy other material goods, including household furnishings (thus assuring his partner's fidelity), gifts for females (enhancing his sexual prowess) and his outside children (being a good provider), a car or a motorbike,[19] and clothing and jewelry. The possession of such items could make a man appear stronger (in terms of money) than he really is, as exemplified in the advice I received from an informant: "Look Whitehead. You talk pretty but that is not enough to get a Jamaican woman. You must dress good. Get you some nice threads [clothes] and a new car. You are a strong man, you can do it. And when you go to these places [nightclubs], let these women see your money because they will then know that you are a strong man and they will become curious about you. Then you got them."

Money and material resources allow a man to exhibit both respectability and reputational traits more adequately in the area of sexual expression—both his own and that of his women (sexual partners and primary female consanguines). While sexual prowess is a core reputational trait, controlling female sexuality (along with being a capable economic provider) is a core respectability trait in that a man is expected to maintain a stable home, economically and sexually. In Haversham, one of the greatest embarrassments for a man is for his female partner to have an affair with another man, not because he has romantic notions of fidelity but because it symbolizes he is not strong enough to prevent his partner's infidelity. A man's control of his partner's (and daughter's) sexuality is threatened by income inadequacies. While all of the men in the male sample were strongly opposed to female infidelity, six of the respondents expressed empathy for the woman who sometimes turned to other men when her partner did not give her what she needed and wanted. Eighteen percent of the male sample in fact defined love as "giving a woman what she wants." If a man provides for a women, he should be assured of her fidelity. The woman who commits adultery after a man has done all he can to provide for her is "wicked." The most wicked woman is one who not only runs off with another man but also takes all the furnishings a man has provided for his home, which happened to three men in the male sample during my fieldwork.

Men in Haversham are generally opposed to their partners' working because they fear the women will be seduced by the men for whom they work.[20] Men with incomes substantiate this belief through their own attempts at, or tales of, seducing their female employees or women they supervise. During the fieldwork period, higher-income men were fond of citing a popular little ditty: "If I can afford it and you can't, my wife is my wife and your wife is my wife." Money and property ownership, therefore, not only assure a man of his partner's fidelity but also give him license to express his sexual prowess.

A little man's prospects are aptly summarized by an informant from the female sample:

> I have no time for a man who can give me nothing. You know that woman across the yard who already has eight children and is pregnant again? Well, she has always done that, taken up with any man, none of them able to help her. Men like that have come after me, but I know that they are only after me because I have a few houses, to see if they can get them away from me. People are always asking me why I married Mr. C. because he is so old and I am young. But why would anybody marry a young man who is running around gambling and wasting his money on other women?

Such comments, however, are from mature, experienced women. The inexperienced school girl is highly vulnerable to sweet talk and promises of love, and she becomes easy prey for the sexual prowess ambitions of the little man, who lacks other means of expressing masculine strength. This is exemplified in female informants' reflections of their first sexual encounters:

> I don't know. Him say him loved me so me let him do it. He give me things. Him big [older] and him worked.

> Well, he said he loved me. He had another girlfriend and she always would do it. But if I would do it, he would stop seeing her and just me would have him. I did love him so I do it.

> It was just a passing thing. I saw him at a party and he told me he loved me and we did it.

> We were children together. He lived across the lane with his father. We went to school together. He always loved me. So when we come big, we just do it.

I don't want what happened to me to happen to me daughter. This man see me go to school and he told me he loved me, so I let him. Then me get pregnant and he no longer see me.

The last comment indicates that some mothers are quite concerned about their daughters' being seduced by older men, because it frequently results in early pregnancy and a life cycle of "hazardous reproduction."[21] The concerns of these mothers are frequently informed by their own experiences. One mother asked me for help with her eleven-year-old adopted daughter: "Mr. Whitehead, will you please talk to Constance. She spent all night with that man. She too young for that. She say the man, him loves her. But, they all say that. She say she love this man. But she's a baby. How can she know love. She say I can't tell her what to do 'cause him loves her. But me can't talk to her. Me gon' send her back to her mother. Me gon' get me some other picni [children]."

Unfortunately, economic circumstances and overcrowded housing conditions lead other parents to welcome their daughters' liaisons, as evidenced in the comment of another female informant: "I have eight picni to take care. She big enough to find a man to take care of her. It is time for her to have some picni herself. Taking care of her own house and picni will keep her out of trouble, give her some response [responsibility]."

Serial sexual partners, crowded housing, and a lack of money can lead to other situations conducive to serial reproduction without the support of a male. A number of male and female informants talked of early sexual encounters with the children of a parent's partner (unmarried coresidential partner) because they lived in small crowded houses.

Constructs of physical sources of masculine strength may also be related to what I am calling hazardous reproduction (see note 21). Physical attributes cited as sources of masculine strength include brains, blood, caucasian features, and semen. Brains are the source of a man's intellect and his sweet-talking characteristics, thus improving his sexual prowess. Hot blood is a source of sexual prowess and hell-raising tendencies. Conversely, then, sexual prowess (and the all-too-frequent consequence of reproduction) becomes a way by which a man demonstrates the level of his brain and his blood.

Caucasian features in men are symbolic of bigness and the potential for achieving bigness and attracting women.[22] Because Jamaicans with these characteristics are attractive to women, they have a greater opportunity to seduce women. Furthermore, some women desire to have children exhibiting caucasian features in the belief that through the child they will have access to their partner's bigness (material resources) and the child will have greater opportunity for bigness as an adult.

Yet, of all the physical sources of masculine strength in Haversham, none was discussed by men as much as semen. Men frequently talked about the loss of semen as a loss of strength and about children as an expression of the strength semen provides. As C.·P. McCormack and A. Draper (1987) have stated in their review of literature on Jamaican sexuality, "In Jamaica . . . for both men and women, perceptions of self-identity and social power are contingent upon sexual potency, which is confirmed by the birth of children." Peter J. Wilson (1973:150) talks further of the importance of children as a symbol of a man's strength:

> But what is also important about a man's relation to his children is that they are the evidence and embodiment of his maturity and manhood, and through them he earns respect in the society at large, especially among his peers. Fathering children is a sign of strength, not necessarily in the muscular sense but in the sense of character and spirit. . . . This sense of a man's strength is the foundation of his reputation. . . . If there is a minimum requirement it is that a man should father children . . . even if he becomes the richest, toughest man around, yet has no children, he can still be sneered at and be the butt of jokes that even the humblest can crack at his expense.

Such sentiments were similarly strong in Haversham. It is interesting that whereas family planning professionals viewed the high fertility rates of lower income males as irresponsible, both higher- and lower-income men and women in Haversham thought it was irresponsible for a thirty-year-old man not to have children. I was even asked numerous questions regarding my lack of offspring. The following conversations took place with a school principal and a little man:

Principal: How many children do you have, Whitehead?

Whitehead: None.

Principal: That is shucking responsibility, man! That is the epitome of irresponsibility. What do you have to live for if you don't have children? That is selfish and irresponsible. Everything that you earn in life you keep it to yourself, then you die and what happens to it? There is nobody to show that you have ever lived. Your existence goes unrecorded.

Little Man: How old are you, Mr. Whitehead?

Whitehead: Thirty-two.

Little Man: How many children do you have?

Whitehead: None, I am not married.

Little Man: Yeah, but you have children, here and there.

Whitehead: No, I haven't taken the time.

Little Man: Well, what are you waiting for?

Whitehead: Well, one day I hope to get married and have two or three.

Little Man: But you are old, when you are fifty your children will be babies. That is a shame, Mr. Whitehead, you are wasting your life.

A female social worker asked me: "It is unnatural for a man your age not to have children. Are you sick? Can you get children?"

For women there is the popular sentiment not only that children make them feel more "complete" or "natural" but also that one of the joys of sex is the knowledge you can get pregnant (Whitehead 1976:158), as is reflected in women's answers to the question, "Who enjoys sex more, the man or the woman?"

The woman because she can have the baby while the man can't.

The woman because she gets everything. She can get pregnant and so forth.

It is also apparent in their response to the question, "What happens during sexual intercourse that most satisfies a woman?"

The knowledge that she can get a baby when she wants it.

She knows that her boyfriend loves her and that she can have babies for him.

The following comments from both men and women are in response to a question about the possibility of marriage to a person who could not have children:

A home without children is no home at all. [A very common answer.]

No, man! A yard without picni is like a yard without a dog, no yard a'tall a'tall!

No, I would not marry such a man because him would have no children to save for.

No, because a man then labors in vain and there is no one to get his property when he is gone.

You should have children to give things to.

No, I wouldn't feel complete without two, three picni.

No, I don't feel good now that I only have two children. I go to the doctor so that I can have more.

Both big and little men in Haversham take great pride in their outside, as well as their inside, children. Outside children are evidence of both success in sexual prowess and independence from the inside woman (current cohabitant). Some little men believe that having children by several women can help a man achieve bigness in two ways. First, the more children a man has, the more financial support he might receive once these children are productive adults. Second, children create affinal ties with the mother's kinship group, sometimes allowing the men to form alliances for economic ventures (see Whitehead 1978). Economic ventures between a father and his children, or his children's maternal kinsmen, exist in two forms. Some "partners" combine their resources in money-making ventures, such as the purchase of a taxi, a rum shop, or a transport truck. Others simply provide a body of laborers that could be hired out to a big man on short notice.

In most cases in Haversham, however, the economic links that men and women could forge through children are decreasing with the complexities of modern economic realities. Outside children are not being supported by fathers, and their mothers are incapable of supporting them. The women spend most of their time caring for a continual stream of children throughout their reproductive years, including the offspring of kins, placing further strain on already meager economic resources.

Sweet Talk and Pretty Words: Multiple Levels of Social Meaning

Working in Haversham forced me to go beyond concepts of contrasting pairs (see, e.g., Levi-Strauss 1978; Needham 1979) for understanding meaning. The Haversham data taught me that, while contrasting pairs may exist at one level of cognition, there may be other levels of interpretation, as Geertz (1973) has implied. Some semantic pairs may appear to have different meanings at one level of analysis; at another, such pairs may be *different ways of expressing concepts that are in fact similar.* For example, material possessions and independence are presented as attitudes of both respectability and reputation (see Figure 1). In the case of material possessions, the contrast is in what these possessions are, which in time also reflect status differences, particularly differential access to such material resources as money. "Flashy" clothes and jewelry may be admired by little men as expressions of strength but seen by others as an unproductive and irresponsible use of scarce resources. On the other hand, such material possessions as expensive clothes and jewelry, a home, land, and the like are considered respectable.

Reputationally, one way that independence is expressed is through the expansion of other reputational traits: defiance of authority, toughness, and bucking the massa. However, the big man doesn't have to exhibit such reputational traits to express independence because he doesn't experience the little man's ever-present burden of potential embarrassment by people bigger than he. In any event, the motivating theme of both respectable and reputational independence is to be viewed as not having to display "buccra-massa" behavior.

Even the intellect expressed as the respectability trait of "talking pretty" (speaking standard English) in Haversham can be interpreted as the same intellect that a man uses in sweet-talking women. Big men who talk pretty are also expected to be sweet talkers. Understanding this phenomenon helped me overcome my own biased interpretations of why big men who took me out were more active in demonstrating their sexual prowess through sweet-talking and visiting mistresses than were little men. (Another factor in this behavior was the "definitions of responsibility" associated with giving these women money, to be discussed in more detail in the next section.)

Other little men may consider a sweet-talking little man as strong as, or stronger than, a pretty-talking man in terms of the physical source of intellect (brains), because they know the big man's native intellect has been supplemented by his having the good fortune to obtain more education. The self-educated little man who keeps himself current on national and world events, or develops philosophies that represent universal symbolisms of being and suffering, is greatly admired by other little men as having very strong intellect. Because they know how to talk to big men, such persons become brokers, not only in terms of information but also in terms of providing help in meeting basic survival needs.

Another aspect of this dynamic is that big men may go to night spots frequented by little men so they can display their sweet-talking strengths and their bigness through little men deferring to them. But they must be careful of little men engaging them in debates where the little men can demonstrate their stronger intellect and shame big men who have had educational advantages. The final point is that because of their educational advantages, their social status, and so forth, big men have had more opportunities to develop pretty-talking capabilities and are expected to outperform little men in these engagements. In the social environments available to the little man, people don't talk pretty, so he has few opportunities or reasons to do so. That does not, however, necessarily prevent him from being a strong man. A little man can be a strong man by sweet-talking, communicating about current events, and entering into debates with big men.

Fertility and the Concerns of the "Responsible" Man

As indicated earlier, men in Haversham view irresponsible behavior not as the fathering of an abundance of children but as not having children at all. Those in the male sample (see note 5) who opposed family planning in general or opposed specific types of contraception thought a woman was wicked if she did not have "all the children in her belly." They also believed that some forms of contraception can cause health problems in men and women and infertility in women. The use of contraceptives can thus mean weakness either in a physical sense (illness) or in the sense of not having children.

Men talked about condoms and vaginal jellies as "wearing a man down," making him tired and nervous because he cannot ejaculate as easily when these contraceptives are used. Others talked about contraceptives as making a man or a woman want sex more often, resulting in the emission of too much of a man's strength (semen). A strong man must have children, but he wants them to be strong and healthy. Some believed that contraceptive foams can lead to the birth of children with severe skin problems and intrauterine devices (I.U.D.s) pressed against the fetus can cause deformity in a child. Some women's health problems can also be traced to the use of contraceptives. The pill sometimes causes incessant bleeding, and condoms can slip off, become lodged in the woman's body, and kill her. The responsible man is concerned about the health and strength of not only himself and his children but also his partner.

Toward a Strategy of Change: Balance, Weakness, and Wickedness

For a number of years, I refused to publish work based on my dissertation research regarding males and family planning attitudes and practices because even though Jamaican males of all socioeconomic statuses demonstrated both respectability and repu-tational attitudes, I was afraid readers would dwell only on the rep-utational attributes, already associated with family irresponsibility. My thoughts on publishing began to change during a return to Ja-maica in 1983. During that trip, I found that beliefs among family planning professionals about the irresponsibility of lower-income males, including their supposed opposition to birth control, still per-sisted. They believed that these men, upon learning their partners had had intrauterine devices inserted, would pull them out. With this misperception in mind, one family planning professional argued that all family planning resources should be used to vaccinate the fe-male population with a three-month contraceptive injection: "With the three-month shot, the male never knows, and his attitude and be-havior are rendered insignificant."

My 1974–75 data did not support the belief of family planning per-sonnel that men engage in irresponsible family behavior and are op-posed to contraception (see note 5). In fact, the men I studied were eager for more information on contraception.[23] What they strongly opposed was their exclusion from the decision to adopt contracep-tion. They viewed it as another example of big people (as family plan-ning professionals were frequently perceived) using a man's woman to undermine his highly desired position as head of the family. My research also indicated women felt more strongly than men that chil-dren were a symbol of ideal adult status (Whitehead 1976:157). When women ceased using a contraceptive device, they therefore fre-quently told the doctor or nurse that "he made me do it" or "he snatched it out." By blaming her partner, a little woman was pro-tected from the scorn of a big person.[24]

The adoption of the contraceptive injection as the only family plan-ning strategy, simply to avoid having to deal with men, would fur-ther aggravate already difficult male-female relationships. Such a strategy would negate the male interest in family planning that I found and would fuel existing male opposition to contraception. It also would not fully address the various sources of hazardous repro-ductive behavior and would further exacerbate the broader family and social problems associated with these behaviors. Moreover, pos-sible negative side effects of injections are still not fully known, and I question now, as I did in 1976, whether the Jamaican government should risk the health of its female population and its future gener-ations with extensive use of this contraceptive device (Whitehead 1976:183).

My recommendation to the Jamaicans is not to adopt a family plan-ning strategy that excludes males but to develop one that makes a special effort to include them. The key to the success of such an effort lies within the male gender construct—within the concept of balance. *Balance* as defined by Havershamians suggests that a man could be interpreted as weak or wicked through either an overexpression or an underexpression of attributes associated with masculine strength and goodness. Although a man is considered both physically and morally weak if he does not have children, he is also seen as weak if he has so many children that it jeopardizes his economic ability to maintain his home. Being a good economic provider is a core component of masculine strength in Haversham.

While being a good provider is a core attribute of respectability, sexual prowess is a core attribute of reputation. A man, however, has to be careful because an overexhibition of sexual prowess can lead to a depletion of his strength in terms of both money and semen, as well as his ability to maintain his home. The acquisition of women, both inside and outside, means providing economic support or at least providing gifts. If the woman has children and scarce economic resources, the man is morally obligated to give her something, lest he be viewed as wicked. In fact, the economic circumstance of many female-headed families supports the idea of big men taking on these women as outside partners as a form of social responsibility (sharing material resources with those in need).[25] Yet the man of meager resources is considered wicked if he sacrifices the welfare of his inside partner and children to have outside women. He must also be careful not to deplete his strength through semen loss, which can leave him "tired, run down and nervy" (Whitehead 1976:119–20). The coital ideal of engaging in sexual intercourse less than five times per month (reported by 80 percent of the male sample) and only once during a lovemaking session would mean little sexual activity for both inside and outside women[26]—if they were to depend on a single male for sexual satisfaction.

More than half of the male sample (forty-two individuals or 52.5 percent) stated they thought women enjoyed sex more than men did. Most of these men said women have a stronger "nature" (sex drive) then men do. Six men stated the woman enjoys sex more because the man gives up his strength when he "discharges" (ejaculates) and the woman takes it. Two of these six men talked of using a "french letter" (condom) when "sexing" so that "when a man loses his strength, the woman won't get it" (Whitehead 1976:120).

Unlike Wilson, I think that change in West Indian mating behavior can be achieved to the extent that respectability ideations can be strengthened and reputational ones weakened within the masculine cognitive construct of balance. Family planning programs have long addressed the core attribute of male respectability: being a strong economic provider. For example, in 1983, one of the most popular mass media educational slogans of the National Family Planning Board was "Two [children] ARE TOO MANY!" This implies that even two children can be an economic burden for most Jamaican couples.

The problem with this slogan is that the idea of two children does not represent the boundary of balance with regard to male fertility. Two children are not *culturally defined* as "enough" before a man is considered weak from overexhibiting his reproductive strength. The problem is exaggerated by the traditional pattern of fathering children with serial sexual partners. "Four" was the most frequent response to my question, "How many children would you like to have?" The men meant four with their present partner, but they also wanted four with their next partner. If every Jamaican male had three reproductive unions in his lifetime and had the ideal four children with each partner, it would indeed contribute to a serious population problem for this small nation.

The evidence in this essay strongly suggests the need for male-focused family planning education in Jamaica. Such a program should consider the cultural fact of reproduction with a number of different partners, the ideational dialectic of respectability and reputation attributes of masculinity, and the various configurations of attributes of the concept of balance as they apply to strength and achieving bigness. I believe men would prefer to express core respectability traits (particularly economic provider) over core reputational traits (particularly sex prowess and fertility), but ecological, economic, and historical circumstances contribute greatly to the persistence of reputational traits. In assisting lower-income men to express core respectability traits over core reputational traits, family planning programs could exploit the dynamics of balance by helping men shift their masculine cognitive construct and the boundaries of balanced/unbalanced wherein greater emphasis is placed on respectability traits. Such a program would concentrate not only on family planning but also on the healthy family and the man's strength as family leader and contributor to the economic security of the family. The program could focus on how dangerous excessive drinking, gambling, sexual prowess, and fathering of outside children are to a man's economic capacities while emphasizing the rewards of even minimal economic capabilities.

The idea of equating loss of semen and money with a loss of masculine strength should also be further explored, and if found to be a prevalent construct, it should be integrated into male-focused family planning programs. Some readers may be uncomfortable with using the concept of semen loss as part of an education program because of the sexual explicitness of such material and the absence of scientific documentation of ill effects from semen emission. Yet the gap between scientific knowledge and folk knowledge is not as wide as once thought.

Research on adolescent fertility repeatedly documents that early reproduction can have negative physical, social, and economic consequences. Within the Haversham male gender construct is the view that boys should not engage in sexual activity until they are old enough and strong enough to handle it both physically and emotionally.[27] Two comments from the male sample illustrate this point:

> A boy should be eighteen or nineteen. When a boy has sex too early, he automatically hampers his brain and his body.

> A boy should wait until he is twenty-one because then his body will be physically fit for a girl and what she can do [an indication of the stronger sexual drive of the woman].

Moreover, the exploitation of the masculine symbols of strength, semen, and sexual prowess need not be explicitly stated in mass media education approaches, as a very popular television commercial for beer demonstrated in 1974. The commercial showed a small bespectacled man walking into a bar, nudging between two big men wearing hard hats, ordering Guiness beer, and then leaving with the barmaid, while the narrator booms—"Guiness! The beer that puts it all back." Family planning programs need the creativity found in the business sector's product-marketing divisions.

At the same time, it would be a mistake to underestimate the motivating power of the concept of sexual prowess among Jamaican men. For example, they may believe too much sex can weaken a man through the loss of too much semen, but they also believe too little sex can weaken them because the "semen builds up, goes to the brain and it explodes, running a man crazy." The tendency to ignore or belittle this core reputational attribute is a principle weakness of current family planning campaigns on the island.

Reputational traits can be constructively used in mass media campaigns because the little man in Haversham is already concerned about "mashing up his home" by depleting both material (money) and physical (semen) resources. The little man can perhaps be convinced that the best path to "bigness" is to take care of his inside affairs first and to exhibit his sexual prowess capabilities outside in verbal displays, without engaging in the sex act itself.

Such an effort might work because boasting of sexual conquests already exists as a form of discourse among men in Jamaica (and elsewhere) and games of flirtation are also enjoyed between men and women in Jamaica (as elsewhere). Verbalizations of sexual prowess were frequently observed in Haversham during the 1974–75 fieldwork. Included among these acts were tales of sexual conquests and sweet-talking encounters with women in which the man's goal was achieved by winning the word game. Even when the man is not the clear-cut victor, both males and females seemed to enjoy these encounters, without the sex act having to be realized. An example of such an encounter was observed between Murphy, a thirty-three-year-old informant, and a fifteen-year-old barmaid:

Murphy:	You know you should come ride on my bike sometime.
Barmaid:	I have rode on many bikes before. Why should I ride on yours?
Murphy:	Yeah, but you have never rode on mine, and I think that we would have a good time together.
Barmaid:	I don't think so, there are many girls that you can have a good time with.
Murphy:	But I want you.
Barmaid:	But why?
Murphy:	Because you are young and a virgin and me like virgins.
Barmaid:	Well, you must like babies because I don't know any virgins older than one year old.

At this point the exchange breaks up into laughter, and Murphy says, "This young girl is smart," and the game goes no further.

The objective of such a game for a man is to win it verbally, which for a little man concerned about his resources of strength (money and semen) could be more rewarding than an actual sexual conquest. Moreover, all may not be lost even when the man does not win the verbal game. As in Murphy's case, although he was not the winner, the woman allowed him to dig deeper into his repertoire of sweet-talking skills for the admiration of his male peers. Murphy cut it off when he saw he probably could not win, but his reputation for sweet-talking was already so well established among his peers that many of them were convinced that Murphy would have been the victor if the game had continued.

The goal of a family planning education program is not to improve a man's ability to tell tales of sexual conquest or his skills in sweet-talking. However, the content of such dynamics can be utilized in small group sessions as part of videos, simulation games, vignettes, and role-playing scenes that would be analyzed and discussed with the objective of manipulating boundaries of balance to favor attributes of respectability. What is being suggested here is the use of interpersonal and mass media communication techniques, as well as the creation of educational programs that are integrated into the existing cultural system. The latter is very important to the institutionalization of change—i.e., the routinization of normative attributes and behavior that will persist beyond the life of the educational program (Kramer, Thomas, and Whitehead 1981).

Institutionalization will also be enhanced through the use of cultural insiders, in this case, little men's brokers, acting as communication liaisons between the new (scientific?) knowledge and the targeted cultural system. These brokers should be trained in the new knowledge offered by the program so that they can become bicultural, to the extent that they are able to interpret not only the content of the program for members of the cultural community but also the community's culture for the health program's professional staff (Whitehead, Frate, and Johnston 1984). Although these communication strategies might appear complicated, these brokers could be most helpful in creating them and testing them for cultural relevancy.

In Jamaica and other developing countries, formal leaders and influentials have traditionally been selected for such roles because they frequently share a physical community with the targeted population. However, the cultural community is more important than the physical community, especially when class differences are highly significant. Big men's brokers are necessary in programs that target big men; to reach little men, their own brokers are best suited. This has not been the tradition in Jamaica. Because of the little man's lack of education, his low level of employment or chronic unemployment, and his tendency to "buck the massa," the Jamaican human services' professional staff has perceived the little man as shiftless, lazy, socially irresponsible, and a troublemaker. Yet the little men who are willing to buck the big man are the most influential among their peers (Whitehead 1984). Just as little men will (or will not) vote for a certain politician based on the advice of a natural broker (see note 12), they will (or will not) use a service based on the advice of a broker. Just as politicians strengthen a man's brokering capabilities by including him in the political patronage system (periodically using the broker to refer men for short-term jobs), human service programs, such as family planning campaigns, increase the broker's capacities by further projecting a view of his ability to deal with big people (family planning staff) and increase his "smarts" (with the new knowledge). This system would provide little men greater access to the human service system through the little men's own respected brokers.[28]

In summary, the well-trained little men's broker would be most influential in shifting the boundaries of balance in carrying out "arguments" (debates) in the gathering places of little men. He could be trained in the Socratic method of questioning the pros and cons of reputational exploits and shifting arguments toward core respectable traits. The Socratic method of questioning, when correctly employed, not only obtains information but also provides information, which becomes integrated into the existing paradigms of those involved in the dialogue. The method is used today by the effective ethnographer to get at an informant's world view and by the effective change agent, who gives target populations ownership to new knowledge by *helping* them achieve it within their own experiences and cognitive constructs. In training the little men's broker to be such a change agent, a *sustainability* and *diffusion* of the new knowledge is achieved through the broker's and his constituency's assimilation of this new knowledge into their own cultural constructs.

Cross-National Implications and Areas of Further Research

I referred earlier to the difficulty I had in initially publishing work from the 1974–75 research effort. A return trip to Jamaica in 1983 and other research experiences with social problems related to attributes of masculinity changed my mind. I now see perceptions and expressions of gender constructs as potentially related to other research topics in which I have become involved, such as female segregation and subfertility in Cameroon (1981); men, alcoholism, and domestic violence in North Carolina (1978–82); male ideals of sexual prowess and risk for AIDS (Acquired Immune Deficiency Syndrome) in Baltimore (1989–90); and drug trafficking in Washington, D.C. (1990–91). These experiences, coupled with the growth of cross-cultural feminist literature in the past decade, made me wonder how widespread such attributes are. I have also become convinced that not only should I disseminate the Jamaican work but I should call for more research on gender constructs and social problems. It was the emergence of this awareness of the importance of gender issues in an array of social problems that gave rise to the development of the present volume.

I believe that as we continue to explore problems related to male-female and male-male interactions, we will come to see the important role played by the complex of masculine traits that I have categorized in Haversham as reputational. I also hypothesize that such problems persist because although wider societal norms call for replacing reputational traits (irresponsibility) with respectability traits, there is support for the continuation of reputational traits in both social and cognitive constructs among the dominant groups in society.

The basis for this hypothesis lies in the fact that the cognitive constructs I have outlined here as masculine in Jamaica (big, little, strong, weak, good, wicked, reputational, respectable) have been found among men in many regions of the world, although their structure, expression, and exact meaning may differ according to how well they fit with other components of the cultural system of which they are a part.[29] I call on other researchers to try to understand the structure, relationship, and meanings of such constructs and on applied researchers to explore their possible relationships to such social issues as problems related to fertility, sexually transmitted diseases, child and spouse abuse, and decision-making processes.

Drawing on such earlier anthropologists as Leslie White (1959), I am prompted by these cross-cultural findings to offer a second hypothesis: reputational traits are part of a behavioral complex that has emerged from millions of years of human social evolution, during which these traits enhanced group survival and male camaraderie in hunting, defense, and conquest. With continued technological advancement, allowing humans more control of the environment and its resources, reputational traits began to lose some of their significance at the wider societal level in favor of respectability traits, particularly the core trait of maintaining a stable home, economically and sexually. The idea of the stable home can be extrapolated to social stability as well, if one sees the family or domestic unit—based on rules of residence, marriage, and kinship—as the premier building block of society. From this, respectability traits became associated with social order, while reputational traits became associated with social disorder.

I will go even further to propose that the emerging dominance of respectability traits over reputational traits is positively correlated with access to resources both within and across societies. That is, the greater the access and ownership nations and class groups have, the

greater the value placed on respectability traits, and the more negative the value placed on reputational traits. A part of this package is
the use of respectability as a class marker—to distinguish one's self
and one's group from those who have less access to resources.

Because respectability is so closely tied to access to or ownership of
resources, it is hard for lower-income men—or little men, in Havershamian terminology—to achieve it. Not only are the little man's attempts to achieve respectability blocked but circumstances leave him
little room to express anything other than reputational traits. Even
when traits can be seen at a deeper structural level as either reputational or respectability (depending on environmental accessibility for
expression), they may still be defined as reputational by the dominant group, because of the environment in which they are expressed
(the workplace versus the rum shop), or as a class marker. Such difficulties, I suggest, give rise to self-fulfilling prophesies in which reputational traits predominate for the little man because sexual
prowess—or tales of such prowess and sweet-talking—is one of the
few avenues left for him to express masculine strength.

In the male-culture versus the female-environment paradigm of
S. B. Ortner (1974) and others, a lower-income man's sexual partner
and home are the last vestiges of his environment over which he has
some control. The loss of control here, or the fear of it, is a major contributor to a man's decision to move on, to find newer environments
(women) to conquer. In the case of some little men, the repeated frustrations of trying to acquire respectability traits result in de-
emphasizing such traits and placing value on reputational traits as a
way to achieve status and respect among peers. This is a dynamic
among lower-income African-American males in the United States,
as described more than twenty years ago by Elliot Liebow (1967).

This class-based analysis can also be used extrasocietally in the
West Indies, with its long history of plantation slavery and colonialism. The West Indies experienced the emergence of capitalism at the
expense of the masses. Jamaican males, regardless of their socioeconomic status, still view themselves as little men vis-à-vis males native
to the metropolitan nations of Europe and North America. Regardless of their status within their own society, Jamaican males have
seen their environmental niche controlled by men "bigger" than
they. Historically, the big man lived in big houses, while the enslaved
Jamaican masses lived in shanties. This is still the case in Kingston,
with the big men's mansions on the hill in plain view of the masses
living in shanties below. Even the native Jamaican middle- and
upper-class males have long viewed their environmental niches as

controlled by capitalistic powers of the metropolitan nations. This national sense of smallness is exacerbated by the physical size of the island relative to such nations as the United States and Canada. Even England, though physically small, is cognitively a "big" nation because of its long control over Jamaican society.

Yet while respectability has become the dominant value expectation of men in high-resource societies, I would suggest that respectable big men in these societies also express reputational traits—particularly sexual prowess and hell-raising—similar to the way they are expressed by little men. I would suggest this to be true for several reasons.

In cross-cultural literature on gender roles, it appears that even in those societies in which respectability traits are the dominant role expectations for males and females, not only are boys allowed a longer period of time before expressing respectability traits, but also boys and young men are expected to display reputational traits ("sowing wild oats" in the Anglo-American cultural sphere). Girls, on the other hand, are expected to take on respectability traits at a young age or to possess them "naturally" (see Sanday 1981). As males get older, the attributes of respectability are expected to be more strongly expressed than the reputational ones. But I would expect many respectable big men to continue to express reputational traits because (1) early socialization establishes reputational traits in them; (2) although respectability traits represent the dominant normative expectation, respectability and the resources that make it possible are hard to obtain for the majority of men in these societies; and (3) given that respectability is demanded from women, reputational traits become a way of both differentiating oneself from women (see Sanday 1981 for more on this) and conquering the environment (i.e., women, within the Ortner paradigm).

I hope that my suggestions are provocative to the extent that they motivate further research. I think the hypotheses generated could lead to some interesting theoretical developments about gender constructs, which could also be helpful to those working in applied programs focusing on male-female interactions, family dynamics, reproduction, and related topics. The notion of balance also has theoretical implications for these programs.

In this concluding section, I argue that the social problems related to the masculine construct of reputation originate in ecological constructs of differential access to resources and that valued masculine norms can be embraced only through access to such resources. Although the wider society can provide the resources for overcoming these problems, the final step toward a solution can only come from little men themselves. I would agree with materialist scholars that there is a relationship between the wider political economy that defines a man's position in society and reproduces itself by enculturating little men in that mainstream definition; however, I disagree with the Marxist idea of a proletariat revolution that is always led by the middle class, that is, by big men without a leading role for the little men's broker.

I also disagree with Wilson's notion that the shift must be from the respectable to the reputational. My position is that the shift should be in the other direction, from reputational to respectability traits. I take this position not because I am trying to co-opt little people into the paradigm for easier control by big people (see note 28) but because the Havershamian experience taught me that this is the desire of little men themselves. They view the expression of respectability traits as more conducive to a true improvement of their economic and political status than is the expression of reputational attributes. Their strategies and frustrations come from a lack of access to resources that would earn them respectability.

Reputational traits are used as a means of gaining respectability. For example, a reputational trait, such as defying authority (bucking the massa), can make a little man more influential among other little men—i.e., a broker, who catches the eye of potential patrons because of this influence, not because of the bucking. If successful this behavior could turn into economic or political capital, which can elevate his economic status (and thereby improve his ability to be an economic provider) as well as increase his sphere of influence and sense of independence. Even sweet-talking sexual prowess and the eventual outcome are believed by some men to provide greater access to resources and respectability because, as I have pointed out elsewhere (Whitehead 1978), children provide access to their mother's consanguine kin and hence to their combined resources. The more women by which a man has children, the more kinship groups to which a man potentially has access.

However, as family planning researchers have documented for some time, values associated with children do not translate into economic value in today's industrial and postindustrial societies, as they once did in agrarian communities. What I am proposing here are informational campaigns—similar to those already attempted in family planning—which focus on men and shift the dominant sphere of masculinity from reputational traits to respectability traits. I do not think such shifts will be difficult to achieve because of the concept of balance.

There is reason to believe that the concept of balance found in Haversham exists in a number of societies. It is similar to the notion of moderation which we find in the idea systems of numerous cultures. Peggy Sanday (1981:161) argues for the human universality of the idea of balance in gender constructs, with an apt quote from Doris Lessing's *The Four-Gated City:* "Every attitude, emotion, thought has its opposite held in balance out of sight, but there all the time. Push any one of them to an extreme, and . . . over you go to its opposite."

The types of informational campaigns I propose are oriented toward shifting the *unobservable but tacit* (Spradley 1980) boundaries of reputational and respectability traits of men; they also have the goal of changing the constructs held by human services professionals regarding men, particularly little men. I would recommend that while these informational campaigns might be initiated by big people (because of their training and educational advantages), little men should be totally incorporated into the campaigns' planning and implementation. Finally, I recommend that we no longer view the goals of such programs as "educational," which connotes a unilinear direction of information, but instead view them as a process of "negotiating paradigmatic constructs." Such a notion proposes mutual informational exchange. Such an approach improves the chances that new cognitive constructs for men will develop, and it provides the program with helpful information for more effective male-oriented program planning.

NOTES

1. Because of the masculine weakness/wickedness construct associated with homosexuality, homosexuals in Jamaica have to work hard at being strong men and not revealing their homosexuality. My two homosexual informants were in fact bisexuals; having wives and children was a way of expressing their masculine strength. They said that they loved their wives and that God made man to love women, not men. For them, their homosexual forays into Kingston at night were a needed release from the rigors of being strong men during the day.

2. See, e.g., Clarke 1957; Henriques 1953; Kerr 1963; R. T. Smith 1956; and Stycos and Bach 1964. Exceptions include the work of Gooden 1966; Wilson 1973; and Brody 1981.

3. During the fieldwork periods of 1971, 1974, 1975, and 1983 my primary method was participant observation; however, numerous other methods

were also employed: (1) analysis of historical texts and oral histories to assess the evolution of the town; (2) a household composition survey of 238 households; (3) interviews of community leaders, employers, and human service providers; and (4) four surveys of a male sample of eighty, and of a female sample of the partners of twenty of the men in the male sample. I utilized both structured and ethnographic (in-depth) interviewing techniques. The ethnographic interviews had numerous functions, including obtaining "meaning" regarding gender constructs as used in the language.

4. In making comparative references to higher- and lower-income males, I devised a scheme in which men who earned J$15 or less per week were considered lower-income males, while those who earned J$25 or more per week were considered higher-income males (in 1974, the value of US$1.00 fluctuated between J$0.88 and J$0.91). I decided on these boundaries because from the 238 randomly selected households in the household composition survey, 177 conjugal males fell within the J$15 and below category. The highest salaries ranged up to J$250 per week.

5. Sixty-eight percent of the male sample ($N = 80$) professed no opposition to using contraceptives, while 69 percent had used or had at some time had a partner who used some form of contraceptive device. Moreover, of the men with a contraceptive history, the most popular method was the condom, a male contraceptive. Their knowledge of what were considered by professionals as the better methods of contraception was faulty at the time, but I found most men in Haversham eager to know more about effective contraceptives. Those men who had been sterilized or had a partner who had been involuntarily sterilized seemed glad that it had happened, because they saw themselves as being "weakened" by having too many children they could not take care of properly. Although almost 63 percent of the sample agreed with the statement that female contraception leads to female promiscuity, not one man gave this as a reason for opposing family planning.

6. In the randomly selected household composition survey (see note 3), 57 (32 percent) of the 177 conjugal males were chronically unemployed, while another 7 (4 percent) were irregularly employed. Another 26 (14.7 percent) had been laid off by the sugar factory, the principal employer in the area. Two of the most difficult times for me were collecting data for the household composition survey and for the male sample, because I encountered household after household with no regularly employed adults. The families continued to ask me, as a "big" (high-status) man, to help them find employment in one of the factories—something that was impossible for me to do.

7. Local educators estimate the adult (eighteen years of age and over) illiteracy rates range from 66 to 75 percent. This high rate exists despite the high value placed on education, a very active national literacy program, and the fact that sixty (75 percent) of the eighty men in the male sample (see note 3) professed to have gone to school four or more years as children. According to local educators, the history of the plantation economy was a primary contributor to the problem. Low wages resulted in children's being used either to contribute to the family income or to provide baby-sitting services while

adults and older children worked. Children are said to be a regular part of the labor market by grade seven or eight, but even many of those in the early years (grades one to three) attend school only two and a half days a week. In the primary grades, most children thus attend school 60 to 100 (out of a possible 280) school sessions a year (Whitehead 1976:50).

8. Peggy Sanday (1981:78) maintains that cross-culturally, women have natural ways of signaling womanhood and men do not have equivalent signals of manhood; thus, men must find ways to display their manhood. This role is usually defined as being what the female is not.

9. J. Spradley (1979:21–24) tells us that it is only in our analysis of the native language that we can truly understand cultural meaning, whereas the descriptive language of social science can contribute to both a bias in interpretation and a lack of understanding.

10. Although this essay is on males, these same descriptions were used regarding females. I do not have the space to go into the use of these adjectives for females. Briefly, however, as a primary description, strength is a natural state of man and is not appreciated in women by men. A strong woman prevents a man from exhibiting his own strength, thus resulting in his being perceived as weak.

11. These adjectives (*big, little, weak, strong, good,* and *wicked*) are not my words but those of Havershamians.

12. When discussing their voting behavior, most of the lower-income males in the study talked about voting a certain way not because the candidate meant anything to them (except the candidate for prime minister) but because certain little men/brokers advised them to do so. Local politicians were aware of this dynamic and often used these brokers to help in their campaigns, as well as to supply laborers for short-term menial jobs.

13. Havershamians use the word *argument* in the sense of debate, an enjoyable exercise providing men the opportunity to show verbal and intellectual skills.

14. The little man who "bucks" is clever in terms of the big man he selects for his display of strength. It is usually someone who he is sure will not be offended by the behavior, or someone who even invites it (such as an ethnographer whose collection of data is enhanced by getting little men to talk to him—a big man—without the barriers of the "buccra-massa"), or someone who does not have the potential to be a patron.

15. A common saying in 1974 was that the ambition of young Jamaican males was to be a "gunman" or a reggae star (or ideally both, as projected in the Jimmy Cliff movie *The Harder They Come*). At the same time, gun-related violence was the greatest public concern and gave rise to the "gun court," a prison built in the middle of downtown Kingston to hold those arrested for gun-related crimes.

16. Metaphysical sources of strength are not directly related to the theme of this essay and therefore are not discussed in the text. They are primarily religious in nature (and in some cases, magical). The man who has "God in him" is expected to be strong and good, which will help him achieve bigness

(either in heaven or on earth). He is also expected to be tough, intelligent, skillful, paternal, generous, secure, independent, loyal, and dependable and, above all, to exhibit balance (a concept discussed later).

17. Following emancipation, many ex-slaves bought or squatted on small plots of land on hillsides and other areas undesirable to the large-estate owners. These small plots of land become known as family land, and they were passed down from generation to generation. In 1973, more than 71 percent of Jamaican farms were less than five acres in size (Jamaica Government, Department of Statistics 1973). In Haversham, almost half (115, or 48 percent) of the residential property in the household sample was owned by members of the household or their extended kin. Eighty percent of these plots were less than one-half acre; 60 percent were less than one-fourth acre.

18. In Haversham, men also view marrying a woman late in her life cycle as possibly protecting them against cuckoldry, since they believe older women are not as desirous of sex and are not as desirable to big men for sexual purposes. This sentiment was strongly supported by younger men in the male sample who were cohabitating with older women. They also appreciated the fact that their partners frequently had property or money inherited from a consanguine kinsman or a dead husband (Whitehead 1976:130).

19. In Haversham, cars and motorbikes are also associated with being strong, because they are possessions and are indicative of the man's skills. In lower-income male peer gatherings, exploits with cars and motorbikes are frequent topics of conversation. In the absence of ownership of a motor vehicle, even the simple possession of a driver's license becomes an indicator of a man's ability to drive a car. Men in this situation often had stories of some prior experiences when they were employed as chauffeurs.

20. In fact, the big man's sexual prowess is ensured through such patterns as brokerage and the buccra-massa. From my first day in Haversham, I was frequently in the company of big men who had little men clients with sweet-talking abilities who introduced them to low-income women, who in turn would allow them to express their sexual prowess.

21. In examining the male fertility patterns in Haversham, I did not find such popular family planning jargon as "unwanted pregnancies," "desired" or "ideal" family size, and so on. It was difficult to distinguish births that were desired from those that were unwanted, and the ideal family size depended on the man's current partner. In the prevalent pattern of serial mating, men had past and usually future ideal family sizes. I define *hazardous reproduction* as that which economically, socially, or physically can negatively affect the parents' or child's health or well-being.

22. The status given to caucasian features has long been a part of the West Indian ideational system (see, e.g., Clarke 1957; Henriques 1953; Kerr 1963; Lowenthal 1972; McCartney 1970; Nettleford 1972). Even after the "Black Power" movement in many parts of the West Indies during the 1960s and 1970s, I still found a strong psychological association between skin color and social strength in Haversham in 1974. In male peer gatherings, dark-skinned men frequently deferred to men of lighter skin color. When light-skinned

men boasted about their achievements, they could usually count on dark-skinned cronies to confirm their stories (Whitehead 1976:106–7). Lighter-skinned males were expected to be more successful with women than were men of darker skin color. Some people associated light skin color with honesty and dark skin color with dishonesty. For example, when an informant was swindled by a boarder, she expressed great disappointment, not because she lost her money but because she "could not understand such behavior from a brown-skinned man."

Not only were people of light skin color sometimes given false social status, but people with a particular social status were given lighter skin color. People in Haversham would refer to my very dark-skinned visitor from the Sugar Board as "browner" than they were because of her education, her use of standard English, her late-model luxury car, and her supervisory position. At the same time, the same reference of brown was ascribed to caucasian expatriate graduate students and Peace Corps volunteers who would visit the community.

23. Asking family planning questions was difficult during interviews with the male sample because they frequently used the session to gain knowledge from me. When asked a question like, "What contraceptive method do you think works better in preventing pregnancy?" the men would often respond, "I don't know. Which ones are best?"

24. One of many instances of big people insulting little people occurred one day as I was walking with Mrs. Heinz, a social worker. As a pregnant young woman walked past us, Mrs. Heinz yelled, "Your first picni? Can you support a baby?" The young girl held her head down and said nothing. "Haven't you heard of the Pill?" The girl did not respond. "Why don't you use the Pill? Me girl, can you support a baby? Where your boyfriend work? In the sugar factory?" The girl nodded to the latter question. "You sure of that?" Although such public encounters brought a "buccra-massa" type response during the encounter, they were the topic of bitter discussion in gatherings of little people later (Whitehead 1976:165).

25. Early in my fieldwork, I interpreted big men who complained of the pressure to take on more women as exploitative of the unfortunate economic circumstances of lower-income women. Then I began to receive the same pressures. Men and women criticized me sharply as being socially irresponsible for not taking a girlfriend in the community and "sharing my wealth" with the many unfortunate women and children in the community.

26. I was surprised at what some would consider the low level of sexual activity, particularly given the great emphasis on sexual prowess. T. C. McCartney (1970) talks about a similar low behavioral ideal but a high verbal value placed on sexual activity by lower-income males in the Bahamas.

27. When men in the male sample were asked how old they thought a boy should be before he begins having sex, fifteen of the eighty men (18.8 percent) gave a specific age and gave as a reason for their answer that only then would a boy's body be able to withstand the rigor of sex. Five other men would not give an exact age because they did not believe that age was as

important as the boy's physical development and his ability to withstand the rigor of sex.

28. I have been accused of advocating the "co-optation" of lower-income leaders, thereby putting them in political danger by exposing their influences. Conversely, I have also been accused of advocating greater political strength for men (little men's brokers), whose interests are selfish quests for power at the expense of the community. I consider the first accusation patronizing to the intelligence of these men. I question whether they would let a "big man" anthropologist influence their decision to do something they would see as not in their best interest. I know of no examples of any of my informants experiencing ill effects politically as a consequence of my work. As for the second accusation, most little men's brokers are motivated by a commitment to improving their constituency's quality of life, as well as their own personal status. The two concerns should be viewed not as mutually exclusive but as complementary.

29. The characteristics described for Havershamians are very similar to the "honor and shame" complex described as characteristic of men in southern European societies (e.g., see Campbell 1964; Cronin 1974; Davis 1975; Gilmore and Gilmore 1979; Pitt-Rivers 1977; Schneider and Schneider 1976; and Brandes 1980). Although many of these authors interpret their findings in dialectical material terms (e.g., Brandes 1980:17–35), most of them go beyond materialism to include symbolic interpretations as well. One of the most widespread symbols of masculine strength is the same organic one I found in Haversham, semen. A similar association of semen with masculine strength has been documented in Mediterranean societies, among Hindu people, and in the Pacific, where R. C. Kelly (1976:45) describes a practice in which young boys are injected with semen because it is believed they are born without strength. This ideation has also been found among people who most likely had no early contact with each other, such as the Fore of New Guinea and Moroccans of North Africa. Among both of these groups, it is stated that a man can come under another's influence if a drop of his semen is found and manipulated in a culturally defined manner (Forge 1970; Dwyer 1978:75). Even in the United States, coaches and athletes sometimes say that sex prior to a sporting event can deplete the athlete of his strength.

REFERENCES

Agar, Michael. 1982. "Toward an Ethnographic Language." *American Anthropologist* 84:779–95.

Beckford, George L. 1972. *Persistent Poverty: Underdevelopment in Plantation Economies of the Third World.* New York: Oxford University Press.

Blake, Judith. 1961. *Family Structures in Jamaica: Social Context of Reproduction.* New York: Free Press.

Brandes, Stanley. 1980. *Metaphors of Masculinity.* Philadelphia: University of Pennsylvania Press.

Brody, E. 1981. *Sex, Contraception and Motherhood in Jamaica.* Cambridge, Mass.: Harvard University Press.

Campbell, J. R. 1964. *Honour, Family and Patronage: Study of Institutions and Moral Values in a Greek Mountain Community.* Oxford: Clarendon Press.

Clarke, Edith. 1957. *My Mother Who Fathered Me: A Study of the Family in Three Selected Communities in Jamaica.* London: George Allen and Unwin.

Cronin, Constance. 1970. *The Sting of Change: Sicilians in Sicily and Australia.* Chicago: University of Chicago Press.

Davis, N. Z. 1975. *Society and Culture in Early Modern France.* Stanford, Calif.: Stanford University Press.

Demas, W. G. 1965. *The Economics of Development in Small Countries with Special Reference to the Caribbean.* Toronto: McGill University Press.

Dwyer, D. H. 1978. *Images and Self-Images: Male and Female in Morocco.* New York: Columbia University Press.

Forge, Anthony. 1970. "Prestige, Influence and Sorcery: A New Guinea Example." In *Witchcraft, Confessions and Accusations,* ed. Mary Douglas. New York: Tavistock.

Gadamer, H. G. 1975. *Truth and Method.* New York: Continuum.

Geertz, Clifford. 1973. *The Interpretation of Cultures.* New York: Basic Books.

Gilmore, M. M., and D. D. Gilmore. 1979. "Machismo: A Psychodynamic Approach." *Journal of Psychological Anthropology* 2(3):281–99.

Gooden, S. S. 1966. "Adolescent Attitude to Sex and Related Matters." Dissertation for Diploma in Education, University of the West Indies, Kingston.

Henriques, Fernando. 1953. *Family and Colour in Jamaica.* London: Eyre and Spottiswoode.

Jamaica Government, Department of Statistics. 1973. *Statistical Yearbook of Jamaica.* Kingston: Jamaica Government Department of Statistics.

Jefferson, Owen. 1972. *The Post War Economic Development of Jamaica.* Kingston: Institute of Social and Economic Research, University of the West Indies.

Kelly, R. C. 1976. "Witchcraft and Sexual Relations: Exploration in the Social and Semantic Implications of a Structure of Belief." In *Man and Woman in the New Guinea Highlands,* ed. P. Brown and G. Buchbinder. Washington, D.C.: American Anthropological Association.

Kerr, Madeline. 1963. *Personality and Conflict in Jamaica.* London: Collins.

Kramer, J. M., A. E. Thomas, and T. C. Whitehead. 1981. "Primary Social Supports and Their Relationships to Health Care Delivery." In *Systems Science in Health Care,* ed. C. Tilquin. London: Pergamon.

Levi-Strauss, Claude. 1978. *Myth and Meaning.* London: Routledge and Kegan Paul.

Liebow, Elliot. 1967. *Tally's Corner: A Study of Negro Street Corner Men.* Boston: Little, Brown.

Lowenthal, David. 1961. "Caribbean Views of Caribbean Land." *Canadian Geographer* 5 (2):1–9.

McCartney, T. C. 1970. *Neuroses in the Sun.* The Bahamas: Executive Printers of the Bahamas.

McCormack, C. P. and A. Draper. 1987. "Social and Cognitive Aspects of Female Sexuality in Jamaica." In *The Cultural Construction of Sexuality,* ed. P. Caplan. London: Tavistock.

Manley, M. 1974. *The Politics of Changes: A Jamaican Testament.* London: Andre Deutsch.

Needham, Rodney. 1979. *Symbolic Classifications.* Santa Monica, Calif.: Goodyear.

Nettleford, Rex. 1972. *Identity, Race and Protest in Jamaica.* New York: William Morrow.

Ortner, S. B. 1974. "Is Female to Male as Nature is to Culture?" In *Woman, Culture and Society,* ed. M. Z. Rosaldo and L. Lamphere. Stanford, Calif.: Stanford University Press.

Pitt-Rivers, Julian. 1977. *The Fate of Shechem, or the Politics of Sex: Essays in the Anthropology of the Mediterranian.* Cambridge: Cambridge University Press.

Rodman, Hyman. 1963. "The Lower Class Value Search." *Social Forces* 42:205–15.

Sahlins, M. D. 1963. "Poor Man, Rich Man, Big Man, Chief: Political Types in Melanesia and Polynesia." In *Comparative Studies in Society and History* 5:285–303.

Sanday, Peggy. 1981. *Female Power and Male Dominance: On the Origins of Sexual Inequality.* New York: Cambridge University Press.

Schneider, Jane, and Peter Schneider. 1976. *Culture and Political Economy in Western Sicily.* New York: Academic Press.

Smith, M. G. 1962. *West Indian Family Structure.* American Ethnological Society Monograph 36. Seattle: University of Washington Press.

———. 1966. "Introduction." In *My Mother Who Fathered Me,* ed. Edith Clarke. London: George Allen and Unwin.

Smith, R. T. 1956. *The Negro Family in British Guiana.* London: Routledge and Kegan Paul.

Spradley, J. 1979. *The Ethnographic Interview.* New York: Holt, Rinehart and Winston.

Stycos, J. M. and K. W. Bach. 1964. *The Control of Human Fertility in Jamaica.* Ithaca, N.Y.: Cornell University Press.

Vincent, Joan. 1968. *African Elite: The Big Men of a Small Town.* New York: Columbia University Press.

Weiner, A. B. 1983. *Women of Value, Men of Renown: New Perspectives in Trobriand Exchange.* Austin: University of Texas Press.

White, Leslie. 1959. *The Evolution of Culture.* New York: McGraw-Hill.

Whitehead, T. L. 1971. *The Feasibility and Practicality of Implementing a Family Planning Related Ethnographic Investigation as a Complement to a KAP Survey in Jamaica.* W I Consultation Report. Washington, D.C.: United States Agency for International Development, Contract AID/la-668.

————. 1976. "Men, Family and Family Planning: Male Role Perception and Performance in a Jamaican Sugartown." Ph.D. diss. University of Pittsburgh.

————. 1978. "Residence, Kinship and Mating as Survival Strategies: A Jamaican Example." *Journal of Marriage and Family* (November):817–28.

————. 1984. "The Buccra-massa Personality and the Little Man Broker in a Jamaican Sugartown: Implications for Community Health and Education Programs." *Social Science and Medicine* 19 (5):561–72.

————. 1986. "Breakdown, Resolution and Coherence: The Fieldwork Experiences of a Big, Brown, Pretty-Talking Man in a West Indian Community." In *Self, Sex and Gender in Cross-Cultural Fieldwork*, ed. T. L. Whitehead and M. E. Conaway. Urbana: University of Illinois Press.

Whitehead, T. L., D. A. Frate, and S. A. Johnson. 1984. "Control of High Blood Pressure from Two Community Based Perspectives." *Human Organization*, 43:163–67.

Wilson, Peter J. 1973. *Crab Antics: The Social Anthropology of English-Speaking Societies of the Caribbean*. New Haven, Conn.: Yale University Press.

Margaret A. Eisenhart and Dorothy C. Holland

Gender Constructs and Career Commitment: The Influence of Peer Culture on Women in College

When we first met Paula[1] in 1979, she had come to college with a straight *A* average from high school and planned to major in biology and become a doctor. During her freshman year, she did not find her courses, including calculus and chemistry, particularly difficult, but she did find them "boring" and often could not make herself go to class or study. By the end of her freshman year, she decided to switch her concentration to nursing ("because my grades aren't high enough for med school"). During the first semester of her sophomore year, she missed the deadline for application to the nursing program and decided instead to try for an education degree. In the middle of her sophomore year, Paula had this to say about her career-related decisions during college: "Since I've been here, I've changed my mind about 1,000 times. . . . And, like right now, I feel like . . . just not working would be the greatest thing in the world—just taking care of children and not studying." Paula eventually settled on a social science field as her major and graduated in 1983. After graduation, she enrolled in a management trainee program, worked in a department store, and got married. In 1987, she had this to say about careers: "[My husband and I] want to have successful careers . . . his is a career where I feel like mine is a job. So, my career goals are for his career more so than mine. . . . I'm trying to be there to help [him] when I can."

Paula's case is not atypical of the college women we have been following since 1979. Despite the removal of legal barriers to women's participation in high-status occupations, the implementation of affirmative action programs, and the efforts of the women's movement, we found women—with the opportunity to attend college, with strong high school records, and with expressed commitments to pursue careers—who continued to make "career decisions" like Paula's, decisions that seemed to be leading them into "traditional" roles for women in the work force.[2] This essay is about the social processes that encourage bright young college women in the United States to continue to make career-related choices like Paula's.

Some researchers have suggested that the underrepresentation of women with careers is declining, especially for privileged young women. R. W. Connell, D. J. Ashenden, S. Kessler, and G. W. Dowsett (1982:96–97) in their study of one hundred Australian middle school students report that some of the girls at elite schools were seriously considering professional careers. The authors predict that these girls will grow up to challenge the traditional model of adult femininity as wife, mother, and volunteer and, by becoming career women, they will redefine work and family and instigate changes in gender relations in Australia (175–77; see also Kessler et al. 1985). Several studies of American college freshmen in the late 1970s and early 1980s reveal large increases in the percentage of women enrolled in traditionally male fields of engineering, math, and science (Astin et al. 1983; Boli, Allen, and Payne 1983; Hafner 1985). These authors hope that this trend will continue and presumably set the stage for more women to pursue careers in these high-status, traditionally male-dominated fields.

Although we take these increases to be a sign of change, we are not convinced that this cohort of privileged young women will, in large numbers, continue into careers—careers in the sense of "job sequences that require a high degree of commitment and that have a continuous developmental character" (Rapoport and Rapoport 1976:9). Our longitudinal study (1979–87) of university women,[3] many of whom started college with interests in math and science majors at two southern universities, revealed that their commitment to careers remained low or diminished during college. Why do such women "decide" not to pursue careers?

Many others have tried to answer this question before, citing such factors as nonsupportive socialization, gender-specific motivation patterns, and subtle forms of institutional discrimination. In this essay we argue that school-based peer groups and their associated cultures play an important—and relatively unrecognized—role in guiding women toward traditional positions in the work force. These peer cultures encourage women to see themselves as (potential) romantic partners with men, and they are virtually silent on the subject of academic work or future careers. In such a context, individual women find that commitment to academic work and a career is difficult to preserve or expand. Ideas about the importance and value of academic work and careers—ideas that the women bring with them to college and which we will refer to as their "cultural models of schoolwork"—are not compelling enough to keep many women from being redirected by the pull of the peer culture.

We believe that our answer and the ethnographic approach that led us to it are unusual in the literature on women and careers. Unlike most other researchers, we focused on discovering the social world in which the women lived during college, the cultural meanings that seemed to guide the women's thoughts and actions at college, and, in that context, the decisions they made related to their careers. In previous studies of women's career choices, women have been treated as though they were making decisions and choices as separate (although well-socialized) individuals. Further, women's interpretations of the world of work and its relationship to their lives have been relatively ignored. It has not been common to explore the context in which women make career-related decisions or to ask how girls and women themselves interpret and organize career-related information (Eisenhart 1985). These topics are important because, as we found in our study, the women's orientations or models of schoolwork affected their abilities to withstand the forces for "career derailment" they met at college. One model protected the women; the other two—held by a majority of the women—did not.

Previous Explanations of Women's Career Commitment

Most studies of women and their careers attempt to demonstrate the antecedent variables, such as mother's career experiences, father's support, attitudes toward locus of control, or sex-role orientation, that are statistically significant predictors of women's selections of courses of study, college majors, or jobs. The supposed ways these variables influence career choice have rarely been tested (Eisenhart 1985), however. We thus know little about the process by which women fail to pursue high-status professions. We do not even know whether they "decide" their future in the sense of consciously choosing among several options.[4]

The literature on women and careers relies primarily on two explanations for women's career commitment (or lack of it) and their career-related decisions: (1) socialization of gender roles, and (2) need fulfillment during stages of women's life course. A third explanation, reproduction of subordinate status, is relevant to this literature but not consistently part of it. We will briefly review these approaches before describing our study. The first two approaches stress the social and cognitive processes that begin in early childhood and function to differentiate the skills and preferences of girls and boys as they grow older. In both approaches, the school and the peer group are thought to play complementary, supporting roles to the primary socialization activities of parents during early childhood. The third approach, which is closest to our own, stresses the dynamic role of the school and significant others, especially from the middle grades on, in reflecting differentiated opportunities for adults in society and thereby creating the conditions for student responses that tend to reproduce society, including the gender status quo.

Socialization of Gender Roles

According to this perspective, females and males experience different socialization pressures from the moment of birth. These divergent experiences shape their behaviors, preferences, and values to fit the gender-specific roles they will occupy as adult women and men (see, e.g., Brophy and Good 1974; Eccles 1987; Eccles and Jacobs 1986). Girls are encouraged, for example, to be nurturant, to develop good verbal skills, and not to be aggressive; boys, in contrast, are encouraged to be aggressive and to develop good mathematical skills but not their nurturing capacity or their verbal skills. Pressures to behave in ways consistent with gender roles are seen as pervasive in family and school interactions. As children grow up, opportunities for nontraditional socialization are few and easily eclipsed by the more prevalent traditional pressures. Although this work has emphasized socialization pressures enacted through parents' or teachers' expectations for males versus females, some recent work in this tradition has drawn attention to the institutional contribution, that is, to the ways in which the organizational features of high school and college coursework favor one group over the other. Jacquelynne Eccles (1989), for example, described classroom activities, such as frequent use of cooperative learning and infrequent use of individualized learning, which correlate with girls' preferences for and success in high school courses. She argues that the absence of these "girl-friendly" activities in high school and college mathematics and science classes contributes to the low numbers of females in them. By the time young women and men are selecting courses and degree programs in high school and college, they have been socialized for quite some time and in numerous and redundant ways, and their "choices" are likely to be consistent with the divergent abilities and orientations they have learned. If privileged women continue to make career-related choices traditionally associated with women, it is because their parents, their schools, and the society in general have, for many years, been preparing them to be more skilled at, to feel more comfortable with, and thus to prefer such pursuits.

Need Fulfillment

The second major explanation focuses on personal needs, the ways these needs are affected by the differential socialization experiences of males and females, and the impact of a gender-segregated occupational structure on socialization experiences (Astin 1983; Goffredson 1981; J. L. Holland 1985; Tittle and Weinberg 1984). From this perspective, women's tendency to choose lower-status courses and jobs can be explained by the fact that from a very early age women are socialized to fulfill their personal needs differently from men, even though their basic presocialized needs are the same as men's. In particular, girls, more so than boys, are socialized to interpret their intrinsic needs in terms of courtship, marriage, and raising children. When women think about work, they consequently think about jobs, not about careers, and they expect to obtain only extrinsic rewards from their jobs. They worry that their work will interfere with the rewards they hope to obtain from domestic activities. Thus, young women are prepared not to want, or not to think they need, to invest themselves in jobs and careers. Later events, such as divorce, the "empty nest," or widowhood, may alter the particular way in which women manage to meet their needs, but in general their understanding of their needs is set before these events occur. Even in the face of such catastrophes, women are disinclined to turn to a career as a source of need fulfillment.

These first two explanations stress the conservative effects of early childhood socialization and needs internalization processes on the career-related decisions of women. These processes, however, do not seem sufficient to explain why women like Paula, who have been academically successful for many years and who have planned, at least until they entered college, to pursue traditionally male fields, suddenly reduce their career commitment or show little interest in further pursuing their fields of study. The third explanation is more applicable to such reversals.

Reproduction of Subordinate Status

The third major explanation of women's career choices focuses on the macro-level social and economic forces that differentiate the alternatives available to women and men. A sexual division of labor in which female labor, both paid and unpaid, is subordinated to male labor is seen as a fundamental structure of Western societies (Hunter College Women's Studies Collective 1983; Kessler et al. 1985). Schools (together with other social institutions) sort students into gender-specific tracks to future careers and reflect the evaluative subordination of female labor in such forms as the organization of courses (Gaskell 1985), the presentation of knowledge (Anyon 1981), and the extracurricular activities they sponsor (Eder 1985; Eder and Parker 1987; Kessler et al. 1985).

Earlier proponents of "social reproduction" theory (e.g., Bowles and Gintis 1976) assumed that children absorbed society's differential expectations of them primarily in schools and then translated these expectations directly into their own aspirations, expectations, and choices. According to this perspective, women learn from their families but especially from schools that they are suited for certain jobs and that the work performed in those jobs is less valuable than the work performed in men's jobs.

This perspective has been challenged in several ways. A number of studies show that women as well as members of other subordinated social groups (e.g., working-class men and black Americans) do not simply agree to the school's sorting of them. They do not necessarily accept the school's ideology that they deserve lower status and poorer future opportunities. They may often end up in inferior positions but for reasons of their own rather than for reasons given by the school.

Jane Gaskell (1985), for example, in a study of young working-class women who selected a vocational/business curriculum in high school, argues that the women purposely chose to pursue business, a career track that reproduced both their subservient class and gender positions. They did so not because they accepted the way the school categorized people like themselves or because the school, their family, or friends made it difficult for them to respond in any other way but because they decided that business was the most beneficial route for them to take, in light of their desired and probable futures (see also Valli 1986). They knew they wanted to marry soon after high school graduation and wanted to work for pay. According to Gaskell, the women determined (correctly) that married, working women were better off than any other adult women and that the greatest number of jobs for women were in clerical positions. In assessing the school offerings in light of these determinations, they found the academic courses irrelevant and the business courses "useful" to them. These courses could give them the skills they needed to qualify for a clerical job immediately after graduation. Without the typing and other skills learned in these courses, they knew they would be seriously disadvantaged in the job market. Thus, according to Gaskell, these women decided, based on the opportunities available to them in the school and community, what their best chances for success in society were and made career-related choices accordingly. They chose the school curriculum that seemed most advantageous to them and, in so doing, reproduced their lower-status class and gender position. To have chosen otherwise, on the off-chance that an academic route might allow them to improve their class position or that a male-dominated route might allow them to improve their position as women, would seem to them rather foolish.

Other revisions of social reproduction theory are more compatible with our approach. Similar to Gaskell's work, Paul Willis's now classic *Learning to Labor: How Working Class Kids Get Working Class Jobs* (1977) describes the active, collective response of people in oppressed groups to their situations. However, unlike Gaskell, he emphasizes peer groups and their formation of a collective (cultural) response to social barriers. In our view, these peer groups and their cultures are extremely important aspects of the context in which individuals "decide" what to do about their futures.

Willis devotes most of his analysis to the active role working-class male students play in the re-creation of classes in British society. Willis argues that these young working-class males, and by implication other dominated groups in a society, come to realize, at some level, that societal structures, as reflected in schools, are organized to oppress them. Their collective response is to produce a counterculture, that is, a set of ideas and behaviors that denies the values promoted by oppressive structures. In Willis's case, the working-class "lads" valorized things, such as manual labor and disruptive behavior, that the school discouraged. Willis goes on to suggest that such responses, despite their apparently oppositional character, functioned in the end to re-create the social status quo. For various reasons, the lads' rebellion led them to celebrate working-class values and to seek working-class jobs. Further, by enacting values discouraged by the school, the lads, as individuals, forfeited their chance of moving out of the working class—the chance afforded by a good school record and a school credential.

R. W. Connell et al. (1982) provide another example of this "social reproduction" approach. They begin from Willis's perspective in an attempt to understand the role of schools in the reproduction of Australian society. Their study reveals how concurrent dynamic interactions within families and middle schools lead girls to apprehend their opportunities in such a way as to reproduce "femininities"—ways of being feminine—in the family and school that are, for the most part, complementary and subordinate to masculinities and appropriate to their class position. Oppositional femininities are possible and are enacted by a few individuals and in an occasional small group, but because most are oppositional to the girls' class and gender position, they are so thoroughly discredited by family members, teachers, and peers that they cannot be sustained in any collective sense for very long. The single exception is the case of privileged girls who want to have careers. They reject traditional femininities associated with women's work but accept those associated with family; in other words, they expect to have careers and to be wives and mothers.

Cultural Reproduction and the Influence of Peers

In this essay we follow some of the assumptions of the "cultural reproduction" framework just described. In particular, we take the position that young women's campus peer groups, like the young men's group in Willis's study, may develop collective responses to their situations and, thereby, to the larger society. The cultural reproduction literature links the creation of youth cultures to structural features of the larger society, particularly class. In Willis's case, he located the elements of the lads' culture in their working-class backgrounds. The work of John Ogbu (1974, 1978), although it is not derived from a Marxist social theory, links the emergence of peer cultures to race. In his early work, Ogbu suggested that black students' apprehension of limited opportunities for good positions in the work force—on account of racial discrimination—led them, as a group, to reject the value of success in school. More recently, Signithia Fordham and John Ogbu (1986) have described the peer culture in a Washington, D.C., high school. Within the peer groups at the school, achievement and participation in certain extracurricular clubs and some sports were associated with "acting white." In this and other work (1988), Ogbu identified the black community's response to discrimination as a major source of elements for the high school peer culture. In both Willis's and Ogbu's work, the peer culture forms in response to structural barriers raised in schools and in the wider society and is constructed as an oppositional form from elements taken from other parts of the students' experiences.

In our earlier study of elementary school students (Eisenhart and Holland 1983), we argued that gender relations became the special province of peer groups by default. Because the elementary school defined students as children, the school and school adults (corroborated by many parents) downplayed the emergent romantic and sexual aspects of the children's interests. The schools and to a large extent parents thus left the children dependent on one another, older siblings, and public sources, such as the media, to develop their own attitudes and practices regarding sex and romance. Since these sources of information about sex and romance were all around them and an indicator of an older, more grown-up status, it was hardly surprising that the students were interested. Because such interests were prohibited by the child identity, they became, by necessity, a part of the peer underground. In what can be seen as an extension of this pattern, we found the college women in our present study were immersed in a campus peer culture that emphasized a model of romantic identities for women and that provided distraction from, not support for, the development or maintenance of school- and career-related interests.[5]

The Study

The primary data on which this essay is based come from three sources: interviews and participant observations with twenty-three women—twelve blacks at Bradford University and eleven whites at Southern University (SU)—during their first three semesters of college (1979–80); follow-up interviews with most of these women in 1983 and 1987; graduation records on the women; and a survey administered to 362 women at Bradford and SU in 1981. These data were gathered as part of a study designed to investigate the college experiences and future plans of black and white women on the two campuses (Holland and Eisenhart 1981).

Historically, Bradford is a black school; SU, a white school. Demographic information on the two universities suggests that SU draws students of predominantly white, middle-class backgrounds while Bradford draws students of predominantly black, lower-middle-class backgrounds. The two schools are quite similar in other respects. Both are state universities. At both schools the ratio of women to men is about the same (60:40). Also at both places 50 percent of those who apply are admitted, and 60 percent of those admitted are enrolled, although Bradford is a smaller school.

The ethnographic sample was selected to include women with a range of college majors, extracurricular interests, size and density of peer networks, and ideas about the future from each university. All of the women selected had records of strong academic performance in high school, and approximately half at each school were, at the time they entered college, planning to major in math- or science-related fields.[6] During preliminary interviews, all of these women expressed a definite intention to pursue a career in the future.

A three-semester period, from near the beginning of the informants' freshman year to the middle of their sophomore year, was chosen for intensive study of the ethnographic sample. During the three-semester period, researchers conducted monthly observations of informants engaged in campus activities. Informants were also interviewed nine times over the course of the three semesters. These "talking diary" interviews were open-ended and designed to encourage respondents to discuss their experiences and concerns in their own terms. For the most part, the women talked, and were encouraged to talk, about their college coursework, majors, activities, and friends. A second type of interview, the "life history" interview, was conducted near the end of the study, in the middle of the women's sophomore year.

It is important to note at this point that all of the women we studied were in the process of making the transition from home to college. They were adjusting to new demands from their schoolwork and were forming friendship groups. It is likely they were particularly susceptible to college peer group influence during these years.

Analysis of the ethnographic cases involved reading through approximately two hundred pages per informant, in search of evidence of the women's career-related decisions and the social and cultural context in which these decisions were made. In our analysis, we attempted to maintain an inductive appreciation of our data. We categorized the women's college experiences into four types, based on our initial reading of the data: schoolwork, romantic relationships, friendships, and family. We then organized the data into these categories and several subcategories. Following the general procedures outlined by James P. Spradley (1979, 1980), we searched for patterns within and across these categories. When this essay was written, we had completed the analysis of twenty-one cases—eleven from Bradford and ten from SU. They are listed in Table 1, along with their anticipated majors when they entered college.

In 1981 we developed the survey instrument, based on a preliminary analysis of the ethnographic data. The survey was designed to examine the factors affecting women's choice of major and commitment to their major. The survey, administered to random samples of sophomore women at each university, investigated changes in

Table 1: Category of Majors and Changes in Majors of Women in the Ethnographic Sample, by Schoolwork Model

Name	University	Entering Major	Interim Major	Major at Graduation
Getting Over				
Cynthia	Bradford	business	no change	business
Rosalind	Bradford	applied biology	left school	
Cylene	Bradford	business	left school	
Phyllis	Bradford	business	no change	business
Deidre	Bradford	social science	left school	
Charlotte	Bradford	applied biology	no change	applied biology
Della	Bradford	business	no change	business
Sybil	Bradford	social science	no change	social science
Sandy	SU	arts/humanities	left school	
Doing Well				
Linda	SU	biological science	scaled down[a]	applied biology
Kelly	SU	biological science	scaled down	social science
Susan	SU	physical science	scaled down	computer science/math
Kim	SU	biological science (B.S.)	scaled down	biological science (B.A.)
Paula	SU	biological science	scaled down	social science
Natalie	SU	computer science/math	no change	computer science/math
Velma	Bradford	business	left school	
Learning from Experts				
Valecia	Bradford	arts/humanities	switched to something better for her	business

Aleisha	Bradford	education	added double major	education/ social science
Karla	SU	arts/humanities	switched to something better for her	physical science
Kandace	SU	social science	no change	social science
Exception				
Lisa	SU	arts/humanities	change spurred by boyfriend	education

[a]These designations are based on the perspective of the woman making the change.

women's chosen major during their freshman a..d sophomore years and tested a model of factors hypothesized, from the ethnographic study, to affect women's declared commitment to pursuing training in a chosen major. Using the instrument, we surveyed 362 women at the two universities.[7]

Data from the survey indicate that the women at Bradford and SU were pursuing a variety of majors, including some in nontraditional fields. (See Table 2 for a summary of their majors.) They seemed to be, as a whole, serious about pursuing a career. At Bradford, 93.3 percent said they wanted a full-time career within two years of graduating from college. At SU, the figure was 84 percent. When asked to rate their commitment to pursuing their chosen major (possible range: 0 to 100), the mean commitment score at Bradford was 88.44 (s.d. = 17.68, N = 179); at SU, it was 79.10 (s.d. = 22.45, N = 182).[8] In this essay we use results from the survey primarily to support assertions drawn from the ethnographic data. Thus, unless otherwise indicated, the data reported about the women's time in college come from the ethnographic work (1979–80).

In 1983, when members of the ethnographic sample should have been graduating from college, and again in 1987, an attempt was made to recontact them and learn about their current activities and plans. Nineteen of the twenty-three were contacted in 1983; seventeen were contacted in 1987. Information on the graduation status of all the women was obtained from each university in 1987. Table 1 includes the graduation status of the women as of 1987. In this essay, all the data about the women's postcollege experiences come from the follow-up interviews with members of the ethnographic sample.

Table 2: Entering and Sophomore-year Majors of Surveyed Sample, by University

Major	Bradford (N = 176)		SU (N = 179)	
	Entering (%)	Sophomore (%)	Entering (%)	Sophomore (%)
Applied biology (includes premed., nursing, therapy)	11.4	10.2	21.7	20.1
Arts/humanities	7.4	6.8	16.1	14.0
Biological sciences	2.3	2.8	12.2	5.6
Business	29.0	29.0	14.4	19.6
Computer sciences/ math	0.0	3.3	5.5	3.2
Education	20.5	15.3	3.9	10.6
Engineering	0.0	0.0	0.0	0.0
Physical sciences	1.7	2.3	10.0	6.2
Social sciences (includes "pure" and applied areas, e.g., social work, criminal justice)	19.9	22.2	5.6	14.0

Note: Adapted from Holland and Eisenhart (1981:72). Seven respondents did not answer this question.

The 1983 and 1987 follow-up interviews were collected by researchers who had not participated in the original study. At the time, we were busy analyzing the ethnographic data, and we did not consult the follow-up data until after the ethnographic analyses were complete. We were therefore not aware of the close associations between the women's experiences in school and their occupational choices until long after all the data were compiled.

Gender Constructs and Career Paths

In the ethnographic study, the women we talked to and observed led us to the realm of their informal peer groups and the powerful mediating role of these groups in creating a context for college women's career-related decisions. The school's contribution seemed pale by comparison.

What we found was that the meaning of gender for these college women was being learned and enacted primarily in peer group interactions and that this process, though surely begun much earlier in the women's lives, was still unfolding and changing while the women were in college. The peer cultures at both schools (although different in some respects) encouraged women to assess themselves in terms of their romantic relationships with and their attractiveness to men. In contrast, women's success at schoolwork or in future careers was not of much consequence in the peer culture. As far as the peer culture was concerned, women could excel or not in schoolwork, and they might or might not have serious career plans. These areas were viewed as matters of individual capability, effort, and preference. What was appraised and rated in the peer culture was how successful women were in their romantic relationships. Thus, to understand the effect of gender constructions on the women's schoolwork models and career plans, it is first necessary to discuss the peer system and the way it construes gender.

The Pull of the Peer System

Ostensibly, women and men go to college for the purposes of furthering their "education" and acquiring the credentials necessary for future careers; yet, there is more to college life than studying, classes, and examinations. Helen Horowitz (1987), in her historical account of college life in the United States, argues that, since the late eighteenth century, the campus peer system has dominated most students' lives at college: "[There is a tradition of] peer consciousness sharply at odds with that of the faculty . . . dating from the late eighteenth century. . . . Classes [were] the price one had to pay for college life . . . 'a little space of time . . . where the young made a world to suit themselves' " (11–12).

When the women in our study went to college, they found themselves in a world of peers. The women spent most of their time around age-mates; were constantly exposed to peer-organized activities; learned age-mates' interpretations and evaluations of all aspects of university life; had most of their close, intimate relationships with age-mates on campus; and learned ways to understand and evaluate themselves from these peers. The women were, of course, familiar with peer cultures when they came to college. Peer groups are an important feature of American students' lives in high school (Coleman 1961; Schwartz 1972) and even in elementary school (Eisenhart and Holland 1983); however, at Bradford and SU, the peer groups were more intense. As at other residential colleges, students lived, worked, and played with their peers, and they had contact with other groups, such as family, much less frequently and perhaps only at long distance.

Especially for women students, the peer culture was organized around male-female relationships. Activities were evaluated according to the opportunities they offered to meet men or to enact romantic relationships. Such activities as being invited to parties, going to mixers and bars, and assisting at male-dominated events were highly appraised in the peer culture. It was considered, for example, more desirable to be a fraternity sweetheart or little sister than a sorority sister and more fun to support men's sports as cheerleaders, majorettes, flag girls, managers, and even spectators than to be involved in women's sports.

In the survey we conducted, respondents were asked how much importance they attributed to fifty-five different kinds of campus activities, which were identified during the ethnographic study. Of these fifty-five activities, thirteen were directly related to schoolwork or a career. Almost twice as many (twenty-three) were peer-dominated, and most of these, including socializing, friendships, and romantic relationships, were rated equal to or more important than work-related activities (Holland and Eisenhart 1981:23–27).

In the ethnographic interviews and observations, the women's talk concerned men, their own and others' physical appearances, and social activities. Paula put it this way: "[When I'm with my girlfriends,] we always talk about our boyfriends, or how we wish we had boyfriends, or how fat we are—we all say that. . . . None of us have to lose weight, but we just want to be thinner. . . . I'm gonna lose weight and clear up my face and [grow] my hair out, so I'll be all beautiful this summer." Aleisha described a long and detailed conversation she had with her "girlfriends": "I came back [to school] and there was actually a list of five [guys]. . . . It just accumulated. . . . All of them are so hard to choose from. . . . Me and my girlfriends were sitting in the room and I am telling them this, and they said, 'All right, who's got the most money? Who's got the most prestige? Who's the nicest? Who's the best looking?' We just debated it back and forth. . . . It was just really even because of all of them, each person had something the other four didn't have. . . . I had the hardest time making up my mind."

Another study at SU suggested that the students had a cultural model of intimate male-female relationships that consisted of a taken-for-granted scenario of how such relationships develop (Holland and Skinner 1987) and that the model informed women's talk, feelings, and thoughts about such relationships (D. C. Holland n.d.). Interviews from Bradford suggest a very similar model.[9]

According to the model, an attractive man and an attractive women are drawn to each other. The man shows his interest by appreciating the woman's special qualities and by treating her well, as demonstrated, for example, in giving her gifts and taking her nice places. The woman, in turn, reveals her affection for him and allows the relationship to become more intimate. By participating in romantic relationships, one gains prestige as well as intimacy. Because men and women tend to match up by attractiveness, men—especially attractive men—validate a women's prestige and vice versa.

Women, it should be noted, were more dependent on romance for prestige than were men. For women, attractiveness to men was the main source and indicator of prestige in the peer culture. Men had several sources of prestige, such as sports or campus offices (see also Horowitz 1987:208). To gain some measure of prestige in the peer system at Bradford and SU, women had to be involved in romantic relationships. One of the women summed it up this way: "Girls always want to have the guy everybody would talk about. . . . You *have* to have a boyfriend for this and that."

A desire for heterosexual intimacy also was considered "natural." A woman could not singly declare a lack of interest in men that she could for, say, mathematics, history, or any or all of her courses. For various reasons, including the inability to find a good match, limited knowledge or expertise about how to find or keep a romantic partner, and in a few cases other salient interests, the women in our study were not equally successful in this peer system (see D. C. Holland n.d. and Holland and Eisenhart 1988a for more detail about this). They were, however, all liable to evaluation in terms of the system, and they all knew it.

In the peer system with its emphasis on romantic relationships, other aspects of college life were important but secondary. On both campuses, women's relationships with other women were formed in the shadow of relationships with men. Although the women went about their female-female relationships differently at Bradford and SU, the outcome was the same: weaker and secondary relationships among women. The women at Bradford emphasized self-reliance and control over information about their relationships with men to the point that it was difficult for them to achieve trusting relationships with women. The women at SU relied on their female friends to support them in their efforts to find and keep desirable men, but once a romantic partner was found, they tended to spend time with female friends only when their boyfriends were unavailable (Holland and Eisenhart 1989).

The Place of Schoolwork

Schoolwork was also a peripheral concern in the peer systems at Bradford and SU. Amidst all the talk about romantic relationships, there were relatively few conversations about the content of courses, the value of various majors, or the viability of various careers. When the women did talk to their peers about schoolwork, they tended to complain: classes required too much work, professors were "unfair," or someone was not able to study enough for a test.

In general, peers seemed to know very little about each others' schoolwork or career interests. For example, in the life history interview each woman was asked to describe what her high school friends did when something went wrong in her schoolwork. Almost without exception in the ethnographic sample, the women said their friends would do very little, because they either would not know about it or would pretend not to know about it. Paula and most of the others felt this was appropriate. Paula, for example, said, "I felt like it was none of their business."

When Paula was asked directly whether she and her high school friends ever talked about why they chose the majors they did, she said, "No. . . . It's just that we all picked things that we did well in in school." When Della was asked whether she and her high school friends ever got together and talked about schoolwork, she said, "No, no; schoolwork didn't play with our minds."

In general, schoolwork and career-related matters seemed to be thought of as a matter of individual choice, not as a matter for (peer) group discussion or debate. The women made repeated references to "making my own decision" and "making up my own mind" about what field to pursue or what major to choose. Aleisha, who spent hours talking with her girlfriends about her many romantic interests, had this to say when asked what her girlfriends were majoring in: "I don't know; I never asked them."

This finding that the women tended to deal with academic matters on their own was further supported by the survey. When asked to rate the importance they attributed to the thirteen academic or career-related activities and relationships, the women rated individual academic activities more highly than peer activities oriented around academic or career interests. The average importance of individual academic activities (on a 5-point scale, where 1 was of little importance and 5 was very important) was 3.93 (s.d. = .69) at Bradford and

3.41 (s.d. = 1.00) at SU. By comparison, the average importance of peer-related academic activities was 3.45 (s.d. = .38) at Bradford and 2.84 (s.d. = .81) at SU (Holland and Eisenhart 1981:31–32). Overall, it appears the women, immersed in a world of peers, tended to academic matters on their own.

Correspondingly, status in the peer system was not determined by academic success. Some references were made to "brains" and "intellectuals," but there was often a negative connotation to these labels. For example, one woman said, "People thought that I studied a lot more than I did and that was always looked on negatively: the brain syndrome." Another said something similar about herself: "Some of my friends . . . and my father call me 'the brain,' but they're just kidding. I'm glad they didn't take it too far." Paula told a story about a "guy with a [perfect grade point average of] 4.0 who wanted to go to Harvard Medical School" but couldn't get in because "all he did was study."

The people in math and science courses, especially, were sometimes considered "weird," at least in part because they were so serious about schoolwork. Paula presented the following picture of science students when she was looking for someone to talk to about getting into medical school: "I need to talk to somebody who knows what's going on . . . all the people I know are business majors . . . except, I guess, the people in chemistry class. And I don't want to get into a detailed conversation [with them] . . . half the people in chemistry are weird. . . . They could be mad scientists, . . . hunchback, running around with their lab coats on."

Struggles to Manage Schoolwork and Peers

Although schoolwork was de-emphasized in the peer group system, doing schoolwork could not be relegated to a secondary place as easily as some other things, such as female-female relationships. No system existed to propel women into close female-female relationships, but the academic system did exert pressure on women, making it necessary for them to pay some attention to schoolwork if they wanted to stay in school. The dynamic created between the peer and academic systems on the two campuses produced a tension that most women mentioned. During the course of the ethnographic study, all of the women in our study struggled—some more, some less—with what they perceived to be the competing demands of schoolwork and peers.

For most, the two systems were viewed as competing domains: time spent studying was time spent away from peers, and time with peers meant little schoolwork was accomplished. One SU woman described the situation as a choice of identity: one could be a "bookworm" or a person who liked to "have fun." Della at Bradford described the same dichotomy in another way: "The ones that did all the book studying, they had no social life; the ones that didn't do no book work, they had a lot [of social life]."

None of the women wished to be viewed as one or the other of these extreme types. When they arrived at college, they all wanted, and expected, to be successful in both school and in the peer system. Almost from the beginning though, they talked about needing to study more and "party" less. Most were surprised to find schoolwork took more time than they had given it in high school, and they struggled to complete it and do other things as well. One woman at SU had this to say: "I always liked school, ever since I was very young . . . but here I haven't done anything for enjoyment in so long. . . . All I do is work. . . . It always came so easy for me in high school, and now I've got to *compete* with somebody just to get a spot [in medical school], so I almost never have time to do anything with my friends . . . I'm going crazy."

This struggle with the demands of schoolwork was evident in the survey responses too. One of the survey questions asked about people and activities that had taken more time than expected over the semester and thus caused the women to cut back on the other things they normally did. Schoolwork was felt to be extraordinarily demanding by the largest percentage; over 80 percent of the women on both campuses felt that some aspects of schoolwork had taken an unexpectedly large amount of their time. Jobs and peer relationships were much less likely to be seen as taking up an untoward amount of time (see Table 3).

The women said their peers complained if they devoted too much time to schoolwork. One Bradford woman put it this way: "Guys will tell you, 'Come on, let's go out.' And if you tell him you have to study, he'd probably be upset. Some of my friends tell me I'm a party-pooper . . . cause I usually have to study. A lot of times when [my two closest friends] have somewhere to go, they won't ask me. . . . This sort of bothered me 'cause they were having a good time and I wasn't."

Jobs, unlike both schoolwork and peers, could be ignored. One woman described her typical day as follows: "[I] go to class, go to work, go out to dinner with some friends, relax with [friends], and watch TV [with friends]." When she got a couple of Cs on tests, she decided, "Work's [the job's] the bother; there's no time left for study-

Table 3: Percentage of Sample for Whom People and Activities Took Extraordinary Amounts of Time, by University

Extraordinary time spent on:	Bradford	SU
Trying to make good grades	84.8	75.4
Trying to do well in major	88.2	68.7
Job or volunteer work	38.8	34.1
Boyfriends	31.4	36.5
Girlfriends	26.3	29.1
Partying	20.7	30.6
Dating	20.1	32.8

Note: The questions for this item were (1) "Have you spent an abnormally large amount of time this semester on any of the following activities: That is, have you spent *such a large amount of time and energy* on them *that you ended up cutting down on the other things that you normally do?*" (2) "Have any of the following people taken up an unusually large amount of your time and energy this semester? That is, has anything *unexpected* or *extraordinary* happened which caused you to spend more time with them than you had planned?" See Holland and Eisenhart (1981:34).

ing. . . . I think I'm going to have to quit work. You think I'm gonna let that work bother me? Nah!"

Occasionally, the women spoke admiringly of other women who could keep peer activities from getting out of control. For example, Della described an older "girl" on her hall as follows: "She's a girl that sets a good example as a very studious person. . . . I see her studying all the time. . . . She lets you know that studying is very important . . . that you can't just all the time have a bunch of friends over to go out all the time. There's a time for everything; she lets you know." Della knew that failure to manage both could have long-term implications: "My sister . . . has messed up her life along the way, and she's still messing up . . . having so many men until she don't even have [time] to work."

The women expressed a need to study more, but they often would also remark that they studied a lot already and were not very motivated to do more. Correspondingly, the women often let themselves be drawn into peer activities. One student explained what happened as she and her suitemates were preparing to leave her room for a night of studying for the next day's exams: "We had a spontaneous party . . . everyone was here . . . till two in the morning. We made all kinds of daiquiris. . . . My parents called [during the party] and I never knew it. They couldn't believe we partied the night before exams. I can't believe we did. I've never done anything like that in my life." Another said, "I've been doing a lot of things with guys. I know my grades are going to suffer. . . . I guess I'll have to buckle down one of these days." And a third had this to say: "If I do homework every night and on the weekends, I can probably do a good job in my courses . . . [but] during the week I'm pretty lazy. . . . I try to study but I just go to sleep . . . or, you know, somebody'll come along and want to do something."

The survey indicated that, particularly at SU, peer-related factors affected "energy available for schoolwork." One variable, "extraordinary demands from peers," was negatively correlated with "energy available." At both schools, the relationship was in the expected direction: women who said that demands from peers were high also said that energy available for schoolwork was low, and vice versa; but only at SU was the correlation significant (Holland and Eisenhart 1981:96).

It appears the women at Bradford and SU wanted and expected to do well both in schoolwork and with their peers, but schoolwork seemed to interfere with peer activities by demanding too much time. Peer-related activities, on the other hand, were more fun and readily available; hence, they threatened to overwhelm schoolwork.

Schoolwork and Careers

Given this peer culture and the constant invitations to women to develop themselves as romantic and social types, how do college women understand and prepare for careers? What happens to their views of themselves as learners or schoolworkers? How do they further their commitment to career?

We found that although the women shared basic ideas about schoolwork, classes, grades, and professors, they differed in their views of the purpose of college work. We have elsewhere described these alternative views as "cultural models" (Holland and Eisenhart 1988b). The women brought to college a view of both the purpose of schoolwork and themselves in school, in the form of these models or orientations. The peer culture provided a system that competed with schoolwork. It derailed some women but not others, and some sooner than others, depending on the woman's model of schoolwork.

We identified three distinctive models of schoolwork held by the women in our ethnographic study. The models were organized around the motives for doing schoolwork and can be described as (1) work in exchange for "getting over" (i.e., finishing college and thereby obtaining college credentials); (2) work in exchange for "doing well" (i.e., receiving good grades or other academic accolades);

and (3) work in exchange for learning from experts. These models of schoolwork affected the women's interpretation of grades, evaluation of teachers, decisions about studying, choices of courses and majors, and feelings about their own performance. During the three-semester period of the main study, each woman seemed to hold one model as a dominant one; however, some were aware of the alternative models and sometimes entertained other models themselves or at least pieces of them (see Holland and Eisenhart 1988b for a detailed presentation of the models).

"Getting Over" and Enjoying Peers. Nine women (eight at Bradford and one at SU) held the first model of schoolwork. All the women in this group seemed to be quite certain what they wanted to major in. They came to college with a major chosen in high school or before, said they fully intended to pursue that major through college, and kept the same major as long as they remained in college (see Table 1). These women did not believe they needed to make outstanding grades or otherwise demonstrate special mastery in academic areas; they were simply trying to make good enough grades to finish school and get the credential they believed necessary to make them eligible for the type of future job they envisioned. They did not find the content of schoolwork compelling. Della's comment was typical: "I just did enough [schoolwork] to get over; hey, that's all."[10]

Elsewhere we have argued that these women had "marginalized worker identities" in the sense that, for them, schoolwork was not expressive of the self (Holland and Eisenhart 1988b). They did not identify with the world of learning. On the other hand, their view of themselves as (potential) romantic partners to men was, consonant with the peer culture, important for all but one—the one at SU—of the women in this group. This marginalization of career identity progressed as the women went through their college years.

All of the Bradford women had steady boyfriends or an ongoing series of romantic relationships with men during their freshmen and sophomore years. All of these women devoted considerable time to managing and maintaining these relationships (see Holland and Eisenhart 1988a for a discussion of the women's efforts to handle their romantic relationships).

Sandy, the SU woman in this group, also seemed to be affected by the peer culture. As described elsewhere (Holland and Eisenhart 1988a), she felt rejected by and had rejected the peer culture at SU. She became involved in a close and time-consuming relationship with another woman.

With two exceptions, the women with the "getting over" model (all of whom had been good students in high school) had no serious trouble doing "well enough" in their schoolwork and having time enough for friends. For them, only minor adjustments were necessary to participate in both worlds. One woman in this group put it this way: "I like biology; it wasn't hard at all. I came out with a *B*. . . . I didn't ever go to class. . . . I was doing a lot of things with my friends. . . . I didn't learn anything, but I passed all my tests." Another said, "I never did bad to where I needed to change my ways." Della provides another example. As mentioned earlier, when she started to have some trouble in her classes, she decided to quit her part-time job, but with no regrets, to have more time to study and to preserve her "free time" with her friends and boyfriends.

Others decided to spend more time at the library or in their rooms to get their studying done, but these alterations did not seriously interrupt their peer relationships. Usually, extra studying was done in the company of friends or boyfriends or timed to coincide with the schedules of others the women wanted to be with or see. Della, who had always studied at home alone during high school, excitedly told the researcher one day during the middle of her freshman year: "I found a new way to study—with my friends."

Whereas they tended to study less than the other women, those with the "getting over" view sometimes wondered if their distant goal of finishing a degree was worth the effort. For example, Della, at one point, said, "I'm here for an education . . . [but it isn't very important to me] because if I can get me a job in my field, where I want to be, . . . school would have no value." In such cases, friends or boyfriends might keep the women going. When Della's resolve faltered, she said, "I was thinking of quitting school and [my boyfriend] told me, 'If you quit,' he was gonna whip my butt. . . . So, I can't quit." One woman and a group of her friends at Bradford decided to rearrange their self-imposed study schedule so that another friend, who was in danger of flunking out because she fell asleep during the study period (it was too late at night for her), could get her studying done.

In two cases (Deidre and Sandy) though, friends pulled the women in other directions, and the women's models of schoolwork were not motivating enough to keep them in school: the women dropped out before the end of the ethnographic study. Deidre came to believe that her goal of "getting a good job" could be better achieved elsewhere: "It's boring here . . . studying for four years. And most of the two-year colleges will find you a job. It's like guaranteed employment, and here it's not." Being at Bradford also inter-fered with Deidre's relationship with her hometown boyfriend and some close girlfriends from high school who attended the commu-nity college in her hometown. Before the end of her second semester in college, she had stopped going to class or studying. She stayed un-til the end of the semester only because another "homegirl" was struggling to complete her courses and wanted Deidre's company. As a friend, Deidre thought it was her "obligation" to attend the other woman's classes with her and to help her with homework.

Sandy dropped out of school too, apparently because she wanted to devote as much time as possible to her developing relationship with her woman friend. About this she said, "[T]here's probably not gonna be another time in my life when I can just sit down and just be friends."

Thus immersed in a peer-dominated system that paid little atten-tion to academic work or career preparation and holding a cultural model of schoolwork that focused on getting credentialed to get a job, there was insufficient incentive for some of the women to stay in school, and even for those women who remained in school, there was no support for developing or further elaborating their views of themselves in a career, regardless of their majors, grades, or announced aspirations for future jobs. It is not surprising then that of the nine of them, four never graduated, and of those we con-tacted who were working after 1983, all but two held clerical or tech-nician jobs.

The survey data from Bradford tend to reflect ethnographic mate-rial from the women with the "getting over" model of schoolwork. According to the survey results, the Bradford women tended to change their majors infrequently and to be certain about the career they wished to pursue. What ambivalence they had was, like that of their compatriots from Bradford in the ethnographic study, focused on the worth of the credential relative to its costs. Costs included time, energy, anxiety, money, and the sacrifice of other interests (e.g., "competing peer" relationships and activities). Those who felt that the costs were unfair or not relevant indicated less commitment to pursuing training in their major (path coefficient = .175, p = .06, Holland and Eisenhart 1981:89).

"Doing Well" and Succumbing to Peers. The seven women (one at Bradford; six at SU) who held the model of schoolwork for doing well were the most vulnerable to *reducing* career commitment in college as they tried to handle the demands of both peer and academic systems.

These women viewed the work they did in college as a way of gaining recognition for their natural abilities and skills. One of them put it this way: "I always wanted to achieve the best, to be the best that I could academically. I always wanted to make As . . . if I made a B, I felt I was a failure within." From the vantage point of this model, doing well in college should be easy for those who are naturally good at the kinds of tasks or the subject matter of school. That is, good grades should be attainable without a lot of hard work; it should be possible to make high grades *and* have time to be with friends and do other enjoyable things.

All of the women in this group, like most of the others, faced the situation of having to work harder in college to get the same grades they did in high school. In general, those with the "getting over" models chose not to work harder and so made lower grades. For those whose major orientation toward schoolwork was the idea of doing well, there was more of a problem. Not being able to do well was a challenge to their identity as a "good student." Not doing well in a particular subject area was a blow to their notion of why they were in college—to study a subject at which they were naturally good.

Five of the seven women with the "doing well" model responded to the demands of college work by reconsidering what courses to take and what to major in. Their difficulties with schoolwork led them to question what coursework and, by extension, what type of occupation they were best suited for. One woman, who was having a great deal of trouble deciding what to major in, put it this way: "I really don't know what I'm going to get into. I guess I should start talking to somebody. It makes me nervous so I always keep pushing it back in my mind."

Eventually, these five women scaled down their ambitions and notions of self. They came to see themselves as "average" rather than "good" students and switched to what they believed were less demanding courses and majors before the end of their sophomore year (see Table 1). Kelly, for example, was faced with reconciling herself to a lower rank after only a few weeks of college. In response, she dropped her goal of becoming a doctor and switched to a social science field before the end of her first semester. About what happened to her, Kelly said, "I came from a background of good grades, tops in the class, never really worrying about it," but in college, "I'm just a face in the crowd . . . just average here. . . . It's a lot harder than I thought . . . I wish I could have done a lot better." Linda, another SU woman who scaled down her commitment to schoolwork and switched her major to a field she perceived as less demanding, also talked about the problem of "being average" at college: "I don't want to be average. . . . But, right now, I guess that's what I'll have to content myself with because I don't know if I can do any better."

Kelly, like Linda, came to believe that she could not do any better. She described her difficulty as not having learned to study well enough to make the grades she wanted without having to give all her time to studying. At the end of her freshman year, she seemed to be resigned to a diminished commitment to doing well academically and decided to increase her extracurricular activities. She stated that next year she planned to get more involved in nonacademic activities "because I wouldn't use this time any better. . . . It's just like the time would be wasted." The changes these women made were not explained as carefully thought-out decisions to pursue a better major or career. Rather, they were explained as ways to reduce the burden of schoolwork and be able to spend time doing other things that the women like to do—as ways to scale down their commitment to schoolwork.

As they reduced their commitment to schoolwork, these five women began to devote more time and energy to romantic and other peer relationships. They all spent their freshmen and sophomore years worried about finding the right man with whom to share a romantic relationship. All five continued relationships with high school boyfriends once at college. For one reason or another, all but Linda decided they were not satisfied with these relationships and looked, ever more desperately as time went on, for better prospects. Linda "broke up" with her high school boyfriend during her freshman year and spent some time dating other men. However, she and her boyfriend soon got back together, and she spent more and more time away from SU and with him at his apartment.

Paula, who came to college interested in becoming a doctor, was perhaps an extreme case of what happened to those women with a "doing well" orientation. By the end of her freshman year, she seemed to plan her coursework with boyfriends in mind. First, she lost sight of her original goal of becoming a doctor before the end of her first semester in college. At the same time, she began having trouble going to class, staying awake in class, and reading the material. She said, "It's so hard to get into studying . . . or going to class. I just feel like, oh well, I'll do it tomorrow." She complained about classes being "boring" and about not being able to see how they were "relevant" to anything she might actually do. Bemoaning her situation at the end of her freshman year, she said, "I want to do something constructive . . . [like] get into a relationship with someone [a man]."

Paula, once she gave up her original goal, at first relied on her girl-friends' course selections to provide her direction in choosing courses for her sophomore year: "You think it'll be fun 'cause you'll have a friend in the class . . . maybe it'll make you go to class more. . . . Like chem, last semester: I could have done better if I'd gone to class more, but I knew three out of four hundred in there, and I'd just met them. So, I didn't feel bad about missing class 'cause I didn't know anybody in it." Paula hoped that with someone to walk with to class, someone to see and talk to once she got there, and someone to study with, she might be motivated enough to do the work she needed to do to get through her courses.

During her sophomore year Paula was still struggling but not as much; she had gotten a better sense of what she liked about her classes: "My chem lab is a lot better than last year. I'm surrounded by eight boys—it helps!" She also had decided that schoolwork was worthwhile because it allowed her to develop interests that would make her attractive to men: "I heard that each person of the marriage needs to develop their own interests so that you can be a more inter-esting person. . . . If you had nothing but the house [i.e., as a house-wife would] . . . and you got a divorce, then you wouldn't be appealing to anyone else."

Paula was the only woman in our ethnographic study (of those who stayed in college) who had not settled on what was to become her final college major by the time the ethnographic study ended. She did not seem too worried about her indecision, however: "Some-one told me that [employers] don't really care what you major in or what your grades are . . . I guess in some ways I want to be a house-wife, a mother. . . . It would be the greatest thing in the world . . . just not working . . . just taking care of children and not studying." Not surprisingly, Paula married shortly after college. Paula, as is ev-ident in the opening vignette, did not, in 1987, have much invested in her career.

In sum, it appeared that as these women divested themselves of strong student or schoolwork-related identities, they invested more of themselves in romantic identities. As schoolwork became less cen-tral to their lives, romantic relationships became more important. (For a detailed description of this process, see Holland and Eisenhart 1990).

Lisa, one of the women at SU, may have held a "doing well" ori-entation, but we were not able confidently to place her in this group because her views about schoolwork were so affected by her boy-friend. Unlike any of the others during their first two years of college,

Lisa had an interest in maintaining a particular romantic relationship that seemed to overwhelm completely her own ideas about her career and future. Although Lisa was exceptional in our study, her orientation toward schoolwork and her future work, like some of her other experiences at college, seemed to presage what some of the other women, especially in the "doing well" group, would face as they became more heavily involved in and committed to their romantic relationships.

Lisa had a steady (older) boyfriend who attended SU before her. When asked why she selected SU, she said, "I always wanted to go here because [my boyfriend] was here." In most things that Lisa did at college, including her academic work, she followed her boyfriend's lead: "He has a lot to do with the way I am. . . . He is the main person who . . . I imitate—not imitate, I wouldn't say, but base my behavior. That's it: base my behavior. . . . He's like a big brother who really cares a lot. . . . You know, the big brother is all the time: 'Well, I don't think you should do this,' or 'That guy's just taking advantage of you,' or something like that . . . just pointing out situations I wasn't aware of at the time . . . because they were, you know, new to me or something."

One specific way Lisa based her behavior on her boyfriend's advice was evident when she was reconsidering her college major. She had begun college planning to major in art but soon came to feel, after some questioning by her boyfriend, that she would need to find something else: a field in which she could hope to get a job. At first she thought about art therapy, but her interest was really captured by a course she was taking in her boyfriend's major. When she mentioned her interest to her boyfriend, he told her that she was not suited for that field. He also pointed out that if they majored in the same field, they would have to find two jobs in that field later. Lisa subsequently settled on education with her boyfriend's approval, saying, "He probably knows best. . . . He knows me so well." Lisa also noted that she did not expect to be well paid in education, but at least she would be able to find work: "There are a lot of jobs in that, even around here." It appeared that Lisa was letting her boyfriend take the lead in determining how she would think about her coursework and her future job prospects. As she envisioned her future life with him, she allowed him to set the parameters of her occupational future.

Velma at Bradford seemed at first to escape. In contrast to those described above, she seemed able to make the grades she wanted and resist, though just barely, the temptation to join in more peer activities: "I know one night I had a biology exam the next day, and I came so close to that campus dance, but something was saying, 'No, you stay and study for your biology exam.' And I did well on that exam and I was so glad I stayed. . . . I think I still could have went to the party and took my exam too, but I probably wouldn't have made as high." At the same time, she claimed to have a boyfriend at home and to be very shy around men on campus: "I have a hard time to look in a [man's] face. I play with my nails, anything. It happened this past weekend. This guy said, 'All I could see was your ear.' I'm going to try to do better. . . . I think I'm nervous if I look in their face. I start trembling, heart beating fast. If I'm turned the other way, it's ok. . . . It's just the opposite sex. If it's a female, [I'm] ok." It became evident by her sophomore year that Velma was not going to be able to maintain her momentum. She became more and more popular with men and dropped out of college before 1983.

Of the women in this group, only one, Natalie at SU, was able to continue to do as well in college as she had done in high school. She did not change her major, and she did not feel that she had to sacrifice time spent with friends to accomplish her academic goals. She also did not become very involved in romantic relationships. She never had a "boyfriend" during the ethnographic study, although she participated actively in campus social activities, such as parties and mixers, where romantic relationships were enacted.

In addition, Natalie, unlike the others with the "doing well" model, seemed to have a special kind of support from her family. She had ongoing help and assistance in learning about her specific career choice from her father, who introduced her to people he knew in her field and arranged for her to visit several firms. She also got advice about courses and professors from her older brother who had attended SU and had majored in the same field.

Everyone in this group, except Velma, graduated from college. By 1987, Linda and Natalie had begun careers based on their college majors, but the others were working in clerical or "odd" jobs (waitressing, cleaning, and the like). Lisa pursued a career in education, but she and Linda described themselves as "following" their husbands or husbands-to-be, that is, choosing their jobs or residences according to their husbands' careers. Only Natalie, who still had no serious romantic relationship, was pursuing her own "career" in the sense we defined earlier.

As a group (based on the survey) the women at SU were similar to those in the ethnographic sample who held the "doing well" model of schoolwork. Many were not very certain whether their major was the best one for them. Many were still in the process of winnowing their best subject from among their perceived abilities. They were sensitive to experiences and indications that could be taken as either confirming or disconfirming their own suitability for a major. For them, "comparative evaluation of major"—that is, the balance of rewards, perceived ability to succeed, and costs to them that were associated with the major—was the main predictor of "commitment to pursue training in the chosen major" (path coefficient $= .572$, $p =$ .0001, see Holland and Eisenhart 1981:89). Their assessments of the legitimacy of the costs of pursuing training in general were not associated with their commitment to pursue training as was the case for the women at Bradford. As far as career path went, the SU women appeared to be uncertain what aspects of themselves they should develop, whereas the Bradford women were more likely to be uncertain whether the costs of college were worth the benefits. Although the SU women also expressed pragmatic concerns, they were less likely than the Bradford women to view college primarily as a place where one goes to obtain the credentials needed to pursue a career.

The survey data also suggested that, for SU women, peer activities and relationships affected commitment to pursue their major. Peer activities and relationships affected commitment through the intervening variable of "energy available for studies." "Extraordinary demands from peers" was inversely related (path coefficient $= -.240$, $p = .005$) and "indirect help/happiness from others" was positively correlated (path coefficient $= .386$, $p = .0001$) with "energy available for studies." At Bradford, none of the peer-related variables was strongly associated with "energy available for studies" (Holland and Eisenhart 1981:94).

Learning from Experts and Managing Peers. The women with this model (two at Bradford, two at SU) believed the purpose of doing academic work at college was to master an area of expertise one wished to pursue into the future. Although concerned about grades and obtaining their degrees, these women were more concerned about finding people in the university setting they considered "expert," especially in their subject of interest. For them, low grades were setbacks but were taken as an indication of one's lack of mastery, not of one's unsuitability for major or career. Professors were sought out not because they were easy or entertaining but because they could teach a subject of interest. One woman in this group said, "I love speech and English. I like writing and I like talking about what I write, but it's the proper way of [doing it] that I have trouble comprehending. I want to major in [English] and I want to get it down solid. . . . It's a lot to learn. But since I got to college . . . the instructor . . . he's an expert and I'm an amateur. . . . He's published five or six books and he knows every corner of a good paper. . . . I always wanted an instructor that was real strict on the way I write and he is. . . . He's been critiquing me hard. That's why if I get a good grade, I'll feel like I've accomplished something."

These women also participated in peer activities and romantic relationships; however, they had a sense of wanting to contain these activities so they could pursue their other interests. One of the women in this group, Karla, chose a boyfriend with extraordinary demands on his time and had this to say about dates: "[My boyfriend] is my favorite date. . . . He's very busy; he usually can get free for only one night a week. He's a workaholic. . . . [But] he allows me as much freedom as I want. . . . My main complaint [about another guy who wants to go out with her] is that he is continually calling me. He wants to take up all my time. . . . I feel like a dog trying to take a walk with this slow little human dragging behind." Because her boyfriend could only go out occasionally and she was not very interested in the activities of her other peers, Karla managed to be free, relative to women in the other groups, to pursue her career interests at college.

The two Bradford women in this group refused to let their relationships with men become "too close." When things got serious, they consistently "cooled off" the relationship and did not jeopardize the time they devoted to academic interests. One said, "I don't believe in getting serious with guys; I think I'm too young. They have a lot on their hands . . . to get an education. And so do I."

Kandace, another woman in this group, viewed college as a place to get to know, and especially to talk at length with, people—professors, other students, townspeople. She was searching for experts who could help her understand and develop herself as an individual.

The women with the "learning from experts" model came to college with a cultural model that made learning important to them, were able to sustain their model throughout our study, and had the ability or luck to keep their romantic and other peer relationships from taking time away from school-related interests. Unlike the women with the "doing well" orientation, these women were not derailed by lower grades. Unlike the women with the "getting over" orientation, these women saw themselves as directly profiting from meaningful activities rather than putting in time doing arbitrary exercises for the purpose of obtaining a degree in the distant future. These women had and were able to maintain a commitment to themselves as students. All of them graduated from college with their original major or with an augmented version of their original major. All of them pursued their college majors into graduate work or a job in their field. In contrast to the few (only three: Linda, Lisa, and Natalie, or 17.6 percent) with other schoolwork orientations who pursued their majors in any way after graduating from college, 100 percent of the women with the "learning from experts" model pursued their college career interests after graduation.

In sum, the competing demands of schoolwork and the peer system were handled in different ways depending on the woman's schoolwork model.[11] The general outcomes fell into two patterns. The first pattern predominated. Sixteen of the twenty-one women whose cases we analyzed from the ethnographic study held the models of schoolwork in exchange for "getting over" or for "doing well." As discussed, they received little support from the peer culture for developing or maintaining a commitment to career during college. One other woman, Lisa, let her boyfriend control her decisions about her schoolwork and her career. Of these seventeen, only one, Natalie, pursued her college major into her own career, without consideration of a man in her life. Perhaps because of the strong support she received for her chosen career from her family, especially from her father, she, unlike the others, did not become very involved in the peer system at college.[12]

The second type of outcome for the ethnographic sample was quite different. The four women who held the view of schoolwork as "learning from experts" were able to maintain and, in some cases, further develop a commitment to career in college.

The pattern that predominated in the ethnographic study appeared to predominate in the survey responses as well. In general, the survey responses from the women on the two campuses were consistent with the pattern found in the ethnographic study. At Bradford, the survey responses suggested that the model of schoolwork for "getting over" was most common among the women on campus; at SU, the model of schoolwork for "doing well" seemed to be the most prevalent. If this is an accurate summary of the situation on the two campuses, it appears a large proportion of the women, regardless of campus, had orientations to schoolwork that easily derailed them. Their experiences on campus eroded their views of their future careers and they were drawn to committing considerable time and energy to the campus peer system.

Conclusion

Although the college women in our study spent more time at school than they ever had before in their lives and although they were required by the university to choose a field of study and, thus indirectly, to choose possible future occupations, these school-related matters did not turn out to be compelling to most of the women we studied. Despite their announced commitment to a major and a career at the beginning of their college experience, a number of the women came to college with vague visions of themselves in a future career. They had few experiences during their first two years of college that encouraged them to develop their vision or bolster their commitment in the peer-dominated environment of college life. Instead, the campus peer system captured their attention and encouraged them to devote time and energy to the development of peer, and especially romantic, relationships.

In the case of those women with the "getting over" model, especially the black women at Bradford, the payoff for completing a degree did not always seem worth the costs. Their views were reminiscent of the views of the black community in the United States as described in Ogbu's (1974) work. For blacks, schooling is a less sure avenue to good jobs than it is for whites. Since the women with the "getting over" model tended to see the content of schoolwork as irrelevant to their future careers *and* often felt doubts about the relationship between getting a degree and getting a job, they sometimes considered it futile to continue college. Even though they had ideas of future careers, they seemed to find schoolwork and the other costs of college too much to pay. Several of these women left Bradford before completing their degrees.

In the case of those women with the "doing well" model, their difficulties maintaining the grade point averages they had easily made in high school, coupled with the pull of the peer system, led them to scale down their ideas of the fields in which they could do well and to redirect their zeal for schoolwork to developing and maintaining romantic relationships.

For a minority of the women—the four with the "learning from experts" model and Natalie—career commitment was sustained and perhaps flourished at college. In a sense, the model they held seemed to protect them from the peer system. They were able to maintain their commitment to schoolwork and career, despite the constant pressure from peers to become more committed to romantic relationships. For the majority (the other seventeen), however, their attention was diverted from career-related pursuits toward peer-related, often gender-oriented, pursuits. For them, the outcomes with respect to their careers were continued vagueness in career identity or a scaled-down commitment to career (relative to what it was when they entered college) in favor of commitment to romantic relationships.

Although a peer culture could conceivably stimulate the development and elaboration of career-related identities for women, this was not the case at either Bradford or SU. Instead, the peer cultures were dominated by social and romantic emphases that tended to compete with and overwhelm, rather than encourage, academic activities and the formation of career identities. The peer culture offered a competing and distracting arena.

For the women in our study, the peer culture provided an arena that required energy and effort from all and supplied alternative opportunities for the women's futures. The peer culture urged on everyone romantic involvement and a concern with being attractive. It also provided a fallback for women with the "getting over" model who tended not to invest themselves in their schoolwork and a fallback for women with the "doing well" model when their grades fell below what they were accustomed to receiving in high school.

Previous explanations for women's career choices have not taken into account peer relationships and particularly the peer culture we found so important in our study. The explanations concerning the socialization of gender roles and need fulfillment do not consider the peer *context* to be a crucial aspect of socialization to career. The cultural reproduction explanations do not consider the peer culture to be a major mediator of gender relations and thus miss its importance in diverting women into traditional roles.

In contrast, our study, like Willis's and Fordham and Ogbu's, suggests the peer culture affects even those who do not directly participate. It promotes a system with which one has to deal and, in the residential college setting at least, provides a large portion of the context for the women en route to possible careers. Depending on individuals' views of school and of self in school, they fall prey—some easily, some not—to peer group activities and values. Peer culture and its emphasis on romantic involvement for women must be added to family socialization patterns, individual personality development, and institutional structures as an important influence on women's career decisions.

Some will read this essay and wonder whether the situation we have described is changing. They will also wonder whether our findings are peculiar to the South. It may be that different orientations would be found among college women now. Perhaps feminist orientations are more widespread. Perhaps women are more cognizant of the feminization of poverty. It is likely, however, that orientations toward schoolwork are slow to change, and there is little evidence to suggest that campus cultures have drastically reoriented from their emphasis on romance and attractiveness. We suspect that women now entering college are facing the same sort of peer groups they faced in the early 1980s, that they have similar models or understandings of schoolwork, and that they are being derailed from careers at roughly the same rates we found.

NOTES

We are indebted to the National Institute of Education, the University of Research Council of the University of North Carolina at Chapel Hill, and the College of Education of Virginia Polytechnic Institute and State University for their funding of this research. We are especially grateful to the women in the study and the interviewers who assisted us.

1. All proper names and place names used in reference to the study are pseudonyms.

2. We use the term *traditional* to refer loosely to the general pattern of female participation in certain college majors, occupations, and other adult activities. Correspondingly, the term *nontraditional* is used to refer to majors, occupations, and other activities conventionally associated with men and usually considered to be higher-status, more lucrative, and more career-oriented than those associated with women.

3. A full account of the study is in Holland and Eisenhart (1990).

4. Based on our research, we would say that women do make some decisions and choices that ultimately affect their futures, including whether they pursue a career; however, it may be quite misleading to speak of them as choosing a career in the sense that "choice" implies knowledge of options, the availability of options, the feasibility of options, or the thoughtful consideration of options (see also Eisenhart 1985).

5. Although our study took place on two university campuses, it focused on the influence of women's peer groups on their career-related decisions— an influence we think has been inadequately recognized in the literature— and not on the influence of the schools' institutional structures. We thus did not attend the women's classes, nor did we try to analyze the organization or structure of their coursework or degree programs. For an interesting study of this aspect of university life, see Nespor 1989.

6. In reviewing the choice of majors among the students who volunteered for the study, we discovered differences in the distribution of math and science majors on the two campuses. A significant number of the white applicants named pure math or science majors, whereas none of the black applicants did. In contrast, many more blacks than whites named business

and therapeutic fields (which might be categorized as "applied" math/science). This situation led us to distinguish "pure" from "applied" math/science fields and to select women with somewhat different majors as representative of the math/science group on each campus. Thus, the white sample included several pure math/science majors, whereas the black sample included only applied math/science majors. In Table 1, the majors of the women in the ethnographic sample are designated by category, rather than by specific field, to preserve the anonymity of the women.

7. The hypothesized factors yielded multiple correlation coefficients of .591—significant at the .0001 level—for Bradford and .676—significant at the .0001 level—for SU (Holland and Eisenhart 1981). This essay relies, in part, on previous analyses of both the ethnographic and survey data. For a fuller account of the ethnographic data, see Holland and Eisenhart (1988a, 1988b, 1990); for a fuller account of the survey data, see Holland and Eisenhart (1981).

8. The question used to ascertain "commitment" was: "All things considered, how certain are you that you will continue with your chosen major? ———% (put a number between 0 and 100." One respondent did not answer this question.

9. Although there were some differences in the peer cultures at Bradford and SU, they are not important to the topic of this essay. For extensive discussions of them, see Holland and Eisenhart (1989, 1990).

10. The predominance of this orientation at Bradford is probably no accident. Ogbu's research has consistently found that black Americans have a skeptical view of schools. After all, they have traditionally faced discrimination in schools as well as job ceilings against which school credentials are useless. See Holland and Eisenhart (1990) for more discussion of this orientation.

11. Sue Lees (1986:118–54), through open-ended interviews in London secondary schools, found fifteen- to sixteen-year-old girls have a somewhat similar variety of orientations to schoolwork. The research she describes was not longitudinal as ours was; however, she did find that those girls who were most alienated from learning or from schools as a place to see friends were the ones most likely to emphasize romance. We review the research on women's response to schooling in Holland and Eisenhart (1990) and suggest that in-depth studies such as ours and Lees's will tend to find similar relationships between work orientations and romance for girls and young women in Britain as well as the United States.

12. In 1987 we learned that Sandy, who dropped out of SU before the end of our ethnographic study, had just begun to develop her own career. Her new career was not based on her college major but on some of her postcollege experiences in the working world.

REFERENCES

Anyon, Jean. 1981. "Social Class and School Knowledge." *Curriculum Inquiry* 11(1):3–42.

Astin, Alexander W., K. C. Green, W. S. Korn, and M. Maier. 1983. *The American Freshman: National Norms for Fall 1983.* Los Angeles: UCLA Higher Research Institute.

Astin, Helen S. 1983. "The Meaning of Work in Women's Lives: A Sociopsychological Model of Career Choice and Work Behavior." *The Counseling Psychologist* 12(4):117–26.

Boli, John, Mary Lou Allen, and Adrienne Payne. 1983. "Women and Men in Introductory Undergraduate Mathematics and Chemistry Courses." Paper presented at the Annual Meeting of the American Educational Research Association, Montreal, Canada.

Bowles, Samuel, and Herbert Gintis. 1976. *Schooling in Capitalist America.* New York: Basic Books.

Brophy, Jere, and Thomas Good. 1974. *Teacher-Student Relationships: Causes and Consequences.* New York: Holt, Rinehart and Winston.

Coleman, James S. 1961. *The Adolescent Society.* New York: Free Press.

Connell, R. W., D. J. Ashenden, S. Kessler, and G. W. Dowsett. 1982. *Making the Difference: Schools, Families and Social Division.* Sydney: George Allen and Unwin.

Eccles, Jacquelynne S. 1987. "Gender Roles and Women's Achievement-Related Decisions." *Psychology of Women Quarterly* 11:135–72.

———. 1989. "Girl Friendly Instruction in Math and the Sciences." Paper presented at the University of Colorado, Boulder.

Eccles, Jacquelynne S., and J. Jacobs. 1986. "Social Forces Shape Math Participation." *Signs: Journal of Women in Culture and Society* 11:367–80.

Eder, Donna. 1985. "The Cycle of Popularity: Interpersonal Relations among Female Adolescents." *Sociology of Education* 58:154–65.

Eder, Donna, and Stephen Parker. 1987. "The Cultural Production and Reproduction of Gender: The Effect of Extracurricular Activities on Peer-Group Culture." *Sociology of Education* 60:200–213.

Eisenhart, Margaret A. 1985. "Women Choose Their Careers: A Study of Natural Decision Making." *Review of Higher Education* 8:247–70.

Eisenhart, Margaret A., and Dorothy C. Holland. 1983. "Learning Gender from Peers: The Role of Peer Groups in the Cultural Transmission of Gender." *Human Organization* 42:321–22.

Fordham, Signithia, and John U. Ogbu. 1986. "Black Students' School Success: Coping with the 'Burden of Acting White.' " *Urban Review* 18(3):176–206.

Gaskell, Jane. 1985. "Course Enrollment in the High School: The Perspective of Working-Class Females." *Sociology of Education* 58:48–59.

Goffredson, Linda S. 1981. "Circumscription and Compromise: A Developmental Theory of Occupational Aspirations" *Journal of Counseling Psychology* 28:545–79.

Hafner, Anne L. 1985. "Gender Differences in College Students' Educational and Occupational Aspirations: 1971–1983." Paper presented at the Annual Meeting of the American Educational Research Association, Chicago, Illinois.

Holland, Dorothy C. n.d. "How Cultural Systems Become Desire: A Case Study of American Romance." Unpublished manuscript.

Holland, Dorothy C., and Margaret A. Eisenhart. 1981. *Women's Peer Groups and Choice of Career: Final Report*. Washington, D.C.: National Institute of Education.

———. 1988a. "Moments of Discontent: University Women and the Gender Status Quo." *Anthropology and Education Quarterly* 19(2):115–38.

———. 1988b. "Women's Ways of Going to School: Cultural Reproduction of Women's Identities as Workers." In *Class, Race, and Gender in American Education*, ed. L. Weis. Albany: SUNY Press.

———. 1989. "On the Absence of Women's Gangs in Two Southern Universities." In *Women in the South: An Anthropological Perspective*, ed. H. Mathews. Athens: University of Georgia Press.

———. 1990. *Educated in Romance: Women, Achievement, and College Culture*. Chicago: University of Chicago Press.

Holland, Dorothy C., and Debra Skinner. 1987. "Prestige and Intimacy: The Cultural Model behind American's Talk about Gender Types." In *Cultural Models in Language and Thought*, ed. D. Holland and N. Quinn. New York: Cambridge University Press.

Holland, J. L. 1985. *Making Vocational Choices: A Theory of Vocational Personalities and Work Environments*. Englewood Cliffs, N.J.: Prentice-Hall.

Horowitz, Helen L. 1987. *Campus Life: Undergraduate Cultures from the End of the Eighteenth Century to the Present*. New York: Alfred A. Knopf.

Hunter College Women's Studies Collective. 1983. *Women's Realities, Women's Choices*. New York: Oxford University Press.

Kessler, S., D. J. Ashenden, R. W. Connell, and G. W. Dowsett. 1985. "Gender Relations in Secondary Schooling." *Sociology of Education* 58:34–48.

Lees, Sue. 1986. *Losing Out: Sexuality and Adolescent Girls*. London: Hutchinson.

Nespor, Jan. 1989. "Gender, Ethnicity, and Organizational Structure in the Choice of a College Major." Paper presented at the American Educational Research Association, April, San Francisco, California.

Ogbu, John U. 1974. *The Next Generation: An Ethnography of Education in an Urban Neighborhood*. New York: Academic Press.

———. 1978. *Minority Education and Caste: The American System in Cross-Cultural Perspective*. New York: Academic Press.

———. 1988. "Class Stratification, Racial Stratification, and Schooling." In *Class, Race, and Gender in American Education*, ed. L. Weis. Albany: SUNY Press.

Rapoport, Rhona, and Robert N. Rapoport. 1976. *Dual-Career Families Reexamined: New Integrations of Work and Family*. London: Martin Robertson.

Schwartz, G. 1972. *Youth Culture: An Anthropological Approach*. Addison-Wesley Module in Anthropology, No. 17. Reading, Mass.: Addison-Wesley.

Spradley, James P. 1979. *The Ethnographic Interview*. New York: Holt, Rinehart and Winston.

————. 1980. *Participant Observation*. New York: Holt, Rinehart and Winston.

Tittle, Carol K., and Sharon L. Weinberg. 1984. "Job Choice: A Review of the Literature and a Model of Major Influences." Paper presented at the Annual Meeting of the American Educational Research Association, New Orleans, Louisiana.

Valli, Linda, 1986. *Becoming Clerical Workers*. Boston: Routledge and Kegan Paul.

Willis, Paul. 1977. *Learning to Labor: How Working Class Kids Get Working Class Jobs*. New York: Columbia University Press.

PART 2

Medical Issues

Dona Lee Davis

Gender and Elective Surgery in a Newfoundland Fishing Village

Within the last twenty years Newfoundland health policy makers concerned with high rates of both population growth and uterine cancer instituted provincewide birth control and cervical cancer screening programs. Soon after the introduction of these programs, Newfoundland rates for surgical removal of the uterus and interruption of the fallopian tubes became among the highest in Canada. Health professionals have assumed that local acceptance of these two surgical procedures was based on informed decision making of a sort similar to that of medical models or the reasoning of the physicians themselves. An examination of notions of biology and gender, which characterize women's sense of self in an isolated Newfoundland fishing community, demonstrates how rapid growth in the rates of two kinds of elective surgical procedures—hysterectomy and tubal ligation—was affected by local sociocultural factors as well as medical ones.

A preference for operations and drastic means of female health maintenance cannot be understood apart from the village value system and social structure. On the village level, the young woman's preference for tubal ligation (as the major means of contraception) and the older woman's preference for hysterectomy (as a preventative measure against problems of "the change") cannot be understood apart from an analysis of recent culture change and its effect on local values and the relationships between the generations of older and younger females. Also intrinsic to surgical decision making are local, gender-specific notions of health, such as blood and purging, which are instrumental in the acceptance of and demand for these two operations as cure-alls for a wide variety of female health complaints.

Data on both hysterectomies and tubal ligations are considered, although the data on hysterectomies are far more plentiful. The two operative procedures may be quite distinct to the epidemiologist, but to the village Newfoundlander they represent two facets of the same phenomenon. Although locals understand the primary purposes are different, they see an overlap in the secondary purposes. Both operations involve notions of blood and purging, images of the good woman, and the idea of "limited good" (a gain in one area results in loss in another). Young women are receptive to a surgical sterilization for the same reasons older women are receptive to a hysterectomy.

Medical issues concerning rates of elective surgery in general, and hysterectomy and tubal ligation in particular, are discussed first. Analysis of recent trends in rates for these two procedures in the Province of Newfoundland follows. Then attention is focused on one specific outport, Grey Rock Harbour, and the local factors affecting women's medical/health decision making. The ethnographic material from Grey Rock Harbour is discussed in terms of current theories on class, community, and gender constructs. Finally, strategies for alleviating problems in the abuse of surgical procedures are presented.

Medical Issues

Medical researchers have documented variation in the rates of hysterectomies (Mindell, Vayda, and Cardillo 1982; Walton 1976) and tubal ligations (Presser and Bumpass 1972) through time and space. Although both surgical procedures can be treated as elective surgery, hysterectomies may be curative (e.g., cancer of the cervix) as well as prophylactic, whereas tubal ligations are always prophylactic. Factors influencing the rates of hysterectomy and tubal ligation as elective surgical procedures include (1) the process of surgical decision making among physicians in a male-dominated profession; (2) the number of doctors, hospital beds, and health facilities in a specific area; and (3) the role of the patient or potential patient in medical and surgical decision making. A brief review of the literature shows how the sociocultural dynamics of the third factor have been overlooked—especially in terms of hysterectomy rates.

Hysterectomy

Hysterectomy is the most frequently performed major operation in North America. In the United States and Canada, the late 1960s ushered in dramatic increases in the number of hysterectomies performed (Cole and Berlin 1977; Dyck, Murphy, and Korchinski 1977a, 1977b; A. B. Miller 1981; Sofer, Roos, and Nelson 1983; Vayda, Mindell, and Rutkow 1982). The change cannot be attributed solely to changes in the age structure of the female population or to a higher incidence of diseases of the uterus. Frequencies increased due to greater use of elective indicators, such as uterine cancer prophylaxis, contraception, and menopausal problems, especially bleeding (Cole and Berlin 1977:117–18). There is considerable geographical variation in the number of hysterectomies performed. In the 1960s, annual hysterectomy rates per 1,000 females ranged from 4.7 for Canada and 4.3 for the United States to a low of 2.1 for Wales and England (Cole and Berlin 1977:118). In Canada the rise of hysterectomy rates, as well as the rise in other elective surgical procedures, coincided with the introduction of universal health insurance in the late 1960s (Sofer, Roos, and Nelson 1983:104).

Between 1964 and 1971 the number of hysterectomies in Saskatchewan increased by 72.1 percent. In 1972 the College of Physicians and Surgeons of Saskatchewan, concerned about the increase, appointed a committee to study hysterectomies. The committee, even granting that bleeding and pelvic congestion syndrome were justifiable indicators for hysterectomy, found 30.8 percent of the operations to be unacceptable (N. F. Miller 1976:804). After the findings of the committee were published, hysterectomy rates dropped dramatically both in Saskatchewan and throughout Canada (Dyck, Murphy, and Korchinski 1977b:1326–27).

As in the Saskatchewan case, most studies look to the medical profession itself to explain variation in the incidence of elective surgeries. Ira M. Rutkow, Alan A. Gittelsohn, and George D. Zuidena (1979:409) conducted a randomized, controlled survey of surgical specialists in an attempt to discover patterns for recommending (or not recommending) surgery, including hysterectomies. The data revealed a marked divergence of opinion among surgeons concerning the need for surgery. The researchers concluded that surgical decision making is, at best, a semiexact scientific process. Similar investigations have shown that for many common elective surgical situations, the opinions rendered will differ significantly from one surgeon to the next (Lewis 1969; LoGerfo 1977; N. F. Miller 1976; Vayda, Mindell, and Rutkow 1982).

Surgeons' attitudes toward an operation partly determine its frequency. Although many surgeons refuse to perform unnecessary surgery (Dyck, Murphy, and Korchinski 1977a:1363), some surgeons feel the so-called prophylactic surgery or "birthday hysterectomy" is justifiable and urge it for all women (Cole and Berlin 1977:118). The strongest advocacy of prophylactic hysterectomy in the medical literature comes from the dated but often-quoted statement by Ralph C. Wright (1969:561): "today, because of widespread training of competent gynecologists, improvements in hospital care, the lab, blood bank, anesthesia and antibiotics, the safety of pelvic operations has permitted us to broaden our indications for hysterectomy. . . . the uterus has but one function: reproduction; after the last planned pregnancy, the uterus becomes a useless, bleeding, symptoms-producing, potentially cancer-bearing organ and therefore should be removed."

Feminists have criticized such attitudes as the "useless uterus syndrome" and attribute them to the paternalist, masculinist, and misogynic structure of medicine (Klee 1988; Seaman 1975). There is a rich and expanding body of critical literature by women's health advocates that provides evidence for continued high rates of unnecessary gynecological surgery and challenges women to resist male domination of obstetrics-gynecology as an assault on female gender identity and as a product of a sexist, racist, and classist society (Bart and Grossman 1979; Keyser 1984; Klee 1988; Seaman 1975; Scully 1980).

Fluctuation in the rates of elective surgical procedures have also been related to the availability of resources, such as number of surgeons and hospitals (Dyck, Murphy, and Korchinski 1974; Miller, Lindsay, and Hill 1976; Scully 1980). The "hysterectomy epidemic" in Canada has been blamed on national health insurance (Lee 1977:671), yet rates in the United States have also gone up. Frank Dyck and Fergus Murphy (1977:670) state the increase is not altogether related to doctors' profit, explaining that when medical services are "free," patients request various services as a "right" and one of the operations most frequently requested is the prophylactic hysterectomy.

The role of the patient in high hysterectomy rates has been overlooked. The patient—her opinions, her questions, and her participation, as well as that of her family, friends, and community, in the surgical decision-making process—is a vital component in clinical decision making that is often ignored by medical researchers (Hanlon 1979:417). Patients frequently do not appreciate the risks of the surgery they request, although that might be changing. Frank Dyck, Fergus Murphy, and Barbara Korchinski (1977a:1366) state that a "few years ago women might have consulted their physicians to request or

even demand a hysterectomy, but patients now insist on a good reason for its performance." Medical analysts recognize the problem,
but they fail to address the patient's role as medical consumer. This is
especially true if the patient is not a middle-class, white North American.

Similar critiques are found in the women's health literature. In a
recent review article on the social significance of hysterectomies; Linnea Klee (1988) concludes that we know almost nothing about the following: how popular folk beliefs about female organs and
reproductive processes and sociocultural beliefs about women's roles
in the family and society influence women's attitudes toward hysterectomies; how hysterectomies affect women's self-concepts of sexuality, femininity, and aging; how women's own assessments of risk
(including fear of pain and confidence in medicine) and expectations
of treatment coincide with those of physicians; and how information
networks and interpersonal relations affect surgical decision making.

A close examination of recent and dramatic change in the opportunities for elective surgery in Newfoundland can shed some light on
these issues. Hysterectomy rates in Newfoundland are unique
among the Canadian provinces in two respects. First, since Newfoundland has the lowest per capita rates of physicians and hospital
beds of all the provinces, one would expect per capita rates for elective surgeries to be low. This is true for prostatectomy, colonectomy,
tonsillectomy, adenoidectomy, and cholecystectomy. Newfoundland
rates for hysterectomies and cesareans, however, were the highest in
Canada and remain high today. In 1974–76, hysterectomy rates were
the second highest (Nova Scotia was first). Second, while during the
1960s to late 1970s, the hysterectomy rates for Canada in general increased and then decreased, Newfoundland rates remained consistently high (Mindell, Vayda, and Cardillo 1982) until after 1978, when
they dropped and Newfoundland was ranked fifth among the ten
provinces. Hysterectomy rates for Newfoundland remained fairly
constant through 1986.[1]

High hysterectomy rates for Newfoundland can be partially explained by two important factors: (1) over the last two decades Newfoundland has had the highest mortality rates from cervical cancer in
Canada, and (2) Newfoundland has had a cervical cancer screening
program since 1962 (Miller, Lindsay, and Hill 1981:655). Taking into
account the incidence of cervical cancer and the screening programs,
to what extent can high hysterectomy rates also be explained by consumer preference for the operation as well as physicians' willingness

to perform prophylactic hysterectomies? This question will be addressed after a brief discussion of another type of commonly performed elective surgery: tubal ligation.

Tubal Ligation

From 1965 to the present, there has been a dramatic increase in rates of contraceptive sterilization in societies with modern, comprehensive health care institutions (Presser and Bumpass 1972:510; Westoff and Jones 1977:156). Trends in patterns of sterilization, however, are not uniform across all groups. According to medical researchers, blacks have more positive attitudes toward female sterilization than do whites, and women with low levels of income and education are more likely to be sterilized than are women at higher levels of income and education (Presser and Bumpass 1972:566). Rochelle N. Shain and Harold D. Dickson (1982:1069) cite access to medical services, high parity, and distrust of other means of contraception as factors in low-income women's positive attitudes toward tubal ligations and their willingness to get sterilized. More radical scholars attribute high rates of contraceptive sterilization among black and lower-class women to medical eugenics and racism (Scully 1980).

The sociocultural dynamics of consumer preferences for contraceptive surgery are much better understood than are those for hysterectomies. The increase in tubal ligations results from the worldwide family planning movement and its attempt to increase the use of fertility-regulating methods cross-culturally. Steven Polgar and John Marshall (1976) note that cross-culturally the adaptive value of various forms of fertility regulation is dependent on societal values, beliefs, preferences, and material conditions. They present five attributes of fertility-regulation methods that govern their acceptability to the user: (1) duration of the fertility-regulating action; (2) side effects; (3) routes of administration; (4) gender of user; and (5) miscellaneous attributes, such as reliability, reversibility, and coitus dependence. Polgar and Marshall, however, recognize that the introduction of new technologies does not always meet with planned results. Locals may react to innovations in unanticipated ways.

Newfoundlanders have been among the world's most prodigious producers of children. Today, there are more than a half-million Newfoundlanders, over 96 percent of whom are native born. The high birth rate and low death rate that caused Newfoundland's population to surge during the nineteenth century continued into the twentieth century; during the postwar baby boom the birth rate reached unprecedented levels. The Newfoundland government had made no effort to impede it; in fact, the government has reveled in the high birth rate (Matthews 1976:17). As the baby boom was ending elsewhere, Newfoundland joined Canada, expecting to enter a new era of hope and prosperity. The Newfoundland boom of the 1940s continued well into the 1960s, giving the province the highest birth rate in Canada and close to the highest in North America. Newfoundland's population has tended to grow so rapidly that its economic gains after 1949 have been largely negligible (Matthews 1976:14–15, 17).

Prior to 1969, it was illegal to distribute literature on contraception or to sell contraceptives in Newfoundland. Family planning in Newfoundland started in 1972 and aimed to provide education for doctors, nurses, social workers, teachers, and welfare officers as well as programs for students in these fields. Around the island, services were poor or nonexistent (Innis 1973; Alderdice et al. 1973). All medical advice came from local doctors.

From 1972 to 1974, rates of tubal ligations almost doubled, reaching a high again in 1976–77, only to decrease dramatically in 1979 to become the lowest in Canada.[2] Tubal ligation was the most commonly used nontraditional fertility-regulating method in Grey Rock Harbour. Provincial family planning advocates cite large families, high illegitimacy rates, early marriage, high unemployment, and low income as reasons for the increased use of fertility-regulating methods in Newfoundland (Innis 1973), but factors leading to the dramatic rise in tubal ligation rates are far more complex. Moreover, they are linked to a high incidence of hysterectomies. How are high rates of elective surgery reflected in the everyday lives of women as members of a specific community? These phenomena cannot be understood apart from the local context of gender, women's status, village egalitarianism, and folk concepts of female biology—(e.g., the theory of limited good applied to the female body).

Grey Rock Harbour

Although conceptually distinct in the medical and scientific literature, hysterectomies and tubal ligation are linked in the Newfoundland mind-set. Local women are highly cognizant of the increased rates of these two operations. While hysterectomies are in the domain of older women and tubal ligations are in the domain of younger women, gender and notions of purging blood act to make these operations conceptually analogous. They are requested, accepted, or rejected on the same premises. The following analysis of the community setting examines the factors of patient consumerism and its meaning in the wider community and the nonhealth-related sphere of women's lives.

The term *outport* commonly refers to the necklace of small, rural, comparatively isolated fishing villages surrounding the shores of the province. Located on the southwest coast of Newfoundland, the outport of Grey Rock Harbour is populated by approximately eight hundred inhabitants of English descent. The major source of employment is a year-round, inshore fishery. Most villagers (74 percent of the work force) earn their livelihood by fishing or working at the fish plant. Settled less than two hundred years ago, Grey Rock Harbour is a comparatively new village by Newfoundland standards. As in other outports, the history of Grey Rock Harbour is largely a chronicle of dismal poverty, isolation, and struggle for survival in a harsh environment. Since confederation with Canada in 1949, however, material conditions have steadily improved. In the mid-1960s, a dirt road was built connecting the village to larger population centers, where health service facilities and consumer products are readily available. Today, Grey Rock Harbour has all the modern conveniences and welfare and unemployment benefits that other rural areas of Canada have. Locals continue to take a great deal of pride in the tradition of the fishery. Their stoic endurance of hard times in the past and their preservation of valued traditions are seen as intrinsic elements in the Newfoundland character.

Fieldwork was conducted from October 1977 to December 1978.[3] During this time tubal ligation and hysterectomy rates were on the rise. Women of all ages in Grey Rock Harbour were fully aware of the sudden increase in surgical rates for operations that could be performed only on women. Sterilization was actively sought and positively valued by young women, as were hysterectomies by older women, and both became a major topic of everyday village gossip.

The most remarkable contemporary change in Grey Rock Harbour family life during the 1970s was the choice that young couples made to have surgical sterilization in their early twenties or thirties. "Tying the tubes," "tubals," or "tubal 'gations" were done in the hospital of a nearby village. The operation supposedly took place in secret, but community gossips were hard to deceive. Through self-admissions and gossip, one could conservatively estimate that over one-half (five) of the village women between the ages of twenty and thirty-five have "been fixed," and 16 percent between the ages of thirty-five and fifty-five have undergone hysterectomies.[4]

This can be partially explained by the commonly offered explanations of the new acceptability of these operations to the medical profession, free health insurance, and the rising number of medical care facilities. Yet sociocultural factors in the community are central to understanding local women's ready acceptance of the operations. The local context of these two forms of elective surgery is discussed in terms of (1) medical myths, (2) an unethical doctor, (3) mother-daughter relationships and the image of the "good woman," and (4) notions of blood and purging.

Medical Myths

Although relatively insular with a very strong sense of community, outporters are not unaware of the changes in the world about them. Health of individuals, personalities of health care practitioners, and evaluation of the treatment and kinds of health care provided are important topics of village conversation networks (Davis 1984). Medical or public health educators tend to depend on the media (e.g., television and print) in their attempt to make outporters responsible health care consumers. No matter how well intentioned public health educators may be, however, they often fail to take account of the process by which information is filtered through local communication networks and reinterpretated in light of folk beliefs and common experience. There is a great deal of medical misinformation in Grey Rock Harbour. In the following section, the local versions of the impact of modern medical technology are presented. This includes myths about tubal ligations and alternative forms of birth control as well as local ignorance and myths about the nature of hysterectomies.

Birth Control

A family planning survey found that 93 percent of Newfoundlanders knew about the pill as a method of family planning. According to family planning personnel (Innis 1973), this is a good sign. The assumption, however, that the convenience and effectiveness of the pill will result in its use is unwarranted. Close examination of Grey Rock Harbour shows that although people know about the pill, their understanding of how it works is erroneous and attitudes concerning use of the pill are consequently extremely negative.

Teenage women in Grey Rock Harbour make excellent informants. They talk freely and at length about their relations with boyfriends and the nature of "courting" (a euphemism for intercourse). The following information is based on my conversations with young women. Young women who use the pill are considered immoral. Girls usually start to date early, at ages eleven to thirteen, choosing boys two to four years older. As a consequence, marriage occurs at an early age. Sexual intimacy is thought to be a natural outcome of romantic attraction. Courting females depend on males for contraception, which usually consists of withdrawal or the condom (not available in the village). The belief prevails that "if he loves you and respects you, he will use something [a condom]." Since contraception is the man's responsibility, it is his fault if his methods fail and she becomes pregnant, and he is obligated to marry her. Use of condoms is not considered a dependable form of contraception, and their use implies a recognized risk of pregnancy. A young woman who uses the pill and is sexually active forfeits the "if it fails, I'll marry you" commitment from her lover and is considered loose or wayward. The reasoning behind this is that the use of an extremely effective means of contraception would mean a woman could risk having sexual relations with someone she was not committed to marrying. Sex without enough love to promise marriage is frowned upon, and women who use the pill are labeled promiscuous.

The status and use of the pill are further undermined by the following beliefs. First, they believe the pill is dangerous. Everyone in town knows a story about a woman who, after using the pill, bled to death during an operation—supposedly her blood would not clot. The important point about this story is not whether it is true but that women believe it and often repeat it.[5] Second, they believe that anything strong enough to kill all those germs (i.e., sperm) cannot be good for the rest of your body. Third, many women believe that if you start taking the pill too early, you may somehow use up its magical properties and will be unable to plan your family when you really want to do so. Fourth, people resent doctors who push any kind of contraception. They believe that doctors look down on them and urge them to use birth control so "their kind" will not reproduce. All of these beliefs undercut the credibility of both the pill and the doctor who prescribes it.

Despite the rumors that "local doctors hand them out like candy," young girls are fairly ignorant of the various methods of contraception and their availability. Although young women are hesitant to use effective birth control methods for both moral (good girls do not plan ahead) and rational (evidence from gossip) reasons, they are very interested in birth control, and it is a frequent topic of conversation. Since few girls read magazines or have any access to factual information or education on birth control, local gossip, which remains the major source of contraceptive education, is characterized by myth and falsehoods.

Other fertility-regulating devices also fare poorly in local lore. Intrauterine devices (I.U.D.s) are called the "the loop." The major "loop" horror story involved Esther "over in the bottoms" who "went to the doctor and got one of those loops. Next thing you know she's pregnant." This was confirmed by Esther herself, who blames the doctor for using her in "some kind of experience [experiment]." The Esther story was corroborated by my landlady's relative "down the coast," who also "got the loop and pregnant at the same time." Diaphragms are unheard of, probably because local doctors fail to recommend them and they are not advertised in any of the magazines or materials read by local women. Foams and jellies, although messy and inconvenient, are used by some women. They are, however, considered too dangerous for regular use, since, like the pill, "anything that can burn out all those germs [sperm] can't be good for your insides." Women who depend on these methods of birth control use them only when "I think I could get pregnant."

A few men are rumored to have had vasectomies. One man who recently had the operation was open about it among his peers, and it was the subject of lively gossip. I was asked to explain several times in "blunt terms" what had been done and if he would become a "sissy." It seems people did not differentiate between a vasectomy and castration, and they were surprised to find out how simple the operation really was.

The desire for reliable and easy forms of contraception is strong. Yet women are uncertain about potential side effects. They are consequently left weighing the horror stories about modern contraceptives against the unreliability of more traditional methods. Skepticism about modern contraceptive methods is widespread. This skepticism arises in part from a dependence on misleading and second-hand sources of information, particularly village gossip. The very nature of this gossip prevents women from making what any public health official would call an informed, rational decision about the type of method to use. Rejecting the pill and the I.U.D., most women opt for what they consider the least dangerous (and least effective) methods, such as withdrawal and rhythm, or the most effective method, sterilization.

Hysterectomy

There is far less controversy over the incidence of hysterectomy, which is viewed as a more acceptable operation. Women share views of cancer as a vile and loathsome disease. Like the earlier scourge of tuberculosis, cancer comes in many forms and has the connotation of being evil. Rates of uterine cancer in Newfoundland have been and are among the highest in Canada (Miller, Lindsay, and Hill 1976:604). Factors postulated to be epidemiologically related to high cervical cancer rates (e.g., early age of intercourse, multiple partners [in Newfoundland's case this is mostly premarital], and high parity) are present in Newfoundland (Walton 1976). The high rate of cervical cancer may partially account for the high rate of hysterectomies; however, only one woman in Grey Rock Harbour gave cancer as a reason for her operation. The majority sought medical attention for heavy and irregular bleeding and believe that is why they had to go "under the knife."

Women who told me they had "ectomies" did not know exactly what had been done to them.[6] They did not know whether the entire uterus had been removed or whether it was a partial operation. In addition, they thought hysterectomy and ovariectomy were the same operation.

Women are aware of the provincewide cervical screening program (A. B. Miller 1978). It does not necessarily work as well as it should, however. One woman, after providing a smear, received a letter in the mail saying her smear was positive. She kept waiting to be called back to the doctor. No request or invitation came. After suffering irregular, heavy bleeding for three years, she finally went to the doctor, who checked her records and told her she had been suffering from cancer for three years. Frustrated and disappointed by the provincial medical system, the young woman went to Nova Scotia to have her operation.

While I was in the field, a young women (age thirty-five) died of cancer of the bowel. Although she had had "troubles" for a long time, from the locals' point of view the doctor's diagnosis of cancer was followed by sudden death (the woman lived six months). There was a general cancer scare among all women of similar age. Many of them went to the doctor convinced that they would be the next sudden victim. Despite the fact that the woman died of bowel cancer, women feared "womb" cancer.[7] Most went to the doctor for a cervical smear. It was months before anyone heard results (some never did). The delay, worry, and fear that accompanied the waiting made women very resentful of what they perceived to be the callousness of the medical profession. One new and inexperienced physician was considered so rude and insensitive to the concerns of local women that he was boycotted, and he eventually left the region to practice elsewhere. Women's attitudes toward individual physicians, however, tend to be more ambivalent, as the next section demonstrates.

Unethical Physicians

Women tend to have a love-hate relationship with medical professionals. Some local women attribute the recent growth in the rate of tubal ligations and hysterectomies to one specific doctor.[8] Village gossip networks made this individual a folk hero/villain. He was an extremely controversial figure. Local attitudes toward him illustrate the combination of pessimism, optimism, and cynicism that characterize community attitudes toward outsiders, as evidenced by the following quotations from different women:

> It was Dr. _____ that sterilized all those women. It wasn't right. He cut [circumcised] all the little boys he birthed, too.

> He used to get $104 for each tubal he did. He made a fortune doing them. He didn't hide his motives. He was real brazen about it. He even asked me [a nurse] if I knew any women who could be talked into one. He even did it to real young women and that is very, very wrong.

> He couldn't have carried on like that with you. He did us in because we were poor and ignorant. To talk to him he was nice as can be . . . real sociable, but he must have felt we weren't fit to have babies.

> He was a criminal. Did it for the money. He's gone now and cannot come back.

> When I had my baby the doctor said I'd die if I ever had another. I asked about the pill. Doctor said that would kill me too. He never told me about anything else. I was seventeen.

> I went to the doctor to have my appendix out and he tied my tubes instead. I'd never had a baby. I was fifteen.

Despite his well-known unsavory reputation women were ready to go to this doctor precisely because he would perform the operation— no questions asked. Likewise, older women who had hysterectomies, although quick to criticize his "mutilation" of young girls, were eager to praise the same doctor for his bedside manner and effective surgery on older women:

> He's not like the others [other physicians]. They'll try to talk you out of it, especially if you were real young and only had one kid. I went to him because I knew he'd do it, no questions asked.

> When he cut you he was a miracle worker. Best doctor ever was. He did my 'ectomy and without that man I would not be here today.

The various attitudes toward this doctor are best explained in terms of the perspectives of two different generations of women.

Mother-Daughter Relationships and the Notion of Limited Good

Although part of the hesitancy to use convenient, effective means of birth control stems form misinformation, education alone would not influence the use of contraceptive methods. This is because the ambivalence displayed toward the more convenient methods reflects a continuity of values between mothers and their grown daughters. In the past, women derived character and high status from their unquestioning acceptance of an unexpected or undesired pregnancy. Women took pride in their stoic acceptance of fate and in their cherished values of self-sacrifice and emotional strength. The "good woman" was a hard worker who cared for her family as well as possible in circumstances of dire poverty and her husband's prolonged absence (Davis 1983b).

Older women believed that it was their fate to have children and any tampering with that fate was wrong. Resources were limited for everybody. According to the belief of "limited good," one person's gain would be another person's loss, or gain in one area of your life would result in loss in some other area. This belief is present today in that those who practice birth control (considered good and desirable) must pay a price. Such a point of view reflects the egalitarian ethic that it is an unfair way to get ahead. The reproductive patterns of today's young differ from those of their middle-aged mothers. Young women complete childbearing early in their marriage—usually in their early twenties—whereas many middle-aged women in their late thirties and forties continue to have children.

Young women's attitudes toward birth control differ from those of women whose reproductive careers began twenty years ago. Older women are ambivalent about the ethics of "being so selfish," but younger women feel that limiting family size is a key to an improved life-style—less work and better material conditions. Although their mothers and grandmothers frequently voice negative attitudes toward birth control, young women are not as resigned to their fate as childbearers as their mothers were. In fact, many women justify the early termination of their reproductive careers by pointing to their mothers's misery.

Mothers and daughters frequently have children the same age. Many young women sterilized today were still living with their parents when their own mothers discovered themselves pregnant with an unplanned "change of life" baby, a condition that was more often received with disappointment than delight. Young women equate poverty and the inability to get ahead in life with having large numbers of children. Young women commonly justify their decision to be sterilized with the belief that it will enable them to do more for the children they do have. Older women envy the freedom and resources of younger women, who often are surgically infertile while their mothers continue to reproduce. One forthright middle-aged woman told me, "The old buddies complain but if they'd of had the chance they'd of got fixed, too."

How do younger women maintain the status of "good woman" and operate within the system of limited good, so that their personal boon (fewer children) does not adversely affect the luck or circumstances of others? In my view, it is not merely coincidence that the preferred means of birth control among the younger women have built-in sacrifices or prices to pay. By choosing a method that allows them to maintain an image of martyr to their reproductive capacity, younger women compromise between the beliefs of their mother's generation and their own desire to limit family size. Withdrawal, rhythm, and sterilization are all practiced at some cost to the self and challenge one's strength of character. The pill is condemned precisely because it is easy, convenient, and effective.[9] As one women aptly put it, "Having no children today is sinfully easy."

A woman who practices withdrawal sees herself as a strong woman, a woman who controls herself in spite of sexual pleasure. Likewise, a woman who practices rhythm also sacrifices sexual pleasure by avoiding her man usually "sometime around the middle of the month." These women also realize they run greater risk of pregnancy. The mothers of daughters who practice withdrawal and rhythm generally approve of them and feel their daughters have not been "weakened" by the changes accompanying modernization.

In choosing sterilization, young women show rebellion against their mother's narrow perspective on birth control and at the same time outdo her in terms of self-sacrifice. Having your "tubes tied" is considered the most effective method. It is convenient and safe, yet one can also emphasize the suffering aspect: first, one must go to the hospital to be "cut up"; second, one sacrifices the option of having any children in the future; third, tying the tubes blocks off or prevents the flow of "natural juices" and can result in "women's problems," such as cramps and abnormal periods that can necessitate a hysterectomy later in life; and fourth, it will make you fat.

In contrast, the role of hysterectomies in relation to the "martyr complex" just described for tubal ligations is much more straightforward. The "good woman" is one who patiently endures all life's trails, overcoming them as best she can (Davis 1983a, 1984). The hysterectomy is just another trial for the woman who can continue to persevere, even when her body "turns against her." Operations enhance the drama of endurance.

In the context of the "good woman" and the ideal of limited good, both tubal ligation and hysterectomy take on an aura of what Robert Bolande (1969:591) calls "ritualistic surgery," or surgery in which the relationship between means and ends is not intrinsic. Aside from community egalitarianism, intergenerational relationships between women, and the mechanism of status enhancement and maintenance, folk notions of blood and purging also contributed to the localized nature of medical reasoning.

Blood and Purging

When it comes to local notions of blood and purging (cleaning the blood), hysterectomies and tubal ligations differ in one important respect: hysterectomies clean out the blood, but tubal ligations block it up. Blood is more than just the "red fluid" in your arteries and veins. The folk notion of blood also includes natural or "vital juices" (hormones and the like).

Concepts of blood are highly elaborated and instrumental in shaping a person's sense of his or her physical self. Health and character may be determined by states of blood—high/low, red/black, thick/thin, good/bad (Davis 1983a). Grey Rock Harbour men, women, and children traditionally subject their bodies to spring and fall cleaning by purges (taking laxatives) to clean the blood. This is particularly important for women, since regular bleeding is a noticeable part of their reproductive processes. Copious menses are seen as a sign of health and the body's own monthly purging. If menstrual blood is deemed too thick or too thin or if the menstrual blood is the wrong color, measures are taken to remedy the problem.[10] Menopause is reckoned as the final cleaning out. Many postmenopausal difficulties are blamed on the fact that the body did not sufficiently clean itself at menopause (menses became sparse too early). The hysterectomy is a remedy for this state of pollution. The statement "he [doctor] cleaned me out, took all of it" refers to a hysterectomy. For this reason women may be inclined to have a hysterectomy, even when a doctor tells them it is not necessary. Moreover, premenopausal women who are disposed to have a hysterectomy are not above using the operation as a means of birth control; however, a woman would be unlikely to admit this and would explain her choice to have the operation in terms of excessive bleeding.

Young girls who have their tubes tied block up the vital juices and prevent their bodies from purging itself or being purged of outside agents. This, in turn, makes them more prone to disease and bad moods. According to local biology, these two operations on the reproductive system have opposite effects.

Finally, a word must be said about the insular nature of village life. Notions about gender and biology in Grey Rock Harbour may not exist in the village twenty miles away. Just as friendship cliques develop an in-group knowledge, orientation, humor, and mode of communication, many of the notions of Harbour folk are continually shaped by a long heritage of common experience. All locals are of the Anglican faith. They share the occupational heritage of fisher family life. The commonly held belief that the survival of community rests on everyone's remaining the same, or equal, is a powerful force against change. The myths of the notorious physician, the individual who died suddenly of cancer, and the young girl who did not get the promised appendectomy become a part of village lore, shaping common experience and influencing collective response.

Class, Community, and Gender Constructs

These ethnographic materials from Grey Rock Harbour should be considered in light of some current theories dealing with the relationships among class, gender, and female body imagery. In her book *The Woman in the Body* (1987), Emily Martin compares middle- and working-class women's views of reproductive processes. Based on interview materials from 165 women in Baltimore, Maryland, Martin concludes that middle-class women have largely bought into the technological aspects of medical accounts of women, which view menstruation and menopause as failed reproduction and which view menstruation, menopause, and childbirth as largely divorced from women's experience. Working-class women, however, resist the hegemonic scientific view, which degrades, fragments, and impoverishes women's lives, as lacking meaning or as being "downright oppressive" (110). According to Martin, among working-class women, in contrast to middle-class women, there is no angst, no mystification of female bodily processes or loss at the mechanics of taking care of them. The detailed practical information these women need comes from their peers (mothers, grandmothers, sisters, and friends). Martin postulates that because working-class women gain less from production and labor in their society, they have rejected the application of models of production to their bodies, and she concludes that there are alternate ideologies of women's bodies reflecting women's different places in the social order.

Although her data are limited to interviews, Martin has challenged us to adopt a new perspective on the culture analysis of reproductive issues. By narrowly focusing only on gender relations (e.g., husband and wife, men and women in a sexist society) and reproductive organs, processes, and roles (e.g., folk beliefs concerning reproductive organs, beliefs about motherhood, desire for children, loss of sexual attractiveness), researchers are in danger of perpetuating a medical view and neglecting the role that more general and more pervasive gender constructs may play as they reflect and shape the social order. Martin's analysis redirects attention to the wider realms of the body in general (all systems, not just the reproductive) and the broader social order (class, race, and the local community). My own experience with the community of women in Grey Rock Harbour and their willingness to initiate and undergo elective surgery on their reproductive organs provides an excellent background for further discussion of the issues raised by Martin.

Despite their receptive attitudes toward elective surgery, it is quite clear that Grey Rock Harbour women, like Baltimore working-class women, have not accepted the medical view. While in the field, I used standardized questionnaires to gather extensive menstrual and reproductive histories from village women (Davis 1983a). However, through daily participation in the villagers' everyday life for a period of fifteen months, I came to realize that my focus on the meaning of reproduction overlooked the more important, overriding gender constructs of the good woman and the stoic endurer. The idealization of the good woman and the stoic endurer are products of the collectively and rigidly imposed egalitarian ethic dominating the social order in Grey Rock Harbour. Martin's characterization of working-class women as resisters of the medical model and as revitalizers of their own more self-respecting body images lends them a sort of heroine status. As one cover-flap reviewer (Thomas Lanquer) states, "These alternative visions are not, however, the product of scientific 'ignorance' but an extraordinary cultural virtuosity through which women struggle to give their own meaning to menstruation, menopause, and birth." By briefly reviewing the Newfoundland data, I would like to pose a more guarded assessment of the strengths and weaknesses of a nonscientific body image.

It is tempting to praise Harbour women's selective rejection of physicians and medical models as attempts to forge their own understanding of their experiences. For example, it was the women themselves who decided which forms of contraception to use. Although physicians recommended the pill, the village women rejected it. When a young physician was judged callous and unsympathetic to women who were concerned about having cancer, the women boycotted his clinic rotation. When a local woman had a confrontation with a physician, community support solidified around the woman. Local women would also assess the opportunities available in the system and exploit specific physicians for their own purposes to obtain elective surgery. Women would also go to considerable effort to get their surgery on the mainland, where they believed the quality of medical care was superior.

In Grey Rock Harbour, medical care decision making is a process primarily influenced by the social interactions of the female community. A collectively held gender ideology of stoic endurer and an egalitarian ethic characterize all social interactions among Harbour women. Individuals are adept at impression management and negotiate their way through a dynamic and vital women's culture that exacts rigid standards for female behavior and maintains the valued status of good woman for all women. This is well illustrated by the way in which young women with tubal ligations successfully manage an impression of themselves as self-sacrificing women.

Like the working-class women in Baltimore (Martin 1987), Harbour women learn about bodily functions from each other. The processes are viewed as normal. Yet the notion of normality does not preclude discomfort, disability, or pain. Difficulties are to be endured rather than fixed. Newfoundland women do not see themselves primarily as producers of the next generation of fishermen. Instead, they are coequals (with husbands), providing emotional and productive support intrinsic to the family fishery (Davis 1989). Although valued, reproduction is not viewed as the sole role of women. Women's instrumental and expressive roles as they relate more directly to the fishing effort are as important as their reproductive roles. The lack of emphasis on reproduction is illustrated by young women's decisions to have a tubal ligation before the age of twenty or after the birth of one child and the grudging acceptance of this decision by the older generations of women.

Nor do the reproductive organs themselves maintain a special place in the body image. Instead, reproductive lore is integrated into an overall schema of growth, bodily functions, and health and illness under the rubric of blood. Like working-class women in Baltimore (Martin 1987), Harbour women describe menstruation in terms of the character of blood that "comes out" rather than in the more middle-class terms of reproductive loss. Moreover, blood is an important concept that governs and explains the healthy functioning of men as well as women.

Yet it is easy to idealize the lay beliefs and strengths of Grey Rock Harbour women. These beliefs do not necessarily make them better health care consumers. The need for medical care is negotiated in the community before a woman ever goes to the physician. Women are encouraged to accept disability and to endure pain. Many women endure unnecessary and uncomfortable vaginal and urinary infections, which are easily treatable, because they are counseled by their peers not to bother the doctor. When they do visit a physician they are resigned and pessimistic: "By the time I set foot in the clinic I mentally prepare for the worst." They are pessimistic about risk: "He told me there's only 10 percent chance of cancer, but with my luck I've got it for sure"; "The safes [condoms] work, but I just know I'd get the one with a hole." Lacking scientific information about their bodies is not necessarily conducive to good health. Women misinform each other. For example, women reject the pill on moral grounds rather than scientific ones, and young women believe that having a tubal ligation means they will have to have a hysterectomy later in life. Ready and open communication among women can also create fear and panic, as occurred in the bowel cancer case.

Newfoundland women may not see themselves as the victims of their reproductive organs, but they do view themselves as victims of a history of poverty, exploitation, and life in a harsh environment. Stoic endurance and self-sacrifice, although valued by women, are not conducive to the emergence of leadership. Nor are they conducive to constructive confrontation with, or implementation of, governmental and provincial health care or development policies. The rigid enforcement of the egalitarian ethic and the prevailing image of limited good also create immense social stress and conflict within the community (Davis 1989).

Conclusion

Differences between regions and changes in the rates of hysterectomies and tubal ligations over time have important implications for health and policy planners. It has long been recognized that policies, publicity, and consumer interest can influence the rates of discretionary operations (Mindell, Vayda, and Cardillo 1982). The place of the consumer in the incidence of operative procedures has tended to be ignored, however. This is especially true for the health care consumer who is separated from the mainstream of the more medically sophisticated middle class.

The foregoing analysis illustrates the extent to which we need to understand women's own thinking when they are faced with a choice of elective surgery. Physicians agree that a woman is the best judge of her own discomfort and willingness to take risks and must participate in the decision for or against surgery.

H. B. Presser and L. L. Bumpass (1972:512) and Rochelle N. Shain and Harold D. Dickson (1982:1071) note the importance of knowing others (friends) who have undergone a tubal ligation. Conversations with friends are said to be instrumental in dispelling fears and misconceptions and result in more favorable attitudes toward sterilization. Yet how much learning from friends is beneficial, especially when researchers have found that many, including students, faculty, and even biology instructors, do not understand the consequences of sterilization (Eisner, Van Tienhoven, and Rosenblatt 1970:337)?

This study demonstrates the extent to which friends create misinformation—their own contraceptive folklore. Population experts are preoccupied with the cultural factors and beliefs inhibiting effective use of fertility-regulating methods. One seldom hears about the problem of misinformation and the potential for abuse or overuse of these methods.

Press releases and questionnaire surveys will have little impact on cervical screening programs for outport women. Physician communication is the key here. Physicians most effectively communicate when they understand how their patients sort out the information they are given. Outport women do not understand how bureaucracies operate. They have undergone cervical smears at considerable cost to their sense of modesty and sense of well-being—"what you don't know won't hurt you." Concerted effort should be made to inform them rapidly of the status of their smears. The screening program's perceived callousness and maliciousness keep local women from participating. This is most unfortunate since cancer rates are very high among this population and doubly frustrating since women are so receptive to reproductive surgery.

One cannot ask or expect the residents of Grey Rock Harbour to become informed, responsible health care consumers, nor can a health professional assume that medical indications for surgery will alone determine the outporter's decision. If health care is to be made universally available, health care personnel must become informed and act on information about how sociocultural factors shape the health care profiles and proclivities of their patients.

Even if local beliefs conveniently and inadvertently support medical purposes, every effort should be made to see that locals are able to make informed choices, with full knowledge of alternatives and the side effects of the operations they so readily seek. More effort should be made to inform local women about alternative means of contraception and to counsel them into trying alternatives. By all too readily giving women hysterectomies and tubal ligations, physicians deny women their right to make informed choices.

The study of elective surgery in a Newfoundland community also demonstrates the wider social context of female body images (Klee 1988; Martin 1987). Gender constructs shape and are shaped by social issues. The high rates of hysterectomies and tubal ligations among Grey Rock Harbour women cannot be dismissed as the simple result of modernization and medical hegemony. Women's desire for these operations must be understood in terms of the local women's culture, which is constantly being negotiated and reformulated. Popular beliefs about women's bodies are not statistically "rooted" in traditional or class-bound beliefs about women's sexuality, their family roles, or their importance in the wider society. In Grey Rock Harbour, it was the very availability of medical services and new opportunities for surgical decision making that stimulated local women to reassess, renegotiate, and adapt (for better or for worse) more traditional gender constructs to bridge the past and the present and to negotiate the future.[11]

NOTES

1. Newfoundland hysterectomy rates per 1,000 insured females over fifteen years of age were 7.30 for 1975–76, 7.88 for 1976–77, 7.67 for 1977–78, 7.47 for 1978–79, and 6.77 for 1979–80. More recent data (Newfoundland and Labrador Department of Health 1987) show little change from 1979 to 1986. The rates for Newfoundland may actually be higher, because many Newfoundland women, believing health care in Nova Scotia is superior to Newfoundland's, travel to Nova Scotia for their hysterectomies.

2. Female sterilization rate per 1,000 insured females age ten to fifty-four were 7.98 for 1972–73, 11.4 for 1973–74, 12.36 for 1974–75, 10.59 for 1975–76, 12.08 for 1976–77, 10.90 for 1977–78, 7.77 for 1978–79, and 5.52 for 1979–80. Recent data (Newfoundland and Labrador Department of Health 1987) show that sterilization rates have remained steady from 1979 to 1986.

3. Research was funded through a two-year traineeship from the U.S. National Institute of Child Health and Development, administered by the Uni-

versity of North Carolina Population Center. For a more detailed account of research methods and life in Grey Rock Harbour, see Davis (1983a).

4. Directly asking a local woman if she has had her "tubes tied" is a gross breach of etiquette. As much as I wanted "hard facts" on this practice, I felt that direct confrontation was an unethical, unwarranted invasion of a woman's privacy. My very conservative "guesstimates" came from sitting in a kitchen with a map of all households in the village spread out on the table and asking informants who, house by house, had had the operation. Information on rates of tubal ligation is not available on a village-by-village basis.

5. Details about which girl, which village, and what kind of operation are lost. When I asked how the pill could possibly have caused such bleeding, my inquiry was parried by the argument that "the doctor told her mother that's what caused it, so he must have been right." In the local view, "that poor dear, who bled to death" provides sufficient proof that the pill interferes with blood clotting.

6. The *h* is silent in outport dialects. All village hysterectomies were abdominal.

7. I cannot explain the connection between bowel and womb. Women were not worried about bowel cancer. The scare was definitely about uterine cancer. The woman's younger sister (age twenty-eight, fearing she may also have cancer, went for a check-up, was discovered to have cervical cancer, and immediately was scheduled for surgery. This young women instantly became the community expert on cancer.

8. This physician had left a couple months before my arrival in the village, so I cannot confirm any of these comments.

9. It may occur to the reader that the risk factor in taking the pill could be used to enhance the martyr image, yet this does not happen. Perhaps this is because so few married women take the pill, which is seen as a specifically teenage contraceptive. More likely, the pill, I.U.D., and jellies do not fit into the martyr complex because they are believed to be potentially harmful to unborn children—a risk that would be unacceptable in any generation's view.

10. For example, vinegar is taken to thin the blood and red jello to thicken it.

11. This essay was written in 1983 and was revised and updated in the summer of 1988. In 1989 I returned to Grey Rock Harbour for an additional seven months of fieldwork. Although the focus of my current research is on the fisheries crisis (the cod stocks have been drastically reduced through poor management of the fisheries), my impression is that hysterectomies and tubal ligations are still frequently performed, but they have lost their importance as status enhancers. This is largely because women who started their families before the road connecting them to larger towns was built have lost their hold over the local moral order. More and more information about the body is now learned from books and filters up from the younger generations to the older ones. The body has become more privatized. Surgical and medical decision making is now less of a community affair; it is pretty much limited to the domains of doctor-patient and immediate family relationships.

Current assessments of the merits of gynecological surgery are expressed not in terms of the character of the woman receiving the surgery but in terms of where and how successfully the operation was performed (there seems to be a considerable problem with postoperative infection). Women continue to complete their families at an early age. Newfoundland's birth rate has dropped to the second lowest (next to Quebec) in Canada. Tubal ligation is still the preferred form of lifelong birth control, despite the fact that tubal ligation in its local form still involves extensive abdominal incisions and week-long hospital stays. Options for belly-button surgery or other outpatient forms of female sterilization are unavailable to local women.

REFERENCES

Alderdice, Kathy, Karen Inkpen, Ross Payne, Lana Rogers, Paul Decker, and Janet Parker. 1973. "Attitudes toward Family Planning in Newfoundland." In *The Planning Association of Newfoundland and Labrador Report.* Prepared for the Provincial Family Planning and Sex Education Conference, St. John's.

Ballinger, Barbara. 1977. "Psychiatric Morbidity and the Menopause: A Survey of a Gynecological Out-patient Clinic." *British Journal of Psychiatry* 131:83–89.

Bart, Pauline, and Marilyn Grossman. 1979. "Taking the Men Out of Menopause." In *Women Look at Biology Looking at Women*, ed. Ruth Hubbard, M. Henifin, and B. Fried. Cambridge, Mass.: Schenkman.

Bolande, Robert P. 1969. "Ritualistic Surgery—Circumcision and Tonsillectomy." *New England Journal of Medicine* 280:591–96.

Cole, P., and J. Berlin. 1977. "Elective Hysterectomy." *American Journal of Obstetrics and Gynecology* 129:117–23.

Davis, Dona L. 1983a. *Blood and Nerves: An Ethnographic Focus on Menopause.* St. John's: Institute of Social and Economic Research, Memorial University of Newfoundland.

———. 1983b. "The Family and Social Change in the Newfoundland Outport." *Culture* 3(1):19–32.

———. 1984. "Medical Misinformation: Communication Difficulties between Newfoundland Women and Their Physicians." *Social Science and Medicine* 18:273–78.

———. 1989. "The Variable Character of Nerves in a Newfoundland Fishing Village." *Medical Anthropology* 11:65–80.

Dyck, Frank, and Fergus Murphy. 1977. "Hysterectomies [Letter to Editor]." *New England Journal of Medicine* 297:671.

Dyck, Frank, Fergus Murphy, and Barbara Korchinski. 1977a. "Surveillance of Hysterectomy in Saskatchewan." *Canadian Medical Association Journal* 117:1363–66.

———. 1977b. "Effect of Surveillance on the Number of Hysterectomies in the Province of Saskatchewan." *New England Journal of Medicine* 296:1326–28.

————. 1974. "The Layered Cake." *New England Journal of Medicine* 291: 253–56.

Eisner, Thomas, Ari Van Tienhoven, and Frank Rosenblatt. 1970. "Population Control, Sterilization and Ignorance." *Science* 167(3917):337.

Hanlon, C. R. 1979. "Discussion in Surgical Decision Making." *Annal of Surgery* 190:417.

Innis, Fran. 1973. "Family Planning in Newfoundland." Paper given at the Family Planning Association of Newfoundland and Labrador Provincial Family Planning and Sex Education Conference, St. John's.

Keyser, Herbert. 1984. *Women under the Knife: A Gynecologist's Report on Hazardous Medicine.* Philadelphia: George F. Stickley.

Klee, Linnea. 1988. "The Social Significance of Elective Hysterectomy." In *Anthropology of Women's Health,* ed. Pat Whelehan. Granby, Mass.: Bergin and Garvey.

Lee, Sydney S. 1977. "Hysterectomies [Letter to the Editor]." *New England Journal of Medicine* 297:670–71.

Lewis, C. E. 1969. "Variation in the Incidence of Surgery." *New England Journal of Medicine* 281:880–84.

LoGerfo, James P. 1977. "Variations in Surgical Rates: Facts vs. Fantasy." *New England Journal of Medicine* 297:387–89.

Martin, Emily. 1987. *The Woman in the Body: A Cultural Analysis of Reproduction.* Boston: Beacon.

Matthews, Ralph. 1976. *"There's No Better Place Than Here": Social Change in Three Newfoundland Communities.* Toronto: Peter Martin.

Miller, A. B. 1978. "Screening for Cancer of the Cervix in Canada Post Walton." In *Screening in Cancer,* UICC Technical Reports Series, Vol. 40, ed. A. B. Miller. Geneva: International Union Against Cancer.

————. 1981. *The Canadian Experience of Cervical Cancer: Incidence Trends and a Planned Natural History Investigation.* Proceedings of the symposium on Trends in Cancer Incidence, Oslo 1980. New York: Hemisphere.

Miller, A. B., J. Lindsay, and G. B. Hill. 1976. "Mortality from Cancer of the Uterus in Canada and Its Relationship to Screening for Cancer of the Cervix." *International Journal of Cancer* 17:602–12.

————. 1981. "The Effect of Hysterectomies and Screening on Mortality from Cancer of the Uterus in Canada." *International Journal of Cancer* 27: 651–57.

Miller N. F. 1976. "Hysterectomy: Therapeutic Necessity or Surgical Racket?" *American Journal of Obstetrics and Gynecology* 51:804–10.

Mindell, William R., Eugene Vayda, and Brenda Cardillo. 1982. "Ten Year Trend in Canada for Selected Operations." *Canadian Medical Association Journal* 127:23–27.

Newfoundland and Labrador Department of Health. 1987. *Statistical Report on Surgical Procedures in Newfoundland and Labrador—1979–1986.* St. Johns: Newfoundland and Labrador Department of Health.

Polgar, Steven, and John Marshall. 1976. "The Search for Culturally Acceptable Fertility Regulatory Methods." In *Culture Natality and Family Planning,* ed. John Marshall and Steven Polgar. Chapel Hill, N.C.: Carolina Population Center.

Presser, H. B., and L. L. Bumpass. 1972. "Demographic and Social Aspects of Contraceptive Sterilization in the United States." In *Demographic and Social Aspects of Population Growth*, ed. C. F. Westoff and R. Parke. Washington, D.C.: Government Printing Office.

Rutkow, Ira M., Alan Gittelsohn, and George D. Zuidena. 1979. "Surgical Decision Making." *Annals of Surgery* 190:409–17.

Scully, Diana. 1980. *Men Who Control Women's Health*. Boston: Houghton Mifflin.

Seaman, Barbara. 1975. "Pelvic Autonomy: Four Proposals." *Social Policy* 6(2):43–47.

Shain, Rochelle N., and Harold D. Dickson. 1982. "Tubal Sterilization: Characteristics of Women Most Affected by the Option of Reversibility." *Social Science and Medicine* 16:1067–77.

Sofer, Tsipporah, Noralou P. Roos, and Norma Nelson. 1983. "Hysterectomy in Manitoba—1970–1978: Patterns of Practice and Changes over Time." *Canadian Journal of Public Health* 74(2):100–105.

Vayda, Eugene, William R. Mindell, and Ira M. Rutkow. 1982. "A Decade of Surgery in Canada, England and Wales, and the United States." *Archives of Surgery* 117(6):846–53.

Walton, R. J. 1976. "Cervical Cancer Screening Programs." *Canadian Medical Association Journal* 114:1003.

Westoff, Charles F., and Elise F. Jones. 1977. "Contraception and Sterilization in the United States, 1965–1975." *Family Planning in Perspective* 9(4):153–72.

Wright, Ralph C. 1969. "Hysterectomy: Past, Present, and Future." *Obstetrics and Gynecology* 33:560–63.

Maureen J. Giovannini

The Relevance of Gender in Postpartum Emotional Disorders

> Because women's biological reproduction has a social func-
> tion—the reproduction of society—any difficulties women have
> with motherhood constitute a social problem."
>
> Ann Oakley, *Women Confined*

Recent evidence indicates that a growing number of women in the United States and Great Britain are suffering from postpartum emotional disorders (Giovannini 1979; Hopkins, Marcus, and Campbell 1984; Howell 1981; Oakley 1980a, 1980b). Since postpartum emotional disorders are intimately bound up with women's reproductive roles, they constitute a social problem as well as an individual concern. This paper explores the relevance of gender-based beliefs, values, and practices for understanding this social problem.

Since gender categories are cultural constructs that order and define what it means to be a woman or a man in a particular social milieu, an examination of gender necessarily includes the symbols, meanings, and images associated with femaleness and maleness in that context. But a problem-oriented study must go beyond the level of cultural meaning to focus on the political-economic and social aspects of gender. This means examining the ways in which gender enters into social relations to affect the differential rights, opportunities, and resources available to people, as well as the difficulties and limitations they face. Such an approach is consistent with socialist feminism, the body of theory that provides the conceptual framework for this essay (Barrett 1980; Barrett and McIntosh 1982; Hartmann 1981;

I. M. Young 1984). Using a socialist-feminist perspective, I explain the increasing incidence of postpartum emotional disorders in the United States and Great Britain in terms of women's experiences as gendered subjects within the broader institutions of these industrial capitalist societies.

The Problem

Postpartum emotional disorders are not a new phenomenon, nor are they necessarily restricted to industrial capitalist societies. But historical and cross-cultural data support the view that, within the United States and Great Britain, such disorders are increasing in intensity and frequency. One review article suggests that up to 20 percent of women in the United States experience some form of emotional disturbance during the first twelve months postpartum (Hopkins, Marcus, and Campbell 1984). Another estimates that four-fifths of all new mothers in the United States have some psychological distress postpartum, while one-sixth of the total experience enough to require professional care (Howell 1981). A London-based study reports that 24 percent of the sample were clinically depressed, while 84 percent experienced mild emotional upsets during their stay in the hospital (Oakley 1980b:135).

A review of the literature on postpartum emotional disorders reveals several conceptual problems. To begin with, a wide variety of signs and symptoms lasting anywhere from one day to several months are subsumed under the term *postpartum depression.* These include crying spells, mild anxiety, more severe and prolonged anxiety; feelings of fear, despondency, hopelessness, or unworthiness (especially as a mother); eating and sleeping disorders; restlessness and agitation; fatigue and listlessness; disinterest in or neglect of the baby; hallucinations or delusions; and suicidal thoughts or attempts (Howell 1981; Oakley 1980b). This raises some key questions. Is postpartum depression one "disease" with these signs and symptoms arranged on a continuum, or are several different "diseases" with diverse etiologies involved? Also, should postpartum depression be viewed as but one form of a more general depression syndrome, or is it a separate entity altogether?

In an attempt to clear up this definitional confusion, several researchers (Hopkins, Marcus, and Campbell 1984; Parlee 1978; Stern and Kruckman 1983; Brown 1979) have converged on a useful approach that divides these signs and symptoms into three categories (see Table 1). The first category is referred to as the "maternity blues"

Table 1: Postpartum Emotional Disorders

Category	Incidence Rates	Symptoms	Onset
"Maternity" or "baby blues"	60–80%	sadness, tension, irritability, crying	1st 2 weeks postpartum
Postpartum depression	10–30%	inadequacy, guilt, anxiety, fatigue, irritability, crying, impaired functioning (in severe cases)	2 weeks–3 months postpartum
Postpartum psychosis	.01–2.00%	delusions, hallucinations, rapid mood change, mental confusion	3–14 days postpartum

or "baby blues." This is very common among women in the United States and Great Britain, with most studies reporting incidence rates between 60 percent and 80 percent. Symptoms and signs associated with the baby blues include sadness, tension, irritability, and crying. They appear during the first two weeks postpartum and are of short duration—one to three days.

The second category is labeled postpartum depression, a disorder comparable to other, nonchildbirth-related depressive neuroses, ranging from mild to severe. Here symptoms involve feelings of inadequacy, guilt, anxiety, fatigue, tearfulness, irritability, and, in more serious cases, the inability to care for the new baby. Postpartum depression seems to manifest itself anytime from two weeks to three months postpartum and can last anywhere from several weeks to a year. The incidence rates for postpartum depression thus defined vary between 10 percent and 30 percent, depending on the study.

The third category, postpartum psychosis (puerperal psychosis), is reported to have a low incidence rate—between .01 and 2.00 per 100 women. Symptoms and signs associated with puerperal psychosis include delusions, hallucinations, rapid mood change, and mental confusion. They have an acute and quick onset, with 80 percent of all cases occurring between three and fourteen days postpartum. Interestingly, the incidence of puerperal psychosis has remained constant in the United States and Great Britain over the past century, while reported rates for both the baby blues and postpartum depressive neurosis have increased significantly (Stern and Kruckman 1983).

Explanatory Models

As with other kinds of emotional disturbances, there may be multiple etiological factors involved in the maternity blues, postpartum depression, and more serious affective psychoses. Yet, until recently, most of the literature on postpartum disorders focused on either biochemical processes or personality variables specific to the female gender. Both approaches can be faulted for excessive reductionism. They must also be critiqued as powerful ideological devices serving to perpetuate the social conditions that make motherhood so problematic for women today. Given the continuing influence of these models (imbued with an aura of scientific validity), it is important to review their conceptual and methodological errors.

Female Biology

The first model, found in medical and psychiatric studies, emphasizes female biology—specifically, hormonal fluctuations—as a major causal factor in postpartum emotional problems (Dalton 1969; Hamilton 1962; Kaij and Nilsson 1972). As K. Dalton (1969:105–6) succinctly put it, "The woman . . . may be upset by this sudden decrease in her progesterone level and may develop a more severe puerperal depression in which she becomes apathetic and tearful, losing appetite, interest, energy, and initiative; she may also become sexually frigid."

Although the hormonal theory is widely accepted in medicine and psychiatry, there is little scientific evidence linking hormonal levels to the incidence and severity of postnatal emotional disorders (Howell 1981). On the contrary, several studies report negative results, and the apparent infrequency of postpartum disorders cross-culturally casts further doubt on the validity of the biological paradigm (Jordan 1980; Mead and Newton 1967; Parlee 1980; Stern and Kruckman 1983). What, then, explains the continued existence and popularity of this model in medical circles? To begin with, it is consistent with the narrow biophysiological and unicausal focus of modern Western medicine. More important, however, it is another example of Western medicine's long-standing tendency to define women, including their emotions and behavior, in terms of female biological processes (Ehrenreich and English 1978). Unfortunately, despite significant challenges from feminist scholars and researchers, the medical establishment still operates under the assumption that female biology is a woman's destiny.

Female Psychodynamics

The second reductionist model, this one prevalent in psycho-analytic and psychological studies of postpartum disorders, explains causality in terms of female intrapsychic dynamics. More specifically, emotional disturbances following childbirth (or any other event in the female reproductive life cycle) are attributed to a woman's intra-psychic conflict surrounding her femininity. L. Chertok (1969:43), for example, states that "maternity appears to be an integrative crisis in women's psychosexual development involving the revival of the con-flicts that have molded her [feminine] identification." N. Morris (1972:150) suggests that "the most frequent and the most important stress factor (in post-partum depression) is psychological and that it arises from unconscious conflicts in the woman about assuming the role and responsibilities of mother," and D. Breen (1975:76) maintains that "femininity refers to those qualities which make for a good ad-justment to the biological female reproductive role." Although the biological paradigm depicts women as passive victims of their hor-mones, here the victim herself is at fault (albeit unconsciously) for failing to achieve mature femininity.

Along with the tendency to blame the victim, the psychodynamic model has other serious limitations as well. First, although it consid-ers those interpersonal relations believed to effect feminine person-ality dynamics (e.g., the mother-daughter dyad), it still focuses narrowly on the individual, to the exclusion of those socioenviron-mental variables of potential relevance to postnatal emotional prob-lems. Second, it tends to view the personality constellation of femininity, including motherhood, as the "natural" outcome of nor-mal psychosexual development. Failure to "develop normally" is then explained in terms of an inadequate femininity profile. The ar-gument is therefore tautological. Third, this model ignores the fact that concepts of femininity are historically and culturally specific gender constructs that may operate to the detriment of women by justifying their subordinate status.

Socioenvironmental Stress

Over the past several years, more holistically oriented health care professionals and social scientists have rejected those reduction-ist (and oftentimes sexist) models in favor of an approach that focuses on socioenvironmental stress as a key etiological factor in postpartum emotional disorders.[1] Childbirth (including the postpartum period) is conceptualized as a life crisis or significant life event that entails learning new behavior and assuming new social roles. This model further assumes that, like other life crises, childbirth involves potentially stressful role uncertainty and ambiguity. To minimize stress and make a successful transition from one set of social roles to another, women undergoing childbirth require emotional support, advice, information, and instrumental assistance. When these kinds of supports are not forthcoming, it is believed that the emotional and even the physical well-being of a woman may suffer. A related assumption is that postpartum problems can be related to other stress-producing factors in a woman's social environment as well (Hopkins, Marcus, and Campbell 1984; O'Hara, Rehm, and Campbell 1983; Parlee 1980; Stern and Kruckman 1983).

Studies of Postpartum Adjustment

Researchers recently have begun to look for the causes of postpartum disorders not in female biology or in feminine psychodynamics but rather in the social worlds inhabited by women during childbirth. One such study was conducted in 1978, when I led a research project designed to uncover the social parameters of postpartum adjustment. My sample consisted of twenty-two married women selected on an opportunity basis. They included both primiparous and multiparous mothers who had given birth during the previous year. Each informant participated in a three-hour, structured home interview that focused on both socioenvironmental stress and support. An attempt was then made to trace the relationship between these variables and the incidence and severity of postnatal adjustment problems as reported by the women themselves (Giovannini 1979, 1980).

Family and Friendship Networks

The twenty-two informants forming the sample were residents of a geographically stable working-class community in the greater Boston area. At the time of the study, all but one was a full-time homemaker. In each case their household was limited to the nuclear family—husband, wife, children. At the same time, however, extended family members often resided within walking distance of the informant and her family, sometimes even in the same apartment building. For example, seven of the twenty-two families lived in the same building that the wife's parents or the husband's parents did. In terms of communication patterns with extended family members, there seemed to be a closer affinity with the wife's family, especially her mother and sisters. Communication included frequent visits and telephone conversations. Six informants stated they saw their mother on a daily basis, while an additional seven informants saw their mother about two or three times a week. In addition, ten informants reported they spoke on the telephone daily with their mother, and seven informants said they talked daily with a sister.

The friendship networks of most informants were also characterized by close-knit ties. For instance, thirteen informants had at least one close friend within walking distance of their home. Eleven informants saw at least one close friend daily, and three additional informants saw one or more close friends on an average of once a week. With regard to joint activities, ten informants reported they participated in structured activities, such as ceramic classes, beano, and bingo, with friends. Finally, in many cases family and friendship networks merged, fourteen informants stated their best friends were also relatives, usually the informant's sister or cousin.

Pregnancy, Labor, and Delivery

When asked if their recent pregnancy was planned, seventeen informants answered in the affirmative, with four others (all multiparous) stating that they had wanted another child but that "the timing for this one wasn't right." None of the informants, however, reported feeling upset, anxious, or depressed during their pregnancy over the thought of a new baby.

Focusing on the kinds of supports they received during pregnancy and when they were hospitalized, informants indicated that instrumental help with household chores and babysitting, information, and advice were more common than emotional support. For all informants, husbands and women relatives were the primary sources of instrumental assistance. In terms of overall advice and information, physicians appeared to be most important. Parity emerged as a significant variable here, with primiparous mothers citing proportionally more sources of information and advice. With regard to emotional support, the informants' women relatives were most frequently mentioned, followed by the physician, the husband, and nurses. As with advice and information, primiparous informants noted more sources of emotional support than multiparous informants did. These differences are probably related to both the perceived and real needs for information, guidance, and reassurance shared by women who are undergoing childbirth for the first time.

The Postpartum Adjustment Period

According to informants, the greatest amount of assistance available during the postpartum period was instrumental support—babysitting, cooking, cleaning, watching the older children, getting up with the baby. In this area, both the informant's family and her husband's family were the major source of assistance. The next category was emotional support, with the informant's family most apt to provide this type of assistance, followed by her husband and friends. Finally, in the area of advice and information—usually surrounding the baby's care—physicians and the informant's family were the chief providers, followed by friends and nurses.

Of the twenty-two informants, eight reported a problem-free postpartum adjustment, while the remaining fourteen stated they suffered from some emotional distress. There was, however, considerable variation in the intensity and duration of these emotional problems. For example, three informants said they were mildly depressed during the first week. Their symptoms were limited to crying spells, which they referred to as the "baby blues." Four other informants reported feeling depressed for the first six to eight weeks postpartum. In two of the four cases, the baby was born in the winter, and the mothers attributed their depression to the fact that it was extremely difficult for them to get out during the first few months. The third informant in this group also related her emotional problems to being "stuck in the house," but her difficulties involved getting out of the house (a third floor walk-up) with a toddler as well as an infant. In the fourth case, the informant, a primiparous mother, attributed her depression to a sense of being overwhelmed by the responsibility of caring for the baby and a lack of sleep related to the baby's colic.

The seven remaining informants reported experiencing prolonged depression, which lasted several months postpartum. These informants described a wide range of symptoms, including crying, feeling confused and disoriented, withdrawing from social contacts, and being unable to care for the baby. As one woman described it, "For six months I felt as though I were alone in a dark room with no way out."

This study did not investigate the psychological makeup of informants; therefore, it cannot attempt to relate the incidence of postpartum emotional problems to the informant's personality characteristics. However, the sociocultural data gathered suggest that other kinds of variables—socioenvironmental supports as well as stressors—may contribute to the incidence and severity of emotional problems during the postpartum period. To compare and contrast the social supports possessed by each informant and the potentially stressful environmental factors each informant had to contend with, simple quantifiable scaling measures were devised and applied to the qualitative data.

The first step was to assess the nature of the informant's relationship with each individual in her family network and her friendship network. This was done by taking information in the following areas: (1) the frequency of contact with that individual during the postpartum period, (2) the amount of instrumental support during that time, (3) the amount of emotional support during that time, and (4) the quality of the relationship (i.e., the degree of trust and harmony during the postpartum period). When this was accomplished, the scores received in the four areas by each member of the informant's family and friendship network were added up, along with the number of individuals in the network. The result was taken to be the informant's overall social support score.

With regard to potential psychosocial stressors, the interviews were examined to determine the socioenvironmental and interpersonal difficulties as well as life changes experienced by individual informants during the postpartum period. Each potential stressor faced by individual informants was assigned a score of one, then added up and used to form a potential social stress score for that informant. It is important to note that, even in cases where the informant mentioned a socioenvironmental difficulty or a life change but did not refer to it as stressful, it was still incorporated into the overall score.

When informants were compared in terms of their scores, some interesting results emerged. To begin with, there was a positive association between the strength of a woman's overall support system (measured in terms of size, frequency of contact, amount of instrumental and emotional support, and quality of the relationships) and minimal or no reported depression. With regard to socioenvironmental stress, informants who experienced no depression or "baby blues" listed few, if any, potential stress factors. In contrast, those women who were depressed for six to eight weeks postpartum reported several socioenvironmental problems, including a sickly baby, problems getting out, and a jealous husband. Likewise, the women who suffered from severe and prolonged depression mentioned some of these same difficulties, but they also described other social stressors, which were of a longer duration and appeared to be more serious (e.g., a dying relative and housing problems). The findings for each of the four groups—average social support scores and average socioenvironmental stress scores—are summarized in Table 2.

The data regarding informants' social support systems and their exposure to potential socioenvironmental stressors indicate that both sets of factors can affect the incidence, intensity, and duration of

Table 2: Comparison of Social Support and Social Stress Scores

Group		Social Support Score	Potential Stress Score
Group 1:	informants reporting no depression ($N = 8$)	77.38	.75
Group 2:	informants reporting the "baby blues" ($N = 3$)	79.00	.88
Group 3:	informants reporting depression for six to eight weeks ($N = 4$)	60.75	2.00
Group 4:	informants reporting depression for six to eight months ($N = 7$)	57.43	3.29

postpartum emotional disorders. Both Group 1 and Group 2 were characterized by relatively high social support scores and low potential social stress scores. The fact that informants in Group 2 experienced the baby blues while the informants in Group 1 were without symptoms could be due to their greater sensitivity to hormonal and fluid changes taking place soon after childbirth. Also, since all three informants in Group 2 were primiparous, their minor and brief symptoms might be related to the confusion and uncertainty that new mothers sometimes experience when assuming their mothering roles for the first time.

While Group 1 and Group 2 had similar social support scores and potential socioenvironmental stress scores, and they contrasted sharply with Group 3 and Group 4, both of which had relatively low social support scores and relatively high potential social stress scores. Based on the scores in all four groups, we can hypothesize that, other things being equal, the incidence and severity of postpartum emotional disorders will be negatively associated with the existence of strong social support systems and positively associated with the existence of potential socioenvironmental stressors.

Although Group 3 and Group 4 had comparable social support scores, they differed in the area of potential social stressors by an average of 1.29. This numerical difference may not appear large enough to account for the prolonged and more severe depression reported by informants in Group 4. However, when assessing the impact of socioenvironmental factors, it is important to note the types as well as the quantity of potential stressors to which informants were exposed. In fact, a number of studies focusing on potential socioenvironmental stressors—specifically, life changes—have attempted to rate different types of life changes according to their stress-producing magnitude

(Holmes and Rahe 1967; Komaroff, Masuda, and Holmes 1968; Rahe 1969). These rating scales were not employed in the present study because, first, they do not deal adequately with the life changes particular to childbirth and, second, they do not address ethnic, class, and gender differences in judgments about the magnitude of life events.

Even without a rating scale, it is possible to examine in more detail the types of potential socioenvironmental stressors found in Group 3 and Group 4 in an attempt to account for the differences in the length and severity of postpartum depressions. In Group 3, the potential socioenvironmental stressors included exhaustion, logistical problems getting out, a sickly baby, uncertainty over mothering, and a jealous husband. In each case the informant explained that these problems subsided after the first month or two. In Group 4, there were also difficulties related to getting out, a sickly baby, and exhaustion, as well as changes associated with an older child starting school for the first time and difficulties breastfeeding, but other potential socioenvironmental stressors existed, which lasted longer and appeared to be more problematic. These included marital problems, serious conflict with relatives, a husband who began night school while continuing to work days, an excessively jealous older child, and a move to a new apartment that the informant "hated." The interview data thus suggest that, compared with Group 3, the informants in Group 4 were under more stress than the numerical scores would indicate, because many of their stress factors were of a greater magnitude and lasted longer.

To summarize, this study suggests that the lack of social supports and the existence of socioenvironmental stressors place a woman at risk for postpartum emotional disorders. Furthermore, among women with relatively equal social support systems who experience postpartum disorders, the amount and type of socioenvironmental stress to which they are exposed may be positively associated with the length and severity of their depression.

Additional Studies

Other, more extensive studies examining the impact of the social environment on postpartum adjustment report findings similar to my own. Using a wide variety of research methods, they have highlighted the importance of specific variables, such as the quality of the marital relationship, including instrumental and emotional support (Belsky 1981; Grossman, Eichler, and Winickoff 1980; O'Hara, Rehm, and Campbell 1983; Paykel et al. 1980); geographical mobility (Heith 1976); financial distress (Heitler 1976); housing

problems (Robson and Kumar 1980); availability of practical assistance, guidance, and emotional support (Gordon, Kapostins, and
Gordon 1965); and an unexpected or recent move (Gordon and Gordon 1967). Additional evidence in favor of a socioenvironmental
explanatory model comes from cross-cultural data documenting the
relative absence of postnatal disorders in non-Western societies
where family and community support mechanisms become activated
during childbirth (Stern and Kruckman 1983).

These studies constitute a significant advance over reductionist
models of female biology or feminine personality disorders. Yet, like
other research on the mental health implications of environmental
stress and social support, they do not go far enough.[2] More specifically, such studies tend to focus on a woman's immediate social
environment instead of relating such conditions to broader social
structures. It is therefore difficult to move beyond statistical aggre-
gates of women to delineate the problematic aspects of their structural position as mothers within a specific sociohistorical context.
Related to this is the assumption that childbirth is a potentially
stressful life crisis like any other, which, if adjusted to successfully,
can lead to emotional growth and development. This approach lacks
any critical analysis of what the transition to motherhood actually entails for women.[3] As Ann Oakley (1979) states, to ask what women
are expected to "adjust" to is a political issue rarely broached. A.
Rossi (1968:27) makes the point even more strongly by asking what
maternity deprives women of in industrialized Western societies.

These essential questions can be most usefully addressed by
examining the ways in which women's postpartum reactions are influenced by their experiences as gendered subjects—women and
mothers—within the ideological, medical, familial, and political-
economic institutions of the wider society. I use this approach to
explain the increasing incidence of postpartum (nonpsychotic) disorders in the United States and Great Britain.

A Socialist-Feminist Perspective

At this point it is important to establish that the patterning of
gender categories and gender-related behavior found in the United
States and Great Britain should not be viewed as a functionally
necessary or generic feature of industrial capitalism. Such an assumption would be much too simplistic. Rather, these particular
constellations have been shaped by a historical process involving
conflicting group interests not only between classes but also between

women and men. In both societies, the resulting gender images, beliefs, and values are linked in complex ways to objective gender relations wherein male dominance prevails.[4]

The Ideology of Motherhood

We can begin to explore this articulation and its relevance to motherhood, both as an institution and an experience (Rich 1976), by looking at the ideological aspects of "woman as mother." In Great Britain and the United States, motherhood is an integral part of the gender category "female." Correspondingly, it is assumed that "normal" adult women have babies and that this is their natural role in life. While similar beliefs exist in many sociocultural contexts, in the industrialized Western world they are legitimized and reinforced by scientific and medical paradigms emphasizing that female biology is a woman's destiny and that rejecting the maternal role can be both a cause and effect of psychological disorders (see the models critiqued above for examples).

Consistent with these assumptions, women are socialized from infancy not just to accept the inevitability of motherhood but to embrace this condition as their primary means to female adulthood, social esteem, respectability, and self-fulfillment. As Linda Gordon (1976) points out, this ongoing socialization process contributes to the formation of a female character structure based on maternal attitudes and aspirations. It follows, then, that women who remain childless often view themselves (and are viewed by others) as anomalies or failures, regardless of their other accomplishments. These attitudes and reactions have ample documentation in the growing body of medical and lay literature on infertility.

The cultural pressures to become a mother are intensified by professional, political, and popular media messages extolling the virtues of mothers and their highly significant social contribution—the bearing and nurturing of future generations. In striking contrast to the idealization of motherhood, women as mothers face very real problems in the United States and Great Britain today. These problems are related to the ways in which women become mothers as well as to the real limitations and constraints faced by mothers in these societies.

Medicalization of Childbirth

In both contexts, women's difficulties adjusting to motherhood are exacerbated by the fact that childbirth has been medicalized by the male-dominated field of obstetrics. The historical processes—

including gender and class relations—that produced this situation have been discussed in several recent works (Barker-Benfield 1976; Ehrenreich and English 1972; Felker 1982). Also well documented is the pervasiveness of negative gender stereotypes in medicine, particularly in obstetrics and gynecology (Ehrenreich and English 1973; Lennane and Lennane 1973; Oakley 1980b; Scully and Bart 1973). In brief, these stereotypes portray women as a special category of person and patient, defined almost exclusively in terms of their reproductive biophysiology. It is this "problematic" reproductive system, deemed responsible for many of the health problems women have, which becomes the object of medical intervention. In addition, women are typified as childlike, emotionally labile, and, as such, in need of firm guidance and direction. Male physicians therefore often adopt an authoritative and patronizing manner toward their female patients that reflects male dominance as well as their differential professional (and sometimes class) status.

All of this becomes particularly problematic during childbirth, when women have more frequent contact with the medical establishment, contact that focuses on the most intimate part of a woman's psychological and physical being. At that time, a woman's experiences with health care personnel may negatively affect her sense of self as an adult, a woman, a sexual being, and a mother. For example, a woman's expectations that self-fulfillment and personal achievement will come from childbirth are likely to be shattered by her real lack of control over personnel and procedures in clinic and hospital settings. Another kind of personal invalidation is faced by women who feel fine physically and wish to give birth naturally but are treated as though they were sick and are subjected to invasive procedures. Adding insult to injury, some male obstetricians seem more concerned about the needs and feelings of the patient's husband than about the woman herself. This is manifested by recommending regional anesthesia so that labor will be easier on the husband as labor coach, conveying important information to the husband rather than to the woman herself, and adding an extra "husband's stitch" to the episiotomy repair to ensure his sexual satisfaction.

These kinds of experiences may very well contribute to the sense of loss and disillusionment that many women report during the postpartum period (Giovannini 1979; Oakley 1980a). Coupled with other dimensions of the medicalization process, they could even play an important role in the high incidence of baby blues as well as prolonged (nonpsychotic) emotional disorders. An additional factor pertains to the hospital experience itself. In fact, one comparative study documented that postpartum depression is significantly higher among women giving birth in hospitals than for those having their baby at home (Cone 1972). In the hospital context women find themselves in an impersonal environment, separated from loved ones, and subjected to bureaucratic rules and regulations. These rules and regulations may interfere in various ways with much-needed rest, mother-infant bonding, and successful breast-feeding.

A final but extremely important aspect of the medicalization of childbirth that may play a part in postpartum emotional disorders relates to the numerous invasive, sometimes surgical, procedures that are routinely employed in the United States and Great Britain. Ann Oakley (1981a:17) has listed a few of these: enemas or suppositories in the first stage of labor; artificial rupture of membranes; pharmacological induction of labor; vaginal examinations in labor; bladder catheterization in labor; mechanical monitoring of the fetal heart; mechanical monitoring of contractions; a glucose or saline drip in labor; epidural analgesics; pain killing/tranquilizing injections; episiotomy; forceps or vacuum extraction of the baby; and accelerated delivery of the placenta by injecting ergometrine or oxytocin and pulling on the cord. In some cases these procedures can actually create risks to mothers or their babies and necessitate even more drastic intervention, such as cesarean delivery. Indeed, cesarean sections are on the rise in Great Britain and the United States, constituting as many as 20 percent of all births in some hospitals.

Ann Oakley (1980b) cites several studies demonstrating that depression is a common reaction to the trauma of surgery, especially if patients were not prepared for the level of pain and discomfort they actually experienced or if the surgery was unexpected. Describing many of the procedures listed above as akin to surgery, she concludes that this aspect of medicalization is significantly related to the high incidence of postpartum disorders in the United States and Great Britain: "Feeling 'depressed' is feeling exhausted, bereft of the skills needed to comfort a crying baby, powerless to change the bondage of remorseless hospital routines. Any man subjected to major surgery and then told to start a new job immediately for which he has had no training and in similarly rigorous conditions would probably also react negatively" (128). Once women leave the hospital, they assume their "new job" in another institutional context of great relevance to the experience of motherhood—the family.

Family and Household

In the industrialized Western world, family and extended kinship are often attenuated. This, coupled with increasing geographic mobility, means that many new mothers cannot rely on traditional sources of advice, information, emotional support, and instrumental assistance during pregnancy and the postpartum period. Even when relatives are close, necessary support and assistance may not be forthcoming for a variety of reasons (Giovannini 1979). Once they leave the hospital many women thus find themselves alone and isolated, with almost total responsibility for the care and well-being of their new baby. Indeed, the theme of isolation, of being "trapped" or "closed in," looms very large in women's own accounts of their postpartum experiences (Giovannini 1979; Oakley 1980a). As my own study indicated, such isolation can be exacerbated by climatic conditions, housing arrangements, and financial resources (Giovannini 1979).

An additional problem relates to the fact that most primiparous women have had little or no experience with infants. In one British survey, 81 percent of middle-class mothers and 65 percent of working-class mothers were so classified (Dally 1983:283). As Ann Dally (1983) notes, this situation can generate a great deal of anxiety and guilt over "doing the right thing." Yet the lack of preparation for mothering has received scant attention in the literature on childbirth. Perhaps this is because childbirth experts—both proponents of medicalization and natural childbirth advocates—all accept the gender-related cultural assumption that, just as motherhood is a woman's natural state, women "naturally" know how to care for babies. Correspondingly, few institutionalized mechanisms or resources exist to teach women about infant care.

A third adjustment difficulty that many women face relates to the abrupt and radical changes in their life-style following the birth of a baby. Babies can be a joy and a pleasure, but they involve considerable additional work, sleep deprivation (especially in early months), and real limitations on one's freedom of movement. A new mother's occupational status and financial situation may also change significantly. While some women willingly choose to be full-time mothers, others are forced to leave paid employment in the absence of adequate childcare facilities. This role loss, coupled with diminished household income and her own financial dependence, may contribute to postpartum emotional disorders. According to Ann Oakley's (1980a) study, this is particularly true for career women, perhaps because work is both rewarding and an integral part of their self-identity. An additional problem for these and other full-time mothers is that often the domestic division of labor shifts so that even "liberated" women find themselves doing most of the household chores. For women who regard such work as boring and tedious, the adjustment is difficult indeed.

To avoid viewing this family-based division of labor as part of the "natural order," we must try to understand it in terms of broader political-economic processes and the structure of male dominance and associated gender ideology that unfolded historically in the United States and Great Britain. In both societies, precapitalist families or households often combined productive labor with domestic work and childcare. Although mothers were primarily responsible for their infants, there were numerous adults and other children around to share this responsibility. A mother's isolation was further lessened by the fact that family systems were embedded in a nexus of community relations. In addition, since many productive activities took place within the household or close by, women could be and often were involved in such activities—farm work, artisanry, the "putting out" system, and forms of wage labor (Clark 1969).

The advent of industrial capitalism brought about many changes, including the privatization of the family, a strict separation between home and workplace, and a more rigid, gender-based division of labor, with women relegated to the domestic sphere while men earned the "family wage." As Heidi Hartmann (1981) has documented, the division of labor not only was the outcome of class struggle but also involved competing interests between working-class women and men, with the men emerging victorious.

The resulting situation was one that benefited men as well as the industrial capitalist state. For their part, men gained important economic privileges both in the family and in the workplace, while their female relatives performed socially devalued, unpaid, and yet necessary work. Within the structures of industrial capitalism, women's maternal and domestic roles ensured that the reproduction of the work force would be undertaken at minimal expense to employers and the state. Women also began to constitute a reserve labor force for industrial capitalism, thus mitigating some of its inherent contradictions. With regard to those women who needed to work on a regular basis, the concept of the family wage, along with more gender-specific stereotypes, justified their low wages, restriction to female-specific jobs, and other discriminatory practices.

In the early decades of the twentieth century, those gender stereotypes were based on the "scientific" assertion that women were biologically and emotionally unfit for certain kinds of labor. During both World War I and World War II, women workers in all fields demonstrated the fallacy of this belief. In the post-World War II era, another gender-related cultural construct emerged and was used to justify the large-scale firing of women workers. This idea, supported by many psychologists, educators, and child-development specialists, emphasized that a child's emotional and physical well-being can only come from a continuous (twenty-four hours-a-day) nurturant relationship with the biological mother. The belief that women need babies to be fulfilled was thus complemented by the scientific dogma that babies need their mothers on a full-time basis to develop. Ann Dally (1983) has documented the historical circumstances, persons, and events involved in legitimating and popularizing this doctrine in Great Britain and the United States. She states that it served as the ideological rationale not only for firing women workers but also for eliminating the public day-care centers established during wartime. At a time of social and economic upheaval, unemployment rates were lowered, public spending was reduced, the family was restored to "normal," and the privileges of male workers were retained—all at the expense of working mothers.

Motherhood and Wage Labor

This historical example parallels the contradiction between the idealization of motherhood and the actual denigration of mothers that still exists today. While the concept of motherhood is glorified by public officials and private interests alike, real mothers continue to be discriminated against in terms of their unpaid domestic work, differential employment opportunities ("mothers' hours" usually means minimum wage for less than twenty hours a week, thus rendering the working mother ineligible for benefits), and decreasing access to public funds and services. These problems are, of course, compounded by the growing number of mothers who must work to subsist or who depend on public support for their survival.

This contradiction, as well as the real hardships it entails for some mothers, may be a key factor in the increased rates of postpartum emotional disorders in the United States and Great Britain. Women are socialized to believe in the idealized concept of motherhood only to be faced with very real limitations and constraints when they become mothers. As Ann Oakley (1980b) puts it, depression is a human way of reacting to frustration and misery, especially when the individual finds him/herself in a state of helplessness, against overwhelming odds.

Another aspect of the problem relates to the fact that mothers who cannot conform to the demands of full-time motherhood, because of their temperament or financial situation, often feel guilty and deficient. These sentiments can certainly contribute to emotional disorders in the postpartum period.

One final note, in recent years the women's movement in the United States and Great Britain has challenged many aspects of subordination. As a result, some important changes in the economic, occupational, legal, and political status of women have been forthcoming. Yet the contradiction described above is very much operative, with the additional ideological input (in the United States, at least) of the "super mom" concept. Today, many young women are no longer socialized to believe they must be full-time mothers. Rather, they are encouraged to seek out fulfilling careers, which will then be combined with motherhood. Examples of "super moms" who have accomplished this abound in newspapers, women's magazines, and television. However, because of continuing structural barriers (e.g., lack of good affordable childcare facilities, inadequate maternity leave, virtually no paternity leave), this image will be impossible for most women to realize. The "super mom" construct masks these objective barriers so that mothers who find they can not "have it all" are deemed failures by themselves and others. This could constitute an additional reason for increasing postpartum emotional problems. According to some researchers, depression may occur not when things are at their worst but when there is a possibility of improvement and a discrepancy exists between one's rising aspirations and the likelihood of fulfilling them (Klerman and Weissman 1980:86).

Conclusion

I have explained the increasing incidence of postpartum emotional disorders in the United States and Great Britain in terms of gender-related constructs surrounding motherhood and women's concrete experience as mothers in medical, familial, and political-economic contexts. One major factor is the contradiction between the idealization of motherhood and the actual denigration of women and mothers within the interlocking structures of capitalism and male domination. One important conclusion is that both the institutionalization of motherhood and the problems that new mothers face are intimately bound up with the overall position of women in society. Yet, as Ann Oakley (1980a) notes, it is perhaps only when they become mothers that women experience the full impact of their subordination.

I am, of course, not denying that, for many women, motherhood can bring great joy, gratification, and personal fulfillment. To realize this potential fully, however, the substantive problems outlined above must be addressed. This would involve qualitative changes in gender constructs—separating out motherhood from definitions of female adulthood—and in related cultural ideas about the social role of mothers. It would also require major structural transformations in health care, family relations, and broader political-economic institutions. In directing our professional and personal efforts toward such change, we will be contributing to a more positive experience for new mothers—one without the postpartum emotional disorders that many women face today.

NOTES

This is a substantially revised version of a paper originally presented at the Eleventh International Congress of Anthropological and Ethnological Sciences in Vancouver, Canada (Summer 1983). I wish to thank Chiara Saraceno and Tony Leeds, along with his graduate study group, for their helpful comments on the original paper.

1. This conceptual approach, which views health and illness in more holistic terms, owes much to the work of W. B. Cannon (1946), H. Selye (1956), and other pioneers in the field of stress research.

2. See A. Young (1980) for a comprehensive critique of the concept of stress.

3. I began to perceive the limitations of this approach following the birth of my own child in 1983. The "lived experience" of motherhood made me reassess my earlier assumptions about childbirth as a life crisis and seek out more powerful explanations for the problems facing new mothers in the United States today. This essay is one outcome of that process.

4. Here I am following I. M. Young's (1984:136) definition of male domination: "Male domination refers to the organization of a particular institution or the pattern of institutional organization in a whole society, in which men have some degree of unreciprocated authority or control over women, and/or men have greater control than women over the operations of the institutions or set of institutions. . . . " See her article for further elaboration of this definition.

REFERENCES

Barker-Benfield, G. J. 1976. *The Horrors of the Half-Known Life.* New York: Harper and Row.
Barrett, Michele. 1980. *Women's Oppression Today.* London: Verso.
Barrett, Michele, and M. McIntosh. 1982. *The Anti-social Family.* London: Verso.
Belsky, J. 1981. "Early Human Experience: A Family Perspective." *Developmental Psychology* 17:3–23.

Breen, D. 1975. *The Birth of a First Child.* London: Tavistock.

Brown, W. A. 1979. *Psychological Care during Pregnancy and the Post-Partum Period.* New York: Raven.

Cannon, W. B. 1946. "The General Adaption Syndrome and the Diseases of Adaption." *Journal of Clinical Endocrinology* 6:117.

Chertok, L. 1969. *Motherhood and Personality: Psychosomatic Aspects of Childbirth.* London: Travistock.

Clark, Alice. 1969. *The Working Life of Women in the Seventeeth Century.* New York: Kelly.

Cone, B. A. 1972. "Puerperal Depression." In *Psychosomatic Medicine in Obstetrics and Gynecology,* ed. N. Morris. Basel: S. Krager.

Dally, Ann. 1983. *Inventing Motherhood.* New York: Schocken.

Dalton, K. 1969. *The Menstrual Cycle.* Harmondsworth, England: Penguin.

Ehrenreich, B., and D. English. 1972. *Witches, Midwives and Nurses: A History of Women Healers.* New York: Feminist Press.

———. 1973. *Complaints and Disorders: The Sexual Politics of Sickness.* New York: Feminist Press.

———. 1978. *For Her Own Good.* New York: Doubleday.

Felker, Marcia. 1982. "The Political-Economy of Sexism in Industrial Health." *Social Science and Medicine* 16:3–13.

Giovannini, Maureen. 1979. "The Post-Partum Adjustment Process: A Relevant Primary Care Issue." Research report prepared for the Boston University School of Medicine and the East Boston Neighborhood Health Center.

———. 1980. "Social Networks and Post-Partum Depression." Paper presented at the Society for Applied Anthropology Annual Meeting, Philadelphia, Pennsylvania.

Gordon, Linda. 1976. *Woman's Body, Woman's Right.* New York: Grossman.

Gordon, R. E., and K. K. Gordon. 1967. "Factors in Post-Partum Emotional Adjustment." *American Journal of Orthopsychiatry* 37:369–80.

Gordon, R. E., E. E. Kapostins, and K. K. Gordon. 1965. "Factors in Postpartum Emotional Adjustment." *Obstetrics and Gynecology,* 25:158–66.

Grossman, F. K., L. S. Eichler, and S. A. Winickoff. 1980. *Pregnancy, Birth and Parenthood.* San Francisco: Jossey-Bass.

Hamilton, J. 1962. *Post-partum Psychiatric Problems.* St. Louis: Mosby.

Hartmann, Heidi. 1981. "The Unhappy Marriage of Marxism and Feminism: Towards a More Progressive Union." In *Women and Revolution,* ed. Lydia Sargent. Boston: South End Press.

Heitler, S. K. 1976. "Post-partum Depression: A Multi-dimensional Study." *Dissertation Abstracts International* 11–B:5792–93.

Holmes, T., and R. Rahe. 1967. "The Social Readjustment Rating Scale." *Journal of Psychosomatic Research* 11:213–18.

Hopkins, J., M. Marcus, and S. Campbell. 1984. "Post-partum Depression: A Critical Review." *Psychological Bulletin* 95:498–515.

Howell, Elizabeth. 1981. "Psychological Reactions of Postpartum Women." In *Women and Mental Health,* ed. Marjorie Bayes. New York: Basic Books.

Jordan, B. 1980. *Birth in Four Cultures*. Montreal: Eden Press.

Kaij, L., and A. Nilsson. 1972. "Emotional and Psychotic Illness following Childbirth." In *Modern Perspectives in Psycho-Obstetrics*, ed. John G. Howells. London: Oxford University Press.

Klerman, G., and M. Weissman. 1980. "Depression among Women: Their Nature and Causes." In *The Mental Health of Women*, ed. M. Guttentag, S. Salasin, and D. Belle. New York: Academic Press.

Komaroff, A., M. Masuda, and T. Holmes. 1968. "The Social Readjustment Rating scale: A Comparative Study of Negro, Mexican, and White Americans." *Journal of Psychomatic Research* 12:121–28.

Lennane, K. Jean, and R. John Lennane. 1973. "Alleged Psychogenic Disorders in Women: A Possible Manifestation of Sexual Prejudice." *New England Journal of Medicine* 288:288–92.

Mead, M., and N. Newton. 1967. "Cultural Patterning of Perinatal Behavior." In *Childbearing: Its Social and Psychological Aspects*, ed. S. Richardson. Baltimore: Williams and Williams.

Morris, N. 1972. *Psychosomatic Medicine in Obstetrics and Gynecology*. New York: S. Karger.

Oakley, Ann. 1979. "A Case of Maternity: Paradigms of Women as Maternity Cases." *Signs: Journal of Women in Culture and Society*. 4:607–31.

———. 1980a. *Becoming a Mother*. New York: Schocken.

———. 1980b. *Women Confined*. New York: Schocken.

O'Hara, Michael, Lynn Rehm, and Susan Campbell. 1983. "Postpartum Depression: A Role for Social Network and Life Stress Variables." *Journal of Nervous and Mental Disease* 171:336–41.

Parlee, M. B. 1978. "Psychological Aspects of Menstruation, Childbirth and Menopause." In *The Psychology of Women: Future Directions in Research*, ed. J. A. Sherman and F. L. Denmark. New York: Psychological Dimensions.

———. 1980. "Social and Emotional Aspects of Menstruation, Birth and Menopause." In *Psychosomatic Obstetrics and Gynecology*, ed. D. Yound and A. Ehrhardt. New York: Appleton-Century-Crofts.

Paykel, E. S., E. M. Emms, J. Fletcher, and E. S. Rassaby. 1980. "Life Events and Social Support in Puerperal Depression." *British Journal of Psychiatry* 136:339–46.

Rahe, R. H. 1969. "Multi-cultural Correlations of Life Change Scalings: America, Japan, Denmark, and Sweden." *Journal of Psychosomatic Research* 13:19–25.

Rich, A. 1976. *Of Woman Born*. New York: W. W. Norton.

Robson, K. M., and R. Kumar. 1980. "Delayed Onset of Maternal Affection after Childbirth." *British Journal of Psychiatry* 13:437–53.

Rossi, A. 1968. "Transition to Parenthood." *Journal of Marriage and the Family* 30:26–39.

Scully, D., and P. Bart. 1973. "A Funny Thing Happened on the Way to the Orifice: Women in Gynecology Text Books." *American Journal of Sociology* 78:1045–50.

Selye, H. 1956. *The Stress of Life*. New York: McGraw-Hill.

Stern, G., and L. Kruckman. 1983. "Multidisciplinary Perspectives on Post-Partum Depression: An Anthropological Critique." *Social Science and Medicine* 17:1027–41.

Young, A. 1980. "The Discourse on Stress and the Reproduction of Conventional Knowledge." *Social Science and Medicine* 14B:133–46.

Young, I. M. 1984. "Is Male Gender Identity the Cause of Male Domination?" In *Mothering: Essays in Feminist Theory*, ed. Joyce Trebilcot. New Jersey: Rowman and Alanheld.

PART 3

Violence against Women

Lee Ann Hoff

Gender-Specific Network Influences on Battered Women

Victimization by crime is commonly recognized as a crisis situation calling for social support. Instead of assistance, however, many suffer double victimization through neglect or by being held accountable for the violent action of their assailants. Such victim blaming or neglect can often be traced to social network members, that is, family members who convey certain values and professionals whose ideological assumptions influence their practice with distressed people.

This essay draws on research with battered women in an eastern American city (Hoff 1990). The study, *Battered Women as Survivors*, shows how victim blaming is related to values and social structural factors that place certain victims at a disadvantage because of their gender, the type of crime, and inadequacies in the health and criminal justice systems. When such secondary victimization occurs, the probability of the victim's emotional healing from the crisis of victimization is reduced, while the victim's vulnerability to emotional and mental scars increases.

Analysis in this essay focuses on selected aspects of the original study. Specifically, it includes three parts: (1) an overview of the larger study; (2) a data excerpt and in-depth analysis regarding the social network members' values concerning gender and accountability for violence and victimization; and (3) a crisis paradigm developed from this research, which highlights network factors in clinical practice with victims of violence.

Overview of Original Study

The central research question of the original study (Hoff 1990) concerned the influence of values and social support on battered women, as expressed through a woman's social network. That is, what is the link between the distress and crisis of individual women (micro-factors) and broader social and cultural issues (macro-factors)? My working hypothesis was that a women's social network might constitute the intermediate structure (or the concrete, visible avenues) between the micro-world of an individually troubled woman and the macro-structure of society, with its political, economic, and other institutions upholding values and norms about women, marriage, the family, and violence. Depending on the values held by a woman's network members and their material resources, it seemed probable that these people were either a source of aid and support or a hindrance to a battered woman in crisis.

A related theoretical concern was to examine how the concepts of sexism and patriarchy are linked to an interpretation of why men batter women, without reifying these concepts. In this study, *sexism* describes behavioral patterns complementary to a social structure of male dominance (i.e., a patriarchal society) in which individual men can, with basic social approval, behave violently against women. The same sexist attitudes, I thought, would influence what a natural or formal network member did or did not do for a battered woman in crisis. I was especially interested in uncovering the processes involved in a battered woman's decision to remain in a violent relationship or to return to such a relationship after leaving a shelter where she got relief from violence. A related question focused on how economic dependence and social and material support influenced the continuation or disruption of violence.

Using primarily qualitative methods in a naturalistic setting, I explored these questions with 9 battered women and 131 network members for approximately one year. Three other battered women took part in the study by facilitating access to potential participants and providing feedback about methodology. Data were gathered through participant observation, open-ended questionnaires, in-depth interviewing, and personal journal material. A total of 367 direct contact hours were spent with the women and their network members, and another 50 hours in directly interviewing network members. A life-history perspective was employed to examine values, overall functioning, and network factors operating in the lives of the women before, during, and after their experience of violence. The framework for the life-history examination was a 17-item Self-Evaluation Guide, which included the following topics: physical health; self-acceptance/self-esteem; vocation/occupation; immediate family; intimate relationships; residence; financial situation; decision making/cognitive functions; life philosophy/goals; leisure time/community involvement; feeling management; violence experienced; lethality toward self; lethality toward other; substance use; legal issues; and agency use. This tool was adapted from a record system of a comprehensive community mental health service that incorporated routine crisis assessment and social network factors into every intake interview (Hoff 1989).

To explore values and network factors further, a 47-item Values Index and a 25-item Social Network Questionnaire were constructed. The Values Index was designed to reveal feminist and traditional values regarding women, marriage, the family, and violence. The Social Network Questionnaire—adapted from J. S. Norbeck, A. M. Lindsey, and V. L. Carrieri's (1981) instrument—was used to identify and compare the following aspects of a woman's social network: reachability, density, range, content, directness, intensity, frequency, and durability.

Data from these sources were analyzed using sensitizing concepts from critical theory and the sociology of knowledge, symbolic interaction and crisis theory, network concepts, ethnomethodology, and related feminist and anthropological analysis of kinship, ritual, and belief systems. The approach to networks in this study grew from three strands in the development of the field: (1) network analysis in social anthropology (Barnes 1972; Boissevain 1979; Bott 1957; Mitchell 1969); (2) network intervention strategies in clinical practice with people in crisis (Hansell 1976; Polak 1971; Garrison 1974; Hoff 1989); and (3) interdisciplinary research on the role of social support as a buffer against stress in individuals experiencing traumatic life events (Gottlieb 1981; Kaplan, Cassel, and Gore 1977; McKinlay 1981).

In this research, *network* includes family, friends, clergy, employers, self-help groups, and anyone else significant to the woman—as C. B. Stack (1974:90) states, "those you count on," or, as clinicians put it, "significant others." *Social support* in this study includes not only the gratification of emotional needs, such as approval from significant others (Kaplan, Cassel, and Gore 1977:50), but also the material, social, and cultural requisites for avoiding crisis. This notion is drawn from G. Caplan's (1964) concept of "supplies" for mental health and N. Hansell's (1976:31–49) expansion of Caplan's work in his description of "essential attachments" (or "life functions"). The disruption of such attachments results in "signals of distress" and possible crisis.

A central concern in this research was a context-specific interpretive analysis, not hypothesis testing through statistical techniques. Also informing the study was the practice-research-practice link. General outcomes of the study demonstrate links between individual battered women in crisis, their social networks, and the larger society, and they form the foundation for a crisis paradigm that includes previously neglected network and political aspects of personal crisis.

Network members were categorized as "natural" (family, friends, and neighbors) or "formal" (institutional representatives, such as nurses and social workers). Social network analysis revealed that the women's families (with the exception of two fathers), as well as friends, were largely supportive of them both during and after crisis around violence. This finding contradicts the stereotype of family members' indifference to a battered woman. Natural network members generally responded positively, in spite of their quite traditional (as opposed to feminist) values regarding women, marriage, the family, and violence. Family members' responses on the Values Index pointed to generally more traditional attitudes than the battered women themselves had. Women network members were generally more feminist in orientation than the men, particularly regarding egalitarian ideals about housework and childrearing. Family members expressed dismay when they learned that the abused women had often deliberately kept knowledge of the violence from them. This finding underscores the extent to which women have absorbed the social value that they are personally responsible for their victimization and resolution of crises around it. It also supports feminist and critical analyses of depression theories that locate women's problems in their biology or in psychological attributes (Hoff 1985; Sayers 1982). Emerging from the logic of depression theories is the notion that "if women could just change their negative attitudes, they would be less suicidal." In contrast to such reductionist theorizing, the research reveals the process whereby women are socialized to channel stress and conflict inward (Cloward and Piven 1979; Gerhardt 1979), with depression and suicide attempts some of the most common results (an example of this process is cited in the next section).

Responses of formal network members (nurses, physicians, counselors, police, and welfare workers) to the women both during and after the violence were either negative or indifferent for the most part. For example, they directly probed for what the woman did to "provoke" the violence; they prescribed tranquilizers instead of crisis counseling; they fell asleep during therapy sessions; they gave no feedback; they failed to say or do anything when a woman confided she had been battered; they behaved in a way that suggested to the woman that battering was a "taboo" topic or that to interact with her meant one would somehow be "contaminated." As one woman said, "You say you're battered and they act like, 'Oh my God! I'm gonna catch that disease!' " Another woman said:

> I used to come in to my hospital job with bruises and they [the nurses] would talk about it. . . . "How can a woman be so stupid and stay with a guy like that?" The nurses were so unsympathetic . . . I couldn't have been bothered talking to any of them about my situation. But I couldn't help seeing how the doctors would put them down and they stood there and took it. Women are too competitive with each other. . . . They get that from men. They [the nurses] would complain about how they were treated by doctors and the hospital, but in their relationships you'd have thought they were perfect the way they acted and talked.

Housing authorities and political figures in the metropolitan area of the study were particularly indifferent to the plight of homelessness some of the women suffered for months after leaving emergency shelters. Also significant was the relative absence of support groups and childcare assistance for women after they left the shelter. If such services existed, either they were inconveniently scheduled or the women could not afford them. Follow-up interviews with the women five years later (in 1988) revealed that most of them were still struggling with the same issues and problems. Press accounts about battering reveal that public response has not changed much either.

Ethnomethodological Analysis of a Data Excerpt

An ethnomethodological perspective in studying violence analyzes rules of conduct and methods of reasoning employed by victims and perpetrators of violence. N. Quinn and D. Holland (1987:4) refer to such reasoning methods as "cultural models," the taken-for-granted beliefs about the world that are widely shared by a society's members. Ethnomethodological analysis in this study focused on how a battered woman makes sense out of her own and others' behavior, what "counts" for them as "support," and what counts as a "public" matter for institutional representatives of a woman's social network.

Such analyses presuppose that the cultural rules and common-sense logic used by battered women and others are publicly—and therefore, empirically—available for analysis in language and other interaction. Thse data of interaction can make publicly visible the beliefs, attitudes, and structure characterizing a particular linguistic community or society. They fill in gaps left by political and ideological discourse and causal analysis of deviance, stress, and coping. To avoid reductionism in such analyses, however, it is important to acknowledge that cultural rules themselves are historically situated (Keesing 1987:387). In this case, beliefs about women, men, and battering reside in a society with continuing patriarchal values that intersect with such social processes as the women's movement.

Two ethnomethodological techniques were used in this study: (1) "presupposition analysis," which assumes that people's beliefs and attitudes are revealed in what people say and do, and (2) the "Membership Categorization Device" (MCD), which refers to the organized ways humans describe and understand people and their activities (Sacks 1974, Coulter 1979b; Benson and Hughes 1983:132). One such categorization device is the Relational Pair (e.g., parent/child, male/female, deserving homeless/undeserving homeless, nature/culture).

General empirical examples of everyday reasoning in this study of violence include: (1) "He beat me because he didn't like what I cooked . . . it was my fault," which presupposes a woman's belief that she is responsible for the violence of her assailant; (2) after beating up his wife, a husband says, "I'll take you to the police station and tell them how stupid you are," which presupposes a man's confidence that the police will not hold him accountable for his violence, that he will "get by"; and (3) the Housing Authority's omission of "battering" as a criterion qualifying one as "homeless through no fault of one's own," which implies that public officials categorize the homeless into the Relational Pair of "deserving homeless/undeserving homeless" and believe battered women are homeless through their own fault.

The following excerpt from an extensive interview with the parents of a battered woman further illustrates the use of ethnomethodological analysis in this study. The father is educated at the master's degree level, while the mother is from New England WASP (white Anglo-Saxon Protestant) ancestry, with some college education.

Father: To our amazement we didn't know [about the violence] for years.

Interviewer: Why do you think she didn't tell you?

Father: It bothered me very greatly because I wondered what in heck I had done wrong in our upbringing of her in not having given her the self-confidence to say "Nobody's going to treat me like that. . . . Get the hell out of here." Somehow or other I feel I'm amiss on that score.

Interviewer: You mean that you feel it's a failure of your parenting?

Father: Yes, I feel that very strongly, both of us do. . . . You know, one of the things I kidded her about was, "You don't need to go to college. . . . You're pretty enough to find a nice man. . . . You don't have to go to college." I was kidding. . . . I had no intention of not letting her go to college—no way, but apparently it was misunderstood and taken wrong.

Interviewer: Did she tell you that?

Father: I found out about it much later when she told me I had told her that when she said she *was* going to college anyway.

Mother: It was more like, "Thank goodness you're a girl. . . . We don't have to worry about the expense of putting you through college."

Father: In whatever way it was said it was unfortunate. . . . You know it's amazing that she would take it that way because my mother was one of the first people that was emancipated in that sense in [a northern European country]. We came from a nouveau rich family. . . . She [his mother] had the gumption to say, "I'm going to do it [take up a career]."

Mother: I would always try to counteract and say, "Your father doesn't mean it . . . girls have to go [to college] just as well as boys."

This interview illustrates the complexity of how natural network members' values (in this case, sex-role stereotyping) are absorbed and may intersect with the occurrence of violence and the victim's endurance of it. The interview offers empirical evidence for the claim that sexist values are linked to violence against women. Specifically, these data were interpreted using the enthnomethodological techniques of the Membership Categorization Device (MCD) and presupposition analysis (Coulter 1979b) to analyze through language the existence of beliefs, values, and the reasoning process of a battered woman's natural network member: her father.

This father's painful recall of his teasing his daughter about not needing a college education presupposes his belief in a connection between this parental behavior and his daughter's later battering (Coulter 1979a). He thinks her lack of self-respect accounts for her battering, and he connects this personal attribute to their parental failure in bringing her up. The childhood inculcation of the traditional roles of wife and mother, rather than college and career, seems borne out in this woman's case.

Even though she is now educated at the graduate level like her father and is highly successful in her career, she expressed her "failure" as a wife and mother more keenly than any of the other study participants: "My mother had been *very* tied up with her ability to have children [she had sixteen pregnancies, with only four living . . .]. I was thinking about it the other day and if someone told me I have only a year to live, what do I want to do, to have accomplished? And the first thing that popped into my mind is that I would want to be pregnant, to have a child." She also said that her decision to conceal her suffering from her parents as long as she did was influenced by her sense of failure as a wife and mother, her shame in not living up to the ideal of her mother as a woman who would not put up with violence, her mother's frequent depressions, her strong tendency to take responsibility for the problems of those around her, and a two-year physical absence of her parents, who were living abroad. Interestingly, she did not include her father's teasing about not having to pay for her to go to college; only the father brought up this item. (This woman, incidentally, was depressed and periodically suicidal for two years after divorcing her violent husband.)

Although the daughter did not refer to her father's teasing in her accounts, some excerpts from the interview can be examined using the Membership Categorization Device, together with further presupposition analysis. An example of MCD displayed in this interview is "gender," which includes the categories "male" and "female."

This man's daughter is "pretty enough to find a nice man," and he tells her, "You don't need to go to college." This statement implies that the male member of the category "gender" does have to go to college. Several times the father expresses guilt about his parenting, which presupposes the belief that failure as a parent may be connected to his daughter's putting up with beating. He attempts to mitigate his guilt, however, by defining his statement as "kidding" and disclaiming any intention of "not letting her go to college—no way." The fact that his daughter focuses on a mothering role in spite of her graduate degree suggests at the very least some ambiguity around what twenty-five years later he calls "kidding." His connecting this "kidding" to his daughter's imputed lack of self-confidence to say "Nobody's going to treat me like that—Get the hell out of here," could be an expression of his desperate attempt to understand his daughter's situation—grasping at any straw, so to speak, for an explanation. On the other hand, this kind of kidding itself, even if sincerely intended *only* as kidding, presupposes certain beliefs about the male/female Relational Pair and the necessity of a college education for boys but not for girls. It also presupposes certain beliefs about a girl's dependency on something other than a college education for her future as an adult. Specifically, she can depend on being "pretty enough" and finding "a nice man" as a result of being "pretty enough." These statements also tie the female/male members of the category "gender" to the traditional association of "female" with marrige and the categories "body/nature/private" ("pretty enough"), and the male with paid occupation and the categories "mind/culture/public" ("college") (Ortner 1974).

The father's disclaimer, "I was kidding," is challenged and the presupposition of traditional beliefs about women verified on two counts: (1) the daughter apparently took his kidding seriously—"She said she was going to college anyway"; and (2) the mother redefines his "kidding" as "Thank goodness you're a girl. . . . We don't have to worry about the expense of putting you through college."

After a joint two-hour interview, each of these parents was also interviewed individually, focusing on the items in the Values Index. At the end of the father's individual interview, after the tape recorder had been shut off, he told about his son's acceptance of his wife's nagging and how the son "shook her" once as "the only way to stop her," because he couldn't take it anymore. He described this shaking as "necessary." I asked if this was any different from his daughter's staying and "taking it" (i.e., if he can't take her nagging anymore, why doesn't he just leave instead of dealing with it by force?). From my question during this brief interchange, this father seemed to develop an awakening to the double standard he had described. He had just elaborately interpreted his daughter's staying and putting up with violence as an indication of her lack of "self-respect." For his son who doesn't leave, self-respect seems enhanced by violence, and, the use of force is seen as a "necessary" solution to conflict.

Here we observe the father again associating the category "gender" with certain behaviors around violence. Gender and violence are inversely related in this man's reasoning. If women have violence used against them and fail to leave, they lack self-respect; if men are stressed by nonviolent behavior (e.g., nagging), their use of violence is seen as necessary and their self-respect is not lost as a result. This reasoning presupposes the traditional belief that a man's self-respect almost depends on the use of violence in such a case.

This man's language points to deeply embedded beliefs about women's responsibility for their victimization, the necessity of men's use of violence as a problem-solving tactic in social relations, and the practice of excusing male violence or redefining it as an "illness" to be treated rather than as a social action for which the man is accountable. This analysis should not be interpreted as suggesting a causal relationship between the father's beliefs, his teasing, and the daughter's later response to battering. Rather, such traditional socialization created a *climate* in which male violence, and female victim blaming and self-blame, could flourish. Perhaps nowhere are the sociocultural roots of such victim blaming and self-blame more dramatically illustrated than in the most frequently asked question about battered women—"Why do they stay?"—a question uppermost in the mind of this battered woman's father.

I propose it is no accident that this question is favored over other ones in mainstream research and lay speculation about woman abuse. This particular line of questioning relates to historic silence about violence against women, a silence signaling the traditional belief that battering is a private matter between the married couple (Dobash and Dobash 1979; Stark, Flitcraft, and Frazier 1979). Such silence also supports traditional ideology, with the man in charge at home and abroad, while the woman fulfills her supposedly "natural" destiny as reproducer and nurturer of children and men and preserver of the marital bond (Elshtain 1981; Rosaldo 1974; Smith 1987).

From this ideology logically follows a focus on a battered woman's responsibility for her victimization by asking why *she* does not leave. Also, traditional ideology created a climate that repressed the probability of asking more appropriate questions about violence against women. Is it not ironic that we have not asked, for example, why violent men are *allowed* to stay? The significance of having asked the wrong questions is particularly striking when considering the intensive socialization of women over hundreds of years to think of their "proper" place as the home.

One can assume that either a strange reversal of logic or scarcely disguised ideology explains why researchers and others have not asked, "Why should battered women, the victims—rather than their assailants—be expected to leave?" The failure to have asked more appropriate questions suggests the depth of society's tendency to blame abused women for their plight and to hold them responsible for the violent action of their assailants. In practical terms, of course, so long as assailants know they can usually get by with violence, it is absolutely necessary for women to leave in order to save their lives. But that is another issue.

To return to the interview example, several factors seemed to operate in a complex interplay to keep this woman isolated during crises around violence: absorption of traditional sex-role values and their expression in the primacy of the wife and mother goal; her corresponding sense of responsibility to make the marriage work; and long-term physical distance from her parents. In short, values seem to intersect with social, psychological, and material factors in this particular instance to prevent the woman from breaking out of the violent partnership sooner. For this financially independent, highly educated woman, economic factors did not play a part in her staying with a violent husband for eight years.

Instead, her case supports the arguments of N. Chodorow (1978), D. Dinnerstein (1977), and E. F. Keller (1983) that early childrearing practices, and in this instance the mother's dominant role-model and depression, have a powerful influence on the development of the individual's self-concept. Her father's professional career did not impress her nearly as much as her mother's desire to have children did. This woman's vision of marriage and motherhood as her most important life work is probably related more to the structural features of her family that strongly reinforced the traditional view of women (Poster 1978; Barrett and McIntosh 1982) than to the notion that biology determines a woman's destiny (Sayers 1982).

Practice Implications

The practice implications of this research cross political and human service domains and illustrate the significance of social network factors in linking the individual and sociocultural aspects of wife abuse. These factors are illustrated in a crisis paradigm that addresses both the political and human service aspects of battering (see Figure 1). The tandem approach to crisis management suggested in the paradigm can prevent collusion in victim blaming (Hoff 1989, 1990). The tandem approach simply means attending to the individual needs of a woman in crisis while not losing sight of the origins of her crisis. Basic to this crisis paradigm is the interactional relationship between crisis origins, personal crisis manifestations, and the outcomes of crisis for various individuals. Crisis intervention and follow-up strategies thus need to be tailored to the distinct *origins* of the crisis to foster positive crisis resolution and to avoid the possible negative outcomes of crisis, such as suicide, homicide, addictions, or emotional breakdown.

For example, a battered woman may lose her home and her husband (see top circle in Crisis Origins in Figure 1) and be forced into a status change from married to single (lower circle), not because she wants to be single but only because of the threat to her life. These two sources of crisis, however, spring from the primary origins of crisis for battered women: the social structure and cultural values (right circle). That is, a battered woman's crisis originates in deeply embedded values about women, marriage and the family, the social inequalty of women, and the deviant behavior of another person, which is basically approved socially inasmuch as so little legal or political action is taken to stop it or to hold violent men accountable. Such social indifference to violence against women is strikingly revealed in the commonly asked question, "Why do battered women stay?" If society really disapproved of violence against women, then researchers, clinicians, and the public could have pointed out that it is the assailants rather than their victims who forfeited their right to stay. The misplacement of social accountability has added to the misery of countless women in crisis from battering.

The emotional healing process of crises stemming from such sociocultural sources differs from those in which the crises can be explained by "an act of God" or fate, such as losses from a natural disaster (Lifton and Olson 1976; Antonovsky 1980; Silver, Boon, and Stones 1983). This is because part of the crisis resolution process includes whatever people do to explain to themselves why certain terrible things happen to them; the event somehow must fit into one's meaning system.

Experiencing violence and neglect rather than nurturance and support from one's spouse and network members represents a certain reversal of the moral order. It also suggests that men fail to contextualize their behavior appropriately. That is, the aggression and violence expected of men in the public domain of, for example, war is carried over to the domestic context in which men are expected to protect and defend their wives. Two women in the study poignantly expressed their shock and disappointment in being beaten during pregnancy, a time they felt more vulnerable and in greater need of protection. The process of emotional healing for people whose crises stem from a social source like this seems to demand some kind of social response, either from themselves or from social network members and others on their behalf.

An appropriate social response is commonly expressed in the form of victim compensation of some kind. This, along with linkage to a peer support group and knowledge that public action is being taken to stop violence against women, helps a woman make sense out of her experience. In the paradigm these responses are depicted as

Figure 1: Crisis Paradigm

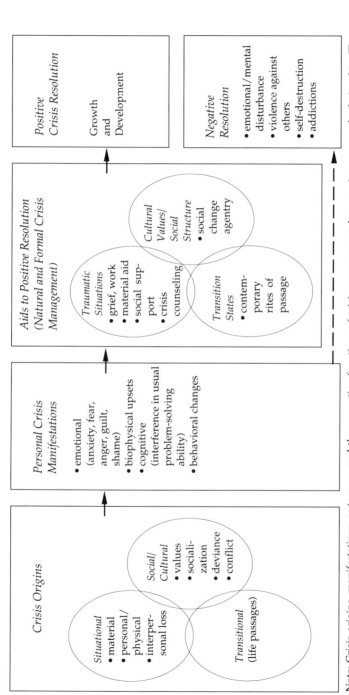

Note: Crisis origins, manifestations, outcomes, and the respective functions of crisis management have an interpersonal relationship. The intertwined circles represent the distinct yet interrelated "origins" of crisis and "aids to positive resolution," even though personal manifestations are often similar. The solid line from origins to positive resolutions illustrates the *opportunity* for growth and development through crisis; the broken line depicts the potential *danger* of crisis in the absence of appropriate aids. From Lee Hoff's *Battered Women as Survivors* (1990:77), with the permission of Routledge.

"contemporary rites of passage" and "social change agentry" (see lower and right circles in Aids to Positive Crisis Resolution in Figure 1). It is encouraging and therefore helpful for a woman to know that her suffering has not been in vain, that something is being done to change the circumstances that contributed to her victimization. In this, battered women have something in common with survivors of the Holocaust, the atom bombs, and other man-made disasters.

Conclusion

To summarize, this research-based paradigm underscores the limits of psychologically oriented crisis intervention when the crisis does not originate in a person's psyche. Social analysts must make explicit the values informing their research, and clinicians must move beyond narrow intrapsychic approaches to network intervention and social change, if they are to make a difference to people in crisis because of their disadvantaged position in the social structure or because of deeply embedded values motivating action or inaction around violence.

Sexist, racist, and classist values and policies leave women, children, the poor, and people of color particularly vulnerable to crises. While natural and formal network members are the medium through which these values are conveyed and policies upheld, these same network members can be a positive force in the lives of battered women in crisis. Psychological support for a battered woman is not enough, however. Crises stemming from sociocultural, political sources demand a social, political response.

REFERENCES

Antonovsky, A. 1980. *Health, Stress and Coping.* San Francisco: Jossey-Bass.

Barnes, J. A. 1972. *Social Networks.* Reading, Mass.: Addison-Wesley.

Barrett, M., and M. McIntosh. 1982. *The Anti-Social Family.* London: Verso.

Benson, D., and J. A. Hughes. 1983. *The Perspective of Ethnomethodology.* London: Longman.

Boissevain, J. 1979. "Network Analysis: A Reappraisal." *Current Anthropology* 20(2):392–394.

Bott, E. 1957. *Family and Social Networks.* London: Tavistock.

Caplan, G. 1964. *Principles of Preventive Psychiatry.* New York: Basic Books.

Chodorow, N. 1978. *The Reproduction of Mothering: Psychoanalysis and the Sociology of Gender.* Berkeley: University of California Press.

Cloward, R. A., and F. E. Piven. 1979. "Hidden Protest: The Channeling of Female Innovation and Resistance." *Signs: Journal of Women in Culture and Society* 4:651–69.

Coulter, J. 1979a. "Beliefs and Practical Understanding." In *Everyday Language: Studies in Ethnomethodology,* ed. G. Psathas. New York: Irvington.

———. 1979b. *The Social Construction of Mind.* Totowa, N.J.: Rowman and Littlefield.

Dinnerstein, D. 1977. *The Mermaid and the Minotaur: Sexual Arrangements and Human Malaise.* New York: Harper Colophon Books.

Dobash, R. P., and R. E. Dobash. 1979. *Violence against Women: A Case against the Patriarch.* New York: Free Press.

Elshtain, J. B. 1981. *Public Man, Private Woman: Women in Social and Political Thought.* Princeton, N.J.: Princeton University Press.

Garrison, J. 1974. "Network Techniques: Case Studies in the Screening-Linking-Planning Conference Method." *Family Process* 13:337–53.

Gerhardt, U. 1979. "Coping and Social Action: Theoretical Reconstruction of the Life-event Approach." *Sociology of Health and Illness* 1:195–225.

Gottlieb, B. H., ed. 1981. *Social Network and Social Support.* Beverly Hills: Sage.

Hansell, N. 1976. *The Person in Distress.* New York: Human Sciences Press.

Hoff, L. A. 1985. "Review of Suicidal Women: Their Thinking and Feeling Patterns, C. Neuringer and D. J. Lettieri." *Suicide and Life-Threatening Behavior* 15(1):69–73.

———. 1989. *People in Crisis: Understanding and Helping.* 3d. ed. Redwood City, Calif.: Addison-Wesley.

———. 1990. *Battered Women as Survivors.* London: Routledge.

Kaplan, Bl H., J. Cassel, and S. Gore. 1977. "Social Support." *Medical Care* 15:47–58.

Keesing, R. M. 1987. "Models, 'Folk' and 'Cultural': Paradigms Regained?" In *Cultural Models in Language and Thought,* ed. D. Holland and N. Quinn. Cambridge: Cambridge University Press.

Keller, E. F. 1983. "Gender and Science." In *Discovering Reality,* ed. S. Harding and M. B. Hintikka. Boston: D. Reidel.

Lifton, R. J. and E. Olson. 1976. "The Human Meaning of Total Disaster: The Buffalo Greek Experience." *Psychiatry* 39:1–18.

McKinlay, J. B. 1981. "Social Network Influences on Morbid Episodes and the Career of Help-seeking." In *The Relevance of Social Science for Medicine,* ed. I. Eisenberg and A. Kleinman. The Hague: D. Reidel.

Mitchell, J. B. 1969. *Social Network Influences in Urban Situations.* Manchester, England: University of Manchester Press.

Norbeck, J. S., A. M. Lindsey, and V. L. Carrieri. 1981. "The Development of an Instrument to Measure Social Support." *Nursing Research* 30(5): 264–69.

Ortner, S. B. 1974. "Is Female to Male as Nature is to Culture?" In *Woman, Culture and Society,* ed. M. Z. Rosaldo and L. Lamphere. Stanford, Calif.: Stanford University Press.

Polak, P. R. 1971. "Social Systems Intervention." *Archives of General Psychiatry* 25:110–17.

Poster, M. 1978. *Critical Theory of the Family.* New York: Seabury.

Quinn, N., and D. Holland. 1987. "Culture and Cognition." In *Cultural Models in Language and Thought*, ed. D. Holland and N. Quinn. Cambridge: Cambridge University Press.

Rosaldo, M. Z. 1974. "Woman, Culture and Society: A Theoretical Overview." In *Woman, Culture and Society*, ed. M. Z. Rosaldo and L. Lamphere. Stanford, Calif.: Stanford University Press.

Sacks, K. 1974. "On the Analyzability of Stories by Children." In *Ethnomethodology*, ed. R. Turner. Harmondsworth, England: Penguin.

Sayers, D. 1982. *Biological Politics*. London: Tavistock.

Silver, R. L., C. Boon, and M. H. Stones. 1983. "Searching for Meaning in Misfortune: Making Sense of Incest." *Journal of Social Issues* 39(2):81–102.

Smith, D. E. 1987. *The Everyday World as Problematic: A Feminist Sociology*. Boston: Northeastern University Press.

Stack, C. B. 1974. *All Our Kin*. New York: Harper and Row.

Stark, E., A. Flitcraft, and W. Frazier. 1979. "Medicine and Patriarchal Violence: The Social Construction of a 'Private' Event." *International Journal of Health Services* 9:461–93.

Barbara V. Reid

A Man's Home Is His Castle: Spousal Rape In Western Society

Only in the last fifteen years has the rape of a woman by her spouse been considered a criminal offense in the United States. Even today many states have not yet abolished the "marital rape exemption," which prevents prosecuting men for the crime of rape when the victim is related through marital vows. The expansion of the meaning of rape to include nonstranger forms, such as marital rape, date rape, acquaintance rape, celebrity rape, incestuous rape, and same-sex rape, is part of a broader trend involving two components. First is the movement directed toward ensuring the right to control one's body at the individual level, as exemplified in struggles around abortion, gay rights, sexual harassment, childbirth, incest, weight control, eating disorders, pornography, and new reproductive technologies. To quote Donna Haraway (1990:141), one of the most prescient of feminist scholars today, "It is possible to argue nonfacetiously that every major public issue in the last two decades in the United States has been pervaded by the symbols and stakes of sexual politics." Second is the redefinition of the meaning of public and private or domestic spheres of activity as they affect the rights of individuals in society. This second trend is also related to shifts in the meaning of both production and reproduction.

In this essay I explore the legal origins of the marital rape exemption and then discuss marital rape in the broader context of biological politics. I contend that the metaphor of women as property underlies the practice of not only marital rape but also stranger rape. I conclude that the redefinition of the demarcation of public as opposed to private spheres has been concurrent with the redefinition of women as independent agents and decision makers, in contrast to previously held cultural definitions that viewed women primarily as the property of men.

Historical Roots of the Marital Rape Exemption

Marital rape was a virtually unstudied social problem prior to the ground-breaking work of Diana E. H. Russell (1982) and David Finkelhor and Kersti Yllo (1983). Russell's study was important in establishing that marital rape was prevalent enough to warrant concern. Fourteen percent of her San Francisco informants reported they had been sexually assaulted by their husbands sometime during their lives. Similarly, in a comparative study done in Boston, Finkelhor and Yllo found that 10 percent of respondents had experienced spousal rape.

What prevented the recognition of spousal rape as a criminal offense? The legal justification for denying the existence of marital rape stems from three historical roots identified by an anonymous contributor to the *Harvard Law Review* (1986): (1) the notion of implied consent, (2) the unities theory, and (3) the theory of separate spheres.

The Notion of Implied Consent

The most frequently cited basis in law for a marital rape exemption is the notion of implied consent as defined by Matthew Hale, chief justice of England in the seventeenth century. According to Hale, a wife has implicitly consented to engage in sexual activities with her husband by virtue of her marriage contract with him. Hale stated the belief that upon marriage a woman has made a binding contract with her husband to meet his sexual needs for the duration of the union. A related custom is the woman's promise, during the wedding ceremony, to "love, honor and obey." Since many contemporary wedding ceremonies do not include the vow to obey, this basis for upholding a marital rape exemption is breaking down. Implied consent is consistent with the archaic Anglo-Saxon legal definition of rape as a man's forcible vaginal penetration of a woman who is not his wife.

Felicity Kaganas (1986:457) notes that under South African law, rape is defined as "carnal connection [by a man] with a woman [not his wife] without her consent." The historical roots of this definition are found in Roman-Dutch law, which in 1656 stated that "husbands have, in the first place, such authority over their wives as is given by the laws of nature, of God, and all nations, namely that wives must be subject to their husbands in all things which do not clearly conflict with honour and virtue. Since no power in the world can be effective without compulsion, the husband must also possess certain means of compulsion, in case the wife refuses to bow to his sway in reasonable matters" (457).

This type of reasoning has been challenged by recent court decisions. For example, in 1984 the New York State Court of Appeals ruled that the state's marital rape exemption was invalid because it did not provide equal rights for married women as compared to unmarried women (Center for Constitutional Rights 1986).

The Unities Theory

The unities theory, which dates from the days of the eighteenth-century British jurist Sir William Blackstone, has been used as a rationale for exempting husbands from prosecution for rape. According to this point of view, when a husband and wife marry they cease to be separate individuals and become one person, both of whom are subsumed under the being of the husband. This precludes the possibility of a husband's raping his wife, because she has no separate identity as a human being apart from him. The *Harvard Law Review* author points out that under the unities doctrine, rape was treated as a crime committed by one man against another, involving essentially the theft and despoiling of another man's property (see also Brownmiller 1975). If the married woman is the property of her husband, then he can hardly steal from himself.

English conventions included marriage by capture of the bride by her husband and the common law custom of divorcing a wife by "selling" her to a new husband (Menefee 1981), once again transferring the rights of ownership of a woman from one man to another. This transfer is also symbolized by the now outmoded marriage ceremony in which the father of the bride "gives her away" to the groom. Once again the ceremony of marriage can be seen as reinforcing the legal premise of a marital rape exemption, even though in the United States this would seem to contradict the separation of church and state when church weddings are involved.

Separate Spheres Theory

The third source of the marital rape exemption dates to the theory of separate spheres, which the *Harvard Law* article claims came to replace the unities theory as the legal justification for sexual inequality. This notion of separate spheres, women in the private or domestic arena and men in the public domain, represents a structural opposition that often demarcates the boundaries within which the law is applied. There came to be an unwritten injunction in common law that the public sphere should not interfere with the private/domestic sphere, hence the reluctance of the law to "invade the privacy" of the home, even when the lives and well-being of women and children are threatened, as in cases of incest and other forms of child or spousal abuse (popularly viewed as "domestic" or "family" matters). Formal, state-controlled, public law sought not to intrude into the home, which was considered to be under the control of the male head of the family.

One exception to the generally sexist applications of public-private interpretations was the use of this reasoning to argue for a woman's right to control her fertility as a private matter, thereby establishing her option to terminate unwanted pregnancy, which served as one basis for the Roe v. Wade decision (Colker 1983). This ruling extended to women autonomous rights in the private sphere, challenging the earlier common law edicts that were based on a hierarchy within the family, where the husband's rights were primary and his word was the law.

Susan S. M. Edwards (1987) has also written in a similar vein about roles in the private realm. She traces the history of the husband's right to chastise his wife, upheld throughout British history and to a certain extent in Canada and the United States, which exempts husbands from charges of assault when wives are not "exemplary" in performing their ideal wifely roles. This reduction of the woman to less than fully privileged adult status is one example of a double standard in the application of the law. The right of chastisement, also implied in Roman-Dutch law, can be traced further to its roots in Greek philosophy (O'Brien 1981).

The Legal Challenge to the Marital Rape Exemption

Until recently, marital rape was considered a "family problem" (Pagelow 1984; Finkelhor and Yllo 1983, 1985; Shields and Hanneke 1983). Categorizing it as a family problem instead of a criminal act is one further manifestation of the public versus domestic gender ideology. It follows from such popular beliefs or folk maxims as "a man's home is his castle," the contents of which, presumably, are his possessions; in the minds of some men, this includes their wives and children. In the last ten to fifteen years, however, there has been an active campaign in the United States and abroad to gain recognition of marital rape as a criminal offense (Russell 1984; Estrich 1987; Anonymous 1986). As women enter the public sphere of activity in greater numbers, it becomes more and more difficult to uphold the gendered distinction between public and private.

The legal challenge to marital rape exemptions has been successful in many parts of the world and in some states within the United States. Mildred Daley Pagelow (1984) mentions that several countries outside the Anglo-Saxon tradition were the first to strike down this exemption. Since 1932 Poland has allowed prosecution for marital rape, as the Soviet Union, Czechoslovakia, Israel, Sweden, Norway, and Denmark now do. In fifteen states in the United States it is not yet possible to prosecute husbands, but in thirty-five states marital rape is acknowledged as a crime under some or all circumstances (Center for Constitutional Rights 1986). The marital rape exemption has been completely abolished in Alaska, Florida, Georgia, Kansas, Maine, Massachusetts, Montana, Nebraska, New Jersey, New York, Oregon, Vermont, and Wisconsin. In other states, prosecution is conditional on one or more of these requirements: the husband and wife live apart; one partner has filled for annulment, divorce, separation, or separate maintenance; or a legal separation or divorce has been obtained.

The Conceptual Challenge to the Marital Rape Exemption

Nicholas Groth's (1979) well-known study suggests marital rapists have the same motives that other rapists have; they differ only in terms of their sexual objects. He maintains that, like other forms of rape, marital rape involves power, anger, and sadism, in varying degrees of emphasis. If these same factors motivate all rapists, perhaps all forms of rape stem from the premise underlying the marital rape exemption: women are viewed by men, and in the past by the law and the church, mainly as property, theirs or other men's. That women are viewed as property is clear from the rationale behind making stranger rape a crime: it is a crime of one man against another man rather than against the woman involved. In fact, in earlier times, when women were not accorded the status of full adult citizenship, it was not possible to commit a crime (any crime) against a woman. According to this interpretation, implied consent, the unities theory, and the separate spheres ideology are implicated in justifying rape of all types.

Although marital rape has been distinguished from stranger rape under the law in the past, the similarities are clear. Blaming the victim is common in both forms. According to several writers, including Susan Brownmiller (1975) writing on the United States and Jennifer

Temkin (1986) corroborating for England, Scotland, Canada, New Zealand, and the Scandinavian countries, law enforcement officials have been inclined to hold the rape victim responsible. Women have been systematically persecuted by police and defense attorneys, and in some instances even by judges, to the point that rape is difficult to prove.

Much of the problem in prosecuting stranger rape has to do with myths about women's complicity or their "implicit consent" in their own rapes. This victim blaming is rooted in such hard-to-shake myths as "a woman provocatively dressed invites rape"; "women secretly want to be raped"; "when she says no, she really means yes." The courts have been more interested in the victim's previous sexual history than in the rapist's, which reflects the assumption that once a woman sleeps with one or more men out of wedlock, she somehow becomes the property of all men.

Rape is particularly difficult to prosecute when the perpetrator is known to the victim. Susan Estich's (1987) study suggests that the better the victim knows the rapist, the less likely she will either define the act as rape or report it to the police. Even when it is reported to the police, it is treated less seriously. Paradoxically, even though we expect those closest to us to treat us better than strangers do (see Hoff and Storer, herein), we punish strangers more severely for the crimes of rape, abuse, and even murder than we do those who know their victims and violate their trust. Both the law and the public consider stranger rape the most serious kind of crime, harking back to the time when rape was by definition the violation of a woman's sexuality by a stranger, a crime committed by one man against another man.

The unities theory, though perhaps less directly involved in justifying nonmarital rape, does serve to emphasize the point that women lack personhood except in relation to men, which both demeans and objectifies women by turning them into chattel. Indirectly, then, the unities theory also contributes to the psychology that legitimates rape.

The theory of separate spheres is important to stranger rape and marital rape alike. One of the myths involved in stranger rape is that women should not be outdoors, in the public sphere, especially at night. Rape is a reminder to them to stay inside where they supposedly belong, in the relative safety of the private or domestic arena, under the protection of male family members. The theory of separate spheres enjoins women to stay in the home or suffer the consequences, and it tells the courts to stay out of domestic affairs.

Christine Delphy (1987) notes the futility of explaining gender and sexuality in terms of values and ideology unless these factors are, in turn, related to the structures and hierarchies of society. The feminist interpretation of rape in general, and of marital rape as a variety of rape, concentrates on the rewards that accrue to males as a group when men commit rape. Men who never commit rape recognize that they are still beneficiaries of the social control consequences of the crime. This is evidenced by the victim-blaming and wrist-slapping attitude that has characterized the U.S. legal system's treatment of rape, including marital rape, in the past. Rape, looked at in such structural terms, upholds the gendered separation between public and private, because it claims the public turf for men and threatens women who venture into it with bodily harm. When rape occurs in the marital context, it emphasizes the control men have over women in the family, and it demonstrates to women that they cannot look to the public authority of the law for protection. Ultimately, a patriarchal system of male dominance is maintained through the use of sexuality as a means of social control (Schecter 1982; Hanmer and Maynard 1987).

Trends Discouraging the Legal Acceptance of Marital Rape

Two interrelated trends have come to the forefront in recent decades that challenge the acceptability of marital rape: the struggle to attain control over one's body as an individual and the redefinition of public and private spheres.

The Struggle to Attain Individual Control over the Body

The use of sexuality to uphold the patriarchal system has been recognized in numerous contexts, and there is a wide-scale struggle centering on the individual's right to claim integrity of the self through control over one's own body. The struggle embraces many issues. The gay rights movement seeks the right to exercise one's own sexual orientation and to have this recognized legally as a protection of one's civil right to nondiscriminatory treatment. Similarly, the campaign to limit the dissemination of pornography, spearheaded by Catharine MacKinnon and Andrea Dworkin, has invoked the civil rights of women (see Kappeler 1986; MacKinnon, herein).

Other issues are more directly reproductive in nature, including the liberalization of abortion laws, the right to regulate fertility through the use of contraceptives, and the rights of women to control the process of childbirth (Sachdev 1988). This constellation of issues, along with gay rights, is particularly threatening to the patriarchal order because it breaks down the connection that has been established in American culture between sexuality and procreation, and in the process it questions the dichotomization of male and female into the categories of producers and reproducers respectively (D'Emilio and Freedman 1988; Ginsburg 1989).

Several other social issues also pertain to control over the individual's body: to name but a few, such eating disorders as anorexia and bulimia, virtually exclusive to women; incest and child (sexual) abuse, now recognized as widespread in society; the commercialization of sexuality and the denigration of womanhood, not only in sadistic and violent pornographic materials but also in advertising; the exploitation of prostitutes; the right to determine one's biological sex as well as one's sexual orientation (see Bolin on transsexuals, herein); and the right to be free from sexual harassment in school and the workplace.

The struggle over spousal rape is but one among several currently waged struggles serving to promote the deconstruction of the gender system of American and other Western societies, which emphasizes the differences between males and females and then places the males in the favored position in the hierarchy.

Public Minds versus Private Bodies: Separate Spheres Revisited

Historically, men have dominated the public sphere; until recently, women have been relegated to the private sphere, where they were treated as the private property of men and were responsible for domestic tasks within the family; and the civil rights accorded to those in the public sphere were not extended to those in the private sphere. The legal system has thus disproportionately favored men in granting legal rights. That women think of moral problems more in terms of response and consequences than in terms of rights (Gilligan 1982) is one consequence of differentially socializing men into the public sphere and women into the domestic and depriving women of their full civil rights, evident in the failure to pass the Equal Rights Amendment to the Constitution.

The recent redefinition of rape as occurring not only in public space but also in the private arena represents a major challenge to the separation of these spheres where the law is concerned. One aspect of the struggle to recognize that women have rights in the private world is to suggest that they are to be recognized as equals to men in all areas of life. Ultimately, abolishing the' marital rape exemption promotes the general welfare of women by challenging the legal and cultural notion that women are the property of men and by fostering the realization of the vision of women as independent and equal human beings in society.

REFERENCES

Anonymous. 1986. "To Have and To Hold: The Marital Rape Exemption and the Fourteenth Amendment." *Harvard Law Review* 99:1239–73.

Brownmiller, Susan. 1975. *Against Our Will*. New York: Bantam Books.

Center for Constitutional Rights. 1986. *Stopping Sexual Assault in Marriage: A Guide for Women, Counselors and Advocates*. New York: Center for Constitutional Rights.

Colker, Ruth. 1983. "Pornography and Privacy: Towards The Development of a Group Based Theory for Sex Based Intrusions of Privacy." *Law and Inequality* 1:191–237.

Delphy, Christine. 1987. "Protofeminism and Antifeminism." In *French Feminist Thought*, ed. Toril Moi. Oxford: Basil Blackwell.

D'Emilio, John D., and Estelle B. Freedman. 1988. *Intimate Matters: A History of Sexuality in America*. New York: Harper and Row.

Edwards, Susan S. M. 1987. " 'Provoking Her Own Demise': From Common Assault to Homicide." In *Women, Violence and Social Control*, ed. Jalna Hanmer and Mary Maynard. Atlantic Highlands, N.J.: Humanities Press International.

Estrich, Susan. 1987. *Real Rape*. Cambridge, Mass.: Harvard University Press.

Finkelhor, David, and Kersti Yllo. 1983. "Rape in Marriage: A Sociological View." In *The Dark Side of Families: Current Family Violence Research*, ed. David Finkelhor, Richard J. Gelles, Gerald T. Hotaling, and Murray A. Straus. Beverly Hills, Calif.: Sage.

———. 1985. *License to Rape: Sexual Abuse of Wives*. New York: Holt, Rinehart and Winston.

Gilligan, Carol. 1982. *In a Different Voice*. Cambridge, Mass.: Harvard University Press.

Ginsburg, Faye. 1989. *Contested Lives*. Berkeley and Los Angeles: University of California Press.

Groth, Nicholas. 1979. *Men Who Rape: The Psychology of the Offender*. New York: Plenum.

Hanmer, Jalna, and Mary Maynard. 1987. "Introduction: Violence and Gender Stratification." In *Women, Violence and Social Control*, ed. Jalna Hanmer and Mary Maynard. Atlantic Highlands, N.J.: Humanities Press International.

Haraway, Donna. 1990. "Investment Strategies for the Evolving Portfolio of Primate Females." In *Body/Politics: Women and the Discourses of Science*, ed. Mary Jacobus, Evelyn Fox Keller, and Sally Shuttleworth. New York: Routledge.

Kaganas, Felicity. 1986. "Rape in Marriage: Developments in South African Law." *International and Comparative Law Quarterly* 35:456–61.

Kappeler, Susanne. 1986. *The Pornography of Representation.* Minneapolis: University of Minnesota Press.

Menefee, Samuel P. 1981. *Wives for Sale: An Ethnographic Study of British Popular Divorce.* New York: St. Martin's.

O'Brien, Mary. 1981. *The Politics of Reproduction.* London: Routledge and Kegan Paul.

Pagelow, Mildred Daley. 1984. *Family Violence.* New York: Praeger.

Russell, Diana E. H. 1982. *Rape in Marriage.* New York: Macmillan.

———. 1984. *Sexual Exploitation: Rape, Child Sexual Abuse, and Workplace Harassment.* Beverly Hills, Calif.: Sage.

Sachdev, Paul, Ed. 1988. *International Handbook on Abortion.* Westport, Conn.: Greenwood.

Schecter, Susan. 1982. *Women and Male Violence.* Boston: South End Press.

Shields, Nancy M., and Christine R. Hanneke. 1983. "Battered Wives' Reactions to Marital Rape." In *The Dark Side of Families: Current Family Violence Research,* ed. David Finkelhor, Richard J. Gelles, Gerald T. Hotaling, and Murray A. Straus. Beverly Hills, Calif.: Sage.

Temkin, Jennifer. 1986. "Women, Rape and Law Reform." In *Rape,* ed. Sylvana Tomaselli and Roy Porter. Oxford: Basil Blackwell.

Catharine A. MacKinnon

Francis Biddle's Sister: Pornography, Civil Rights, and Speech

Topically, I will first situate a critique of pornography within a feminist analysis of the condition of women. I will discuss what pornography means for the social status and treatment of women. I will briefly contrast that with the obscenity approach, the closest this government has come to addressing pornography. Next I will outline an argument for the constitutionality of the ordinance Andrea Dworkin and I conceived, in which we define pornography as a civil rights violation.[1] Here I will address what pornography *does* as a practice of sex discrimination, and the vision of the First Amendment with which our law is consistent. Evidence, much of it drawn from hearings on the ordinance in Minneapolis,[2] supports this argument. The Supreme Court has never considered this legal injury before, nor the factual support we bring to it. They have allowed the recognition of similar injuries to other people, consistent with their interpretation of the First Amendment. More drastic steps have been taken on a showing of a great deal less harm, and the courts have allowed it. The question is: Will they do it for women?

This is the horizontal structure, the threads I will pull through this discussion, the themes that underlie it. My formal agenda has three parts. The first treats pornography by connecting epistemology—which I understand to be about theories of knowing—with politics—which I will take to be about theories of power.[3] For instance, Justice Stewart said of obscenity, "I know it when I see it."[4] I see this as a statement connecting epistemology—what he knows through his way of knowing, in this case, seeing—with the fact that his seeing determines what obscenity *is* in terms of what he sees it to be, because of his position of power. I have to wonder if he knew what I know when I see what I see, given what's on the newsstands—and that's not a personal comment about him.

Another example of the same conceptual connection is this. Having power means, among other things, that when someone says, "This is how it is," it is taken as being that way. When this happens in law, such a person is accorded what is called credibility. When that person is believed over another speaker, what was said becomes proof. Speaking socially, the beliefs of the powerful become proof, in part because the world actually arranges itself to affirm what the powerful want to see. If you perceive this as a process, you might call it force, or at least pressure or socialization or what money can buy. If it is imperceptible as a process, you may consider it voluntary or consensual or free will or human nature, or just the way things are. Beneath this, though, the world is not entirely the way the powerful say it is or want to believe it is. If it appears to be, it is because power constructs the appearance of reality by silencing the voices of the powerless, by excluding them from access to authoritative discourse. Powerlessness means that when you say "This is how it is," it is *not* taken as being that way. This makes articulating silence, perceiving the presence of absence, believing those who have been socially stripped of credibility, critically contextualizing what passes for simple fact, necessary to the epistemology of a politics of the powerless.

My second thematic concern is jurisprudential. It is directed toward identifying, in order to change, one dimension of liberalism as it is embodied in law: the definition of justice as neutrality between abstract categories. The liberal view is that abstract categories—like speech or equality—define systems. Every time you strengthen free speech in one place, you strengthen it everywhere. Strengthening the free speech of the Klan strengthens the free speech of Blacks.[5] Getting things for men strengthens equality for women. Getting men access to women's schools strengthens women's access to education. What I will be exploring is the way in which substantive systems, made up of real people with social labels attached, are *also systems*. You can reverse racism abstractly, but white supremacy is unfudgeably substantive. Sexism can be an equal abstraction, but male supremacy says who is where. Substantive systems like white supremacy do substantively different things to people of color than they do to white people. To say they are *also systems* is to say that every time you score one for white supremacy in one place, it is strengthened everyplace else.

In this view, the problem with neutrality as the definition of principle in constitutional adjudication[6] is that it equates substantive powerlessness with substantive power and calls treating these the same, "equality." The neutrality approach understands that abstract systems are systems, but it seems not to understand that substantive systems are also systems. This criticism frames a problem that is the same for equal protection law under the sex-blind/color-blind rubric[7] as it is for the First Amendment under the absolutist rubric—the systematic defense of those who own the speech because they can buy it or have speech to lose because they have the power to articulate in a way that counts.[8] Although absolutism has never been the law of the First Amendment, it has left its impression upon it. Its contributions include helping to make the marketplace of ideas, the original metaphor for how the First Amendment was supposed to work,[9] rather more literal than figurative.

If this argument is right, it makes sense that Herbert Wechsler's seminal exposition of the neutral principles approach[10] would be couched as an abstract defense of *Plessy v. Ferguson*[11]—in which separate but equal in the racial context was found equal—and an abstract attack on *Brown v. Board of Education*,[12] which recognized the inequality in racial separation in a racially hierarchical society. *Plessy* was neutral toward racism; *Brown* recognized its substantivity, therefore its inequality. Similarly noticing the substantive context within which many of the big systemic constitutional debates have been carried out reveals that much of the legal tradition on the evils of substantivity as such—*Lochner* and so on[13]—revolves around cases that substantively concern the treatment of women. Yet nobody talks about these as cases about women. Women are substantively absent.[14] Just as the struggle of Blacks for an education was a vehicle for Wechsler's exposition of the virtues of neutrality, women's lives provide the occasion for confronting the issues the legal system regards as the real issues, the abstract issues, to which the treatment of women is as invisible in law—just as essential and just as marginalized—as women's substantive framing of social existence is invisible in life.

The *Lochner* line of cases created concern about the evils of their substance, which, as women were erased, came to stand for the evils of substantivity *as such*. There has been correspondingly little discussion, with the partial exception of the debate on affirmative action,[15] on the drawbacks of abstraction as such. Granted, trying to do anything on a substantive basis is a real problem in a legal system that

immediately turns everything into an abstraction. I do hope to identify this as something of a syndrome, as a risk of abuse. Considering
it the definition of principle itself ensures that nothing will ever basically change, at least not by law.

When these two frames converge—epistemology and politics on
the one hand with the critique of neutrality on the other—they form
a third frame: one of political philosophy. Here is how they converge.
Once power constructs social reality, as I will show pornography constructs the social reality of gender, the force behind sexism, the subordination in gender inequality, is made invisible; dissent from it
become inaudible as well as rare. What a woman is, is defined in pornographic terms; this is what pornography *does*. If the law then looks
neutrally on the reality of gender so produced, the harm that has
been done *will not be perceptible as harm*. It becomes just the way things
are. Refusing to look at what has been done substantively institutionalizes inequality in law and makes it look just like principle.

In the philosophical terms of classical liberalism, an equality-
freedom dilemma is produced: freedom to make or consume pornography weighs against the equality of the sexes. Some people's
freedom hurts other people's equality. There is something to this, but
my formulation comes out a little differently. If one asks whose freedom pornography represents, a tension emerges that is not a dilemma among abstractions so much as it is a conflict between groups.
Substantive interests are at stake on *both* sides of the abstract issues,
and women are allowed to matter in neither. If women's freedom is
as incompatible with pornography's construction of our freedom as
our equality is incompatible with pornography's construction of our
equality, we get neither freedom nor equality under the liberal calculus. Equality for women is incompatible with a definition of men's
freedom that is at our expense. What can freedom for women mean,
so long as we remain unequal? Why should men's freedom to use us
in this way be purchased with our second-class civil status?

Substantively considered, the situation of women is *not really
like anything else*. Its specificity is not just the result of our numbers—
we are half the human race—and our diversity, which at times has
obscured that we are a group with an interest at all. It is, in part, that
our status as a group relative to men has almost never, if ever, been
much changed from what it is. Women's roles do vary enough that
gender, the social form sex takes, cannot be said to be biologically determined. Different things are valued in different cultures, but whatever is valued, women are not that. If bottom is bottom, look across

time and space, and women are who you will find there. Together with this, you will find, in as varied forms as there are cultures, the belief that women's social inferiority to men is not that at all but is merely the sex difference.

Doing something legal about a situation that is not really like anything else is hard enough in a legal system that prides itself methodologically on reasoning by analogy.[16] Add to this the specific exclusion or absence of women and women's concerns from the definition and design of this legal system since its founding, combined with its determined adherence to precedent, and you have a problem of systemic dimension. The best attempt at grasping women's situation in order to change it by law has centered on an analogy between sex and race in the discrimination context. This gets a lot, since inequalities are alike on some levels, but it also misses a lot. It gets the stigmatization and exploitation and denigration of a group of people on the basis of a condition of birth. It gets that difference, made an issue of, is an excuse for dominance, and that if forced separation is allowed to mean equality in a society where the line of separation also divides top from bottom in a hierarchy, the harm of that separation is thereby made invisible. It also gets that defining neutrality as principle, when reality is not neutral, prevents change in the guise of promoting it. But segregation is not the central practice of the inequality of the sexes. Women are as often forcibly integrated with men, if not on an equal basis. And it did help the struggle against white supremacy that Blacks had not always been in bondage to white people.

Most important, I think it never was a central part of the ideology of racism that the system of chattel slavery of Africans really was designed for their enjoyment and benefit. The system *was* defended as an expression of their true nature and worth. They *were* told to be grateful for good treatment and kind masters. Their successful struggle to organize resistance and avoid complicity while still surviving is instructive to all of us. But although racism *has* been defended by institutionalizing it in law, and then calling that legal; although it has been cherished not just as a system of exploitation of labor but as a way of life; and although it *is* based on force, changes in its practices are opposed by implying that they are really only a matter of choice of personal values, for instance: "You can't legislate morality."[17] And slave owners *did* say they couldn't be racist—they loved their slaves. Nonetheless, few people pretended that the entire system existed *because* of its basis in love and mutual respect and veneration, that white supremacy really treated Blacks in many cases *better* than whites, and that the primary intent and effect of their special status was and is their protection, pleasure, fulfillment, and liberation. Crucially, many have believed, and some actually still do, that Black people were not the equals of whites. But at least since *Brown v. Board of Education*,[18] few have pretended, much less authoritatively, that the social system, as it was, *was equality for them*.

There is a belief that this is a society in which women and men are basically equals. Room for marginal corrections is conceded, flaws are known to exist, attempts are made to correct what are conceived as occasional lapses from the basic condition of sex equality. Sex discrimination law has concentrated most of its focus on these occasional lapses.[19] It is difficult to overestimate the extent to which this belief in equality is an article of faith for most people, including most women, who wish to live in self-respect in an internal universe, even (perhaps especially) if not in the world. It is also partly an expression of natural law thinking: if we are inalienably equal, we can't "really" be degraded.

This is a world in which it is worth trying. In this world of presumptive equality, people make money based on their training or abilities or diligence or qualifications. They are employed and advanced on the basis of merit. In this world of just deserts, if someone is abused, it is thought to violate the basic rules of the community. If it doesn't, victims are seen to have done something they could have chosen to do differently, by exercise of will or better judgment. Maybe such people have placed themselves in a situation of vulnerability to physical abuse. Maybe they have done something provocative. Or maybe they were just unusually unlucky. In such a world, if such a person has an experience, there are words for it. When they speak and say it, they are listened to. If they write about it, they will be published. If certain experiences are never spoken about, if certain people or issues are seldom heard from, it is supposed that silence has been chosen. The law, including much of the law of sex discrimination and the First Amendment, operates largely within the realm of these beliefs.

Feminism is the discovery that women do not live in this world, that the person occupying this realm is a man, so much more a man if he is white and wealthy. This world of potential credibility, authority, security, and just rewards, recognition of one's identity and capacity, is a world that some people do inhabit as a condition of birth, with variations among them. It is not a basic condition accorded humanity in this society, but a prerogative of status, a privilege, among other things, of gender.

I call this a discovery because it has not been an assumption. Feminism is the first theory, the first practice, the first movement, to take seriously the situation of all women from the point of view of all women, both on our situation and on social life as a whole. The discovery has therefore been made that the implicit social content of humanism, as well as the standpoint from which legal method has been designed and injuries have been defined, has not been women's standpoint. Defining feminism in a way that connects epistemology with power as the politics of women's point of view, this discovery can be summed up by saying that women live in another world: specifically, a world of *not* equality, a world of inequality.

Looking at the world from this point of view, a whole shadow world of previously invisible silent abuse has been discerned. Rape, battery, sexual harassment, forced prostitution, and the sexual abuse of children emerge as common and systematic.[20] We find that rape happens to women in all contexts, from the family, including rape of girls and babies, to students and women in the workplace, on the streets, at home, in their own bedrooms by men they do not know and by men they do know, by men they are married to, men they have had a social conversation with, and, least often, men they have never seen before.[21] Overwhelmingly, rape is something that men do or attempt to do to women (44 percent of American women according to a recent study)[22] at some point in our lives. Sexual harassment of women by men is common in workplaces and educational institutions.[23] Based on reports in one study of the federal workforce, up to 85 percent of women will experience it, many in physical forms.[24] Between a quarter and a third of women are battered in their homes by men.[25] Thirty-eight percent of little girls are sexually molested inside or outside the family.[26] Until women listened to women, this world of sexual abuse was *not spoken* of. It was the unspeakable. What I am saying is, if you *are* the tree falling in the epistemological forest, your demise doesn't make a sound if no one is listening. Women did not "report" these events, and overwhelmingly do not today, because no one is listening, because no one believes us. This silence does not mean nothing happened, and it does not mean consent. It is the silence of women of which Adrienne Rich has written, "Do not confuse it with any kind of absence."[27]

Believing women who say we are sexually violated has been a radical departure, both methodologically and legally. The extent and nature of rape, marital rape, and sexual harassment itself, were discovered in this way. Domestic battery as a syndrome, almost a habit, was discovered through refusing to believe that when a woman is assaulted by a man to whom she is connected, that it is not an assault. The sexual abuse of children was uncovered, Freud notwithstanding, by believing that children were not making up all this sexual abuse.[28] Now what is striking is that when each discovery is made, and somehow made real in the world, the response has been: it happens to men too. If women are hurt, men are hurt. If women are raped, men are raped. If women are sexually harassed, men are sexually harassed. If women are battered, men are battered. Symmetry must be reasserted. Neutrality must be reclaimed. Equality must be reestablished.

The only areas where the available evidence supports this, where anything like what happens to women also happens to men, especially in terms of numbers, involve children—little boys are sexually abused—and prison.[29] The liberty of prisoners is restricted, their freedom restrained, their humanity systematically diminished, their bodies and emotions confined, defined, and regulated. If paid at all, they are paid starvation wages. They can be tortured at will, and it is passed off as discipline or as means to a just end. They become compliant. They can be raped at will, at any moment, and nothing will be done about it. When they scream, nobody hears. To be a prisoner means to be defined as a member of a group for whom the rules of what can be done to you, of what is seen as abuse of you, are reduced as part of the definition of your status. To be a woman is that kind of definition and has that kind of meaning.

Men *are* damaged by sexism. (By men I mean the status of masculinity that is accorded to males on the basis of their biology but is not itself biological.) But whatever the damage of sexism to men, the condition of being a man is not defined as subordinate to women by force. Looking at the facts of the abuses of women all at once, you see that a woman is socially defined as a person who, whether or not she is or has been, can be treated in these ways by men at any time, and little, if anything, will be done about it. This is what it means when feminists say that maleness is a form of power and femaleness is a form of powerlessness.

In this context, all of this "men too" stuff means that people don't really believe that the things just described are true, though there really is little question about their empirical accuracy. The data are extremely simple, like women's fifty-nine cents on the dollar pay figure.[30] People don't really seem to believe that either. Yet there is no question of its empirical validity. This is the workplace story: what women do is seen as not worth much, or what is not worth much is seen as something for women to do. *Women* are seen as not worth much, is the thing. Now why are these basic realities of the subordination of women to men, for example, the fact that only 7.8 percent of women have never been sexually assaulted or harassed,[31] effectively not believed, not perceived as real in the face of all this evidence? Why don't *women* believe our own experiences? In the face of all this evidence, especially of systematic sexual abuse—subjection to violence with impunity is one extreme expression, although not the only expression, of a degraded status—the view that basically the sexes are equal in this society remains unchallenged and unchanged. The day I got this was the day I understood its real message, its real coherence: *This is equality for us.*

I could describe this, but I couldn't explain it until I started studying a lot of pornography. In pornography, there it is, in one place, all of the abuses that women had to struggle so long even to begin to articulate, all the *unspeakable* abuse: the rape, the battery, the sexual harassment, the prostitution, and the sexual abuse of children. Only in the pornography it is called something else: sex, sex, sex, sex, and sex, respectively. Pornography sexualizes rape, battery, sexual harassment, prostitution, and child sexual abuse; it thereby celebrates, promotes, authorizes, and legitimizes them. More generally, it eroticizes the dominance and submission that is the dynamic common to them all. It makes hierarchy sexy and calls that "the truth about sex"[32] or just a mirror of reality. Through this process pornography constructs what a woman is as what men want from sex. This is what the pornography means.

Pornography constructs what a woman is in terms of its view of what men want sexually, such that acts of rape, battery, sexual harassment, prostitution, and sexual abuse of children become acts of sexual equality. Pornography's world of equality is a harmonious and balanced place.[33] Men and women are perfectly complementary and perfectly bipolar. Women's desire to be fucked by men is equal to men's desire to fuck women. All the ways men love to take and violate women, women love to be taken and violated. The women who most love this are most men's equals, the most liberated; the most participatory child is the most grown-up, the most equal to an adult. Their consent merely expresses or ratifies these preexisting facts.

The content of pornography is one thing. There, women substantively desire dispossession and cruelty. We desperately want to be bound, battered, tortured, humiliated, and killed. Or, to be fair to the soft core, merely taken and used. This is erotic to the male point of view. Subjection itself, with self-determination ecstatically relinquished, is the content of women's sexual desire and desirability.

Women are there to be violated and possessed, men to violate and possess us, either on screen or by camera or pen on behalf of the consumer. On a simple descriptive level, the inequality of hierarchy, of which gender is the primary one, seems necessary for sexual arousal to work. Other added inequalities identify various pornographic genres or subthemes, although they are always added through gender: age, disability, homosexuality, animals, objects, race (including anti-Semitism), and so on. Gender is never irrelevant.

What pornography *does* goes beyond its content: it eroticizes hierarchy, it sexualizes inequality. It makes dominance and submission into sex. Inequality is its central dynamic; the illusion of freedom coming together with the reality of force is central to its working. Perhaps because this is a bourgeois culture, the victim must look free, appear to be freely acting. Choice is how she got there. Willing is what she is when she is being equal. It seems equally important that then and there she actually be forced and that forcing be communicated on some level, even if only through still photos of her in postures of receptivity and access, available for penetration. Pornography in this view is a form of forced sex, a practice of sexual politics, an institution of gender inequality.

From this perspective, pornography is neither harmless fantasy nor a corrupt and confused misrepresentation of an otherwise natural and healthy sexual situation. It institutionalizes the sexuality of male supremacy, fusing the erotization of dominance and submission with the social construction of male and female. To the extent that gender is sexual, pornography is part of constituting the meaning of that sexuality. Men treat women as who they see women as being. Pornography constructs who that is. Men's power over women means that the way men see women defines who women can be. Pornography is that way. Pornography is not imagery in some relation to a reality elsewhere constructed. It is not a distortion, reflection, projection, expression, fantasy, representation, or symbol either. It is a sexual reality.

In Andrea Dworkin's definitive work, *Pornography: Men Possessing Women*,[34] sexuality itself is a social construct gendered to the ground. Male dominance here is not an artificial overlay upon an underlying inalterable substratum of uncorrupted essential sexual being. Dworkin presents a sexual theory of gender inequality of which pornography is a constitutive practice. The way pornography produces its meaning constructs and defines men and women as such. Gender has no basis in anything other than the social reality its hegemony constructs. Gender is what gender means. The process that gives sexuality its male supremacist meaning is the same process through which gender inequality becomes socially real.

In this approach, the experience of the (overwhelmingly) male audiences who consume pornography is therefore not fantasy or simulation or catharsis but sexual reality, the level of reality on which sex itself largely operates. Understanding this dimension of the problem does not require noticing that pornography models are real women to whom, in most cases, something real is being done; nor does it even require inquiring into the systematic infliction of pornography and its sexuality upon women, although it helps. What matters is the way in which the pornography itself provides what those who consume it want. Pornography *participates* in its audience's eroticism through creating an accessible sexual object, the possession and consumption of which *is* male sexuality, as socially constructed; to be consumed and possessed as which, *is* female sexuality, as socially constructed; pornography is a process that constructs it that way.

The object world is constructed according to how it looks with respect to its possible uses. Pornography defines women by how we look according to how we can be sexually used. Pornography codes how to look at women, so you know what you can do with one when you see one. Gender is an assignment made visually, both originally and in everyday life. A sex object is defined on the basis of its looks, in terms of its usability for sexual pleasure, such that both the looking—the quality of the gaze, including its point of view—and the definition according to use become eroticized as part of the sex itself. This is what the feminist concept "sex object" means. In this sense, sex in life is no less mediated than it is in art. Men have sex with their image of a woman. It is not that life and art imitate each other; in this sexuality, they *are* each other.

To give a set of rough epistemological translations, to defend pornography as consistent with the equality of the sexes is to defend the subordination of women to men as sexual equality. What in the pornographic view is love and romance looks a great deal like hatred and torture to the feminist. Pleasure and eroticism become violation. Desire appears as lust for dominance and submission. The vulnerability of women's projected sexual availability, that acting we are allowed (that is, asking to be acted upon), is victimization. Play conforms to scripted roles. Fantasy expresses ideology, is not exempt from it. Admiration of natural physical beauty becomes objectification. Harmlessness becomes harm. Pornography is a harm of male supremacy made difficult to see because of its pervasiveness, potency, and, principally, because of its success in making the world a pornographic place. Specifically, its harm cannot be discerned, and will not be addressed, if viewed and approached neutrally, because it *is* so much of "what is." In other words, to the extent pornography succeeds in constructing social reality, it becomes invisible as harm. If we live in a world that pornography creates through the power of men in a male-dominated situation, the issue is not what the harm of pornography is, but how that harm is to become visible.

Obscenity law provides a very different analysis and conception of the problem of pornography.[35] In 1973 the legal definition of obscenity became that which the average person, applying contemporary community standards, would find that, taken as a whole, appeals to the prurient interest; that which depicts or describes in a patently offensive way—you feel like you're a cop reading someone's *Miranda* rights—sexual conduct specifically defined by the applicable state law; and that which, taken as a whole, lacks serious literary, artistic, political, or scientific value.[36] Feminism doubts whether the average person gender-neutral exists; has more questions about the content and process of defining what community standards are than it does about deviations from them; wonders why prurience counts but powerlessness does not and why sensibilities are better protected from offense than women are from exploitation; defines sexuality, and thus its violation and expropriation, more broadly than does state law; and questions why a body of law that has not in practice been able to tell rape from intercourse should, without further guidance, be entrusted with telling pornography from anything less. Taking the work "as a whole" ignores that which the victims of pornography have long known: legitimate settings diminish the perception of injury done to those whose trivialization and objectification they contextualize. Besides, and this is a heavy one, if a woman is subjected, why should it matter that the work has other value? Maybe what redeems the work's value is what enhances its injury to women, not to mention that existing standards of literature, art, science, and politics, examined in a feminist light, are remarkably consonant with pornography's mode, meaning, and message. And finally—first and foremost, actually—although the subject of these materials is overwhelmingly women, their contents almost entirely made up of women's bodies, our invisibility has been such, our equation as a sex *with* sex has been such, that the law of obscenity has never even considered pornography a women's issue.

Obscenity, in this light, is a moral idea, an idea about judgments of good and bad. Pornography, by contrast, is a political practice, a practice of power and powerlessness. Obscenity is ideational and abstract; pornography is concrete and substantive. The two concepts represent two entirely different things. Nudity, excess of candor, arousal or excitement, prurient appeal, illegality of the acts depicted, and unnaturalness or perversion are all qualities that bother obscenity law when sex is depicted or portrayed. Sex forced on real women so that it can be sold at a profit and forced on other real women; women's bodies trussed and maimed and raped and made into things to be hurt and obtained and accessed, and this presented as the nature of women in a way that is acted on and acted out, over and over; the coercion that is visible and the coercion that has become invisible— this and more bothers feminists about pornography. Obscenity as such probably does little harm.[37] Pornography is integral to attitudes and behaviors of violence and discrimination that define the treatment and status of half the population.

At the request of the city of Minneapolis, Andrea Dworkin and I conceived and designed a local human rights ordinance in accordance with our approach to the pornography issue. We define pornography as a practice of sex discrimination, a violation of women's civil rights, the opposite of sexual equality. Its point is to hold those who profit from and benefit from that injury accountable to those who are injured. It means that women's injury—our damage, our pain, our enforced inferiority—should outweigh their pleasure and their profits, or sex equality is meaningless.

We define pornography as the graphic sexually explicit subordination of women through pictures or words that also includes women dehumanized as sexual objects, things, or commodities; enjoying pain or humiliation or rape; being tied up, cut up, mutilated, bruised, or physically hurt; in postures of sexual submission or servility or display; reduced to body parts, penetrated by objects or animals, or presented in scenarios of degradation, injury, torture; shown as filthy or inferior; bleeding, bruised, or hurt in a context that makes these conditions sexual.[38] Erotica, defined by distinction as not this, might be sexually explicit materials premised on equality.[39] We also provide that the use of men, children, or transsexuals in the place of women is pornography.[40] The definition is substantive in that it is sex-specific, but it covers everyone in a sex-specific way, so is gender neutral in overall design.

There is a buried issue within sex discrimination law about what sex, meaning gender, is. If sex is a *difference*, social or biological, one looks to see if a challenged practice occurs along the same lines; if it does, or if it is done to both sexes, the practice is not discrimination, not inequality. If, by contrast, sex has been a matter of *dominance*, the issue is not the gender difference but the difference gender makes. In this more substantive, less abstract approach, the concern with inequality is whether a practice *subordinates* on the basis of sex. The first approach implies that marginal correction is needed; the second requires social change. Equality, in the first view, centers on abstract symmetry between equivalent categories; the asymmetry that occurs when categories are not equivalent is not inequality, it is treating unlikes differently. In the second approach, inequality centers on the substantive, cumulative disadvantagement of social hierarchy. Equality for the first is nondifferentiation; for the second, non-subordination.[41] Although it is consonant with both approaches, our antipornography statute emerges largely from an analysis of the problem under the second approach.

To define pornography as a practice of sex discrimination combines a mode of portrayal that has a legal history—the sexually explicit—with an active term that is central to the inequality of the sexes—subordination. Among other things, subordination means to be in a position of inferiority or loss of power, or to be demeaned or denigrated.[42] To be someone's subordinate is the opposite of being their equal. The definition does not include all sexually explicit depictions *of* the subordination of women. That is not what it says. It says, this which *does* that: the sexually explicit that subordinates women. To these active terms to capture what the pornography *does*, the definition adds a list of what it must also contain. This list, from our analysis, is an exhaustive description of what must be in the pornography for it to do what it does behaviorally. Each item in the definition is supported by experimental, testimonial, social, and clinical evidence. We made a legislative choice to be exhaustive and specific and concrete rather than conceptual and general, to minimize problems of chilling effect, making it hard to guess wrong, thus making self-censorship less likely, but encouraging (to use a phrase from discrimination law) voluntary compliance, knowing that if something turns up that is not on the list, the law will not be expansively interpreted.

The list in the definition, by itself, would be a content regulation.[43] But together with the first part, the definition is not simply a content regulation. It is a medium-message combination that resembles many other such exceptions to First Amendment guarantees.[44]

To focus what our law is, I will say what it is not. It is not a prior restraint. It does not go to possession. It does not turn on offensiveness. It is not a ban, unless relief for a proven injury is a "ban" on doing that injury again. Its principal enforcement mechanism is the civil rights commission, although it contains an option for direct access to court as well as de novo judicial review of administrative determinations, to ensure that no case will escape full judicial scrutiny and full due process. I will also not discuss various threshold issues, such as the sources of municipal authority, preemption, or abstention, or even issues of overbreadth or vagueness, nor will I defend the ordinance from views that never have been law, such as First Amendment absolutism. I will discuss the merits: how pornography by this definition is a harm, specifically how it is a harm of gender inequality, and how that harm outweighs any social interest in its protection by recognized First Amendment standards.[45]

This law aspires to guarantee women's rights consistent with the First Amendment by making visible a conflict of rights between the equality guaranteed to all women and what, in some legal sense, is now the freedom of the pornographers to make and sell, and their consumers to have access to, the materials this ordinance defines. Judicial resolution of this conflict, if the judges do for women what they have done for others, is likely to entail a balancing of the rights of women arguing that our lives and opportunities, including our freedom of speech and action, are constrained by—and in many cases flatly precluded by, in, and through—pornography, against those who argue that the pornography is harmless, or harmful only in part but not in the whole of the definition; or that it is more important to preserve the pornography than it is to prevent or remedy whatever harm it does.

In predicting how a court would balance these interests, it is important to understand that this ordinance cannot now be said to be either conclusively legal or illegal under existing law or precedent,[46] although I think the weight of authority is on our side. This ordinance enunciates a new form of the previously recognized governmental interest in sex equality. Many laws make sex equality a governmental interest.[47] Our law is designed to further the equality of the sexes, to help make sex equality real. Pornography is a practice of discrimination on the basis of sex, on one level because of its role in creating and maintaining sex as a basis for discrimination. It harms many women one at a time and helps keep all women in an inferior status by defining our subordination as our sexuality and equating that with our gender. It is also sex discrimination because its victims, including men, are selected for victimization on the basis of their gender. But for their sex, they would not be so treated.[48]

The harm of pornography, broadly speaking, is the harm of the civil inequality of the sexes made invisible as harm because it has become accepted as the sex difference. Consider this analogy with race: if you see Black people as different, there is no harm to segregation; it is merely a recognition of that difference. To neutral principles, separate but equal was equal. The injury of racial separation to Blacks arises "solely because [they] choose to put that construction upon it."[49] Epistemologically translated: how you see it is not the way it is. Similarly, if you see women as just different, even or especially if you don't know that you do, subordination will not look like subordination at all, much less like harm. It will merely look like an appropriate recognition of the sex difference.

Pornography does treat the sexes differently, so the case for sex differentiation can be made here. But men as a group do not tend to be (although some individuals may be) treated the way women are treated in pornography. As a social group, men are not hurt by pornography the way women as a social group are. Their social status is not defined as *less* by it. So the major argument does not turn on mistaken differentiation, particularly since the treatment of women according to pornography's dictates makes it all too often accurate. The salient quality of a distinction between the top and the bottom in a hierarchy is not difference, although top is certainly different from bottom; it is power. So the major argument is: subordinate but equal is not equal.

Particularly since this is a new legal theory, a new law, and "new" facts, the situation of women it newly exposes deserves to be considered on its own terms. Why do the problems of 53 percent of the population have to look like somebody else's problems before they can be recognized as existing? Then, too, they can't be addressed if they do look like other people's problems, about which something might have to be done if something is done about these. This construction of the situation truly deserves inquiry. Limiting the justification for this law to the situation of the sexes would serve to limit the precedential value of a favorable ruling.

Its particularity to one side, the *approach* to the injury is supported by a whole array of prior decisions that have justified exceptions to First Amendment guarantees when something that matters is seen to be directly at stake. What unites many cases in which speech interests are raised and implicated but not, on balance, protected, is harm,[50] harm that counts. In some existing exceptions, the definitions are much more open-ended than ours.[51] In some the sanctions are more severe, or potentially more so. For instance, ours is a civil law; most others, although not all, are criminal.[52] Almost no other exceptions show as many people directly affected. Evidence of harm in other cases tends to be vastly less concrete and more conjectural, which is not to say that there is necessarily less of it.[53] None of the previous cases addresses a problem of this scope or magnitude— for instance, an eight-billion-dollar-a-year industry.[54] Nor do other cases address an abuse that has such widespread legitimacy. Courts have seen harm in other cases. The question is, will they see it here, especially given that the pornographers got there first. I will confine myself here to arguing from cases on harm to people, on the supposition that, the pornographers notwithstanding, women are not flags.[55]

I will discuss the four injuries we make actionable, with evidence in the voices of the women and men who spoke at our hearing.

The first victims of pornography are the ones in it. To date, it has only been with children, and male children at that, that the Supreme Court has understood that before the pornography became the pornographer's speech, it was somebody's life.[56] This is particularly true in visual media, where it takes a real person doing each act to make what you see. This is the double meaning in a statement one ex-prostitute made at our hearing: "[E]very single thing you see in pornography is happening to a real woman right now."[57] Linda Marchiano, in her book *Ordeal*,[58] recounts being coerced as "Linda Lovelace" into performing for *Deep Throat*, a fabulously profitable film,[59] by being abducted, systematically beaten, kept prisoner, watched every minute, threatened with her life and the lives of her family if she left, tortured, and kept under constant psychological intimidation and duress. Not all pornography models are, to our knowledge, coerced so expressly, but the fact that some are not does not mean that those who are, aren't. It only means that coercion into pornography cannot be said to be biologically female. The further fact that prostitution and modeling are structurally women's best economic options should give pause to those who would consider women's presence there a true act of free choice. In the case of other inequalities, it is sometimes understood that people do degrading work out of a lack of options caused by, say, poverty. The work is not seen as *not* degrading "for them" because they do it. With women, it just proves that this is what we are really for, this is our true nature. Why is it that when a woman spreads her legs for a camera, she is assumed to be exercising free will? Women's freedom is rather substantively defined here. And as you think about the assumption of consent that follows women into pornography, look closely sometime for the skinned knees, the bruises, the welts from the whippings, the scratches, the gashes. Many of them are not simulated. One relatively soft-core pornography model said, "I knew the pose was right when it hurt."[60] It certainly seems important to the audiences that the events in the pornography be real. For this reason pornography becomes a motive for murder, as in "snuff" films, in which someone is tortured to death to make a sex film. They exist.[61]

Coerced pornography models encounter devastating problems of lack of credibility because of a cycle of forced acts in which coercion into pornography is central. For example, children are typically forced to perform the acts in the pornography that is forced on them; photographs are taken of these rapes, and the photographs are used to coerce the children into prostitution or into staying in prostitution. They are told that if they try to leave, the pictures will be shown to the authorities, their parents, their teachers (whoever is *not* coercing them at the time), and no one will believe them. This gets them into prostitution and keeps them there.[62] Understand, the documentation of the harm as it is being done is taken as evidence that no harm was done. In part, the victim's desire for the abuse is attributed to the victim's nature from the fact of the abuse: she's a natural-born whore; see, there she is chained to a bed. Too, the victims are often forced to act as though they are enjoying the abuse. One pornographer said to a woman he abducted and was photographing while bound: "Smile or I'll kill you. I can get lots of money for pictures of women who smile when they're tied up like you."[63] When women say they were forced, they are not believed, in part because, as Linda Marchiano says, "What people remember is the smile on my face."[64]

Pornography defines what a woman is through conditioning the male sexual response to that definition, to the unilateral sexuality pornography is part of and provides. Its power can be illustrated by considering the credibility problems Linda Marchiano encounters when she says that the presentation of her in *Deep Throat* is not true, in the sense that she does not and did not feel or enjoy what the character she was forced to portray felt and enjoyed. Most concretely, before "Linda Lovelace" was seen performing deep throat, no one had ever seen it being done in that way, largely because it cannot be done without hypnosis to repress the natural gag response. *Yet it was believed.* Men proceeded to demand it of women, causing the distress of many and the death of some.[65] Yet when Linda Marchiano now tells that it took kidnapping and death threats and hypnosis to put her there, that is found *difficult to believe.*[66]

The point is not only that when women can be coerced with impunity the results, when mass-produced, set standards that are devastating and dangerous for all women. The point is also that the assumptions the law of the First Amendment makes about adults—that adults are autonomous, self-defining, freely acting, *equal* individuals—are exactly those qualities that pornography systematically denies and undermines for women.[67] Some of the same reasons children are granted some specific legal avenues for redress—relative lack of power, inability to command respect for their consent and self-determination, in some cases less physical strength or lowered legitimacy in using it, specific credibility problems, and lack of access to resources for meaningful self-expression—also hold true for the social position of women compared to men. It is therefore vicious to suggest, as many have, that women like Linda Marchiano should remedy their situations through the exercise of more speech. Pornography makes their speech impossible, and where possible, worthless. Pornography makes women into objects. Objects do not speak. When they do, they are by then regarded as objects, not as humans, which is what it means to have no credibility. Besides, it is unclear how Linda Marchiano's speech is supposed to redress her injury, except by producing this legal remedy, since no amount of saying anything remedies what is being *done* to her in theaters and on home videos all over the world, where she is repeatedly raped for public entertainment and private profit.

What would justice look like for these women?[68] Linda Marchiano said, "Virtually every time someone watches that film, they are watching me being raped,"[69] Nancy Holmes, who was forced to perform for pornography by her father and who, like many such victims, has been searching for the film for years, says,

> You wonder who might have seen the film. In some back-alley adult book shop someone has dropped a quarter and maybe it might be you they are looking at. You would not ordinarily mix company with this person under these circumstances . . . [b]ut in some back alley, in someone's dark mind you are worth 25 cents. Someone has just paid 25 cents to see you being brutally raped and beaten. And some total stranger gets to gain sadistic and voyeuristic pleasure from your pain. It costs you your sanity and years of suffering and psychological turmoil. It cost him only a quarter, and he gained tremendous pleasure. It robbed you of your childhood; it gave him satisfaction.[70]

Now think about his freedom and her powerlessness, and think about what it means to call that "just the construction she chooses to put upon it."

As part of the relief for people who can prove this was done to them, our law provides an injunction to remove these materials from public view. The best authority we have for this is the *Ferber* case, which permits criminal prohibitions on child pornography.[71] That case recognized that child pornography need not be obscene to be child abuse. The Court found such pornography harmful in part because it constituted "a permanent record of children's participation and the harm to the child is exacerbated by circulation."[72] This was a film, by the way, largely of two boys masturbating.[73] The sensitivities of obscenity law, the Court noted, were inapt because "a work which, taken on the whole, contains value may nevertheless embody the hardest core of child pornography."[74] Whether a work appeals to the prurient interest is not the same as whether a child is physically or psychologically harmed to make it.[75]

Both of these reasons apply to coerced women. Women are not children, but coerced women are effectively deprived of power over the expressive products of their coercion. Coerced pornography should meet the test that "the evil to be restricted . . . overwhelmingly outweighs the expressive interests, if any, at stake."[76] Unless one wishes to retain the incentive structure that has introduced a profit motive into rape, pornography made this way should be able to be eliminated.[77]

We also make it actionable to force pornography on a person in employment, education, in a home, or in any public place.[78] Persons who are forced cannot, under this part of the law, reach the pornography, but they can reach the perpetrator or institution that does the forcing. In our hearings we heard the ways in which pornography is forced on people. It is used to show children how to perform sex acts, to duplicate exactly these so-called natural childish acts;[79] on men's jobs, it is used to intimidate women into leaving;[80] in women's jobs, to have or set up a sexual encounter;[81] it is used to show prostitutes or wives what a "natural woman" is supposed to do.[82] In therapy, it is seen as aiding in transference, meaning submitting to the therapist;[83] in medical school, it desensitizes doctors so that when patients say they are masturbating with a chicken or wondering if intercourse with a cow will give them exotic diseases, the doctor does not react.[84] In language classes, it becomes material to be worked over meticulously for translation.[85] It is used to terrorize children in homes, so they will keep still about its use in the rape of their mothers and sisters: look at this; if you tell, here's what I'll do to you.[86] Sometimes it ends there; some children "only" have the pornography forced on them. Some of them later develop psychological diffi-culties that are identical to those of children who had the *acts* forced on them.[87] Do a thought-act distinction on that one.

Women who live in neighborhoods where pornography is concen-trated, much of it through state and local legal action called "zon-ing," report similar effects on a broad scale.[88] Because prostitutes know what others seem to have a lot staked on denying, which is that pornography makes men want the real thing, they sometimes locate around it. This means that any woman there may be considered a prostitute, which is dangerous enough if you are one, but becomes particularly dangerous if you are not. The threat of sexual harass-ment is constant. The presence of the pornography conditions wom-en's physical environment. Women have no place to go to avoid it, no place to avert their eyes *to*.[89] Certainly not home, where the presence of pornography is so sanctified[90] we don't even challenge it in this law. One woman, who as a child was a victim of incest and now lives in a community saturated with pornography, relates a Skokie-type injury.[91] She relives the incest every time she walks by the pornog-raphy she cannot avoid. "[L]ooking at the women in those pictures, I saw myself at 14, at 15, at 16. I felt the weight of that man's body, the pain, the disgust . . . I don't need studies and statistics to tell me that there is a relationship between pornography and real violence against women. My body remembers."[92] Now recall that more than a third of all women are victims of child sexual abuse; about the same propor-tion are victims of domestic battery; just under half are victims of rape or attempted rape. I am not saying that every such presence of the pornography is legally force, but what does it mean for targeted survivors to live in a society in which the rehearsal and celebration and ritual reenactment of our victimization is enjoyed, is an enter-tainment industry, is arguably a constitutional right?

Specific pornography does directly cause some assaults.[93] Some rapes *are* performed by men with paperback books in their pockets.[94] One young woman testified in our hearings about walking through a forest at thirteen and coming across a group of armed hunters read-ing pornography. As they looked up and saw her, one said, "There is a live one."[95] They gang-raped her at gunpoint for several hours. One Native American woman told us about being gang-raped in a reen-actment of a video game on her. "[T]hat's what they screamed in my face as they threw me to the ground. 'This is more fun than Custer's Last Stand.' They held me down and as one was running the tip of his knife across my face and throat he said, 'Do you want to play

Custer's Last Stand? It's great, you lose but you don't care, do you? You like a little pain, don't you, squaw? . . . Maybe we will tie you to a tree and start a fire around you."[96]

Received wisdom seems to be that because there is so little difference between convicted rapists and the rest of the male population in levels and patterns of exposure, response to, and consumption of pornography, the role of pornography in rape is insignificant.[97] A more parsimonious explanation of these data is that knowing patterns of exposure to, response to, or consumption of pornography will not tell you who will be reported, apprehended, and convicted for rape. But the commonalities such data reveal between convicted rapists and other men are certainly consistent with the fact that only a tiny fraction of rapes ever comes to the attention of authorities.[98] It does not make sense to assume that pornography has no role in rape simply because little about its use or effects distinguishes convicted rapists from other men, when we know that a lot of those other men *do* rape women; they just never get caught. In other words, the significance of pornography in acts of forced sex is one thing if sex offenders are considered deviants and another if they are considered relatively nonexceptional except for the fact of their apprehension and incarceration. Professionals who work with that tiny percentage of men who get reported and convicted for such offenses, a group made special only by our ability to assume that they once had sex by force in a way that someone (in addition to their victim) eventually regarded as serious, made the following observations about the population they work with. "Pornography is the permission and direction and rehearsal for sexual violence."[99] "[P]ornography is often used by sex offenders as a stimulus to their sexually acting out." It is the "tools of sexual assault,"[100] "a way in which they practice" their crimes, "like a loaded gun,"[101] "like drinking salt water,"[102] "the chemical of sexual addiction."[103] They hypothesize that pornography leads some men to abusiveness out of fear of loss of the control that has come to mean masculinity when real women won't accept sex on the one-sided terms that pornography gives and from which they have learned what sex is. Because pornography is reinforcing, and leads to sexual release, it "leads men to want the experience which they have in photographic fantasy to happen in 'real' life."[104] "They live vicariously through the pictures. Eventually, that is not satisfying enough and they end up acting out sexually."[105] "[S]exual fantasy represents the hope for reality."[106] These professionals are referring to what others are fond of terming "just an idea."

Although police have known it for years, reported cases are increasingly noting the causal role of pornography in some sexual abuse.[107] In a recent Minnesota case, a fourteen-year-old girl on a bicycle was stopped with a knife and forced into a car. Her hands were tied with a belt, she was pushed to the floor and covered with a blanket. The knife was then used to cut off her clothes, and fingers and a knife were inserted into her vagina. Then the man had her dress, drove her to a gravel pit, ordered her to stick a safety pin into the nipple of her left breast, and forced her to ask him to hit her. After hitting her, he forced her to commit fellatio and to submit to anal penetration, and made her use a cigarette to burn herself on her breast and near her pubic area. Then he defecated and urinated on her face, forced her to ingest some of the excrement and urine, and made her urinate into a cup and drink it. He took a string from her blouse and choked her to the point of unconsciousness, leaving burn marks on her neck, and after cutting her with his knife in a couple of places, drove her back to where he had gotten her and let her go. The books that were found with this man were *Violent Stories of Kinky Humiliation, Violent Stories of Dominance and Submission*—you think feminists made up these words?—*Bizarre Sex Crimes, Shamed Victims*, and *Water Sports Fetish, Enemas and Golden Showers*. The Minnesota Supreme Court said, "It appears that in committing these various acts, the defendant was giving life to some stories he had read in various pornographic books."[108]

To reach the magnitude of this problem on the scale it exists, our law makes trafficking in pornography—production, sale, exhibition, or distribution—actionable.[109] Under the obscenity rubric, much legal and psychological scholarship has centered on a search for the elusive link between harm and pornography defined as obscenity.[110] Although they were not very clear on what obscenity was, it was its harm they truly could not find. They looked high and low—in the mind of the male consumer,[111] in society or in its "moral fabric,"[112] in correlations between variations in levels of antisocial acts and liberalization of obscenity laws.[113] The only harm they have found has been harm to "the social interest in order and morality."[114] Until recently, no one looked very persistently for harm to women, particularly harm to women through men. The rather obvious fact that the sexes *relate* has been overlooked in the inquiry into the male consumer and his mind. The pornography doesn't just drop out of the sky, go into his head, and stop there. Specifically, men rape, batter, prostitute, molest, and sexually harass women. Under conditions of inequality, they also hire, fire, promote, and grade women, decide how much or whether we are worth paying and for what, define and approve and disapprove of women in ways that count, that determine our lives.

If women are not just born to be sexually used, the fact that we are seen and treated as though that is what we are born for becomes something in need of explanation. If we see that men relate to women in a pattern of who they see women as being, and that forms a pattern of inequality, it becomes important to ask where that view came from or, minimally, how it is perpetuated or escalated. Asking this requires asking different questions about pornography than the ones obscenity law made salient.

Now I'm going to discuss causality in its narrowest sense.[115] Recent experimental research on pornography[116] shows that materials covered by our definition cause measurable harm to women through increasing men's attitudes and behaviors of discrimination in both violent and nonviolent forms. Exposure to some of the pornography in our definition increases the immediately subsequent willingness of normal men to aggress against women under laboratory conditions.[117] It makes normal men more closely resemble convicted rapists attitudinally, although as a group they don't look all that different from them to start with.[118] Exposure to pornography also significantly increases attitudinal measures known to correlate with rape and self-reports of aggressive acts, measures such as hostility toward women, propensity to rape, condoning rape, and predicting that one would rape or force sex on a woman if one knew one would not get caught.[119] On this latter measure, by the way, about a third of all men predict that they would rape, and half would force sex on a woman.[120]

As to that pornography covered by our definition in which normal research subjects seldom perceive violence, long-term exposure still makes them see women as more worthless, trivial, nonhuman, and objectlike,[121] that is, the way those who are discriminated against are seen by those who discriminate against them. Crucially, all pornography by our definition acts dynamically over time to diminish the consumer's ability to distinguish sex from violence. The materials work behaviorally to diminish the capacity of men (but not women) to perceive that an account of a rape is an account of a rape.[122] The so-called sex-only materials, those in which subjects perceive no force, also increase perceptions that a rape victim is worthless and decrease the perception that she was harmed.[123] The overall direction of current research suggests that the more expressly violent materials accomplish with less exposure what the less overtly violent—that is, the so-called sex-only materials—accomplish over the longer term. Women are rendered fit for use and targeted for abuse. The only thing that the research cannot document is which individual women will be next on the list. (This cannot be documented experimentally largely because of ethics constraints on the researchers—constraints that do not operate in life.) Although the targeting is systematic on the basis of sex, for individuals it is random. They are selected on a roulette basis. Pornography can no longer be said to be just a mirror. It does not just reflect the world or some people's perceptions. It *moves* them. It aggravates attitudes that are lived out, circumscribing the status of half the population.

What the experimental data predict will happen actually does happen in women's real lives. It's fairly frustrating that women have known for some time that these things do happen. As Ed Donnerstein, an experimental researcher in this area, often puts it, "We just quantify the obvious."[124] It is women, primarily, to whom the research results have been the obvious, because we live them. But not until a laboratory study predicts that these things *will* happen do people begin to believe you when you say they *did* happen to you. There is no—*not any*—inconsistency between the patterns the laboratory studies predict and the data on what actually happens to real women. Show me an abuse of women in society, I'll show it to you made sex in the pornography. If you want to know who is being hurt in this society, go see what is being done and to whom in pornography and then go look for them other places in the world. You will find them being hurt in just that way. We did in our hearings.

In our hearings women spoke, to my knowledge for the first time in history in public, about the damage pornography does to them. We learned that pornography is used to break women, to train women to sexual submission, to season women, to terrorize women, and to silence their dissent. It is this that has previously been termed "having no effect." The way men inflict on women the sex they experience through the pornography gives women no choice about seeing the pornography or doing the sex. Asked if anyone ever tried to inflict unwanted sex acts on them that they knew came from pornography, 10 percent of women in a recent random study said yes.[125] Among married women, 24 percent said yes.[126] That is a lot of women. A lot more don't know. Some of those who do testified in Minneapolis. One wife said of her ex-husband, "He would read from the pornography like a textbook, like a journal. In fact when he asked me to be bound, when he finally convinced me to do it, he read in the magazine how to tie the knots."[127] Another woman said of her boyfriend, "[H]e went to this party, saw pornography, got an erection, got me . . . to inflict his erection on . . . There is a direct causal relationship there."[128] One woman, who said her husband had rape and bondage magazines all over the house, discovered two suitcases full of Barbie dolls with rope tied on their arms and legs and with tape across their mouths.[129] Now think about the silence of women. She said, "He used to tie me up and he tried those things on me."[130] A therapist in private practice reported:

> Presently or recently I have worked with clients who have been sodomized by broom handles, forced to have sex with over 20 dogs in the back seat of their car, tied up and then electrocuted on their genitals. These are children, [all] in the ages of 14 to 18, all of whom [have been directly affected by pornography,] [e]ither where the perpetrator has read the manuals and manuscripts at night and used these as recipe books by day or had the pornography present at the time of the sexual violence.[131]

One woman, testifying that all the women in a group of ex-prostitutes were brought into prostitution as children through pornography, characterized their collective experience: "[I]n my experience there was not one situation where a client was not using pornography while he was using me or that he had not just watched pornography or that it was verbally referred to and directed me to pornography."[132] "Men," she continued, "witness the abuse of women in pornography constantly and if they can't engage in that behavior with their wives, girl friends or children, they force a whore to do it."[133]

Men also testified about how pornography hurts them. One young gay man who had seen *Playboy* and *Penthouse* as a child said of such heterosexual pornography: "It was one of the places I learned about sex and it showed me that sex was violence. What I saw there was a specific relationship between men and women . . . [T]he woman was to be used, objectified, humiliated and hurt; the man was in a superior position, a position to be violent. In pornography I learned that what it meant to be sexual with a man or to be loved by a man was to accept his violence."[134] For this reason, when he was battered by his first lover, which he described as "one of the most profoundly destructive experiences of my life,"[135] he accepted it.

Pornography also hurts men's capacity to relate to women. One young man spoke about this in a way that connects pornography—not the prohibition on pornography—with fascism. He spoke of his struggle to repudiate the thrill of dominance, of his difficulty finding connection with a woman to whom he is close. He said, "My point is that if women in a society filled by pornography must be wary for their physical selves, a man, even a man of good intentions, must be wary for his mind . . . I do not want to be a mechanical, goose-stepping follower of the Playboy bunny, because that is what I think it is . . . [T]hese are the experiments a master race perpetuates on those slated for extinction."[136] The woman he lives with is Jewish. There was a very brutal rape near their house. She was afraid; she tried to joke. It didn't work. "She was still afraid. And just as a well-meaning German was afraid in 1933, I am also very much afraid."[137]

Pornography stimulates and reinforces, it does not cathect or mirror, the connection between one-sided freely available sexual access to women and masculine sexual excitement and sexual satisfaction. The catharsis hypothesis is fantasy. The fantasy theory is fantasy. Reality is: pornography conditions male orgasm to female subordination. It tells men what sex means, what a real woman is, and codes them together in a way that is behaviorally reinforcing. This is a real five-dollar sentence, but I'm going to say it anyway: pornography is a set of hermeneutical equivalences that work on the epistemological level. Substantively, pornography defines the meaning of what a woman is seen to be by connecting access to her sexuality with masculinity through orgasm. What pornography means *is* what it does.

So far, opposition to our ordinance centers on the trafficking provision. This means not only that it is difficult to comprehend a group injury in a liberal culture—that what it *means* to be a woman is defined by this and that it is an injury for all women, even if not for all women equally. It is not only that the pornography has got to be accessible, which is the bottom line of virtually every objection to this law. It is also that power, as I said, is when you say something, it is taken for reality.[138] If you talk about rape, it will be agreed that rape is awful. But rape is a conclusion. If a victim describes the facts of a rape, maybe she was asking for it or enjoyed it or at least consented to it, or the man might have thought she did, or maybe she had had sex before. It is now agreed that there is something wrong with sexual harassment. But describe what happened to you, and it may be trivial or personal or paranoid, or maybe you should have worn a bra that day. People are against discrimination. But describe the situation of a real woman, and they are not so sure she wasn't just unqualified. In law, all these disjunctions between women's perspective on our injuries and the standards we have to meet go under dignified legal rubrics like burden of proof, credibility, defenses, elements of the crime, and so on. These standards all contain a definition of what a woman is in terms of what sex is and the low value placed on us through it. They reduce injuries done to us to authentic expressions of who we are. Our silence is written all over them. So is the pornography.

We have as yet encountered comparatively little objection to the coercion, force, or assault provisions of our ordinance. I think that's partly because the people who make and approve laws may not yet see what they do as that. They *know* they use the pornography as we have described it in this law, and our law defines that, the reality of pornography, as a harm to women. If they suspect that they might on occasion engage in or benefit from coercion or force or assault, they may think that the victims won't be able to prove it—and they're right. Women who charge men with sexual abuse are not believed. The pornographic view of them is: they want it; they all want it.[139] When women bring charges of sexual assault, motives such as veniality or sexual repression must be invented, because we cannot really have been hurt. Under the trafficking provision, women's lack of credibility cannot be relied upon to negate the harm. There's no woman's story to destroy,[140] no credibility-based decision on what happened. The hearings establish the harm. The definition sets the standard. The grounds of reality definition are authoritatively shifted. Pornography is bigotry, *period*. We are now—*in* the world pornography has decisively defined—having to meet the burden of proving, once and for all, for all of the rape and torture and battery, all of the sexual harassment, all of the child sexual abuse, all of the forced prostitution, *all* of it that the pornography is part of and that is part of the pornography, that the harm *does happen* and that when it happens it looks like this. Which may be why all this evidence never seems to be enough.

It is worth considering what evidence has been enough when other harms involving other purported speech interests have been allowed to be legislated against. By comparison to our trafficking provision, analytically similar restrictions have been allowed under the First Amendment, with a legislative basis far less massive, detailed, concrete, and conclusive. Our statutory language is more ordinary, objective, and precise and covers a harm far narrower than the legislative record substantiates. Under *Miller*, obscenity was allowed to be made criminal in the name of the "danger of offending the sensibilities of unwilling recipients, or exposure to juveniles."[141] Under our law, we have direct evidence of harm, not just a conjectural danger, that unwilling women in considerable numbers are not simply offended in their sensibilities, but are violated in their persons and restricted in their options. Obscenity law also suggests that the applicable standard for legal adequacy in measuring such connections may not be statistical certainty. The Supreme Court has said that it is not its job to resolve empirical uncertainties that underlie state obscenity legislation.[142] Rather, it is to determine whether a legislature could reasonably have determined that a connection might exist between the prohibited material and harm of a kind in which the state has legitimate interest. Equality should be such an area. The Supreme Court recently recognized that prevention of sexual exploitation and abuse of children is, in its words, "a governmental objective of surpassing importance."[143] This might also be the case for sexual exploitation and abuse of women, although I think a civil remedy is initially more appropriate to the goal of empowering adult women than a criminal prohibition would be.[144]

Other rubrics provide further support for the argument that this law is narrowly tailored to further a legitimate governmental interest consistent with the goals underlying the First Amendment. Exceptions to the First Amendment exist. The reason they exist is that the harm done by some speech outweighs its expressive value, if any. In our law a legislature recognizes that pornography, as defined and made actionable, undermines sex equality. One can say—and I have—that pornography is a causal factor in violations of women; one can also say that women will be violated so long as pornography exists; but one can also say simply that pornography violates women. Perhaps this is what the woman had in mind who testified at our hearings that for her the question is not just whether pornography causes violent acts to be perpetrated against some women. "Porn is already a violent act against women. It is our mothers, our daughters, our sisters, and our wives that are for sale for pocket change at the newsstands in this country."[145] *Chaplinsky v. New Hampshire* recognized the ability to restrict as "fighting words" speech which, "by [its] very utterance inflicts injury."[146] Perhaps the reason that pornography has not been "fighting words"—in the sense of words that by their utterance tend to incite immediate breach of the peace—is that women have seldom fought back, yet.[147]

Some concerns that are close to those of this ordinance underlie group libel laws, although the differences are equally important. In group libel law, as Justice Frankfurter's opinion in *Beauharnais* illustrates, it has been understood that an individual's treatment and alternatives in life may depend as much on the reputation of the group to which that person belongs as on their own merit.[148] Not even a partial analogy can be made to group libel doctrine without examining the point made by Justice Brandeis[149] and recently underlined by Larry Tribe:[150] would more speech, rather than less, remedy the harm? In the end, the answer may be yes, but not under the abstract system of free speech, which only enhances the power of the pornographers while doing nothing substantively to guarantee the free speech of women, for which we need civil equality. The situation in which women presently find ourselves with respect to the pornography is one in which more *pornography* is inconsistent with rectifying or even counterbalancing its damage through speech, because so long as the pornography exists in the way it does there *will not be more speech by women*. Pornography strips and devastates women of credibility, from our accounts of sexual assault to our everyday reality of sexual subordination. We are stripped of authority and reduced and devalidated and silenced. Silenced here means that the purposes of the First Amendment, premised upon conditions presumed and promoted by protecting free speech, do not pertain to women because they are not our conditions. Consider them: individual self-fulfillment[151]—how does pornography promote our individual self-fulfillment? How does sexual inequality even permit it? Even if she can form words, who listens to a woman with a penis in her mouth? Facilitating consensus—to the extent pornography does so, it does so one-sidedly by silencing protest over the injustice of sexual subordination. Participation in civic life—central to Meiklejohn's theory[152]—how does pornography enhance women's participation in civic life? Anyone who cannot walk down the street or even lie down in her own bed without keeping her eyes cast down and her body clenched against assault is unlikely to have much to say about the issues of the day, still less will she become Tolstoy. Facilitating change[153]—*this law* facilitates the change that existing First Amendment theory had been used to throttle. Any system of freedom of expression that does not address a problem where the free speech of men silences the free speech of women, a real conflict between speech interests as well as between people, is not serious about securing freedom of expression in this country.[154]

For those who still think pornography is only an idea, consider the possibility that obscenity law got one thing right. Pornography is more actlike than thoughtlike. The fact that pornography, in a feminist view, furthers the idea of the sexual inferiority of women, which is a political idea, doesn't make the pornography itself into a political idea. One can express the idea a practice embodies. That does not make that practice into an idea. Segregation expresses the idea of the inferiority of one group to another on the basis of race. That does not make segregation an idea. A sign that says "Whites Only" is only words. Is it therefore protected by the First Amendment? Is it not an act, a practice, of segregation because what it means is inseparable from what it does?[155] *Law* is only words.

The issue here is whether the fact that words and pictures are the central link in the cycle of abuse will immunize that entire cycle, about which we cannot do anything without doing something about the pornography. As Justice Stewart said in *Ginsburg*, "When expression occurs in a setting where the capacity to make a choice is absent, government regulation of that expression may coexist with and *even implement* First Amendment guarantees."[156] I would even go so far as to say that the pattern of evidence we have closely approaches Justice Douglas's requirement that "freedom of expression can be suppressed if, and to the extent that, it is so closely brigaded with illegal action as to be an inseparable part of it."[157] Those who have been trying to separate the acts from the speech—that's an act, that's an act, there's a law against that act, regulate that act, don't touch the speech—notice here that the illegality of the acts involved doesn't mean that the speech that is "brigaded with" it *cannot* be regulated. This is when it *can* be.[158]

I take one of two penultimate points from Andrea Dworkin, who has often said that pornography is not speech for women, it is the silence of women.[159] Remember the mouth taped, the woman gagged, "Smile, I can get a lot of money for that." The smile is not her expression, it is her silence. It is not her expression not because it didn't happen, but because it *did* happen. The screams of the women in pornography are silence, like the screams of Kitty Genovese, whose plight was misinterpreted by some onlookers as a lovers' quarrel. The flat expressionless voice of the woman in the New Bedford gang rape, testifying, is silence. She was raped as men cheered and watched, as they do in and with the pornography. When women resist and men say, "Like this, you stupid bitch, here is how to do it" and shove their faces into the pornography,[160] this "truth of sex"[161] is the silence of women. When they say, "If you love me, you'll try,"[162] the enjoyment we fake, the enjoyment we learn is silence. Women who submit because there is more dignity in it than in losing the fight over and over[163] live in silence. Having to sleep with your publisher or director to get access to what men call speech is silence. Being humiliated on the basis of your appearance, whether by approval or disapproval, because you have to look a certain way for a certain job, whether you get the job or not, is silence. The absence of a woman's voice, everywhere that it cannot be heard, is silence. And anyone who thinks that what women say in pornography is women's speech—the "Fuck me, do it to me, harder," all of that—has never heard the sound of a woman's voice.[164]

The most basic assumption underlying First Amendment adjudication is that, socially, speech is free. The First Amendment says Congress shall not abridge the freedom of speech.[165] Free speech, get it, *exists*. Those who wrote the First Amendment *had* speech—they wrote the Constitution. *Their* problem was to keep it free from the only power that realistically threatened it: the federal government. They designed the First Amendment to prevent government from constraining that which, if unconstrained by government, was free, meaning *accessible to them*. At the same time, we can't tell much about the intent of the framers with regard to the question of women's speech, because I don't think we crossed their minds. It is consistent with this analysis that their posture toward freedom of speech tends to presuppose that whole segments of the population are not systematically silenced socially, prior to government action. If everyone's power were equal to theirs, if this were a nonhierarchical society, that might make sense. But the place of pornography in the inequality of the sexes makes the assumption of equal power untrue.

This is a hard question. It involves risks. Classically, opposition to censorship has involved keeping government off the backs of people. Our law is about getting some people off the backs of other people. The risks that it will be misused have to be measured against the risks of the status quo. Women will never have that dignity, security, compensation that is the promise of equality so long as the pornography exists as it does now. The situation of women suggests that the urgent issue of our freedom of speech is not primarily the avoidance of state intervention as such, but getting affirmative access to speech for those to whom it has been denied.

While I was thinking about all of this, I had an imagination. I was haunted by an entirely imaginary person: Francis Biddle had a sister. Do not look for her story in the diplomatic or legal sections of the library. She wrote no autobiography, much less two.[166] No legal footnotes embellish her life story. No one endowed a lecture series in recognition of her exemplary life of accomplishment. When she confronted people directly, it was not said, as Dean Fisher gracefully said of her brother, that she was "anti-tact";[167] they simply said she was tactless. People do not recall her elegance or grace on ceremonial oc; casions. Her compassion, her recognition that torture is real even when planned and systematic and carried out against targets defined as appropriate at the time, did not lead, as her brother's did, to sitting in judgment at Nuremburg. Her passion for justice did not express itself in the interstices of procedure. She never acted for her government for well or ill, regretting it or recalling it in pride in later years. Fact is, we don't know a thing Francis Biddle's sister said, much less in her own words. Maybe she spent her life changing typewriter ribbons or diapers or bedpans or beds. If she was lucky, she was well treated, at least most of the time while she was being used. If she was not, meaning that no man ever chose her for more than one night at a time or approved of her for whatever reasons are within their power to bestow or withhold, maybe she ended up walking the streets, talking out loud to no one in particular, until someone locked her up. Maybe, if she could manage it, she retreated to the home, in Andrea Dworkin's words, "that open grave where so many women lie waiting to die."[168] Maybe she hit bottom of women's options. Maybe she did well, carrying around the most whole self any woman can have in a society in which the degradation of her body is enjoyed. Some days she tried. Some days she gave up. In large part because of the society in which she lived, when she died it all came to about the same. Nothing much. Which, especially if you applied the standards her brother lived up to, is about what she was seen as good for.

You may be thinking that there isn't much we can do about this. I think there is something, as Virginia Woolf once wrote about a similar sister she invented for Shakespeare, that is in our power to give her.[169] Those of us who are as much her descendants as Francis Biddle's would apply his passion, his developed skills, his talents, if only some of his commitments, to her life. We would have this law I have been urging. We would have this recognition and institutional support for our equality. If this proposal were to become law and if it were to be used, if it were to be given the life in women's hands for which it is designed, there could come a day when she would speak in her own voice and you would hear her. And I think only then would we understand how unimaginable what she would say is for us now. She would write, she would lecture, she would carry on in public, she would make policy. From that day forward, neutrality might make some sense. Sexual equality would not be an empty standard, a taunting aspiration, or a vicious illusion. And silence would be a choice.

NOTES

This work was first presented as the 1984 Francis Biddle Memorial Lecture at Harvard Law School. It is reprinted, with minor editorial changes, from Catharine A. MacKinnon's *Feminism Unmodified* (1987) by permission of Harvard University Press.

1. We define pornography as "the graphic sexually explicit subordination of women, whether in pictures or in words, that also includes one or more of the following: (i) women are presented dehumanized as sexual objects, things or commodities; or (ii) women are presented as sexual objects who enjoy pain or humiliation; or (iii) women are presented as sexual objects who experience sexual pleasure in being raped; or (iv) women are presented as sexual objects tied up or cut up or mutilated or bruised or physically hurt; or (v) women are presented in postures of sexual submission, servility or display; or (vi) women's body parts—including but not limited to vaginas, breasts, and buttocks—are exhibited, such that women are reduced to those parts; or (vii) women are presented as whores by nature; or (viii) women are presented being penetrated by objects or animals; or (ix) women are presented in scenarios of degradation, injury, torture, shown as filthy or inferior, bleeding, bruised, or hurt in a context that makes these conditions sexual." Pornography also includes "the use of men, children or transsexuals in the place of women." Pornography, thus defined, is discrimination on the basis of sex and, as such, a civil rights violation. This definition is a slightly modified version of the one passed by the Minneapolis City Council on December 30, 1983. Minneapolis, Minn., Ordinance amending tit. 7, chs. 139 and 141, Minneapolis Code of Ordinances Relating to Civil Rights (Dec. 30, 1983). The ordinance was vetoed by the mayor, reintroduced, passed again, and vetoed again in 1984.

The Indianapolis City-County Council passed a version of it eliminating subsections (i), (v), (vi), and (vii), and substituting instead as (vi) "women are presented as sexual objects for domination, conquest, violation, exploitation, possession, or use, or through postures or positions of servility or submission or display." Indianapolis, Ind., City-County General Ordinance No. 35 (June 11, 1984) (adding inter alia, ch. 16, 16-3(q)(6) to the Code of Indianapolis and Marion County) [hereafter cited as Indianapolis Ordinance]. It was signed by the mayor, and a suit immediately followed in federal court. See American Booksellers, Inc. v. Hudnut, 598 F. Supp. 1316 (S.D. Ind. 1984), 771 F.2d 323 (7th Cir. 1985) aff'd 106 S.Ct. 1172 (1986).

2. See *Public Hearings on Ordinances to Add Pornography as Discrimination Against Women*, Committee on Government Operations, City Council, Minneapolis, Minn. (Dec. 12–13, 1983) [hereafter cited as *Hearings*]. All those who

testified in these hearings were fully identified to the City Council. Some are identified here only by their last initials for purposes of privacy.

3. I treat these themes more fully in "Feminism, Marxism, Method and the State: Toward Feminist Jurisprudence," *Signs: Journal of Women in Culture and Society* 8:635 (1983); "Feminism, Marxism, Method and the State: An Agenda for Theory," *Signs: Journal of Women in Culture and Society* 7:515 (1982).

4. Jacobellis v. Ohio, 378 U.S. 184, 197 (1964) (Stewart, J., concurring).

5. For my use of upper-case "Black," see Catharine A. MacKinnon "Not By Law Alone," in *Feminism Unmodified* (1987), note 12.

6. The classic enunciation of the meaning of neutrality as the principled approach to constitutional adjudication is Herbert Wechsler, "Toward Neutral Principles of Constitutional Law," *Harvard Law Review* 73:1 (1959). The doctrine of gender neutrality applies this approach to the area of sex, which goes far toward explaining the predominance of male plaintiffs in the Supreme Court's leading gender discrimination cases, especially among successful plaintiffs. See cases collected in David Cole, "Strategies of Difference: Litigating for Women's Rights in a Man's World," *Law and Inequality: Journal of Theory and Practice* 2:33–34, n. 4 (1984) ("The only area in which male plaintiffs do not dominate constitutional gender discrimination cases involves treatment of pregnancy").

7. For judicial discussions of the color-blindness of the law, see Fullilove v. Klutznick, 448 U.S. 448, 482 (1980); United Steelworkers of America v. Weber, 443 U.S. 193 (1979); Regents of the University of California v. Bakke, 438 U.S. 265, 327 (1978) (Brennan, White, Marshall, and Blackmun, JJ., concurring in part and dissenting in part); Swann v. Charlotte-Mecklenburg Board of Education, 402 U.S. 1, 19 (1971); Plessy v. Ferguson, 163 U.S. 537, 559 (1896) ("Our Constitution is color-blind, and neither knows nor tolerates classes among citizens") (Harlan, J., dissenting). The view that the Constitution should also be sex-blind also animates the leading interpretation of the proposed federal Equal Rights Amendment. See Barbara Brown, Thomas I. Emerson, Gail Falk, and Ann Freedman, "The Equal Rights Amendment: A Constitutional Basis for Equal Rights for Women," *Yale Law Review* 80:871 (1971).

8. The absolutist position on the entire Constitution was urged by Justice Black. See, e.g., Hugo Black, "The Bill of Rights," *New York University Law Review* 35:865–67 (1960), focusing at times on the First Amendment; and E. Cahn, "Justice Black and First Amendment 'Absolutes': A Public Interview," *New York University Law Review* 37:549 (1962). Justice Douglas as well as Justice Black emphatically articulated the absolutist position in the obscenity context. See, e.g., Miller v. California, 413 U.S. 15, 37 (1973) (Douglas, J., dissenting); Smith v. California, 361 U.S. 147, 155 (1959) (Black, J., concurring); Roth v. United States, 354 U.S. 476, 514 (1957) (Douglas, J., joined by Black, J., dissenting). Absolutist-influenced discontent with obscenity law is clear in Justice Brennan's dissent in Paris Adult Theatre I v. Slaton, 413 U.S. 49, 73 (1973).

9. The image of the First Amendment as guaranteeing the "free trade in ideas," in which the "best test of truth is the power of the thought to get itself accepted in the competition of the market," originated with Justice Holmes, dissenting in Abrams v. United States, 250 U.S. 616, 630 (1919) (joined by Brandeis, J.). Some possible shortcomings in this model are noticed in Laurence Tribe, *American Constitutional Law* 576–77 (1978).

10. See Wechsler, "Toward Neutral Principles of Constitutional Law."

11. Plessy v. Ferguson, 163 U.S. 537 (1896).

12. Brown v. Board of Education, 347 U.S. 483 (1954) (Brown I); Brown v. Board of Education, 349 U.S. 294 (1955) (Brown II).

13. See Lochner v. New York, 198 U.S. 45 (1905); Allgeyer v. Louisiana, 165 U.S. 578 (1897) (invalidating maximum hours restrictions on the ground of liberty to freely contract). For the rest of the tradition and its demise, see note 14.

14. See, e.g., Muller v. Oregon, 208 U.S. 412 (1908) (sustaining restrictions on women's hours). Adkins v. Children's Hospital, 261 U.S. 525 (1923) (legislation mandating minimum wages for women violated due process) was overruled in West Coast Hotel v. Parrish, 300 U.S. 379 (1937) (minimum wage laws for women may be legislated). *Parrish* followed Bunting v. Oregon, 243 U.S. 426 (1917) (upholding state law limiting hours). See also Stettler v. O'Hara, 243 U.S. 629 (1909) (upholding state minimum wage requirements for women factory workers). It is not that women as such were invisible to the judges who decided these cases. Indeed, it was their conception of women's distinctive (mostly physical) vulnerabilities as well as family place that justified the rulings upholding these laws, while laws protecting all workers, as in *Lochner*, were disallowed. Because this substantive view of women was so demeaning and so destructive, and because it became part of the critique of substantivity in adjudication as such, which was necessary to establish if social welfare legislation was to be allowed, the possibility was obscured that there might be a substantive analysis of the situation of women that was adequate to women's distinctive social exploitation, which could ground a claim to equality, and which did not license any more wholesale judicial discretion in the direction and to the degree that already existed. If one wants to claim no more for a powerless group than what can be extracted under an established system of power—if only the lines between that group and the powerful can be blurred as much as possible—one strategy is to try to claim that the powerless are entitled to what "everybody" is entitled to: in short, *abstract*. If, however, one's claim is against the distribution of power itself, one needs a critique not so much of the substantivity of the Lochner-era approach per se, but of its substance, with a critique of the tradition that replaced it, in which part of the strategy for hegemony is to present substance as substancelessness.

15. See, e.g., Regents of the University of California v. Bakke, 438 U.S. 265 (1978); John Ely, *Democracy and Distrust: A Theory of Judicial Review* 54–55 (1981). But see Laurence Tribe, "Speech as Power: Swastikas, Spending, and the Mask of Neutral Principles," in *Constitutional Choices* (1985).

16. See Edward Levi, "An Introduction to Legal Reasoning," *University of Chicago Law Review* 15:501 (1948).

17. See, e.g., Derrick Bell, *Race, Racism and American Law* 1–85 (1972).

18. 347 U.S. 483 (1954).

19. In my analysis, the combined effect of Texas Department of Community Affairs v. Burdine, 450 U.S. 248 (1981), and Furnco Construction Corp. v. Waters, 43 U.S. 567 (1978), both purporting to follow the standard first announced in McDonnell Douglas Corp. v. Green, 411 U.S. 792 (1973), is that anyone who has been discriminated against is assumed exceptional and living in that sex-discrimination-free universe that the burdens of proof are allocated to presuppose. The difficulty arises in the attempt to assume that discrimination because of sex neither exists nor does not exist in assessing facts such as those in *Burdine,* in which two persons are equally qualified, the man gets the job, and the woman sues. The Fifth Circuit in *Burdine* had required the employer to prove that the man who got the job was more qualified, but its decision was reversed. Facing the impossibility of neutrality here makes one wonder if there is any difference between nondiscrimination and affirmative action.

20. The following publications are selected from the large body of work that exists. On rape: Susan Brownmiller, *Against Our Will: Men, Women and Rape* (1975); L. Clark and D. Lewis, *Rape: The Price of Coercive Sexuality* (1977); N. Gager and C. Schurr, *Sexual Assault: Confronting Rape in America* (1976); A. Medea and K. Thompson, *Against Rape* (1974); Diana Russell, *Rape in Marriage* (1982); Diana Russell, *The Politics of Rape* (1975); Martha R. Burt, "Cultural Myths and Supports for Rape," *Journal of Personality and Social Psychology* 38:219 (1980); Irene Frieze, "Investigating the Causes and Consequences of Marital Rape," *Signs: Journal of Women in Culture and Society* 8:532 (1983); Gary LaFree, "Male Power and Female Victimization: Towards a Theory of Interracial Rape," *American Journal of Sociology* 88:311 (1982); Diana Russell and Nancy Howell, "The Prevalence of Rape in the United States Revisited," *Signs: Journal of Women in Culture and Society* 8:688 (1983).

On battery: R. Emerson Dobash and Russell Dobash, *Violence against Wives: A Case against the Patriarchy* (1979); R. Langley and R. Levy, *Wife Beating: The Silent Crisis* (1977); D. Martin, *Battered Wives* (rev. ed. 1981); S. Steinmetz, *The Cycle of Violence: Assertive, Aggressive, and Abusive Family Interaction* (1977); L. Walker, *The Battered Woman* (1979); Evan Stark, Ann Flitcraft, and William Frazier, "Medicine and Patriarchal Violence: The Social Construction of a 'Private' Event," *International Journal of Health Services* 3:461 (1979).

On sexual harassment: Catharine A. MacKinnon, *Sexual Harassment of Working Women: A Case of Sex Discrimination* (1979); Donna J. Benson and Gregg E. Thompson, "Sexual Harassment on a University Campus: The Confluence of Authority Relations, Sexual Interest and Gender Stratification," *Social Problems* 29:236 (1982); Phyllis Crocker and Anne E. Simon, "Sexual Harassment in Education," *Capital University Law Review* 10:3 (1981); U.S. Merit Systems Protection Board, *Sexual Harassment in the Federal Workplace: Is it a Problem?* (1981).

On incest and child sexual abuse: L. Armstrong, *Kiss Daddy Goodnight* (1978); Kathleen Brady, *Father's Days: A True Story of Incest* (1979); A. Burgess, N. Groth, L. Holmstrom, and S. Sgroi, *Sexual Assault of Children and Adolescents* (1978); S. Butler, *Conspiracy of Silence: The Trauma of Incest* (1978); D. Finkelhor, *Child Sexual Abuse: New Theory and Research* (1984); D. Finkelhor, *Sexually Victimized Children* (1979); J. Herman, *Father-Daughter Incest* (1981); Florence Rush, *The Best-Kept Secret: Sexual Abuse of Children* (1980); Diana Russell, *The Secret Trauma: Incest in the Lives of Girls and Women* (1986); Arthur C. Jaffe, Lucille Dynneson, and Robert TenBensel, "Sexual Abuse: An Epidemiological Study," *American Journal of Diseases of Chidren* 6:689 (1975); Diana Russell, "The Prevalence and Seriousness of Incestuous Abuse: Stepfathers vs. Biological Fathers," *Child Abuse and Neglect: The International Journal* 8:15 (1984); Diana Russell, "The Incidence and Prevalence of Intrafamilial and Extrafamilial Sexual Abuse of Female Children," *Child Abuse and Neglect: The International Journal* 7:2 (1983).

On prostitution: Kathleen Barry, *Female Sexual Slavery* (1979); Jennifer James, *The Politics of Prostitution* (2d ed. 1975); Moira Griffin, "Wives, Hookers and the Law: The Case for Decriminalizing Prostitution," *Student Lawyer* 10:13 (1982); Jennifer James and Jane Meyerding, "Early Sexual Experience as a Factor in Prostitution," *Archives of Sexual Behavior* 7:31 (1977); "Report of Jean Fernand-Laurent, Special Rapporteur on the Suppression of the Traffic in Persons and the Exploitation of the Prostitution of Others" (a United Nations report), in *International Feminism: Networking against Female Sexual Slavery* (Report of the Global Feminist Workshop to Organize against Traffic in Women, Rotterdam, Netherlands, Apr. 6–15, 1983), K. Barry, C. Bunch, S. Castley, eds. 130 (1984).

On pornography: Andrea Dworkin, *Pornography: Men Possessing Women* (1981); Linda Lovelace and Michael McGrady, *Ordeal* (1980); P. Bogdanovich, *The Killing of the Unicorn: Dorothy Stratten, 1960–1980* (1984); L. Lederer, ed., *Take Back the Night: Women on Pornography* (1980); Edward Donnerstein, "Pornography: Its Effects on Violence against Women," in *Pornography and Sexual Agression*, N. Malamuth and E. Donnerstein, eds. (1984); Martha Langelan, "The Political Economy of Pornography," *Aegis: Magazine on Ending Violence against Women* 5 (1981); Dorchen Leidholdt, "Where Pornography Meets Fascism," *Women's International News* (WIN), Mar. 15, 1983, 18; Daniel Linz, Edward Donnerstein, and Steven Penrod, "The Effects of Long-Term Exposure to Filmed Violence against Women" (unpublished manuscript, Mar. 22, 1984).

See generally: J. Long and P. Schwartz, *Sexual Scripts: The Social Construction of Female Sexuality* (1976); E. Morgan, *The Erotization of Male Dominance/Female Submission* (1975); Diana Russell, *Sexual Exploitation: Rape, Child Sexual Abuse and Workplace Harassment* (1984); D. Russell and N. Van de Ven, *Crimes against Women: Proceedings of the International Tribunal* (1976); E. Schur, *Labeling Women Deviant: Gender, Stigma, and Social Control* (1984); Edith Phelps, "Female Sexual Alienation," in *Women: A Feminist Perspective*, J. Freeman, ed. 16

(1975); Adrienne Rich, "Compulsory Heterosexuality and Lesbian Existence," *Signs: Journal of Women in Culture and Society* 5:4 (1980); E. Stanko, *Intimate Intrusions* (1985) (called "No Complaints: Silencing Male Violence to Women" in manuscript).

21. See Menachem Amir, *Patterns in Forcible Rape* 229–52 (1971); see also Gager and Schurr, *Sexual Assault;* Russell, *Sexual Exploitation.*

22. See Diana Russell, "The Prevalence of Rape in United States Revisited," *Signs: Journal of Women in Culture and Society* 8:689 (1983).

23. See sexual harassment references, note 20.

24. U.S. Merit Systems Protection Board, *Sexual Harassment.*

25. See battery references, note 20.

26. See child sexual abuse references, note 20, especially Russell, "Incidence and Prevalence of Intrafamilial and Extrafamilial Sexual Abuse of Female Children."

27. Adrienne Rich, "Cartographies of Silence," in *The Dream of a Common Language* 16, 17 (1978).

28. See Rush, *The Best-Kept Secret.* See also Jeffrey Masson, *The Assault on Truth: Freud's Suppression of the Seduction Theory* (1983).

29. Finkelhor, *Child Sexual Abuse;* D. Lockwood, *Prison Sexual Violence* 117 (1980): "For the player [the pimp-type prison rapist] to operate his game, however, he must 'feminize' his object of interest. We must remember that prisoners consider queens to be women, not men. As a consequence, the one who dominates the queen is a 'man.' Players live according to norms that place men who play female roles in submissive positions. . . . The happy conclusion . . . is for the target to become a 'girl' under his domination, a receptacle for his penis, and a female companion to accentuate his masculinity." See also Jacobo Timmerman, *Prisoner without a Name, Cell without a Number* (1981).

30. See Employment Standards Administration, U.S. Department of Labor, *Handbook on Women Workers* (1975); U.S. Department of Labor, *Women's Bureau Bulletin* 297 (1975 and 1982 update).

31. Catharine A. MacKinnon "Introduction," in *Feminism Unmodified* (1987), note 18.

32. Michel Foucault, "The West and the Truth of Sex," *Sub-Stance* 20:5 (1978).

33. This became a lot clearer to me after reading Margaret Baldwin, "The Sexuality of Inequality: The Minneapolis Pornography Ordinance," *Law and Inequality: Journal of Theory and Practice* 2:629 (1984). This paragraph is directly indebted to her insight and language there.

34. Dworkin, *Pornography.*

35. For a fuller development of this critique, see Catharine A. MacKinnon, "Not a Moral Issue," in *Feminism Unmodified* 146–62 (1987).

36. Miller v. California, 413 U.S. 15, 24 (1973).

37. See *The Report of the Presidential Commission on Obscenity and Pornography* (1970).

38. For the specific statutory language, see note 1.

39. See, e.g., Gloria Steinem, "Erotica v. Pornography," in *Outrageous Acts and Everyday Rebellions* 219 (1983).

40. See the Indianapolis Ordinance, note 1.

41. See MacKinnon, *Sexual Harassment of Working Women* 101–41.

42. For a lucid discussion of subordination, see Andrea Dworkin, "Against the Male Flood: Censorship, Pornography, and Equality," *Harvard Women's Law Journal* 8:1 (1985).

43. If this part stood alone, it would, along with its support, among other things, have to be equally imposed—an interesting requirement for an equality law, but arguably met by this one. See Carey v. Brown, 447 U.S. 455 (1980); Police Department of Chicago v. Mosley, 408 U.S. 92 (1972); Kenneth Karst, "Equality as a Central Principle in the First Amendment," *University of Chicago Law Review* 43:20 (1975).

44. See KPNX Broadcasting Co. v. Arizona Superior Court, 459 U.S. 1302 (1982) (Rehnquist as Circuit Justice denied application to stay an Arizona judge's order that those involved with heavily covered criminal trial avoid direct contact with press; mere potential confusion from unrestrained contact with press is held to justify order); New York v. Ferber, 458 U.S. 747 (1982) (child pornography, defined as promoting sexual performance by a child, can be criminally banned as a form of child abuse); F.C.C. v. Pacifica Foundation, 438 U.S. 726 (1978) ("indecent" but not obscene radio broadcasts may be regulated by F.C.C. through licensing); Young v. American Mini Theatres, Inc., 427 U.S. 50 (1976) (exhibition of sexually explicit "adult movies" may be restricted through zoning ordinances); Gertz v. Robert Welch, Inc., 418 U.S. 323, 347 (1974) (state statute may allow private persons to recover for libel without proving actual malice so long as liability is not found without fault); Pittsburgh Press Co. v. Human Relations Commission 413 U.S. 376 (1973) (sex-designated help-wanted columns conceived as commercial speech may be prohibited under a local sex discrimination ordinance); Miller v. California, 413 U.S. 15, 18 (1973) (obscenity unprotected by First Amendment in a case in which it was "thrust by aggressive sales action upon unwilling [viewers] . . . "); Red Lion Broadcasting Co. v. F.C.C., 395 U.S. 367, 387 (1969) (F.C.C. may require broadcasters to allow reply time to vindicate speech interests of the public: "The right of free speech of a broadcaster, the user of a sound truck, or any other individual does not embrace a right to snuff out the free speech of others"); Ginzburg v. United States, 383 U.S. 463, 470 (1966) (upholding conviction for mailing obscene material on the basis of the "pandering" theory: "the purveyor's sole emphasis [is] on the sexually provocative aspects of his publications"); Roth v. United States, 354 U.S. 476, 487 (1957) (federal obscenity statute is found valid; obscene is defined as "material which deals with sex in a manner appealing to prurient interest"); Beauharnais v. Illinois, 343 U.S. 250 (1952) (upholding group libel statute); Chaplinsky v. New Hampshire, 315 U.S. 568 (1942) (a state statute outlawing "fighting words" likely to cause a breach of peace is not unconstitutional under the First Amendment); Near v. Minnesota, 283 U.S. 697 (1931) (Minnesota

statute permitting prior restraint of publishers who regularly engage in publication of defamatory material is held unconstitutional; press freedom outweighs prior restraints in all but exceptional cases, such as national security or obscenity); for one such exceptional case, see United States v. Progressive, Inc., 486 F. Supp. 5 (W.D. Wis. 1979) (prior restraint is allowed against publication of information on how to make a hydrogen bomb, partially under "troop movements" exception); Schenck v. United States, 249 U.S. 47, 52 (1919) ("clear and present dangers" excepted from the First Amendment: "The most stringent protection of free speech would not protect a man in falsely shouting fire in a theatre and causing a panic").

45. See Young v. American Mini Theatres, Inc., 427 U.S. 50 (1976); Pittsburgh Press Co. v. Human Relations Commission, 413 U.S. 376 (1973); Konigsberg v. State Bar of California, 366 U.S. 36, 49–51 (1961).

46. In 1984, an Indiana federal court declared the ordinance unconstitutional in a facial challenge brought by the Media Coalition, an association of publishers and distributors. The ordinance is repeatedly misquoted, and the misquotations are underscored to illustrate its legal errors. Arguments not made in support of the law are invented and attributed to the city and found legally inadequate. Evidence of harm before the legislature is given no weight at all, while purportedly being undisturbed, as an absolutist approach is implicitly adopted, unlike any existing Supreme Court precedent. To the extent that existing law, such as obscenity law, overlaps with the ordinance, even it would be invalidated under this ruling. Moreover, clear law on sex equality is flatly misstated. The opinion permits a ludicrous suit by mostly legitimate trade publishers, parties whose interests are at most tenuously and remotely implicated under the ordinance, to test a law that directly and importantly would affect others, such as pornographers and their victims. The decision also seems far more permissive toward racism than would be allowed in a concrete case even under existing law, and it displays blame-the-victim misogyny: "Adult women generally have the capacity to protect themselves from participating in and being personally victimized by pornography. . . . " See American Booksellers v. Hudnut, 598 F. Supp. 1316, 1334 (S.D. Ind. 1984). For subsequent developments, see Catharine A. MacKinnon "The Sexual Politics of the First Amendment," in *Feminism Unmodified* (1987).

47. See, e.g., Title IX of the Education Amendments of 1972, 20 U.S.C. 1681–1686 (1972); Equal Pay Act, 29 U.S.C. 206(d) (1963); Title VII of the Civil Rights Act of 1964, 42 U.S.C. 2000e to 2000e-17 (1976). Many states have equal rights amendments to their constitutions. See Barbara Brown and Ann Freedman, "Equal Rights Amendment: Growing Impact on the States," *Women's Rights Law Reporter* 1:1.63, 1.63-1.64 (1974). Many states and cities, including Minneapolis and Indianapolis, prohibit discrimination on the basis of sex. See also Roberts v. United States Jaycees, 468 U.S 609 (1984) (recently recognizing that sex equality is a compelling state interest); Frontiero v. Richardson, 411 U.S. 677 (1973); Reed v. Reed, 404 U.S. 71 (1971); U.S. Constitution, Fourteenth Amendment.

48. See City of Los Angeles v. Manhart, 435 U.S. 702, 711 (1978) (the Los Angeles water department's pension plan was found discriminatory in its "treatment of a person in a manner which but for that person's sex would be different"). See also Orr v. Orr, 440 U.S. 268 (1979); Barnes v. Costle, 561 F.2d 983 (D.C. Cir. 1977).

49. See Plessy v. Ferguson, 163 U.S. 537, 551 (1896); Wechsler, "Toward Neutral Principles of Constitutional Law," 33.

50. In each case cited in note 44 (except *Near*), a recognized harm was held to be more important than the speech interest also at stake. The Supreme Court has also recognized, if not always in holdings, that the right to privacy or fair trial can outweigh the right to freedom of the press. See Zacchini v. Scripps-Howard Broadcasting Co., 433 U.S. 562 (1977) (a performer has a proprietary interest in his act that outweighs press interest in publishing it); Nebraska Press Association v. Stuart, 427 U.S. 539 (1976) (restraint on press is unconstitutional); Cox Broadcasting Corp. v. Cohn, 420 U.S. 469, 491 (1975) (no civil liability for privacy violations against broadcaster for truthfully publishing court records in which the daughter of the plaintiff was a rape victim, but: "In this sphere of collision between claims of privacy and those of the free press, the interests on both sides are plainly rooted in the traditions and significant concerns of our society"); Time, Inc. v. Hill, 385 U.S. 374 (1967) (magazine has no liability for inaccurate portrayal of private life unless knowingly or recklessly false). But see KPNX Broadcasting Co., 459 U.S. 1302 (1982). See also Globe Newspaper Co. v. Superior Court, 457 U.S. 596 (1982) (state may not require exclusion of press and public from courtroom during testimony of minor victim of sex offense); Richmond Newspapers, Inc. v. Virginia, 448 U.S. 555 (1980). The harm of defamatory speech to personal reputation is also the reason libel is actionable notwithstanding First Amendment protections of speech. See, e.g., Gertz v. Robert Welch, Inc., 418 U.S. 323 (1974). "Defamation has long been regarded as a form of 'psychic mayhem,' not very different in kind, and in some ways more wounding, than physical mutilation." See Tribe, *American Constitutional Law* 649 (discussing issues raised by Gertz). In Los Angeles v. Taxpayers for Vincent, 466 U.S. 789 (1984), the City of Los Angeles's aesthetic interests outweighed a political candidate's speech right to post signs on public property.

51. Under the standard in *Miller*, 413 U.S. 15, 24 (1973), obscenity prohibits materials that, inter alia, are "patently offensive" and appeal to the "prurient interest," terms with no apparent determinate meaning. Offensiveness is subjective. Prurience is a code word for that which produces sexual arousal. See F. Schauer, "Response: Pornography and the First Amendment," *University of Pittsburgh Law Review* 40:605, 607 (1969). See also Justice Brennan's discussion of the vagueness of terms like "lewd" and "ultimate," in *Paris Adult Theatre I*, 413 U.S. 49, 86 (1973) (Brennan, J., dissenting). "Community standards," also part of the *Miller* test, is a standard that is open-ended by design. In F.C.C. v. Pacifica Foundation, 438 U.S. 726 (1978), the Supreme Court allowed a regulatory body to construe the meaning of the term "indecent," which represents a social value judgment. In *Ferber*, 458 U.S. 747,

765 (1982), the Supreme Court did not seem at all bothered by the fact that "lewd," as in "lewd exhibition of the genitals" in the statute's definition of sexual performance, was statutorily undefined. *Beaulharnais*, 343 U.S. 250, 251 (1952), sustained a law that prohibited the publishing, selling, or exhibiting in any public place of any publication that "portrays depravity, criminality, unchastity, or lack of virtue of a class of citizens of any race, color, creed or religion." Although doubt has been cast on the vitality of *Beauharnais*—see, e.g., Collin v. Smith, 578 F.2d 1197, 1205 (7th Cir. 11978)—"*Beauharnais* has never been overruled or formally limited in any way" Smith v. Collin, 436 U.S. 953 (1978) (Blackmun, J., joined by Rehnquist, J., dissenting from denial of stay of Court of Appeals order).

52. Most obscenity laws provide criminal sanctions, with the appropriate procedural requirements. *Roth*, 354 U.S. 476, 478 n. 1 (1957); *Miller*, 413 U.S. 15, 16 n. 1 (1973). However, the injunction proceeding in *Paris Adult Theatre I*, 413 U.S. 49 (1973), was civil, and the statutory scheme discussed in Freedman v. Maryland, 380 U.S. 51 (1964) (under which prior restraints imposed by a censorhip board were legal only if certain procedural requirements were met) was noncriminal. Of course, all a civil injunction can do under our ordinance is stop future profit-making or assault. A potential award of civil damages under our ordinance is not a negligible sanction; it is designed to deter victimization but differently than potential incarceration does. A major purpose of pornography is to make money. Depriving the pornographers of profits by empowering those whom they exploit to make them, directly counteracts one reason pornographers engage in the exploitation at all, in a way that potential incarceration does not. Another not inconsiderable benefit of a civil rather than criminal approach to pornography is that criminal prohibitions, as well as eroticizing that which they prohibit, tend to create underground markets wherein the prohibited commodity is sold at inflated prices, passed hand to hand in secret settings, and elevated in value. If it were not pssible to make or use pornography as it now is without exploiting its victims as they are exploited now, a civil prohibition would create no underground. This approach does not solve the problems of terror and intimidation that keep victims from suing, nor does it give them resources for suit. It does define who is hurt directly (versus the amorphous "community" that is considered hurt on the criminal side), gives victims (and lawyers) the incentive of a potential civil recovery, and leaves control over the legal actions as much as possible in the hands of the victims rather than the state. For further views on civil as opposed to criminal approches to this area, see the opinions of Justice Stevens in F.C.C. v. Pacifica Foundation, 438 U.S. 726 (1978); Young v. American Mini Theatres, Inc., 427 U.S. 50 (1976); and, most fully, his dissent in Smith v. United States, 431 U.S. 291, 317 (1977) (criticizing community standards in a criminal context, but approving their "flexibility [as] a desirable feature of a civil rule designed to protect the individual's right to select the kind of environment in which he wants to live"). Some who oppose or are critical of obscenity restrictions have found it preferable to first adjudicate pornographic materials obscene in a civil or administrative proceeding. See Miller

v. California, 413 U.S. 15, 41 (1973) (Douglas, J., dissenting); Z. Chafee, *Government and Mass Communications* 1:228–31 (1947); William Lockhart, "Escape from the Chill of Uncertainty: Explicit Sex and the First Amendment," *Georgia Law Review* 9:533, 569–86 (1975); William Lockhart and Robert McClure, "Censorship of Obscenity," *Minnesota Law Review* 65:5, 105–7 (1960); American Civil Liberties Union, Policy No. 4(c) (2) (Feb. 14, 1970) (civil proceeding seen as the least restrictive method of censorship).

53. The harm of obscenity recognized in *Miller*, 413 U.S. 15, 19 (1973), was the "danger of offending the sensibilities of unwilling recipients or of exposure to juveniles." This statement was adduced from the Presidential Commission on Obscenity's finding that it could not be concluded that obscenity causes harm: "[The] Commission cannot conclude that exposure to erotic materials is a factor in the causation of sex crime or sex delinquency." See *Report of the Presidential Commission on Obscenity and Pornography* 27 (1970). The harm in F.C.C. v. Pacifica Foundation, 438 U.S. 726, 748–50 (1978), was the possibility that children would overhear indecent speech, since radio intrudes into the home. In United States v. Orito, 413 U.S. 139, 143 (1973), a federal ban on interstate transportaton of obscene materials for private use was sustained on "a legislatively determined risk of ultimate exposure to juveniles or to the public." Throughout, exposure of juveniles to obscenity is assumed to be a risk, but the harm that exposure does per se is unspecified, not to say unsubstantiated and not in evidence. The harm recognized in *Ferber*, 458 U.S. 747 (1982), appears to be that done to a minor male by being seen having sex. The film depicted two boys masturbating; the Court concluded that this was "a permanent record of children's participation and the harm to the child is exacerbated by [its] circulation" (759). This same harm is at times characterized by the Court as "psychological" (759 n. 10) but is otherwise unspecified and in evidence only in the form of the film. In *Chaplinsky*, 315 U.S. 568 (1942), the harm apparently was a combination of the offense given by the speech itself and the risk of imminent breach of the peace occasioned by its utterance. As to group libel, the harm of the racist leaflet to the group as a whole recognized in *Beauharnais*, 343 U.S. 250, 258–61 (1952), was inferred from observed racial inequality and racial unrest.

54. See Galloway and Thornton, "Crackdown on Pornography—A No-Win Battle," *U.S. News and World Report*, June 4, 1984, 84; see also J. Cook, "The X-Rated Economy," *Forbes*, Sept. 18, 1978, 81 ($4 billion per year); Langelan, "The Political Economy of Pornography" 5 ($7 billion per year); "The Place of Pornography," *Harper's*, Nov. 1984, 31 ($7 billion per year).

55. Flags, seen as symbols for the nation rather than mere pieces of brightly colored cloth or even as personal property, receive special solicitude by legislatures and courts, as to both the patriotic value of their protection and the expressive value of their desecration. See, e.g., Spence v. Washington, 418 U.S. 405 (1974); Street v. New York, 394 U.S. 576 (1969). I have not considered the applicability of this line of cases here, in light of my view that women in pornography are not simply symbols of all women but also are women. Of course, under male supremacy, each woman represents all

women to one degree or another, whether in pornography or in bed or walking down the street, because of the stereotyping intrinsic to gender inequality. But that does not mean that, in a feminist perspective, each woman, including those in pornography, can be treated solely in terms of her representative or symbolic qualities, as if she is not at the same time alive and human. An underlying issue has to do with the extent to which women's bodies must be freely available as vocabulary and imagery for the expression of others, such that once they are so converted, whatever the means, women retain no rights in their use or abuse, in the face of evidence of the harm from such expropriation and exposure, ranging from the individual so used to anonymous women subsequently used or treated or seen in light of their availability for such use. (Given the extent to which women now must be men's speech, one might rather be a flag.)

56. *Ferber,* 458 U.S. 747 (1982).

57. II *Hearings* 75 (testimony of a named former prostitute).

58. Lovelace and McGrady, *Ordeal.*

59. As of September, 1978, *Deep Throat* had grossed a known $50 million worldwide. See Cook, "The X-Rated Economy." Many of its profits are untraceable. The film has also recently been made into a home video cassette.

60. Priscilla Alexander, coordinator for the National Organization for Women's Task Force on Prostitution, said she was told this by a woman pornography model. Panel on Pornography, National Association of Women and the Law, Los Angeles, Apr. 1, 1984.

61. "In the movies known as snuff films, victims sometimes are actually murdered." See *Congressional Record* 130:S13192 (daily ed. Oct. 3, 1984) (statement of Senator Specter introducing the Pornography Victims Protection Act). Information on the subject is understandably hard to get. See People v. Douglas, Felony Complaint No. NF 8300382 (Municipal Court, Orange County, Calif., Aug. 5, 1983); "Slain Teens Needed Jobs, Tried Porn" and "Two Accused of Murder in 'Snuff' Films," *Oakland Tribune,* Aug. 6, 1983; MacKinnon, "Not A Moral Issue," note 56; L. Smith, "The Chicken Hawks" (unpublished manuscript, 1975).

62. "We were all introduced to prostitution through pornography, there were no exceptions in our group, and we were all under 18. . . . There were stacks of films all over the house, which my pimp used to blackmail people with." See II *Hearings* 70, 79 (testimony of a named former prostitute). Kathleen Barry, author of *Female Sexual Slavery* (1979), refers to "season[ing]" to prostitution by "blackmailing the victim by threatening to send [photographs of coerced sex] to her family, and selling them to the pornographers for mass production." See I *Hearings* 59 (letter of Kathleen Barry). A worker with adolescent prostitutes reports: "These rapes are often either taped or have photographs taken of the event. The young woman when she tries to escape or leaves is told that either she continues in her involvement in prostitution or those pictures will be sent to her parents, will be sent to the juvenile court, will be used against her. And out of fear she will continue her involvement in prostitution." See III *Hearings* 77 (testimony of Sue Santa).

63. Speech by Andrea Dworkin, in Toronto, Feb. 1984 (account told to Dworkin), reprinted in *Healthsharing*, Summer 1984, 25.

64. Linda Marchiano, Panel on Pornography, Stanford University, Apr. 2, 1982.

65. "When *Deep Throat* was released, we [prostitutes] experienced men joking and demanding oral sex." See II *Hearings* 74 (testimony of a named former prostitute). Increasing emergency room reports of throat rape followed the exhibition of *Deep Throat*. One woman told Flora Colao, C.S.W., an emergency room nurse in New York City at the time, that the men who raped her said, as she was becoming unconscious, "Let's deep-throat her before she passes out." See I *Hearings* 60 (Exhibit 13 [letter], Nov. 10, 1983). She also reported women dead of suffocation from rape of the throat. One woman wrote the Minneapolis City Council the day after Marchiano's testimony before it, in a letter typical of the accounts received by Marchiano since the publication of *Ordeal*: "I read about Linda Lovelace in our morning paper which said that she testified for women's civil rights. I only hope that she is able to undo some of the terrible damage that was done by making her movie. Those years started days of misery for me and a lot of my friends. Linda was so convincing that she enjoyed what she was doing that our husbands began to think they were cheated in life with us upper middle class wives. 'I'm not satisfied!' 'You don't know how to be a woman.' And every young girl in town was brainwashed to show our husbands that they could be a better 'Linda Lovelace' than the wife they had at home. I saw a lot of heartbreaks, nervous breakdowns to women that were being coerced in sex—many tranquilizers taken because they had to keep up with the times or else. Being forced to do something they don't enjoy or 'someone else will gladly go out with me!' I even saw a business fail because the husband was so preoccupied with this type of sex. Why do you think women's lib evolved—women became tired of being exploited, brainwashed and now Linda says she didn't enjoy it. It's too late for us 50 year olds, but help the young girls not to wreck their lives by letting boyfriends and husbands force them to be receptacles instead of cherished wives." See Letter from "a bitterwife" to the Minneapolis City Council, Dec. 14, 1983.

66. The credibility of the pornography, as compared with that of the women in it, is underlined by the following: Vanessa Williams, formerly Miss America, lost her title when pornographic pictures of her were published by *Penthouse*. Williams says she posed for the sexually explicit pictures under the representation that they were for private use, at most for silhouettes, and that she did not consent to their publication. Brian DePalma, director of *Dressed to Kill* and *Body Double* (both "splatter" films of sexualized violence against women) who should know what it takes for a director to create an image of an interaction so that it *looks* like sex, was interviewed concerning the Williams episode. Asked about her version of the events, DePalma said, "I believed her until I saw the pictures." See "Double Trouble: Brian DePalma Interviewed by Marcia Pally," *Film Comment* 20: 13, 16 (Sept-Oct. 1984).

67. I am indebted for this argument's development to Margaret Baldwin, "Pornography: More Than a Fantasy," *The Hennepin Lawyer*, Mar.-Apr. 1984, 8, 25.

68. This question and the paragraph that follows draw directly on Andrea Dworkin's speech. See note 63.

69. I *Hearings* 56.

70. National Task Force on Child Pornography, "Let's Protect Our Children" 17 (1983).

71. 458 U.S. 747 (1982).

72. Ibid. 759.

73. Ibid. 747.

74. Ibid. 761.

75. Ibid.

76. Ibid. 763–64.

77. The harm of child pornography cannot be stopped effectively without also addressing the pornography of adult women. Adult pornography has been commonly used "to show, teach or induce the children into the sexual activity or pornographic modeling" by child-sex rings. See A. Burgess, C. Hartman, M. McCausland, and P. Powers, "Response Patterns in Children and Adolescents Exploited through Sex Rings and Pornography," *American Journal of Psychiatry* 141:656, 657–58 (1984). Given what is done in pornography, it is even more difficult than usual to distinguish between adults and children. Adult women are infantilized in pornography; children are dressed and used as if they were adult women. The resulting materials are then used against both, and they target both for abuse relatively interchangeably. For instance, the "shaved pussy" genre, in which adult women's genitals are made to resemble those of young girls, converges with the "Lolita" or "cherry tarts" genre, in which young girls are presented resembling the pornographers' image of adult female sexuality. It also seems worth observing that a law that has the abuse disappear legally when its victims get one day older is difficult to administer effectively.

78. "The forcing of pornography on any woman, man, child, or transsexual in any place of employment, in education, in a home, or in any public place." See Indianapolis Ordinance. Section 16–17(a) states: "A complaint charging that any person has engaged in or is engaging in a discriminatory practice . . . may be filed . . . in any of the following circumstances: . . . (7) in the case of forcing pornography on a person, against the perpetrator(s) and/or institution."

79. III *Hearings* 71, 76 (testimony of Charlotte K. and Sue Santa).

80. II *Hearings* 85–90 (testimony of Jackie B.).

81. These often arise under the rubric of sexual harassment. See, e.g., MacKinnon, *Sexual Harassment of Working Women* 29. Although not providing the same range of relief, sexual harassment cases recognize concerns related to those underlying the Minneapolis ordinance: "The . . . workplace was pervaded with sexual slur, insult and innuendo, and [the plaintiff] Katz was personally the object of verbal sexual harassment by her fellow controllers.

This harassment took the form of extremely vulgar and offensive sexually related epithets addressed to and employed about Katz by supervisory personnel as well as by other controllers. The words used were ones widely recognized as not only improper but as intensely degrading, deriving their power to wound not only from their meaning but also from 'the disgust and violence they express phonetically.' " See Katz v. Dole, 709 F.2d 251, 254 (4th Cir. 1983) (quoting C. Miller and K. Swift, eds., *Words and Women* 109 [1977]).

Do such words become *not* injurious by virtue of appearing in print? To an extent, Tribe's observation about the words whose regulation was allowed in *Chaplinsky* applies here: "Such provocations are not part of human discourse but weapons hurled in anger to inflict injury or invite retaliation." See Tribe, *American Constitutional Law* 605. The fact that in the case of pornography the projectiles hurled at women are other women, or constructions of one's own gendered anatomy, puts them on a slightly different plane and also helps to explain why pornography's injury has neither been seen by its perpetrators nor retaliated against by its victims: the injury it inflicts, it inflicts in such a humiliating and undermining way that it disables retaliation. Silence has been the usual response.

82. "Women were forced constantly to enact specific scenes that men had witnessed in pornography. They would direct women to copy postures and poses of things they had seen in magazines." See II *Hearings* 73 (testimony of a named former prostitute).

83. Letters from Marvin Lewis to Catharine MacKinnon, Dec. 7, 1983. Attorney Lewis described to me situations in which therapists had women patients act out scenes from *The Story of O.*

84. "The pornographic view of women is one that is prevalent within the medical community unfortunately. This is expressed by the kinds of jokes that are made about women and their bodies, especially when they are under anesthesia and undergoing surgical procedures. This view includes seeing women as not worthy of respect and also seeing them primarily in terms of their sexual functioning. Several years ago when I was teaching at the Rutgers Medical School there was a week-long sexuality program planned annually for students. The first day of this program consisted of all-day viewing of pornographic movies. The intent was to 'desensitize' the students to sex." See letter from Michelle Harrison, M.D., to the Minneapolis City Council, Dec. 9, 1983.

See also P. Bart, "From Those Wonderful People Who Brought You the Vaginal Orgasm: Sex Education for Medical Students" 2 (1976) (paper presented at the meetings of the American Sociological Association, New York). "When I was asked to participate in the sex education program at the University of Illinois 6 years ago it was a joint venture of Gynecology and Psychiatry and its primary purpose was to 'desensitize' the medical students. My first thought was, 'Aren't they insensitive enough as it is?' The term, however, has a technical meaning. It means that the subject will not react emotionally when presented with certain stimuli that previously she/he had such reactions to. . . . In order to achieve this purpose the students were shown porno films." The specifics in the text are drawn from examples many people have recounted to me as a standard part of the program customarily used in medical schools.

85. Students and clients reported this to me in the course of my research into sexual harassment in education.

86. See III *Hearings* 13–16 (testimony of Susan G.) (discussing sexual abuse of an adult woman with whom she lived).

87. See, e.g., III *Hearings* 69–74 (testimony of Charlotte K.); United States v. Roth, 237 F.2d 796, 812 (2d Cir. 1956) (Frank, J., appendix to concurring opinion). *Seduction* here is the term that attributes consent or acquiescence or enjoyment of rape to the rape victim.

88. See II *Hearings* 90–100. A woman who lived in a neighborhood into which pornography had been zoned said, if you think pornography is harmless, "you move into my neighborhood and I will move into yours." See ibid., testimony of Shannon M., 99.

89. Averting one's eyes is supposed to be an alternative to the injury, as it may well have been in Cohen v. California, 403 U.S. 15, 21 (1971) ("Those in the Los Angeles courthouse could effectively avoid further bombardment of their sensibilities simply by averting their eyes"). Or, less so but still arguably, in Erznoznik v. City of Jacksonville, 422 U.S. 205, 212 (1975) (the screen was not "so obtrusive as to make it impossible for an unwilling individual to avoid exposure to it") (quoting Redrup v. New York, 386 U.S. 767, 769 [1967]). The situations that our ordinance is premised upon and is designed to address directly are more like that of the woman who was tied to a chair in front of a video screen in her home and forced to watch pornography. See, e.g., III *Hearings* 24.

90. See Stanley v. Georgia, 394 U.S. 557 (1969) (right to privacy protects possession of obscenity at home). The Court seems to assume that Stanley is at home alone.

91. Many Jewish citizens, survivors of the Nazi extermination, live in Skokie, Illinois. The town's attempts to keep Nazis from demonstrating there produced years of local ordinances, all ultimately held unconstitutional. Dissenting from a denial of certiorari, Justice Blackmun said, "On the one hand we have precious First Amendment rights vigorously asserted. . . . On the other hand, we are presented with evidence of a potentially explosive and dangerous situation, inflamed by unforgettable recollections of traumatic experiences in the second world conflict." See Smith v. Collin, 439 U.S. 916, 918 (1968). Observing that citizens had asserted "that the proposed demonstration is scheduled at a place and in a manner that is taunting and overwhelmingly offensive to the citizens of that place," he thought their claim deserved to be heard, "for 'the character of every act depends upon the circumstances in which it is done' " (919) (quoting Schenck v. United States, 249 U.S. 47, 52 [1919]).

92. II *Hearings* 112 (testimony of Mags D.).

93. The Indianapolis Ordinance, ch. 16, 16-3(g) (8), provides: "Assault or physical attack due to pornography: The assault, physical attack, or injury of

any woman, man, child, or transsexual in a way that is directly caused by specific pornography." No damages or compensation for loss is recoverable from traffickers under this section "unless the complainant proves that the respondent knew or had reason to know that the materials were pornography." Pornography that caused the acts can be reached under this provision, although it would be very difficult to prove "direct cause."

94. "The First Amendment demands more than a horrible example or two of the perpetrator of a crime of sexual violence, in whose pocket is found a pornographic book, before it allows the Nation to be saddled with a regime of censorship." See Memoirs v. Massachusetts, 383 U.S. 413, 432 (1966) (Douglas, J., concurring). One wonders how many bodies must pile up before individual victims will be allowed to enjoin the proven cause, simply because that cause is a book. See also ibid. 452 (Clark, J., dissenting) (noting repeated reports "that pornography is associated with an overwhelmingly large number of sex crimes").

95. II *Hearings* 43 (testimony of Rita M.).

96. III *Hearings* 18–19 (testimony of Carol L.).

97. Ongoing research on sex offenders in Hennepin County, Minn., that documents these similarities was presented by Candace Kruttschnitt to the City of Minneapolis Task Force on Pornography, Mar. 13, 1984. The data are consistent with that of all researchers who find it difficult to document differences between sex offenders and populations of normal men on virtually any dimension. See note 118. My analysis is that the few measurable differences between these populations involve the likelihood of getting caught for sex offenses more than the likelihood of committing them.

98. Only 9.5 percent of all rapes and rape attempts are reported. See Russell, *Sexual Exploitation* 31. The reporting rate of most sexual violations is as low or lower. Six percent of extrafamilial child sexual assault and 2 percent of incestuous assault are reported to authorities. See ibid. 172; see also Herman, *Father-Daughter Incest* 12–15. Another study estimates that only 1 of very 270 incidents of wife abuse is ever reported to authorities. See Steinmetz, *The Cycle of Violence*. This is probably a low figure. Although 42 percent of federal employees had been subjected to sexual harassment in the two years prior to one survey, 29 percent in severe forms, most had not reported the behavior. See U.S. Merit Systems Protection Board, *Sexual Harassment* 35, 71.

99. III *Hearings* 36 (testimony of Barbara Chester, director of the Rape and Sexual Assault Center, Hennepin County, Minn.).

100. III *Hearings* 44–45 (testimony of Jill Seals, director of Sexual Assault Services, Center for Behavior Therapy, Minneapolis, Minn.).

101. III *Hearings* 64 (testimony of Nancy Steele, therapist with sex offenders).

102. Ibid.

103. III *Hearings* 88 (testimony of Michael Laslett, reading a statement by Floyd Winecoff, psychotherapist specializing in services for men).

104. Ibid. 86.

105. III *Hearings* 44 (testimony of Bill Seals).

106. III *Hearings* 59 (testimony of Gerry Kaplan, executive director of Alpha Human Services, an inpatient program for sex offenders).

107. Examples range from the seemingly correlational to the integral to the causal. See, e.g., Hoggard v. State, 277 Ark. 117, 640 S.W.2d 102 (1982), cert. denied, 460 U.S. 1022 (1983), in which the court, in ruling on a challenge that the prejudicial effect of pornography outweighed its probative value in the allegation of the rape of a six-year-old boy, stated, "We readily agree the material was prejudicial, it could hardly be otherwise. But the argument that its probative value was lacking fades under scrutiny. This pornography and the offense being tried had a clear correlation: the pornography depicted deviate sexual acts by young males and the crime charged was deviate sexual acts of a forty-two-year-old man and a six-year-old boy. More importantly, the pornography was used as the instrument by which the crime itself was solicited—the child was encouraged to look at the pictures and then encouraged to engage in it. The value of the evidence as proof of the crime is obvious" (277 Ark. 124–25, 640 S.W.2d 106).

In a case concerning statutory rape, the defendant cared for two children, seven and six, "and while they were there had the children perform various sexual acts with him and each other while he took photographs, some of which he sent to foreign publishers of pornographic magazines." See Qualle v. State, 652P.2d 481, 483 (Alaska Ct. App. 1982). As to his own children: "Documents, photographs, and films seized from Qualle's home in 1979 showed that he had taken sexually explicit films and photographs of his children and had tried to sell at least two rolls of such pictures to European companies. He asked for money or pornographic magazines in exchange for his pictures. One magazine ('Lolita') published a series of pictures of one of his daughters (484).

In State v. Natzke, 25 Ariz. App. 520, 522, 544 P.2d 1121, 1123 (1976), pornography was admissible in a rape case in which the defendant's daughter "expressed a reluctance to perform the requested sexual acts . . . appellant told her that these acts were all right and that 'everybody does it,' and that as proof of this fact, appellant showed his daughter pictures and magazines showing sexual activities."

In People v. Reynolds, 55 Cal. App. 3d 357, 127 Cal. Rptr. 561 (1976), the defendant sought to suppress pornographic pictures of victims in a prosecution for kidnapping and rape. "According to Tracy, the suspect forced her to take some yellow capsules with a can of cola, and she became groggy; he gave her pornography to read, and at one point stopped the car to make a telephone call and she heard him say: 'I have got the girl.' . . . When the officers searched his room they discovered pornographic negatives and photographs, some of which depicted the Konoske girls. . . . More photographs were [later] found which were pornographic" (55 Cal. App. 3d 362, 365, 127 Cal. Rptr. 564, 566).

In another case the defendant was charged with, among other things, encouraging minors to participate in pornographic films and to engage in sexual intercourse with him: "Defendant showed pornographic films to two boys, and defendant was an actor in one of them. He also showed a pornographic film to two of the girls. . . . He suggested to two of the girls that they become prostitutes. Defendant had a movie camera set up to photograph his bed so that, 'in case some of these young girls tried to say that he raped them, he would have this as proof that he did not.' " See State v. Dobbs, 665 P.2d 1151, 1155, 1159 (N.M. Ct. App. 1983).

In yet another case, the defendant was an Episcopal priest who ran a boy's farm, which was supposedly for the benefit of wayward and homeless boys, but was "maintained largely from funds raised . . . from the sale of photographs and slides of the children to some 200 or more 'sponsors.' These photographs depicted the boys (most of whom were eleven to sixteen years of age when photographed) posed in the nude and engaged in various acts of simulated or actual fellatio and sodomy." See Vermilye v. State, 584 S.W.2d 226, 228 (Tenn. Crim. App. 1979).

See also People v. Cramer, 67 Cal. 2d 126, 127, 429 P.2d 582, 583, 60 Cal. Rptr. 230, 231 (1967) ("At the house, they swam, and defendant served Phillip vodka and 7-Up and showed him some *Playboy* magazines"); People v. Hunt, 72 Cal. App. 3d 190, 195–196, 139 Cal. Rptr. 675, 677 (1977) (rape case in which the "defendant told her his name was John and that he was a 'porno' photographer. . . . This time the defendant took a polaroid picture of Chris (the victim) performing the act [oral copulation]"); People v. Mendoza, 37 Cal. App. 3d 717, 721, 112 Cal. Rptr. 565, 567 (1974) ("He then invited Tad and Jim into his apartment, where he gave the boys candy and pointed out a *Playboy* magazine centerfold photograph of a nude girl on the wall"); Whiteman v. State, 343 So. 2d 1340 (Fla. Dist. Ct. App.) (admissibility of pornography in the sexual battery of a niece), cert. denied, 353 So. 2d 681 (Fla. 1977); Brames v. State, 273 Ind. 565, 406 N.E.2d 252 (1980) (attempt to introduce evidence of rape defendant's prior visit to pornographic movie house rejected as part of insanity plea); Allan v. State, 92 Nev. 318, 321, 549 P.2d 1402, 1404 (1976) (minor's testimony concerning defendant's past advances admissible as "tending to show proof of a motive . . . wherein minors were lured to appellant's quarters and, after being 'conditioned' by the showing of his pornographic movies, subjected to his sexual desires"); Stein v. Beta Rho Alumni Association, 49 Or. App. 965, 968, 621 P.2d 632, 634 (1980) (personal injury suffered to a burlesque dancer who performed for a fraternity after "a pornographic movie had been shown"). Finally, in Padgett v. State, 49 Ala. App. 130, 133, 269 So. 2d 147, 149 (Crim.), cert. denied, 289 Ala 749, 269 So. 2d 154 (1972), a husband was convicted for shooting his wife, allegedly accidentally, after he admittedly " 'nagged' [her] about the girls in the *Playboy* magazine 'to try to irritate her.' "

California's spousal rape law, effective January 1980, has made many reports of sexual violence in intimate contexts visible for the first time. "Beglin was watching an X-rated movie [on cable TV] in the family room. Beglin allegedly entered the bedroom, threw her [his wife] on the bed and bound her. Beglin also ripped off her clothing and began taking nude photos of her, [Prosecutor Alphonsus C.] Novick said. He then sexually assaulted her." See

Brown, "Man on Trial Again on Wife Rape Count," *Los Angeles Times*, May 19, 1981. The husband was acquitted after claiming his wife consented. See Kutzmann, "Beglin Innocent of Wife Rape," *Costa Mesa Daily Pilot*, May 29, 1981. Evidence included testimony of crisis center workers and an emergency room doctor and photos of her wrists and ankles, "allegedly marked from being tied to a bed with ropes." The prosecutor said, "The case couldn't have been any better. . . . Unfortunately, we may have to wait until some wife is severely mutilated or murdered until they'll see." See LaGuire, "Spousal-Rape Trial: Husband Cleared, Prosecutor Angered," *Los Angeles Herald Examiner*, May 30, 1981, A-1.

In Merced, California, Victor Burnham was convicted of spousal rape for forcing his wife to have sex with neighbors and strangers (a total of sixty-eight) while he took photographs. See Wharton, "Sex Torture Charges Unveiled in Burnham Trial," *Sun-Star* (Merced, Calif.), May 29, 1981. She was also forced, through assault and holding their child hostage, to stand on the corner and invite men in for sex and to have sex with a dog. See "Burnham Pleads No Contest on Charge of Possession of Automatic Rifle," *Sun-Star* (Merced, Calif.), May 27, 1981; "Man Found Guilty of Spousal Rape," *Times-Delta* (Tulare County, Calif.), June 6, 1981. She testified to "episodes of torture with a battery-charged cattle prod and an electric egg beater. See Wharton, "Sex Torture Charges." The defense attorney, "attempting to show the jury there was no force used by the defendant, quizzed Mrs. Burnham about photographs in the albums showing her smiling during the sexual encounters. Mrs. Burnham said her husband threatened her with violence if she did not smile when the pictures were taken." Two of Burnham's previous wives testified that he had forced them to commit similar acts. See "Wife Testifies in Burnham Sex Case," *Sun-Star* (Merced, Calif.), May 28, 1981. Burnham said Mrs. Burnham agreed to the acts; his lawyer showed the photos to the jury to "see for themselves that the pictures were in complete conformity with Becky's morals." See Wharton, "Guilty Verdict in Sex Trial," *Sun-Star* (Merced, Calif.), June 5, 1981. Burnham's conviction was overturned for failure to instruct *sua sponte* that he might have believed she consented. See People v. Burnham, 222 Cal. Rptr. 630 (Ct. App. 1986), (rev. denied, May 22, 1986). My general impression from rape and sexual harassment cases is that it takes a minimum of three women testifying to the same or similiar treatment to create a chance of overcoming the man's credibility when he defends himself against an accusation of sexual force by saying that the woman consented to the act. (For example, some educational institutions have a covert policy of not moving to investigate claims of teachers' sexual harassment of students until they receive complaints from three different women about the same man. They also do not keep reports over time.)

In another such case, "the woman testified that her husband tortured her on several occasions, including sewing her to the bed, burning her with a lamp until she blistered, cutting her with a razor blade and raping her with objects ranging from a coat hanger to a hair brush. . . . [He] used duct tape to keep her from screaming. . . . When Deputy Attorney Lela Henke asked the woman where her husband got the idea to rape her with a coat hanger, the woman replied they had seen it in a movie on cable television." See "Wife Tells of Assault, Torture," *Press Courier* (Oxnard, Calif.), May 9, 1984. Similarly, a woman told of her husband "sewing her sexual organs with needle and yarn." See Green, "Wife Describes Brutal Attacks by Mate as He Listens in Court," *Star Free Press* (Ventura, Calif.), May 10, 1984.

Apparently 500 to 1,000 deaths occur each year from "autoerotic asphyxia," in which young men asphyxiate, usually from a noose around the neck, something presented in pornography as producing intense erections. Usually "pornographic material is nearby." See Brody, " 'Autoerotic Death' of Youths Causes Widening Concern," *New York Times*, Mar. 27, 1984, C3.

108. State v. Herberg, 324 N.W.2d 346, 347 (Minn. 1982).

109. Indianapolis Ordinance, ch. 16, 16-3(4) states, "Trafficking in pornography: the production, sale, exhibition, or distribution of pornography. (A) City, state, and federally funded public libraries or private and public university and college libraries in which pornography is available for study, including on open shelves, shall not be construed to be trafficking in pornography, but special display presentations of pornography in said places is sex discrimination. (B) The formation of private clubs or associations for purposes of trafficking in pornography is illegal and shall be considered a conspiracy to violate the civil rights of women. (C) This paragraph (4) shall not be construed to make isolated passages or isolated parts actionable." Section 16–17(b) states, "In the case of trafficking in pornography, any woman may file a complaint as a woman acting against the subordination of women and any man, child, or transsexual may file a complaint but must prove injury in the same way that a woman is injured in order to obtain relief under this chapter."

110. See, e.g., U.S. Commission on Obscenity and Pornography, *Commission Report* (1970); Commission on Obscenity and Film Censorship, *Report,* Cmd. No. 7772 (1979) (United Kingdom).

111. Regina v. Hicklin, 3 L.R.-Q.B. 360, 370 (1868) (obscene meaning "calculated to produce a pernicious effect in depraving and debauching the minds of the persons into whose hands it might come").

112. Roth v. United States, 354 U.S. 476, 501–02 (1956) (Harlan, J., concurring in the companion case of Alberts v. California); see also Jacobellis v. Ohio, 378 U.S. 184, 202 (1964) (Warren, C.J., dissenting) ("protection of society's right to maintain its moral fiber").

113. The date of John H. Court and of Berl Kutchinsky, both correlational, reach contradictory conclusions on the relationship between the availability of pornography and the level of crime. Compare Kutchinsky, "The Effect of Easy Availability of Pornography on the Incidence of Sex Crimes: The Danish Experience," *Journal of Social Issues* 29:163 (1973), and Kutchinsky, "Towards an Explanation of the Decrease in Registered Sex Crimes in Copenhagen," *Technical Report of the Commission on Obscenity and Pornography* 7:263 (1971), with Court, "Pornography and Sex-Crimes: A Re-Evaluation in the Light of Recent Trends around the World," *International Journal of Criminology and Pe-*

nology 5:129 (1977). More recent investigations into the relationship between the circulation rates of popular men's sex magazines and the rate of reported rape establish a correlation between them in the United States. See Larry Baron and Murray Straus, "Sexual Stratification, Pornography, and Rape in the United States" in *Pornography and Sexual Aggression*, N. Malamuth and E. Donnerstein, eds. 185 (1984).

114. Roth v. United States, 354 U.S. 476, 485 (1957) (quoting Chaplinisky v. New Hampshire, 315 U.S. 568, 572 [1942]). See also Paris Adult Theatre I v. Slaton, 413 U.S. 49, 57–58 (1973) ("There are legitimate state interests at stake . . . these include the interest of the public in the quality of life").

115. Positivistic causality—linear, exclusive, unidirectional—has become the implicit standard for the validity of a connection between pornography and harm. This standard requires the kind of control that can be achieved only in labortory settings, if at all. When it is found there, as it has been, that pornography causes harm (see note 117), the objection is heard that laboratory settings are artificial. But their artificiality is what makes a conclusion about causality possible under this causal model. In real-world settings, a relation of linear consequentiality between pornography and harm is seldom sufficiently isolable or uncontaminated—indeed, seldom even sufficiently separable, the pornography and its impact being so pervasive and intertwined—to satisfy this standard. I am suggesting that the positivistic model of causation may be inappropriate to the social reality of pornography. See also Werner Heisenberg, *The Physical Principles of Quantum Theory* 63 (1930); Morton Horowitz, "The Doctrine of Objective Causation," in *The Politics of Law*, David Kairys, ed. 201 (1982).

116. Major sources are N. Malamuth and E. Donnerstein, eds., *Pornography and Sexual Aggression* (1984); Dolph Zillman, *Connections between Sex and Aggression* (1984); Edward Donnerstein and Leonard Berkowitz, "Victim Reactions in Aggressive Erotic Films as a Factor in Violence against Women," *Journal of Personality and Social Psychology* 41:710–24 (1981); Neil M. Malamuth and John H. Check, "The Effects of Mass Media Exposure on Acceptance of Violence against Women: A Field Experiment," *Journal of Research on Personality* 15:436–46 (1981); Neil M. Malamuth and Edward Donnerstein, "The Effects of Aggressive-Pornographic Mass Media Stimuli," *Advances in Experimental Social Psychology* 15:103 (1982); Diane Russell, "Pornography and Violence: What Does the New Research Say?" in *Take Back the Night*, L. Lederer, ed. 216 (1983); Dolph Zillman and Jennings Bryant, "Pornography, Sexual Callousness, and the Trivialization of Rape," *Journal of Communication* 32:16–18 (1982); I *Hearings* 13–45 (testimony of Edward Donnerstein); Daniel Linz, Edward Donnerstein, and Steven Penrod, "The Effects of Long-Term Exposure to Filmed Violence against Women," *Journal of Personality and Social Psychology* (forthcoming).

117. In addition to the references listed in note 116, see E. Donnerstein and J. Hallam, "The Facilitating Effects of Erotica on Aggression toward Females," *Journal of Personality and Social Psychology* 1270 (1978); R. Geen, D. Stonner, and G. Shope, "The Facilitation of Aggression by Aggression:

Evidence against the Catharsis Hypothesis," *Journal of Personality and Social Psychology* 31:721 (1975); B. S. Sapolsky and Dolph Zillman, "The Effect of Soft-Core and Hard-Core Erotica on Provoked and Unprovoked Hostile Behavior," *Journal of Sex Research* 17:319 (1981); Dolph Zillman, J. L. Hoyt, and K. B. Day, "Strength and Duration of the Effect of Aggressive, Violent, and Erotic Communications on Subsequent Aggressive Behavior," *Communication Research* 1:286 (1974). See also N. Malamuth, "Factors Associated with Rape as Predictors of Laboratory Aggression against Women," *Journal of Personality and Social Psychology* 45:432 (1983) (valid relation between factors associated with real-world aggression against women and laboratory aggression).

118. Neil M. Malamuth and John Check, "Penile Tumescence and Perceptual Responses to Rape as a Function of Victim's Perceived Reactions," *Journal of Applied Social Psychology* 10:528 (1980); Neil M. Malamuth, Scott Haber, and Seymour Feshbach, "Testing Hypotheses Regarding Rape: Exposure to Sexual Violence, Sex Difference, and the 'Normality' of Rapists," *Journal of Research in Personality* 14:121 (1980). The lack of distinction between the reactions of convicted rapists and those of control groups may be the reason many people have concluded that pornography does not do anything. When all the unreported, undetected, not to mention unconscious or potential, rapists in the control groups are considered, this conclusion stops being mysterious. See text accompanying note 98. See also Gene Abel, Judith Becker, and L. Skinner, "Aggressive Behavior and Sex," *Psychiatric Clinics of North America* 3:133, 140 (1980) (fewer than 5 percent of rapists are psychotic while raping); N. Malamuth, "Rape Proclivity among Males," *Journal of Social Issues* 37:4 (1981); Malamuth and Check, "The Effects of Mass Media Exposure"; N. Malamuth, J. Heim, and S. Feshbach, "Sexual Responsiveness of College Students to Rape Depictions: Inhibitory and Disinhibitory Effects," *Social Psychology* 38:399 (1980).

On the general subject of men's attitudes toward rape, see T. Beneke, *Men on Rape* (1982); P. Burt, "Cultural Myths and Supports for Rape," *Journal of Personality and Social Psychology* 38:217 (1980); MacKinnon, "Introduction," note 20; S. D. Smithyman, "The Undetected Rapist" (Ph.D. diss., Claremont Graduate School, 1978). A currently unknown number of incidents originally reported as rapes are now considered by police to be unfounded, meaning "the police established that no forcible rape offense or attempt occurred." In 1976, the last year the FBI reported its "unfounding" rate, it was 19 percent of reports. See Federal Bureau of Investigation, *Crime in America* 16 (1976).

119. See notes 116 and 118. It is perhaps worth noting that there is no experimental research to the contrary.

120. See John Briere and Neil M. Malamuth, "Self-Reported Likelihood of Sexually Aggressive Behavior: Attitudinal versus Sexual Explanations," *Journal of Research in Personality* 37:315, 318 (1983) (58 percent of college males in the survey reported some likelihood of forcing sex on a women if they knew they would not get caught). See also Mary Koss and Cheryl J. Oros, "Sexual Experiences Survey: A Research Instrument Investigating Sexual Aggression and Victimization," *Journal of Consulting and Clinical Psychology* 50:455 (1982).

121. See I *Hearings* 21–38 (testimony of E. Donnerstein discussing supporting data submitted in the record). See also Zillman and Bryant, "Pornography, Sexual Callousness" (normal males exposed to films like *Debbie Does Dallas* see rape victims as many times more worthless than do men who had not seen the films; they also saw less than half the amount of injury to the victim). In spite of this factual support, it is likely that the Indianapolis version of the ordinance would not apply to trafficking in such materials. See 16-3(8) of the Indianapolis Ordinance, which states, "Defenses: It shall be a defense to a complaint under paragraph (g) (4) . . . that the materials complained of are those covered only by paragraph (q) (6)."

122. See note 121. See also Linz, Donnerstein, and Penrod, "The Effects of Long-Term Exposure." On female subjects, see Carol Krafka, "Sexually Explicit, Sexually Violent, and Violent Media: Effects of Multiple Naturalistic Exposures and Debriefing on Female Viewers" (Ph.D. diss., University of Wisconsin, 1985).

123. See I *Hearings* 37–38 (testimony of E. Donnerstein) ("subjects who have seen violent material or X-rated material see less injury to a rape victim than people who haven't seen these films. Furthermore, they consider the woman to be more worthless"). See also Zillman and Bryant, "Pornography, Sexual Callousness."

124. Donnerstein says this in most of his talks.

125. Russell, *Rape in Marriage* 228.

126. Ibid., 84.

127. See II *Hearings* 68 (testimony of Ruth M.).

128. II *Hearings* 55 (testimony of Nancy C.).

129. III *Hearings* 29 (testimony of Sharon Rice Vaughn, reading a statement by Donna Dunn of Women's Shelter, Inc., in Rochester, Minn., which describes events reported by a woman at the shelter).

130. Ibid.

131. III *Hearings* 83 (testimony of Sue Schafer).

132. II *Hearings* 74 (testimony of a named former prostitute). The use of pornography in the sexual abuse of prostitutes, as well as its use in getting them into prostitution, is documented by Mimi Silbert and Ayala Pines, "Pornography and Sexual Abuse of Women," *Sex Roles: Journal of Research* 10:857 (1984). Even though no specific questions were asked about pornography, 24 percent of the subjects (current and former prostitutes) mentioned references to pornography by the men who raped them, often references to specific materials in which prostitutes were presented as loving and wanting violent abuse and death. Ten percent mentioned being used in pornography as children, again in unsolicited open-ended accounts of their lives. Had they been directly asked, "it is assumed that the actual response to this question would be notably higher" (865).

133. II *Hearings* 74–75 (testimony of a named former prostitute).

134. I *Hearings* 56 (testimony of Gordon C.).

135. Ibid.

136. III *Hearings* 94–95 (testimony of Omar J.).

137. Ibid. 95.

138. See Andrea Dworkin, "The Bruise that Doesn't Heal," *Mother Jones* 3:31, 35 (1978) ("Reality is when something is happening to you and you know it and you say it and when you say it, other people understand what you mean and believe you").

139. See Dworkin, *Pornography* 149 ("She wants it, they all do").

140. I think it is important that when the actual object, for example the pornography, is present, finding facts about it is thought to become more rather than less difficult—compared, for example, with finding facts about a rape. This suggests that the usual process of proof amounts to a credibility contest between conflicting stories, which come to court in personae. Pornography has pervasively written women's side of the story as not a rape. When there is no story about reality to provide a proxy for simplifying it to a question of whose version one believes but the reality itself is there, perhaps—if it is measured against standards devised to described it—women will have a chance.

141. See Miller v. California, 413 U.S. 15, 19 (1973).

142. See Kaplan v. California, 413 U.S. 115, 120 (1973); Paris Adult Theatre I v. Slaton, 413 U.S. 49, 60 (1973); Roth v. United States, 354 U.S. 476, 501 (1957) (Harlan, J., concurring).

143. New York v. Ferber, 458 U.S. 742, 757 (1982).

144. See consideration of civil as opposed to criminal procedures and remedies, note 52. It does seem to me that criminal civil rights legislation might be worth considering at the federal level, but only in addition to providing private civil claimants access to court.

145. III *Hearings* 53 (testimony of Cheryl Champion, member, Sexual Abuse Unit, Washington County, Minn., Human Services).

146. 315 U.S. 568, 572 (1941).

147. Actually, some have. See Ann Hansen, "Direct Action: Sentencing Statements," *Open Road* (Vancouver, B.C.) 17:11–12 (Winter 1984) (on receiving a life sentence for firebombing the Red Hot Video store, among other actions). Nikki Craft, with the Preying Mantis Women's Brigade, engages in disruptive and exemplary acts against pornography, from staging the Myth California Pageant (in opposition to the Miss California Pageant) to destroying copies of *Hustler*, for which she served time. See Linda Hooper, "Preying on Porn Propaganda," *City on a Hill* (Santa Cruz, Calif.), Apr. 5, 1984, 5–7. Women in Europe have also engaged in destruction of property to express their opposition to pornography and to attempt to destroy some of it. See Dworan, "Review," *off our backs*, May 6, 1984, 118–19 (reviewing *Breaching the Peace: A Collection of Radical Feminist Papers* [1983]).

148. See Beauharnais v. Illinois, 343 U.S. 250, 263 (1952) ("The dignity accorded him may depend as much on the reputation of the racial and religious group to which he willy-nilly belongs as on his own merits").

149. See Whitney v. California, 274 U.S. 357, 377 (1927) (Brandeis, J., concurring).

150. See Tribe, *American Constitutional Law* 731.

151. See T. Emerson, "Toward a General Theory of the First Amendment," *Yale Law Journal* 72:877, 879–81 (1963); C. E. Baker, "Scope of the First Amendment Freedom of Speech," *UCLA Law Review* 25:964, 990–1005 (1978).

152 See A. Meiklejohn, *Political Freedom* 24–28 (1960). The importance of participation in civic life is also recognized by Emerson: "Man in his capacity as a member of society has a right to share in the common decisions that affect him." See T. Emerson, *The System of Freedom of Expression* 6 (1970).

153. See Emerson, *The System of Freedom of Expression*. Emerson is entirely aware that some groups lack power in a way that the political process does not accommodate, but he simply considers this a risk posed principally to "the nonbelonging individual" (37), rather than advancing any substantive analysis of who does and does not have power and thus access to the means of speech. In the absence of such a substantive analysis, pornographers can cast themselves as outsiders when they are actually paradigmatic. See also Clark, "Liberalism and Pornography," in *Pornography and Censorship*, D. Copp and S. Wendell, eds. 57 (1983).

154. One case has squarely balanced a municipal ordinance prohibiting sex discrimination in advertising against the First Amendment. Noting that commercial speech is not the highest order of speech—a position with strong parallels to the plurality's treatment of the "sexually explicit" in Young v. American Mini Theatres, 427 U.S. 50 (1976)—the *presumptive* connection between sex segregation in job advertisements and sex segregation in the workplace stated a harm that outweighed freedom of the press. Further, the Supreme Court held that the compelling state interest in eradicating discrimination against women justified the impact of Minnesota's Human Rights Act on First Amendment rights of expressive association. See Roberts v. United States Jaycees, 468 U.S. 609 (1984). Holding that the state's interest in sex equality outweighed the First Amendment interests implicated, the Court stated that the equality interest is not "limited to the provision of purely tangible goods and services" but also includes steps to remove "the barriers to economic advancement and political and social integration that have historically plagued certain disadvantaged groups, including women (626)." In a formulation strikingly apposite to the antipornography ordinance, the Court said, "Acts of invidious discrimination in the distribution of publicly available goods, services, and other advantages cause unique evils that government has a compelling interest to prevent—wholly apart from the point of view such conduct may transmit. Accordingly, like violence or other types of potentially expressive activities that produce special harms distinct from their communicative impact, such practices are entitled to no constitutional protection" (628).

155. In one obscenity case the Supreme Court stated, "Appellant was not prosecuted here for anything he said or believed, but for what he did, for his dominant role in several enterprises engaged in producing and selling allegedly obscene books." See Mishkin v. New York, 383 U.S. 502, 504–5 (1966). The statute upheld in *Ferber*, 458 U.S. 747 (1982), defined publication of child pornography as "promoting a sexual performance by a child," N.Y. Penal

Law 263 (McKinney 1980), logic that was extended to support the law against the pornography's distribution. It is arguable that a major reason obscenity was defined as "nonspeech" is because speech was considered to communicate ideas, and obscenity was understood to function physically rather than ideationally. For some further thoughts on this subject, see MacKinnon, "Not a Moral Issue." To state the obvious, I do not argue that pornography is "conduct" in the First Amendment doctrinal sense.

156. Ginsberg v. New York, 390 U.S. 629, 649 (1968) (Stewart, J., concurring in result) (emphasis added).

157. Roth v. United States, 354 U.S. 476, 514 (1957) (Douglas, J., dissenting) (citing Giboney v. Empire Storage and Ice Co., 336 U.S. 490, 498 [1949]); Labor Board v. Virginia Power Co., 314 U.S. 469, 477–78 (1941). See also Memoirs v. Massachusetts, 383 U.S. 413, 426 (1966) (Douglas, J., concurring) (the First Amendment does not permit the censorship of expression not brigaded with illegal action); Pittsburgh Press Co. v. Human Relations Commission, 413 U.S. 376, 398 (1973) (Douglas J., dissenting) (speech and action are not so closely brigaded as to be one).

158. Rape, battery, assault, kidnapping, and prostitution are all crimes, and they are absolutely integral to pornography as we define and make it actionable. Compare with *Ferber*, 458 U.S. 747 (1982): masturbating is not a crime, nor is watching it; yet making and distributing a film of two boys masturbating is.

159. Speech by Dworkin, note 63.

160. This example is from an interview with a victim done in preparation for the Minneapolis *Hearings*.

161. See Foucault, "The West and the Truth of Sex."

162. "He [her husband] told me if I loved him I would do this. And that, as I could see from the things he read me in the magazines initially, a lot of times women didn't like it but if I tried it enough I would probably like it and I would learn to like it. And he would read me stories where women learned to like it." See II *Hearings* 63 (testimony of Ruth M.).

163. See Rennie Simson, "The Afro-American Female: The Historical Context of the Construction of Sexual Identity," in *Powers of Desire: The Politics of Sexuality*, A. Snitow, C. Stansell, and S. Thompson, eds. 231 (1983) (quoting a Black slave, Harriet Jacobs, who speaks for many women under circumstances of compulsion when she writes of her rape by her white master: "It seems less demeaning to give one's self, than to submit to compulsion." Jacobs subsequently resisted by hiding in an attic cubbyhole, "almost deprived of light and air, and with no space to move my limbs, for nearly seven years" to avoid him.

164. This paraphrases a portion of Andrea Dworkin's speech, note 63.

165. See U.S. Constitution, First Amendment.

166. Francis Biddle, *A Casual Past* (1961), and *In Brief Authority* (1962).

167. A. Fisher, "Francis Biddle," *Harvard Civil Rights—Civil Liberties Law Review* 9:423, 424 (1974) (foreword to Herbert Wechsler, "The Francis Biddle Lectures," *Harvard Civil Rights–Civil Liberties Law Review* 9:426 [1974]). It was

also said that "Mr. Biddle deeply shared what Justice Brandeis called the 'conviction' of Justice Holmes, that 'man should be free in a large way' " (426). So, it seems to me, should woman.

168. Dworkin, "The Bruise that Doesn't Heal" 31, 36.

169. V. Woolf, *A Room of One's Own* 48–50 (1929), inspired the form of this vision.

Notes on Contributors

MICHAEL V. ANGROSINO is a professor of anthropology and public health at the University of South Florida. His research interests are in the area of community mental health and public policy. His recent publications include *A Health Practitioner's Guide to the Social and Behavioral Sciences* and *Documents of Interaction*. He is currently editor of *Human Organization*, the journal of the Society for Applied Anthropology.

ANNE BOLIN received her Ph.D. in cultural anthropology from the University of Colorado. Prior to her position as an assistant professor of anthropology at Elon College in North Carolina, she was on the faculty at the University of Colorado at Denver. She has published articles on the subject of sex, gender, and women. Her book *In Search of Eve: Transsexual Rites of Passage* received a Choice Magazine Award for an Outstanding Academic Book for 1988–89. She is coauthoring an anthropology of human sexuality text and engaging in ethnographic research with competitive women bodybuilders for a book on women and the body.

DONA LEE DAVIS is a professor of anthropology at the University of South Dakota in Vermillion. She received her Ph.D. in anthropology from the University of North Carolina at Chapel Hill in 1980. She is the author of *Blood and Nerves: An Ethnographic Focus on Menopause* and coedited (with Jane Nadel-Klein) *To Work and To Weep: Women in Fishing Economies*. Davis just completed a twelve-year follow-up study of recent social changes and their differential effects on the men and women of Grey Rock Harbour, Newfoundland.

MARGARET A. EISENHART received her Ph.D. in anthropology from the University of North Carolina at Chapel Hill, taught for seven years at Virginia Tech, and is currently associate professor of educational anthropology and research methodology in the School of Education at the University of Colorado at Boulder. Her publications have addressed race and gender relations in U.S. schools and the uses of ethnographic methods in educational research. She recently coauthored (with Dorothy C. Holland) *Educated in Romance: Women, Achievement, and College Culture.*

MAUREEN J. GIOVANNINI is a cultural anthropologist employed by ODI, an international management consulting firm located in Burlington, Massachusetts. She received her M.A. and Ph.D. from Syracuse University and served on the faculty of Boston University from 1975 to 1986. Her academic work centered on gender studies and the anthropology of health. Since joining ODI, she has consulted in the health care, financial, manufacturing, and service industries. She specializes in assessing the quality improvement needs of organizations and helping managers effect organizational change.

LEE ANN HOFF, a nurse-anthropologist and crisis specialist, is an associate professor at Northeastern University, Boston, and is the founder and director of the Life Crisis Institute. She is the author of *Battered Women as Survivors* and the award-winning *People in Crisis* and the coauthor of *Omnicide: Life in the Nuclear Age.* Her research focuses on life crises and women's health issues in the sociocultural context.

DOROTHY C. HOLLAND is a professor of anthropology at the University of North Carolina at Chapel Hill. She has done research in American Samoa, Trinidad, and Nepal, as well as in the American South. She is coeditor (with Naomi Quinn) of *Cultural Models in Language and Thought* and author of publications in cognitive and psychological anthropology and in the anthropology of gender and schooling, including (with Margaret Eisenhart) *Educated in Romance.* She currently has two books in progress: *Mind in Society/Society in Mind* (with Claudia Strauss and *Symbols and the Formation of Self* (with C. Cain, R. Prillaman, and D. Skinner).

CATHARINE A. MACKINNON received a B.A. from Smith College, *magna cum laude* in 1969, a J.D. from Yale Law School in 1977, and a Ph.D. in political science from Yale University in 1987. She has taught law at Yale, Harvard, Stanford, UCLA, the University of Chicago, the University of Minnesota, and Osgoode Hall (York University, Toronto). Her fields are constitutional law (including comparative), focusing on equality, speech, and feminist theory. She participates in litigation, legislation, and policy development on issues of sex equality in the United States and abroad. Her publications include *Sexual Harassment of Working Women; Feminism Unmodified; Pornography and Civil Rights: A New Day for Women's Equality* (with Andrea Dworkin); and *Toward a Feminist Theory of the State.*

BARBARA V. REID has published on the topics of gender and morality, Samoan culture, and medical anthropology. Her most recent research has focused on the experience of chronic illness. She has taught at the University of North Carolina and North Carolina State University and is currently on the faculty of San Jose State University in San Jose, California. Her work in progress includes two books: *Women of Pride and Sympathy: Gender and Samoan Moral Discourse* and *Who Decides? Abortion Stories from East and West*.

JOHN H. STORER received his doctorate from the University of Missouri. He developed his interest in child sexual abuse during a six-year period spent as a child abuse investigator for a state social service agency. He is currently an assistant professor in the Department of Physical Education and Leisure Studies at Iowa State University.

TONY L. WHITEHEAD, an associate professor, is the chair of the Department of Anthropology at the University of Maryland in College Park and the director of the department's Cultural Systems Analysis Group. He received his M.S. degree in public health and his Ph.D. in anthropology from the University of Pittsburgh. He spent two years as a U.S. Peace Corps volunteer in Turkey and has conducted health-related anthropological fieldwork in Jamaica, Cameroon, southwest France, and the rural southeast and the urban north of the United States. His research interests include male gender roles, food and culture, and health-related community diagnostic research, program planning, and evaluation.

LUCINDA J. ZAGNOLI is Director of Quality Assurance at the Northside Centers of Tampa. She received her M.A. in counseling from the University of South Florida and is a licensed mental health and marriage family therapist.

Index

Abelson, G., 47
Abortion, 46. *See also* Privacy rights
Absence, 267. *See also* Harm; Power: and silence
Adaptive behavior scales, 42
Adolescence. *See* Puberty
Adultery: and incestuous fathers, 5, 83, 95–97
Adversarial relationships: between incestuous father and daughter, 84–85.
Advertising: sexuality in, 258
Affirmative action, 263
Agar, Michael, 107
American Association on Mental Deficiency, 42
Analogies: between blacks and women, 265–66. *See also* Racism
Androgyny: transsexuals' views of, 36n5
Angrosino, Michael V., 4, 40–69
Ashenden, D. J., 143
Authority: in incestuous families, 76–77, 80–81, 89–90; defiance of, and reputational strength, 112
"Autoerotic asphyxia," 314n107
Avoidance: as daughter's strategy in incest, 79, 82

"Baby blues": defined, 210–11
Balance: Jamaican concept of, 104, 123, 133
Barry, Kathleen, 305n62

Battered Women as Survivors (Hoff), 235
Battering, 3, 7, 8, 235–48, 267–68, 269, 281, 286; as a private matter, 254; readings on, 297n20
Beauharnais v. Illinois, 289–90
"Benefactors" (of retarded adults), 46
Benjamin, Harry, 14
Berdache Society (pseudonym), 14, 16, 21, 33–34
Biddle, Francis, 292–93
"Big men" (in Jamaica), 103–4, 110, 111, 112, 119, 120–21
"Bill" (retarded television character), 43
Birth control: and retarded adults, 46, 58; Jamaican attitudes toward, 121–22; in Newfoundland, 189, 191–93, 203. *See also* Family planning; Reproductive issues; Tubal ligations
Black men: retarded, 53, 54, 55, 62
Blackstone, William, 253
Black women: experiences at college, 174
Blood: Newfoundland notions about, 183, 184, 189, 198–99, 202. *See also* Menarche; Menopause
Body: individual control over, 7. *See also* Birth control; Privacy rights; Rape; Reproductive issues; Sterilization
Body Double (DePalma), 360n66
Bolande, Robert, 198
Bolin, Anne, 4, 13–39

Bradley, V., 62
Brandeis, Louis, 290
Breen, D., 213
Brokers: in Jamaica, 111, 120; suggested
    use of, in family planning programs,
    127–28
Brownmiller, Susan, 255
Brown v. Board of Education, 263, 266
"Buccra-massa" behavior, 111–12, 120, 127
"Building block" model of analysis, 73,
    89–90, 97
Bumpass, L. L., 203
Burnett, Jaquetta H., 19

Cancer screening programs: in New-
    foundland, 194; recommendations
    for, 203–4. *See also* Cervical cancer;
    Uterine cancer
Caplan, G., 237
Careers: women's decisions about, in
    college, 142–77. *See also* Jobs
Carrieri, V. L., 237
Cars: significance of, in Jamaica, 136n19
Caucasian features: in Jamaica, 116–
    17, 122
Cervical cancer: in Newfoundland, 183,
    187, 194
Chaplinsky v. New Hampshire, 289
Chapple, Elliott, 17, 19
Chertok, L., 213
Child abuse: as a private matter, 254.
    See
    also Child pornography; Incestuous
    families; Sexual abuse: of children
Childbirth: transsexual changes and
    metaphors for, 27; as life crisis, 213–
    14; medicalization of, 221–23
Child molester: and incestuous fathers,
    5, 95–96
Child pornography: and incest, 81; and
    coercion, 278; criminal prohibitions
    on, 280, 289; and pornography using
    adult women, 307n77
Children: as symbol of strength, 117–19,
    121, 122, 124
Children of Retarded Mental Develop-
    ment (CRMD) classes, 41
Chodorow, N., 245
Cicourel, Aaron, 98
Class: and respectability, 129–30

Cliff, Jimmy, 135n15
Cloak of Competence, The (Edgerton), 46
Coercion: incestuous fathers' methods
    of, 75, 76, 79–82, 84; and pornogra-
    phy, 270, 277–80
College of Physicians and Surgeons of
    Saskatchewan, 185
Colonialism: strategies of survivors of,
    likened to retarded adults, 60; linger-
    ing effects of, in Jamaica, 107–8,
    130–31
Coming of Age in Samoa (Mead), 30
"Communitas," 24
Community-based care: of retarded
    adults, 40–64
"Complex networks": defined, 73
Compson, Benjy (as retarded person), 43
Connell, R. W., 143, 148–49
Contraceptives. *See* Birth control
Coon, C. S., 17, 19
"Courtship": as first stage in incest, 77–
    78, 80–82, 93
Credibility: of women victims, 278, 287–
    88, 290, 313n107
CRMD (Children of Retarded Mental
    Development) classes, 41
Cross-dressing, 4, 14–15. *See also* "Full-
    time"; Transsexuals
Cultural models, 239–40

Dally, Ann, 224, 226
Dalton, K., 212
Daughter: pseudomaturity of, in
    incestuous families, 71, 78–79,
    83–84, 87–88, 94; adaptations of,
    to father's incest with, 72, 74–78,
    80, 83–84, 85, 87, 88–97; sexual
    activity of, outside of incestuous
    father, 83–84, 94–95; as trouble-
    maker in incestuous family, 89–92,
    94–95
Davis, Dona Lee, 6, 183–208
Deep Throat (film), 277, 278
Deinstitutionalization, 41, 60, 62–64
Delphy, Christine, 257
Denial: in incestuous families, 101–2
DePalma, Brian, 306n66
Depression: described, 226–27; theories
    of, 238. *See also* Postpartum
    depression

Developmentally disabled. *See* Retarded
adults
Devor, Holly, 22, 23
Dickson, Harold D., 188, 203
Dignity of risk: concept of, 41, 57
Dinnerstein, D., 245
Discovery (of incest): by outsiders, 81,
83, 84–85, 94; by mothers, 90–92
Dissociation, 26
Donnerstein, Ed, 285
Douglas, William O., 291
Dowsett, G. W., 143
"Drag queens," 14–15
Draper, A., 117
Dressed to Kill (film), 306n66
"Dumb brute" view of retarded
people, 43
Dworkin, Andrea, 257, 261, 270, 273,
291, 293
Dyck, Frank, 186–87

EASE (Essential Adult Sex Education)
survey, 49–60
Eating disorders, 258
Eccles, Jacquelynne, 145
Edgerton, Robert, 46
Edmonson, Barbara, 47
Edwards, Susan S. M., 254
Egalitarian ethic: in Newfoundland, 200,
201, 202. *See also* Equality
Eisenhart, Margaret A., 5–6, 142–80
Emerson, T., 319n152
Equality: presumption of, in USA, 266,
271–72, 275–76, 279; appearance of,
in pornography, 269–70, 276; in mu-
nicipal pornography ordinance,
273–75
Equal Rights Amendment, 258, 295n7
Erotica, 273
Essential Adult Sex Education (EASE)
Curriculum. *See* EASE
Estrich, Susan, 256

Family (nuclear): views of, about violence, 7; overriding importance of,
96; work of, 99–100. *See also* Daughter; Father; Father-daughter incest;
Husband; Incestuous families; Moth-
er(s); Parents; Wife
Family networks. *See* Support networks

Family planning: efforts at, in Jamaica,
5, 103–38; perceptions of, professionals, 121–22, 127, 133; Whitehead's
recommendations about Jamaican,
122–28; in Newfoundland, 191–93.
See also Birth control; Hysterectomies;
Reproductive issues; Tubal ligations
Father: adaptations of, to incest with
daughter, 72, 74–84. *See also* Hus-
band; Incestuous families
Father-daughter incest: prevalence of, in
USA, 70; stages in, 73–75, 79–80,
82–84. *See also* Incestuous families
Femininity: postpartum depression and
intrapsychic conflicts about, 6, 213.
See also Physical feminization;
Women
Feminism: and pornography, 266–67,
272, 273
Ferber case, 280
Finkelhor, David, 70, 252
First Amendment: and pornography,
261, 275; and neutrality issue, 263,
266; exceptions to, 276–77, 288–89;
assumptions of, 279, 292. *See also*
Pornography
Fischer, Michael M. J., 36n3
Fisher, Dean, 293
Force. *See* Coercion
Fordham, Signithia, 149, 175
Four-Gated City, The (Lessing), 133
Frankfurter, Felix, 289
Frayser, Suzanne, 25
Freud, Sigmund, 268
Friendships: between college women,
157–58, 159, 163–65. *See also* Support
networks
"Full-time": defined, 14; described, 21–
22, 28–29, 33–36

Gadamer, H. G., 107
Gaskell, Jane, 147–48
Gay female impersonators, 14–15, 30–31
Gay rights movement, 257–58
Geertz, Clifford, 13, 36n3, 119
Gender: early anthropological interest
in, 1; cultural construction of, 1–4, 8
Gender construct(s): defined, 2, 21; and
transsexuals, 15–17, 20–36; retarded
adults' development of, 41–64; and

socialization among retarded adults,
56, 59, 60–62; among Jamaican men,
103–38; and women's career commit-
ments, 142–80; of "good women" in
Newfoundland, 184, 196–98, 200,
201, 202. *See also* Victimization
Gender cues, 22–23, 25
Gender identity: dissatisfaction in, 15;
formation of, 44–48. *See also* Identity
formation
Gender ideology: of transsexuals, 22–23,
29; among retarded adults, 61
Gender status, 22. *See also* Status change
Genitalia: and gender, 22–23
Genovese, Kitty, 291
Ginsburg v. New York, 291
Giovanni, Maureen J., 6–7, 209–31
Gittelsohn, Alan A., 185
Goffman, Erving, 13, 17, 19–20
Goodenough, Ward, 72, 95–96
"Goodness" (in Jamaica), 103, 112
"Good woman": and reproductive is-
sues, 6, 184, 196–98, 200, 201, 202
Gordon, Linda, 221
Gottlieb, Anthony, 30
Grey Rock Harbour (Newfoundland),
183–206
Groth, Nicholas, 255
Group libel law, 289–90

"Habilitation" (of institutionalized re-
tarded adults), 42, 43, 64
Hale, Matthew, 252
Hansell, N., 237
Haraway, Donna, 251
Harder They Come, The (film), 135n15
Harm: unrecognizable under neutrality
principle, 264, 271–72, 276–77, 278,
281, 283–87, 289–92; as criterion for
prosecution, 288
Hartmann, Heidi, 225
Harvard Law Review: article on spousal
rape, 252–53
Haversham, Jamaica (pseudonym),
103–38
"Hazardous reproduction," 116, 122
Head of household: definitions of, in
Jamaica, 114
Hoff, Lee Ann, 7, 235–50
Holland, Dorothy C., 5–6, 142–80, 239

Holmes, Nancy, 279
Homelessness: among retarded adults,
63; among battered women, 239, 240.
See also Deinstitutionalization
Homosexuality: among retarded adults,
55, 59, 61; perceptions of, among Jamaicans, 104. *See also* Gay female impersonators; Gay rights movement
Hormonal changes: as factor in postpartum depression, 6, 212. *See also* Physical feminization
Horowitz, Helen, 155
Husband: adaptations of, to incest with
daughter, 92–97
Hysterectomies, 3, 6, 183–88, 193–94,
197–99, 204

Identity formation: and gender
constructs, 3–4; and women's career
choices, 5–6; in transsexuals' transformation, 13–37; facets of, 40;
among retarded adults, 40–64. *See
also* Gender identity
Identity relationship: defined, 72
Illiteracy: in Jamaica, 108
Implied consent: in rape, 252–53, 256
Incest, 258, 281; as a private matter, 254;
readings on, 298n20. *See also* Incestuous families
Incest taboo, 70, 71
Incestuous families, 3, 4–5, 70–102; patterns among, 70–71, 97–102
Incorporation rite: defined, 18, 24
Independence: in Jamaica, 119–20
Indianapolis City-County Council,
294n1. *See also* Pornography: munici-
pal ordinances regarding
"Innocent children" view of retarded
people, 43
Interaction rates, 19. *See also* Symbolic
interaction theory
Intercourse: its significance to incestuous father, 82–84
Irresponsibility: Jamaican definitions of,
117–19, 121

Jamaica: reproductive issue in, 5, 103–38
Jobs: transsexuals' changes of, 28–29;
college girls' valuing of, 160–61. *See
also* Occupations

Kaganas, Felicity, 252
Keesing, Roger M., 72–73, 97, 100
Keller, E. F., 245
Kerr, Madeline, 104
Kessler, S., 143
Klee, Linnea, 187
Koegel, Paul, 43–44, 47, 62, 64
Korchinski, Barbara, 186–87

Landownership: and masculine strength, 113; and respectability, 129–30
Lanquer, Thomas, 200
Law: bases of, 265. *See also* First Amendment
Leach, Edmund R., 99, 101
Learning to Labor (Willis), 148
Least restrictive environment: concept of, 41
Lessing, Doris, 133
Liebow, Elliot, 130
Life-crisis event: postpartum depression as, 6, 213–14
"Life history" interviews, 151
Life-skills training: for retarded adults, 42
Liminal rites. *See* Transition: rites of
Limited good: concept of, 184, 202
Lindsey, A. M., 237
"Little men" (in Jamaica), 103–4, 110–12, 119, 120–21, 125–26. *See also* Brokers
Lochner v. New York, 263
Lovelace, Linda. *See* Marchiano, Linda

McCormack, C. P., 117
MacKinnon, Catherine A., 7, 257, 261–321
Mainstreaming: concept of, 41
Male dominance: and postpartum depression, 221, 225; and rape, 257; and reproductive issues, 257–58; and status of women, 262, 270–71; and pornography, 269–71. *See also* Authority; Maleness; Masculinity; Ownership; Power; Sexism
Maleness: as a form of power, 268
Marchiano, Linda, 277, 278, 279
Marcus, George E., 36n3
Marital infidelity: perceptions of, in Jamaica, 114–15

Marital rape, 3, 7, 8, 251–59, 268; exemption of, 7, 252–57; laws regarding, around the world, 255, 312–14n107
Marriage: and retarded adults, 45–46, 52–53; in Jamaica, 113–14; and women's career choices, 147–48; in Newfoundland, 192; ceremony, 253. *See also* Marital infidelity; Marital rape; Romantic relationships
Marshall, John, 188
Martin, Emily, 199–200
Martin, M. Kay, 40
Masculinity: meaning of, in Jamaica, 5, 103–38
Masturbation: and retarded adults, 54, 59
Material possessions: in Jamaica, 119–20
"Maternity blues." *See* "Baby blues"
Mead, George H., 17, 20
Mead, Margaret, 30
Meaning: in symbolic interaction theory, 20; in the use of language, 103–38, 241
Medical decision making: in Grey Rock Harbour, 201–2
Medicare and Medicaid Programs (1965), 62
Meiklejohn, A., 290
Membership Categorization Device (MCD), 240, 241, 242
Menarche: and intercourse in incestuous families, 84
Menopause: Newfoundland views of, 198. *See also* Hysterectomies
Mental Health Act (Florida, 1984), 63
Mentally challenged individuals. *See* Retarded adults
Mental Retardation Facilities and Community Mental Health Centers Construction Act (1963), 62
Michigan Gender Identity Test, 47
Miller v. California, 288
Mind, Self and Society (Mead), 20
Minneapolis City Council: antipornography ordinance of, 294n1. *See also* Pornography: municipal ordinances regarding
Modeling (as an occupation), 277
Modesty norms, 75–76, 79

Monat, Rosalyn Kramer, 44
Money: and masculine strength, 113–14; and respectability, 129–30
Morris, N., 213
Mother(s): adult retarded males' fixation on, 54; incapacity of, in incestuous families, 71, 86–88; adaptations of, to husband's incest with daughter, 72, 85–92; ideology about, 221, 226–27; inexperience of new, 224; lifestyle changes of, 224; actual conditions of, 226–27. *See also* Wife
Mother-daughter relationships: and wife battering, 7
Murphy, Fergus, 186–87
Murphy, Gardner, 25
Myerhoff, Barbara, 30

National Family Planning Board (NFPB) of Jamaica, 106, 124
National health insurance: and increase in hysterectomies, 186
Ndembu religious rituals, 24
"Network": defined, 237. *See also* Support networks; "Complex networks"
Neutrality: possibility of, in current legal practices, 7–8. *See also* Power: and neutrality
Newfoundland: acceptance of medical procedures in, 6, 183–206
Norbeck, J. S., 237
Normalization: concept of, 41, 60

Oakley, Ann, 220, 223, 226, 227
Obscenity: contrasted with pornography, 261, 272–73, 283, 288–91, 303n52
Occupations: choices leading women to choose traditional, 5–6, 142–80; and women, in Jamaica, 115. *See also* Jobs
Ogbu, John, 149, 174, 175
Opportunity House (pseudonym), 48, 53–57
Ordeal (Marchiano), 277
Ortner, Sherry B., 1, 130, 131
Ownership (of women): and rape, 7, 251, 253, 255, 257, 259

Pagelow, Mildred Daley, 255

Paluszny, Maria, 47
Parents: of retarded adults, 45, 58, 59; retarded adults as, 46, 52–53, 54, 58–59. *See also* Father; Mother(s)
Participant observation: as methodology, 4, 13, 50, 133n3, 150
"Passing": among transsexuals, 16, 22, 28–29, 33; among retarded adults, 61–62
Patriarchy. *See* Male dominance
Peer group: and college women's career choices, 6, 142–77
Penthouse, 286, 306n66
Personal identity, 20–23, 25
Physical feminization: importance of, to transsexuals, 22, 25, 30–32
Playboy, 286
Plessy v. Ferguson, 263
Polgar, Steven, 188
Polynesian cultures, 4
Population rate: in Newfoundland, 183, 188–89, 206n11
Pornography, 3, 258; legal issues involved in, 7–8, 261–321; as defining of women, 261, 269–73, 278, 284–85, 287; as sex discrimination, 261, 273–75, 284, 303n52; municipal ordinances regarding, 261, 273–88; dangers of, 270–72, 275–76, 281, 283–85; definition of, in municipal ordinance, 273–74, 294n1; injuries caused by, 277–88, 289; causal relationship of, to rape, 281–83, 285–86; trafficking in, 283–88; readings on, 298n20; as desensitizing device, 308n84; crimes involved with, 320n158. *See also* Child pornography; Harm; Power
Pornography: Men Possessing Women (Dworkin), 270–71
Postpartum depression, 3; rise in, and causes of, 6–7, 209–28; symptoms of, 210; defined, 211; cross-cultural incidence of, 212, 220; and socioenvironmental stressors, 217–19. *See also* Life-crisis event; Support networks
Postpartum psychosis, 211
Power: differences in, between men and women, 2; and neutrality, 7–8, 262–64, 276; in incestuous families, 86,

89, 91, 95; and silence, 262, 267, 279, 286, 287–88, 290, 291–92; and pornography, 273, 281. *See also* Authority; Male dominance

President's Committee on Mental Retardation (1965), 62

President's Panel on Mental Retardation (1963), 62

Presser, H. B., 203

Price, John, 45

Prisoners: women likened to, 268

Privacy rights: of retarded adults, 46; of women's reproductive decisions, 254

Private and public. *See* Public and private

Prostitution, 258, 267, 269, 277, 278, 281, 286, 298n20

Psychosexual development. *See* Incestuous families; Puberty

Puberty: transsexuals' use of women's, 4, 16, 29–32. *See also* Menarche; Secondary sexual characteristics

Public and private: boundaries between, 7, 8, 251, 253–55, 256–57

Purging: Newfoundland notions about, 183, 184, 189, 198–99

Quinn, N., 239

Racism: in Wilson's traits paradigm, 109; and substantive systems, 262; differentiated from sexism, 265–66, 276

"Raging hormone" theory of adolescence, 30

Rape, 267, 269, 281; and pornography, 281–83; readings on, 297n20. *See also* Coercion; Implied consent; Marital rape; Rapists; Stranger rape; Throat rape

Rapists: motives of, 255

Refusal: as daughter's strategy in incest, 79–80

Rehabilitation Act of 1973, 63

Reid, Barbara V., 7, 251–60

Reiter, Rayna, 1

Religiosity: among incestuous families, 71

Religious authorities: their approach to incestuous fathers, 96

Reproductive issues: and lower-class Jamaican males, 3, 106, 121–22; in Newfoundland fishing village, 6, 183–206; and women's control of their bodies, 257–58. *See also* Abortion; Birth control; Postpartum depression; Sterilization

"Reputational traits," 104, 107, 109, 110–14, 123, 124, 125, 129–32

"Respectability traits," 104, 107, 109–10, 112, 113–14, 123–24, 129–32

Retardation: nonhereditary nature of, 46

Retarded adults, 3, 40–69; stereotypes concerning, 43; black males as better social compensators, 53, 54, 55, 62; romances between, 58

Rich, Adrienne, 267

Rites of passage: for transsexuals, 13–37

Ritual: definitions of, 19; uses of, 25, 26. *See also* Rites of passage

"Ritualistic surgery," 198

Rodman, Hyman, 104

Roe v. Wade, 254

Roles: in incestuous families, 71, 85–92; defined, 72

Romantic relationships: emphasis on, in college, 150, 155, 156–57, 163, 167, 168, 174, 175. *See also* Marriage

Rooney, Mickey, 43

Rossi, A., 220

Russell, Diana E. H., 252

Rutkow, Ira M., 185

Sanday, Peggy, 2, 133, 135n8

Saskatchewan: number of hysterectomies in, 185

"Scene": defined, 73; changes in, in incestuous families, 76

Schoolwork: as a peripheral concern in college, 150, 158–62, 167, 168; models of, 162–73

Secondary sexual characteristics: as indication of puberty, 30; and incestuous fathers, 74, 84

Secrecy: in incestuous relations, 75–76, 82, 84. *See also* Discovery

Self: in symbolic interaction theory, 20

Semen: and masculine strength, 117, 125

Separate spheres. *See* Public and private

Separation rites: defined, 18, 19

Sex-change surgery. *See* Surgical conversion

Sex discrimination, 266. *See also* Pornography: as sex discrimination

Sex education: need for, for retarded adults, 43, 44–45, 56–57, 64; provided by incestuous father, 80–81

Sexism: defined, 236; as substantive system, 262

"Sex-only" materials, 284–85

Sexual abuse: of retarded adults, 55–56, 57–58; symptoms of, among incest victims, 96–97; of children, 258, 267–68, 269, 277, 281, 298n20; among women, 267–69. *See also* Child pornography; Incestuous families; Pornography

Sexual activity: in Jamaica, 123

Sexual harassment, 258, 267, 269, 280–81, 297n20, 307n81

Sexuality: Jamaican views of, 114–17. *See also* Pornography: as defining of women; Retarded adults

"Sexualization" of incestuous daughter, 83–84, 94–95

Sexual Meanings (Ortner and Whitehead), 1

Sexual stratification, 1, 2–3

Sexual victimization. *See* Sexual abuse; Victimization

Shain, Rochelle N., 188, 203

Shakespeare, William, 293

Silence. *See* Power: and silence

Silverman, Martin, 2

Slavery: lingering effects of, in Jamaica, 107–8, 130

"Slut": incestuous daughter as, 96–97

Smith, M. G., 104

"Snuff" films, 278

Social identity, 25, 72; defined, 21

Social isolation: of incestuous families, 71, 84

Social issues: defined, 1–2; gendered perspective on, 3

Social Network Questionnaire, 237

Social relations: in symbolic interaction theory, 20

"Social reproduction" theory, 147, 148–49

Social Security Act: Title XX, 63

Social status: defined, 72; in Jamaica, 103–4

Social support. *See* Support networks

Spousal rape. *See* Marital rape

Spradley, James P., 135n9, 151

Stack, C. B., 237

Status change: and transsexuals, 17, 24, 25

Status relationship: defined, 72

Sterilization: involuntary, of retarded adults, 46. *See also* Hysterectomies; Tubal ligations

Stewart, Potter, 261, 291

Stigma: and transsexuals, 17, 22, 28–29, 33, 35

Stoic endurer. *See* "Good woman"

Storer, John H., 3, 4–5, 70–102

Stranger rape, 7, 251, 255, 256

"Strength" (in Jamaica), 103–4, 110, 112, 123, 124, 130

Subidentities, 21–22

Substantive systems, 262–64

Suffering: and the "good woman," 197–98

Sugar: and Jamaica's development, 108

"Supermoms," 227

Supplemental Security Income, 63

Support networks: and postpartum depression, 7, 214–19, 223–26; and battered women, 236, 238–39, 246. *See also* Berdache Society

Surgeons: and elective surgery, 185–86, 195, 203–4. *See also* Hysterectomies; Surgical conversion; Tubal ligations

Surgical conversion (of transsexuals), 13, 14, 23, 24, 35–36

Sweet-talking, 120–21, 126–27, 130

Symbolic interaction theory, 13, 17, 19–20, 101

"Talking diary" interviews, 151

"Talking pretty," 120–21

Tarjan, George, 45

Temkin, Jennifer, 256

Tennessee Community Skills Profile, 42

Therapy: transsexual rites of passage likened to, 23–26

"Third sex," 4

Threshold rites. *See* Transition: rites of

Throat rape, 306n65. *See also* Deep Throat

Title XX (Social Security Act), 63
Transition: as stage in transformation of transsexuals, 16–17; rites of, 18, 23–25, 26–36
Transsexuals, 3–4, 13–37; defined, 14; stages in transformation of, 15–17, 18, 20–36; their eventual rejection of that description, 33–36. *See also* Berdache Society
Transvestites, 14–15, 30–31. *See also* Cross-dressing
Tribe, Larry, 290
Tubal ligations, 3, 183–84, 188–89, 190, 197–98, 199, 204. *See also* Hysterectomies
Turner, Jim L., 47–48
Turner, Victor, 13, 17, 24

U.S. Supreme Court: and retarded adults' sexual rights, 46; and pornography, 277, 289. *See also* Obscenity; *Names of individual Supreme Court justices*
Unities theory: in rape, 253, 256
Uterine cancer: in Newfoundland, 183, 194

Values Index, 237, 238, 243
Van Gennep, Arnold, 17, 18–19
Vasectomies, 193
Victimization: of battered women, 235, 242–44; secondary, 235, 244, 255–56. *See also* Battering; Marital rape; Pornography
Violence: gender differences and, 243–44; and sex in pornography, 284–85, 286–87

Virginity: fathers' views of daughters', 83
Voice and speech lessons: for transsexuals, 28
Voorhies, Barbara, 40

Wallace, Anthony, 25
"Weakness" (in Jamaica), 103
Wechsler, Herbert, 263
White, Leslie, 129
Whitehead, Harriet, 1
Whitehead, Tony L., 5, 103–38
White supremacy, 262
Whittemore, Robert D., 47, 62, 64
"Wickedness" (in Jamaica), 103, 104, 115, 121
Wife: adaptations of, to husband's incest with daughter, 85–97
Wife abuse. *See* Battering
Williams, Vanessa, 306n66
Willis, Paul, 148–49, 175
Wilson, Peter J., 103–4, 107, 109, 110, 117, 123, 132
Woman in the Body, The (Martin), 199–200
Women: cultural constructs of, as seen by transsexuals, 16, 22, 29–33; low status us, 264–65. *See also* Black women; Femininity; Male dominance; Ownership; Pornography: as defining of women; Puberty
Woolf, Virginia, 293
Wright, Ralph C., 186

Yalman, Nur, 99, 101
Yllo, Kersti, 252

Zagnoli, Lucinda J., 4, 40–69
Zetlin, Andrea G., 47–48
Zuidena, George D., 185